Faith and Heritage:
A Christian Nationalist Anthology

Faith and Heritage

A Christian Nationalist Anthology

Antelope Hill Publishing

Copyright © 2021 Faith and Heritage

First printing 2021

The separate works of this anthology, which are owned by their authors, were originally published electronically at faithandheritage.com. Permission has been granted to Antelope Hill Publishing by both the original authors and Faith and Heritage to assemble and publish this anthology in the interest of preserving their words in physical format.

Cover art by sswifty
Edited by Margaret Bauer
The publisher can be contacted at
Antelopehillpublishing.com

ISBN-13: 978-1-953730-23-7 Paperback
ISBN-13: 978-1-953730-31-2 EPUB

*From one man he made all the nations, that they should inhabit
the whole earth; and he marked out their appointed times
in history and the boundaries of their lands. God did
this so that they would seek him and perhaps
reach out for him and find him, though
he is not far from any one of us.*

Acts 17:26-27

Contents

Foreword by Myles Poland ix

Davis Carlton

A Biblical Defense of Ethno-Nationalism 3
Divorce, Miscegenation, and Polygamy: A Comparative Approach to Their Morality
    Part 1 17
    Part 2 24
Ten Christian Zionist Myths
    Part 1 29
    Part 2 38
    Part 3 44
    Part 4 50
    Part 5 57
In Defense of Privilege, White or Otherwise 63

Nil Desperandum

Hate the Sin and Hate the Sinner 71
False Sins 79
The Case for Postmillennialism
    Part 1 85
    Part 2 88
    Part 3 93
    Part 4 97
Our Familial and Racial Existence in Heaven 103
Christianity as a Necessary Foundation for White Nationalism
    Part 1: Morality 109
    Part 2: The Glory of God 114
    Part 3: Design, Order, and Kinds 120
    Part 4: Anti-Judaism 129

Adam Grey

Fear Eve, Lose Eden 141
A Time for Choosing in the Church 145
The Alt Right Won't Win with Atheism 147

Thorin Reynolds

There Is No Male and Female 155
A Christian View on Segregation 159

Gic Serry

From Higher Criticism to Marxism: The Treasonous Behavior of the South African Dutch Reformed Churches Towards the Afrikaner People 169
Kinism in the Early Church 173
The Ethnoconfessional Nature of Culture 185

Ehud Would

Alienism: Bramble Path to Oblivion 191
Kinism: The Only Theonomy 195
A Kinist Commentary on the Ten Commandments 203
    The First Word 206
    The Second Word 208
    The Third Word 213
    The Fourth Word 215
    The Fifth Word 221
    The Sixth Word 224
    The Seventh Word 228
    The Eighth Word 242
    The Ninth Word 251
    The Tenth Word 258
The Way We Were 265
"Ecce Homo": Sheepdogs, Alpha Males, and the Man of God 285
The Golden Rule: The Equity of Ethnonationalism 293
Charlottesville and the Kalergi Clergy 301
Nationalism as Christian Apologetics 307
An Open Letter to the American Church: A Response to RAAN's Charlottesville Declaration 311
Ehud Cross-Examined: A Reader Asks Some Pointed Questions 321
The Blackwashing of Christian History and Beyond
    Part 1 331
    Part 2 334
Covenant vs. Coven: Liberalism as Witchcraft 339

Foreword

Faith and Heritage. If you're White in the 2020's, you're told that those two concepts are irreconcilable. We're told over and over that in order to be a "good Christian" we must allow our nations to be overrun with foreigners who want little more than to destroy White civilization and loot the corpse, returning to their squalor once their grisly work is done. We're told that if you don't fling open the doors to your nations, pour out the contents of your wallet, and sacrifice your children on the altar of multiculturalism, then you're surely inviting God's wrath. Nothing could be further from the truth.

"God doesn't care about your politics." That idea — ill-formed at the time — led to the creation of the Godcast. At the time of writing, myself and my co-host, SuperLutheran, comprise the only active ministry that seeks to bring the Gospel to White Nationalists. When the publishers of this impressive volume asked me to write the foreword, I was profoundly grateful for both the opportunity and to have an easily accessible resource for harmonizing seemingly contradictory ideas as ethno-nationalism and Christ's work on the cross.

I must confess, my expectations weren't high when I was told that the book would be a collection of essays by several authors. I went in expecting a series of short blog posts, authors giving their observations on the state of the Christian Church, lamenting the sorry state of mainline denominations, and giving their thoughts on what might be done to turn things around. Instead I was treated to an intellectual *tour de force*. Long-form essays — and series of essays — powerfully argue that the concept of an ethno-nation is well established in Holy Scripture and is embraced by God.

The anthology starts with a series of essays by Davis Carlton with a rather on-the-nose piece called "A Biblical Defense of Ethno-Nationalism." If you've picked up this book right before getting a call from your doctor informing you that you've only got an hour left to live, then this is the essay for you. Several of his essays attack the cancer plaguing Western churches: Christian Zionism, or uncritical support among Christians for both Jews and the nation of Israel. Carlton addresses the most common myths that pastors and other corrupted churchmen use to push support for a country and people that hate our guts and immolates them.

We're then treated to another hefty series by Nil Desperandum where he lays out that the moral, cultural, and logical cornerstone of White Nationalism is Christianity. The case is made in no uncertain terms, and I have trouble thinking of anything approaching a valid counter-argument. He spends much of his writing correcting myriad misconceptions regarding sin. Always a helpful endeavor for Christians.

Several essays deal with ethno-nationalism in historical context and how it relates to our faith, demonstrating that much of the world has gone mad with multiculturalism, and those of us who recognize the obvious have been right all along. Ehud Would takes to task the multicult's fascination with casting every historical figure as a black African, lambasting the notion that salvation comes from blackness. Though my favorite essay by far is "Our Familial and Racial Existence in Heaven," by Nil Desperandum. In it he lays out the critical role our ethnic heritage plays in God's plan of salvation. It is something so important to our existence as human beings that our genetic heritage will be preserved even in the new Heaven and new Earth to come.

I can't say I agree with every jot and tittle written in this book. For example, I personally find Nil Desperandum's case for postmillennialism unconvincing, and I think Ehud Would gets a few points wrong in his Commentary on the Ten Commandments. These differences, however, amount to polite disagreements between Brothers in Christ. As someone who leads the sole active ministry tending to the spiritual hunger within the Dissident Right, I can give this volume my ringing endorsement. Our beliefs are built upon the bedrock of logic and history, and I am pleased to find that I've been standing on the shoulders of these giants all along.

I don't know about you, dear reader, but I'm not ready to roll over and die just yet. Unlike the Amalekites, I haven't received a single message from God about our people's impending destruction. The cause of White Nationalism is righteous—at least when the people championing the cause choose to be.

Myles Poland

DAVIS CARLTON

Davis is a descendant of Swiss-German farmers. He enjoys history, historical fiction, and theology. Davis appreciates traditional European culture as well as classical Christian liturgy and ecclesiology, and he desires to instill these values in the minds of fellow Christians of European descent. Davis considers it his task to do "the exact opposite of the work which the Radicals had to do...to cling to every scrap of the past that he can find, if he feels that the ground is giving way beneath him and sinking into mere savagery and forgetfulness of all human culture."

A Biblical Defense of Ethno-Nationalism

January 19, 2011

Ethno-nationalism is a belief system that affirms a traditional Christian understanding of families, tribes, and nations. Ethno-nationalism holds that nations are defined and rooted in common heredity, and that the foundations of a nation are based on common ancestry, language, culture, religion, and social customs.

What are the primary factors that bind a nation together? Is it common ancestry or common ideas? In a sense, ethno-nationalism is redundant. It is evident that the English word *nation* has been traditionally defined by birth, not merely geographic or political boundaries. The word *nation* in the English language is related to *natal*, which means birth, as in a neo-natal ward. On Christmas we celebrate Christ's nativity. You are a native of the land of your birth. But if this is true, why even speak of ethno-nationalism since it is redundant? Why not simply defend the concept of nationalism? The reason is that in recent history we have seen the ascendancy of the concept of the proposition nation. A proposition nation is supposed to be a group of people who are united by a common ideology rather than by common heredity, but as we shall see, a proposition nation is a contradiction in terms.

The question that we as orthodox Christians must ask is: How does the Bible use the term *nation*? What kind of nation does the Bible promote? Does the Bible endorse a more traditional definition of a nation? Or does the Bible promote the idea of a propositional nation, the proposition being Christian faith? It is my goal to demonstrate that the Bible in fact promotes the traditional concept a nation as an aggregation of people who share a common lineage.

The Meaning and Usage of the Word Nation in the Bible

The Bible is predominantly written in the Hebrew and Greek languages. The Biblical word used in the Greek New Testament and Septuagint translation of the Old Testament is the word *ethnos*.[1] This word is related to our English word *ethnicity* and denotes those of a common lineage. This definition is also consistent

---

[1] The English word nation is an appropriate translation of Biblical concepts expressed in Hebrew and Greek, but its meaning has changed over the course of the 20th century to mean little more than a political construct. A nation was originally defined much differently as this definition in the Sixth Edition of Black's

with how the word nation is used in the Bible. Nations are first mentioned in the Table of Nations listed in Genesis chapter 10. The Table of Nations classifies the people descended from Noah after the Biblical Flood. These nations are all listed by heredity, like branches off a tree that has Noah for its trunk. Nations are enumerated as an extension of families (Gen. 10:5, 20, 31-32), and the usage of the word *nation* is consistent throughout the Bible. After a number of generations had passed after the Flood, a man named Nimrod tried to build an empire. His kingdom was called Babel, and he united several different groups of people by his charismatic leadership. The people under Nimrod set out to build a city and a tower as a monument to their commitment to political unity. God takes notice of this arrangement and proclaims that this will cause evil to go unrestrained (Gen. 11:6). God resolves to confuse the language of the Babel builders in order that men might henceforth be kept from uniting into one body politic. This is a strong passage that demonstrates that national boundaries and divisions are commensurate with the natural order that God has ordained.

Some may argue that the division of nations was only a transient solution to a problem posed several centuries ago and that in Christ these divisions are healed. These people would typically view national boundaries or division as a problem that will ultimately be solved. Ethno-nationalists strongly disagree with this view of the teleology or purpose of race and racial distinctions. Ethno-nationalists affirm that God intended to create separate races, nations, tribes, and families from the beginning, and that ultimately all people would be united under Christ. Since racial distinctions exist in heaven, it is clear that God intended for racial distinctions to exist for his own glory. Nothing in the Bible indicates that racial distinctions or racial identity is a transient solution to a temporary problem. Instead these distinctions are an integral element of our identity that will endure forever (Rev. 5:9, 7:9, 21:24, 22:2). Since we've established that separate nationalities exist in heaven and that there are multiple "nations of them which are saved," it is clear that race does indeed have intrinsic significance. We could no more argue that our resurrected bodies will lack racial identity than we could argue that they lack gender identity.

Racial Pride, Loyalty, and Responsibility

It is common among white Christians today to believe that any sort of pride of race is inherently wrong or evil. Many Christians express the belief that we

---

Law Dictionary demonstrates: "A people, or aggregation of men, existing in the form of an organized jural society, usually inhabiting a distinct portion of the earth, speaking the same language, using the same customs, possessing historic continuity, and distinguished from other like groups by their racial origin and characteristics, and generally, but not necessarily, living under the same government and sovereignty."

should only boast in our identity in Christ. There is a sense in which this is true. The Apostle Paul considered everything that he could claim to be "but dung" in comparison to the "excellency of the knowledge of Christ Jesus my Lord" (Phil. 3:4-8) including his own ancestry! It's extremely important to note that Paul is making a comparison by hyperbole. Paul is saying that in comparison with Christ's righteousness, all that we have and all that we are is worthless! It is also important to point out that Paul is comparing his own righteousness, to the righteousness of Christ. It is in this sense that nothing about us matters for salvation. We are saved solely by the merits of Christ. Even Christ demands that our loyalty to himself exceed our loyalty to our immediate families and spouses (Matt. 19:29, cf. Mar. 10:30). It would be a severe mistake however to conclude that attributes such as ancestry or even marriage are meaningless!

Indeed, the very same Apostle Paul who spoke those words to the Philippians also said that he was "willing to be accursed from Christ" for his "brethren, his kinsman according to the flesh" (Rom. 9:3). The New International Version renders "kinsman according to the flesh" as "race." This is a clear and unashamed expression of racial pride and loyalty. Paul unambiguously expresses solidarity with his people even though they themselves were unbelievers! Paul's commitment for his missionary work to non-Israelite people did not in any way compete with his natural affection for his own people. If it was alright for Paul to express such commitment to the welfare of his own kindred, why is it considered wrong for white people to express the same commitment? White people are usually singled out for any expression of solidarity with each other, even when there is clearly no animosity expressed towards people of different races. This sentiment of love and affection for one's own people should not only be manifested in warm feelings of kind regard, but also should be manifested by outward actions and responsibilities.

Today many people do not believe in family responsibilities or obligations. This should not be so! The Apostle Paul tells his disciple Timothy that "if any provide not for his own, and especially for those of his own house, he hath denied the faith, and is worse than an infidel!" (1 Tim. 5:8).[2] Clearly, our "own" probably cannot be interpreted to mean what we would call race today. Our own in this verse refers to extended family which centers in on the household or immediate family. What Paul is teaching here is that people have familial obligations that radiate outward in concentric loyalties. Our responsibilities to humanity at large are extraordinarily small in comparison to our responsibility to our immediate family. This again demonstrates that family, clan, tribe, nation, and race have meaning in the Biblical paradigm of society.

---

[2] Henry, Matthew. *Complete Commentary on the Whole Bible*. Deuteronomy 23, Verses 1-8

The Purpose of National Distinctions

The purpose that God has for different nations or races will be fleshed out in greater detail in other articles. This should merely serve as a brief overview of the question of what purpose the nations serve. The first observation that we must make is that national distinction based upon heredity already existed at the time of Babel. We are given a relative time frame reference in the Table of Nations when we read that the division of Babel occurring during the lifetime of Peleg (Gen. 10:25). Peleg is the fourth generation from Shem, and the fifth generation from Noah. Therefore, it seems that national identity was rooted in the sons of Noah and their offspring, and that the division at Babel was not a new or innovative arrangement, but was rather a reaffirmation of a preexisting social structure which had existed at least since the time of the Flood. God confused language as an additional tool for maintaining national distinction. This did not create new nations which had theretofore not existed! There had already been several generations of the nations listed in Genesis 10 by the time that Tower of Babel is formed and God was protecting the unique identity of the nations that already existed. It is certainly true that Babel was a punishment for sin, but it was also an act of mercy from God in order to restrain the evil that typically arises in cosmopolitan societies who have lost sight of their tribal identity. Raceless or tribeless societies become decadent due to anonymity and loss of patriarchal authority, which is inevitable in these regimes. When people forget their ancestors they will not regard their children and future descendants!

Deuteronomy 32:8 tells us that nations were divided by a special act of God's providence. We read that the Most High divided the nations their inheritance and separated the sons of Adam, and that God set the boundaries of the nations. God's dividing the inheritance to the various nations is a positive and intentional work of God's providence. This means that God did not merely allow the nations to be divided but that He caused this to happen for man's own good.

Another pivotal passage that addresses the purposes of national distinctions and affirms their propriety is Acts 17:26-27. In this passage we read that God made from one blood (presumably referring again to Adam) "all nations of men for to dwell on all the face of the earth, and hath determined the times before appointed, and the bounds of their habitation; That they should seek the Lord, if haply they might feel after him, and find him, though he be not far from every one of us." It is worth pointing out that traditional Christians firmly believe that all humanity is descended from Adam and Eve, seeing as Eve is referred to as the "mother of all living" (Gen. 3:20). Commonly, detractors of ethno-nationalism erect a straw man that suggests that ethno-nationalists do not affirm the unity of everyone under Adam as a covenant head. Indeed, it is this covenant unity by which original sin is transferred to all mankind (Rom. 5:12). But this common descent from Adam does not change the fact that God intentionally divided the nations of men and appointed them their respective bounds and habitations. Notice also that verse 27 provides us with a reason why God did this. God did this so that man would grope for God and find him! It is important to note that no one can come to God through their own natural ability (1 Cor. 2:14), but it is clear that God uses distinct nations as a means of bringing about salvation by his own sovereignty similar to the way that God uses believing spouses to sanctify and redeem their unbelieving husbands or wives (1 Cor. 7:14).

Some people argue that this may have been a passing purpose of national distinctions, but that these distinctions are blurred or done away with by the descent of the Holy Spirit at Pentecost recorded in Acts chapter 2. The problem with this interpretation is that it does not square with the narrative. If God intended for the people at Pentecost to amalgamate into one body politic then he would have caused them to start speaking one language again, hereby facilitating their unity. Instead we read that God caused those present to hear the Apostle Peter preach to them in their own language! It is important also to point out that those assembled at Pentecost were identified as pious Israelites who had gathered at Jerusalem from the regions where they had been residing. Pentecost would hardly resemble a United Nations gathering today. The people involved were quite homogeneous ethnically. Moreover Pentecost was the baptism of Babel. Dr. Francis Nigel Lee states quite succinctly the relationship between Babel and Pentecost:

> *Pentecost sanctified the legitimacy of separate nationality rather than saying this is something we should outgrow. In fact, even in the new earth to come, after the Second Coming of Christ, we are told that the nations of them which are saved shall walk in the light of the heavenly Jerusalem, and the kings of the earth shall bring the glory and the honor – the cultural treasures – of the nations into it... But nowhere in Scripture are any indications to be found that such peoples should ever be amalgamated into one huge nation.*[3]

What then is the destiny of separate nationality as Dr. Lee calls it? Are separate nations bound to "bleed into one" as the Gospel spreads? Or will separate nationhood persist? Ethno-nationalists strongly believe that separate nationhood will persist even into the next life in the new heavens and the new earth. We read about this chiefly in Revelation, written by the Apostle John, when he writes that "the nations of them which are saved shall walk in the light of it (heavenly Jerusalem): and the kings of the earth do bring their glory and honour into it" (Rev. 21:24). The Apostle John also envisions Christians of every kindred, people, and nation in heaven (Rev. 5:9, 7:9), and also witnesses the Tree of Life in the heavenly Jerusalem which is for the healing of the nations (Rev. 22:2). Within the church, then, we can

---

[3] Dr. Lee, Francis Nigel. *Race, People, and Nationality*. 2 Feb 2005.

boldly assert that there are separate and distinct nations. When you become a Christian, you retain your ethnic and racial identity. These are not done away with in Christ, but rather sanctified and legitimized in the same way that both genders are sanctified in their separate identities within the family and Church. What role do nations play in a Christian civil society? This question is foundational to a traditional Christian understanding of social order.

The Role of Nationhood

As J.C. Ryle has written, "Community of blood is a most powerful tie."[4] In Deut. 23, Israel is given laws regarding who can assimilate into the congregation of the Lord. The congregation of the Lord probably denotes Israel's national church. It is important to notice that assimilation took into account both heredity and history when determining assimilation. The Moabites and Ammonites are more thoroughly excluded due to a bad past history with the children of Israel, and Egypt is more readily assimilated due to Israel being a stranger in their land. Edom and Israel were nations that had a troubled history to say the least. But the Edomites are easily assimilated into the Israelite congregation due to their consanguinity, since both are descended from the patriarch Isaac. This is why Edom is referred to as Israel's brother (Deut. 23:7, Num. 20:14). The significance of consanguinity taught in this passage was not lost on noted commentator Matthew Henry, who writes concerning this that, "The unkindness of near relations, though by many worst taken, yet should with us, for that reason, because of the relation, be first forgiven."[5]

Ethnic identities are the outgrowth of families. The Bible does not endorse the notion of a propositional nation that is simply identified by ideas rather than lineage. Israel serves as an example of nationhood that the rest of the nations are supposed to emulate (Deut. 4:5-7). It stands to reason that if Israel was reckoned hereditarily by lineage, then all nations should be identified the same way. The easiest way to conceive of a nation is to think of a nation in the proper sense as an extended family. Ancient Israel was organized into twelve tribes descended from their patriarch Jacob, and these tribes are listed according to the families that make them up. The first eight chapters of Chronicles are dedicated to listing the families of the tribes because "all Israel were reckoned by genealogies" (See Numbers 1-4 and 1 Chronicles 1-8, 9:1).

Non-Israelites were called strangers or sojourners and were to be treated with courtesy and fairness (Ex. 12:48-49, 22:21, 23:9, Lev. 19:10, 19:33-34, Lev. 23:22, 24:22, Num. 9:14, 15:15-16, 15:29-30). The best way to think of these strangers or

---

[4] Ryle, J.C. *The Family of God.*
[5] Henry, Matthew. *Complete Commentary on the Whole Bible.* Deuteronomy 23, Verses 1-8

sojourners is as invited house guests. Guests in your home should be treated with the utmost courtesy, but at the same time they do not take ownership or possession of what belongs to you. Incidentally, God promises to punish wayward Israel with uncontrolled influx of foreigners who will sap their strength and consume their wealth (Deut. 28:32-36).[6] This is eerily similar to America's current circumstances. Physical blood relationships are significant for civil government through the principle of kin rule as well as for property ownership since only Israelites were allowed to permanently own land that was partitioned based upon tribal identity.

The Principle of Kin Rule

The Bible places familial authority in the hands of husbands and fathers.[7] This is considered "sexist" or "chauvinistic" by today's standard, but God does not answer to man's opinions![8] In the Bible, civil authority is a natural outgrowth of familial authority. The foundational text for this position is Deut. 17:15, which states that Israel should set one from among their brethren to be king over them, and that they were not to put a stranger over them who was not their brother. It's important to keep in mind that brothers does not always refer to Christians in the Bible. Num. 20:14, Deut. 1:16, 23:7, 2 Kings 10:13-14, Neh. 5:7, Jer. 34:9, and Rom. 9:3 are examples of it being used in the ethnic sense in terms of Israel's identity. Gill points out that the King is Israel's brother, both by nation and religion, not exclusively by religion.[9] Keil & Delitzsch point out that the King is not a foreigner or non-Israelite.[10] Knox suggests that based upon Deut. 17:15, all women and strangers are excluded.[11] Again, we cannot simply interpret references to strangers or foreigners as though they were inherently unbelievers. Is. 56:3 is a good example of strangers/foreigners joining God's covenant. Samuel Rutherford also uses Deut. 17:15 as the foundational text of his classic *magnum opus* on civil government in which he comments, "The king is a relative."[12] I would also point out that strangers could be circumcised (Ex. 12:48), but were still reckoned apart from the children of Israel (Num. 11:4), and were not made civil magistrates (Deut. 1:13-16,

---

[6] Interestingly enough the Rev. Jesse Lee Peterson has also applied this passage to blacks in America being displaced due to their own infidelity to the Gospel.
[7] "Fatherly government being the first and measure of the rest, must be the best; for it is better that my father govern over me than a stranger govern me, and, therefore, the Lord forbade his people to set a stranger over themselves to be their king. The Prelate contendeth for the contrary,... {but a man's} father was born only by nature subject to his own father, therefore,...there is no government natural, but fatherly and marital." Samuel Rutherford. *Lex, Rex*. (Q.XIII, pg. 51-52)
[8] On male authority and headship as well as the authority of parents: Gen. 2:18, 3:16, Ex. 20:12 (cf. Deut. 5:16), Num. 30, Is. 3:19, 1 Cor. 11:7-12, 14:34-35, Eph. 5:22-33, Col. 3:18-21, 1 Tim. 2:9-15, Tit. 2:1-8, 1 Pet. 3:1-7.
[9] Gill, John. *Exposition on the Entire Bible*.
[10] Keil & Delitzsch. *Commentary on the Old Testament*.
[11] Knox, John. *The First Blast of the Trumpet Against the Montrous Regiment of Women*. 1558.
[12] Rutherford, Samuel. *Lex, Rex*. Q.XXV, pg. 120-124

17:15). Membership within the nation of Israel was based upon heredity (Deut. 15:12; 23:7, 19-20; Num. 20:14; Lev. 18:26; 22:18). Lev. 18:26 is particularly informative because those who keep God's law and statutes are said to be of the Israelite nation (*ethnos*) and the strangers (non-Israelites) that dwell among them. This is a solid example of how the nation of Israel was considered to be hereditary, not solely covenantal or spiritual.

There are other parallel passages that confirm the familial nature of civil authority. Kings and queens are referred to as fathers and mothers (Is. 49:23). Other parallel passages that should be mentioned are 2 Sam. 5:1 and 1 Chr. 11:1 in which the tribes of Israel affirm David's legitimate claim to rule by stating that they were of David's "bone and flesh."[13] It is clear from the context that "bone and flesh" refers to some finite hereditary relationship that cannot be applied to everyone. That civil rulers should have a close kindred relationship to those they rule seems to be the application of what Moses is communicating in Deut. 1:13-16 and 17:15. This establishes the basic principle upon which all nations are governed.[14] This bone and flesh relationship is the same way that the Bible communicates what is normative for marriage (Gen. 2:23). God created the woman to be a "helpmate" to her husband, and this is best accomplished by the bone and flesh relationship of Adam to Eve. Intermarriage between distant nations breaks this norm mentioned in Gen. 2:23-24 for marriage in a similar way that polygamy or marriage across large age differences goes against the standard rule for marriage based upon the example given by the marriage of Adam to Eve.[15] Civil consideration also prevented marriage with people who were Israel's enemies. The law in Deut. 23:1-8 was applied by Ezra and Nehemiah to prevent marriage to those who would seek Israel's harm.[16] The practical reasons for this rule in Deut. 17:15 is obvious. If a stranger governs a nation then he will naturally expropriate the wealth and property of the native people for the benefit of those who are of his own bone and flesh. This applies both to Christians as well as non-Christians since multiple nations will always exist within the Church and will continue to exist in Heaven (Rev. 21:24). There can be exceptions to this rule. God temporarily used Joseph as a wise regent to Pharaoh in Egypt (Gen. 39:4-6), and King Cyrus' righteous decree allowed the Israelites to return to their homeland under his protection (2 Chr. 36:22-

---

[13] One could also include Jdgs. 9:2 as well.
[14] Ecclesiasticus 17:17. This is a reference to the deuterocanon or apocrypha. There have been different schools of thought on using the deuterocanonical writings throughout Christian history. My usage of deuterocanonical writings is commensurate with their usage throughout most of the Christian church. Christ and the Apostles were very familiar with the deutero-canon, and there are many allusions to deutero-canonical literature in the New Testament.
[15] See Ezr. 9:2, Jer. 25:20, 24, 50:37, Eze. 30:5, and Dan. 2:43 for additional instances in which "mixed" or "mingled" people are mentioned in a context of judgment. Abraham, Isaac, Manoah, and Tobit all counseled their children against marriage outside of their people (Gen. 24:1-4, 37, 41, 26:34-35, 27:46, 28:1-2, 29:14, Jdgs. 14:3, Tob. 4:12).
[16] See Ezr. 10 and Neh. 13 on the application of the law in Deut. 23.

23). These are exceptions to the rule and are a clear case of God bringing the best out of a less than ideal situation.

Tribal Property Ownership

The Bible promotes the private ownership of property. This is inherent in the commandment against stealing (Ex. 20:15, cf. Deut. 5:19). God is the true and proper owner of everything (Ps. 24:1), but He has delegated stewardship over creation so that humanity might take dominion over what God has created (Gen. 1:28-30). Part of this dominion is exercised in ownership of property. God divides the inhabitable land between the different nations (Deut. 32:8, Acts 17:26) and he further subdivides this land between the various tribes, clans, and families. God expects boundaries to be acknowledged and respected (Prov. 22:28, Deut. 27:17). This does not mean that political boundaries will never change. A good example of this was the political schism that divided the nation of Israel into the separate kingdoms of Israel and Judah following King Solomon's death. The fact that political boundaries might change over time does not nullify the principle and relevance of boundaries in general to God.

God's law also provided Israel with a provision that would insure that property stayed within families and clans. The firstborn son would become the primary inheritor of his father's estate and property (Num. 3), and would thus become the head of his father's house after his father's death and the caretaker of his kinsmen. This is called primogeniture and was practiced as a matter of law in European society until very recently. In the absence of a male heir, the eldest daughter's husband would be the primary inheritor of the estate. What if the daughter's husband was from another tribe or clan? Wouldn't this easily transfer property from one family or tribe to another tribe? Yes it would, so God specified that female heirs were to marry within their father's tribe and clan, so as to prohibit this from happening (Num. 27:1-11, cf. Num. 36). Recall that Israel is given to us as an example of how Godly nations are to operate (Deut. 4:5-7). Clearly, then, God cares about physical inheritance, and His law has built-in protections from allowing it to be squandered or permanently lost due to passing financial offers or circumstances. The Bible promotes economic nationalism by allowing Israel to charge royalties to foreigners for the privilege of conducting business with the Israelites, as well as by providing for the Jubilee laws, which allowed the Israelites to redeem their property that they would have to lease or sell for a period of time (Lev. 25). The problem of the mentality of the "global economy" is that this concept is the tool of international bankers and business men who desire to turn a profit at the expense of the well-being of their countrymen and even immediate family!

Contrast this problem with one of the best examples of fidelity to familial inheritance in the person of Naboth. King Ahab offered a large sum of money to

Naboth in exchange for the vineyard that Ahab coveted. Naboth refused, telling Ahab, "The LORD forbid it me, that I should give the inheritance of my fathers unto thee" (1 Kings 21:3). Naboth clearly expresses that his loyalty to his ancestors is stronger than his impulse to make a quick buck. The ironic thing about laissez-faire capitalism is that the desire to get rich quick and frequently exchange property often leads to poverty and over-consolidation of wealth in the hands of a few businessmen and executives. Societies that neglect Biblical wisdom will ultimately pay the price in their inheritance!

Empires and Propositional Nationhood

Against the principle of kin rule and tribal ownership is the existence of empires. An empire is a kingdom that extends over several different tribes, nations, and peoples. Propositional nationhood has its origin in empires. The first recorded attempt at empire was Nimrod forming the city of Babel that was mentioned previously. The prophet Daniel also speaks about a succession of empires that would rule the Mediterranean world in Daniel chapters 2 and 7. Empires are usually relatively short-lived and are maintained by military might and aggression (Daniel 2:37-40, 7:19). As such empires are a cheap imitation of Christ's spiritual kingdom which will grow to encompass all physical nations and people (Dan. 2:44, 7:13-14, Rev. 5:9, 7:9) which is established peacefully by the internal ministry of the Holy Spirit, rather than by military might (Jn. 18:36).

America was not traditionally viewed as a "propositional nation" until recently in history. John Jay, first Chief Justice of the United States, and co-author of the Federalist Papers, writes concerning America's founding:

> With equal pleasure I have as often taken notice that Providence has been pleased to give this one connected country to one united people – a people descended from the same ancestors, speaking the same language, professing the same religion, attached to the same principles of government, very similar in their manners and customs, and who, by their joint counsels, arms, and efforts, fighting side by side throughout a long and bloody war, have nobly established general liberty and independence.[17]

In case you missed it, John Jay means by "descended from the same ancestors" that Americans were identified as Europeans, in the same way that the "same religion" that Americans professed was Christianity.

The underlying problem with propositional nations is that they experience internal conflict due to differences in interpretation of the country's propositions.

---

[17] Jay, John. *Federalist*. Number 2

Take America for example. America is supposed to be a propositional country that unites around the concepts of "freedom" or "democracy" or my personal favorite, "tolerance." Who interprets these concepts in the same way? No one! This is why every election cycle is a heated debate over our meaningless and undefined "values." America has degenerated into a proposition nation in the recent decades, but it is by no means the first proposition nation. The Greek historian Aelius Aristides wrote extensively about Roman universal citizenship of the people it conquered as a means of preserving their rule:

> *Most noteworthy and most praiseworthy of all is the grandeur of your conception of citizenship. There is nothing on earth like it. You have divided all of the people of the empire – and when I say that, I mean the whole world – into two classes; and all the more cultured, virtuous, and able ones everywhere you have made into citizens and nationals of Rome ... Neither the sea nor any distance on land shuts a man out from citizenship. Asia and Europe are in this respect not separate. Everything lies open to everybody; and no one fit for office or responsibility is considered an alien. Rome has never said "No more room!"*

> *No one is a foreigner who deserves to hold an office or is worthy of trust. Rather, there is here a common "world democracy" under the rule of one man, the best ruler and director ... You have divided humanity into Romans and non-Romans, ... and because you have divided people in this manner, in every city throughout the empire there are many who share citizenship with you, no less than the share citizenship with their fellow natives. And some of these Roman citizens have not even seen this city [Rome]!*

Sound familiar? This sounds an awful lot like America's current immigration and naturalization policy! In AD 212, Emperor Caracalla finally declared all freemen of the empire from Britain to Arabia as Roman citizens.[18] When Americans promote this concept of propositional nationhood in the quest to "make the world safe for democracy," we are unwittingly replicating the worst aspects of pagan Rome who tried to set up a "world democracy" under the rule of one man. America's current religious policy is the same is the imperialistic Romans. All religions are tolerated so long as they conform to the obedience of the state, whereas Christ accepts no competitors in matters of religion (Matt. 12:30). For Rome, this meant worshiping Caesar as God in addition to whatever other gods a person might be inclined to worship, and in modern America we look to the state no less than the ancient Romans did for the source of all our material needs and comforts.

---

[18] Called the *Constitutio Antoniniana*:

Was America founded as a Roman style propositional empire? Or was America founded as a biblical nation rooted in history, tradition, kinship, and the Christian faith? America was founded by the settlers in Virginia and the Pilgrims in Massachusetts as a Biblical nation. The Virginia Company's charter seal bore the image of the English King James I. The Pilgrims addressed themselves as "loyal subjects of our dread Sovereign Lord King James" meaning that the colonists saw themselves as English subjects rather than as Christians who had no earthly sovereign.[19] President George Washington insured that immigration and naturalization were restricted to "free white persons of good moral character."[20] If we had continued to heed the wise precedent of many past generations of Americans then non-Christian religions would be essentially non-existent here. Borders have been blurred and in some cases rendered meaningless by allowing imperialism and cultural Marxism to dictate policy rather than God's law. We will not avoid the punishment that God promises to those who disregard His law and precepts (Deut. 28:43-44).

An Appeal to Ethno-Nationalism

It is obvious that there is no alternative to embracing the ethno-nationalism that the Bible prescribes as normative. Europe was made great through the adherence to God's law in all things, including ethno-nationalism. We have fallen far from our previous civilization which was evident only a number of decades ago. During the 1960s, the culturally-Marxist "civil rights movement" carried us toward the unbiblical idea of "equal rights" and away from God's law.

We as Christians have a moral duty to promote Godly order in our lives, as well as for our families and our societies. We can clearly see from the Bible that nations should naturally be tied to blood and soil. We must reject ideologies which reject this Christian notion of ethno-nationalism. It is no coincidence that we have rejected the Christian basis for national identity at the same time as we are rejecting the Christian doctrine of marriage, gender roles, and morality. The rejection of ethno-nationalism is nothing more than a symptom of the rejection of God's law in its entirety, sadly even by professed Christians in many cases.

The foundation of a Biblical nation as defined in the Table of Nations is derived from common ancestry, common religion, common history, and common customs, and mutually possessed ideas and values will be built upon this foundation. In America we have made the same mistake as the Romans before us, and we will not escape their eventual fate. We European Christians who are heirs of Western Civilization are at a crossroads. We can either choose to continue to wantonly

---

[19] See the Mayflower Compact.
[20] The first Constitutional policy was the Naturalization Act of 1790.

follow the paths trod by our Roman imperial pagan forebears in which case we will meet the same impending doom that very nearly ruined the West, or we can revive the spirit of Christian nationalism which saved the West and preserved its civilization for generations of European people. The solution is to return to the old paths that our ancestors once trod (Jer. 6:16), and to once again embrace the God of our fathers. God alone can rebuild our cities and put flesh upon the dry bones of our ancestors (Eze. 37). It is incumbent upon us to embrace the future with optimism that God will preserve a faithful remnant to once again rebuild the ruins which we now dwell among (Is. 1:9).

Divorce, Miscegenation, and Polygamy:
A Comparative Approach to Their Morality

Part 1

May 25, 2012

Throughout my formative years as a budding racially-conscious Christian, I tried to reason through the question of the morality of racial intermarriage. Like many Christians from an evangelical background, it was difficult for me to accept that something could be wrong without an express and specific condemnation of the practice in Scripture. To condemn something that the Bible did not was the essence of legalism, and this was routinely condemned as the worst of sins, since it added to God's Word and dstracted from God's grace. For the record, I certainly believe that legalism is definitely wrong, and I believe that we should make a concerted effort to promote true Christian liberty wherewith Christ has made us free. While I reject legalism, I believe that antinomianism or the anything-goes mentality is also wrong a serious problem that Christians grapple with today.

As I was formulating my opinions on race and other important social concerns, miscegenation still did not sit well with me. At the very least, there was something that seemed odd about racially mixed relationships and marriages. One thing I learned as I was becoming cognizant of the perils of white folks is our declining demographics. By this century's end, we will soon become almost non-existent, even in places in which our ancestors have dwelt for centuries, if current trends continue. This is true in North America as well as in Europe. Intermarriage with non-whites only accelerates this process and hastens our demise as a people. The fact that the Bible teaches that ethnic and racial identity is a positive attribute of our identity led me to continue questioning the practice. Add to this the fact that most of our ancestors seemed to have historically been opposed to race-mixing, which continued until very recently.[21] Can we as Christians make a credible claim to obeying the commandment to honor our parents while simultaneously condemning their opposition to miscegenation as nothing more than the remnants of a more "racist" and "intolerant" era than the one we live in now?

---

[21] Carlton, Davis. "A Response to an Article on Kinism Published in the Puritan News Weekly." *Faith Heritage*, 15 Aug. 2011, faithandheritage.com/2011/08/a-response-to-an-article-on-kinism-published-in-the-puritan-news-weekly/.

Still, while these considerations predisposed me to believe that miscegenation was contrary to God's design, I remained uncommitted for some time as to the exact nature of the morality of miscegenation. Over time, I have developed my own thesis on the morality of miscegenation, which I formulated during discussions with Christians who were both in agreement and disagreement with the kinist approach. My approach is slightly different from the approach that Nil Desperandum takes in his excellent essay, On Interracial Marriage: The Moral Status of Miscegenation.[22] Those reading this brief essay should not consider my argument to be in opposition to Nil's view. To the contrary, I assent wholeheartedly to the positions that Nil takes. This should simply be considered an adjunct to the issues and arguments that Nil brings up while discussing the important topic of miscegenation.

Over the course of many discussions with both proponents and opponents of miscegenation, I noticed that many of those who support miscegenation almost always point out that there is no single verse which either establishes that miscegenation is wrong or provides an exact hereditary distance that is sinful to cross by marriage. Many of our adversaries and friendly opponents wax triumphant at this point, noting that kinism simply seems to be steeped in legalism, making a rule where none exists in God's law. This is a serious charge indeed, and it needs to be confronted. While this typical alienist tactic seems strong when initially encountered, its perceived strength is merely superficial.[23]

This argument is similar to typical Baptist arguments against infant baptism. Baptists argue that because there is no explicit verse in the Bible, especially in the New Testament, then infants should not be baptized. What this argument misses is that the argument in favor of infant baptism is a very strong inferential argument. Far from ignoring what the Bible teaches, those who endorse infant baptism apply principles that are clearly taught in many specific passages. This particular argument against miscegenation works the same way, and it closely parallels the inferential argument Christ used in a confrontation with the Pharisees.

Christ Confounds the Pharisees' Argument for Divorce

Throughout Christ's ministry, the Pharisees were in a panic. They correctly perceived Him as a threat to their own power and influence over the Hebrews. Many of them ostensibly hated their Roman overlords and wanted to reestablish an independent Israel, but they maliciously made the ultimate betrayal by swearing an oath of loyalty to Caesar in order to secure Christ's crucifixion (John 19:15).

---

[22] Though referenced when this essay was originally written, the referenced article is no longer available on Faith and Heritage and is not among the essays Nil wished to reproduce here.
[23] Would, Ehud. "Alienism: Bramble Path to Oblivion." *Faith Heritage*, 14 Mar. 2012, faithandheritage.com/2012/03/alienism-bramble-path-to-oblivion/.

Their encounters with Christ were attempts to stump Him with legal and theological questions. The question with which we are particularly concerned is their question on divorce.[24]

First, the Pharisees ask Christ if divorce is permissible: *"Is it lawful for a man to put away his wife for every cause?"* (v. 3). Jesus responds,

> Have ye not read, that he which made them at the beginning made them male and female, And said, For this cause shall a man leave father and mother, and shall cleave to his wife: and they twain shall be one flesh? Wherefore they are no more twain, but one flesh. What therefore God hath joined together, let not man put asunder (vv. 4-6).

Jesus cites Genesis 2:24: *"Therefore shall a man leave his father and his mother, and shall cleave unto his wife: and they shall be one flesh."* Notice that the verse which Jesus cites contains no express prohibition of divorce. There is no "thou shalt not divorce" statement to be found here. The case that Jesus makes is *inferential*. He is inferring a meaning from the text that agrees with the spirit of what is written. To clarify, Jesus is not reading something into the text that is not already inherent there; the same inference could have been made by anyone else. His case is strong, compelling, and in agreement with what God inspired through Moses.

Christ points out that marriage is something instituted by God. God created Adam and gave him Eve as his wife. Since marriage is a divine institution as old as humanity itself, then humanity has no right to dissolve or alter the nature of marriage. Christ views the marriage of Adam and Eve as archetypal; it thus serves as the foundation upon which subsequent marriages should be based. Christ reasons that since God had created Eve for Adam and inseparably joined them for life, so too should all marriages be lifelong. The Pharisees' legalism here led them to interpret the letter of the law while ignoring its spirit. If God joins a couple together in matrimony, then even the self-righteous Pharisees have no legal basis for rending this union asunder.

The Pharisees do not attempt to dispute the logic that Christ had used to argue for the indissolubility of marriage, because they cannot. Instead, they jump to another passage of the Bible that seems to justify their own perspective on the permissibility of divorce. In a classic case of proof-texting, the Pharisees ask: *"Why did Moses then command to give a writing of divorcement, and to put her away?"* (v. 7). The reason that this constitutes proof-texting is because the Pharisees have cited a verse which permits divorce without taking its context or qualifications into account. The verse they cite is Deuteronomy 24:1, which states:

---

[24] The following verse references are from Matthew 19. This account is also recorded in Mark 10:1-12.

> "When a man hath taken a wife, and married her, and it come to pass that she find no favour in his eyes, because he hath found some uncleanness in her: then let him write her a bill of divorcement, and give it in her hand, and send her out of his house."

Jesus responds to their mishandling of Scripture:

> *Moses because of the hardness of your hearts suffered you to put away your wives: but from the beginning it was not so. And I say unto you, whosoever shall put away his wife, except it be for fornication, and shall marry another, committeth adultery: and whoso marrieth her which is put away doth commit adultery (vv. 8 and 9).*

Jesus acknowledges that Moses had indeed permitted divorce because of the hardness of the people's hearts. However, He again refers back to Genesis 2:24 when He states, *"from the beginning it was not so."* This demonstrates that Jesus considered the creation of man and woman and their permanent joining together as husband and wife to be normative, such that any later developments were to be a mere accommodation to less-than-ideal circumstances. Jesus also clarifies for us the meaning of Deuteronomy 24:1 when He says that it is adultery to divorce and remarry, *"except it be for fornication."* The Pharisees ignored the fact that while Moses did permit divorce and remarriage in Deuteronomy 24, the reason that a wife would find no favor in her husband's eyes was because *"he hath found some uncleanness in her."*

To a legalistic Pharisee, "uncleanness" could mean just about anything if we consult extant rabbinic writings in the time of Jesus. Jesus states in no uncertain terms that the uncleanness to which Moses refers strictly involves illicit sexual intercourse which dissolves the marriage bond. Although God never intends for divorce, He allows it as an accommodation when grievous sin has been committed. Even when one spouse commits adultery, it is still better to reconcile than to allow the marriage to end. This can easily be discerned in the example of Hosea, whom God tells to reconcile with his adulterous wife Gomer as an example of how God reconciles with Israel, even though Israel had gone whoring after heathen gods. The reconciliation of an estranged married couple is a wonderful testament to Christian charity and a demonstration to the unbelieving world of God's love and compassion for erring sinners. Even when divorce and remarriage does happen to be permissible, we miss out on a magnificent opportunity to demonstrate our faith to nonbelievers.

Relevance to the Issue of Miscegenation

At this point, many might be thinking, "Great, you've outlined the classic Christian argument against divorce and remarriage, but what does this have to do with miscegenation? Isn't that what you are supposed to be writing about?" The reason I invoke this passage is because, over the course of several discussions, I have noticed how alienist arguments in favor of miscegenation often parallel the dubious argument that the Pharisees used to argue in favor of divorce and remarriage. We are conditioned to think of legalism, such as the Pharisees represented, as something that prohibits what should otherwise be permitted, only taking into account explicit Bible passages. Thus, kinists who oppose miscegenation are often labeled as legalists or Pharisees. The reality is that legalism can cut both ways. Legalism can indeed argue that something should be forbidden which in reality should be allowed. A good example of this is the prohibition of alcohol amongst the teetotalists. However, legalism can often use crafty legal arguments to argue that something should be permitted which should generally be forbidden. (Think of a lawyer who uses a legal loophole to exonerate a dubious client.) I believe that most arguments that alienists use to promote the general permissibility of miscegenation are of this variety of legalism.

We can easily use the same kind of argument that Christ used against the Pharisees of His day to dispel the alienist arguments of our day. The alienist begins by asking the kinist if there is any objection to a Christian marrying someone outside of his race or ethnicity. The alienist, like the Pharisee centuries before, is looking for a word-for-word condemnation in God's law of the practice that he seeks to permit. Like Christ, however, kinists do not need to give the alienists an exact Bible verse to prove our case. Instead, we can refer back to Adam and Eve as the archetypal marriage, the same way that Christ did when the Pharisees confronted him.

When God created Adam, He noted that it was not good for the man to remain alone. God decided to create a helpmeet for him. Out of Adam's rib, God created woman and presented her to her husband, Adam. Adam commented upon meeting his wife: *"This is now bone of my bones, and flesh of my flesh: she shall be called Woman, because she was taken out of Man"* (Gen. 2:23). Adam's declaration is significant because of the way this expression of a "bone and flesh" relationship is used in the rest of the Bible. One cardinal rule of interpretation is to always interpret Scripture by Scripture. Whatever we think that "bone and flesh" might mean, it is important to allow its usage in the Bible to dictate its meaning.

Many people argue that there is only one race, the human race, since all are descended from the first couple of Adam and Eve (Gen. 3:20; Acts 17:26a). While it is true that all humans share a common origin, it is not true that there are not meaningful distinctions within humanity. The Apostle Paul acknowledges this very fact even as he asserts our common origin in Adam. He states that God has made from *"one blood all nations of men for to dwell on all the face of the earth, and hath determined the times before appointed, and the bounds of their habitation"* (Acts 17:26). The word nation is rendered from the Greek word ethnos, from which we derive our concept of ethnicity. Therefore, it should be clear that Paul is referring to nations as peoples who are distinguished by heredity, and not to simple geo-political entities. This is a modern-day corruption of the original meaning of the word "nation." So, when the Bible uses the idiom "bone and flesh," is it referring to the universal descent all possess from the first man? Or is it referring to some sort of subsidiary ethnic relationship? To determine this, we must look at how this idiom is used elsewhere in the Bible.

Since the first place that the bone-and-flesh idiom appears is with regards to Adam and Eve, and this couple is the source of humanity, many people might think that this expression has no ethnic significance. But this expression does have racial and ethnic significance. It is consistently used to express a close hereditary relationship, often between close family members. It is also used to communicate a broader kinship as well, but never extends beyond ethnic distinctions. Laban uses this phrase to articulate his relationship with his nephew Jacob (Gen. 29:14). This was significant, for Jacob was commanded by his parents to seek out someone from among their relations to marry, and was specifically commanded not to marry someone from among the Canaanites. Laban assures Jacob that they are kin using the expression "bone and flesh." Laban's comment would have been utterly nonsensical if "bone and flesh" were understood merely to denote a common humanity. Obviously, Laban was not suggesting that the Canaanites were not human, only that they were not kin to Jacob in the way that Laban and his family were kin.

The bone-and-flesh paradigm is also used to establish the principle of kin-rule. God tells the Israelites only to allow a brother as opposed to a stranger to rule over them (Deut. 17:15). How did the Israelites interpret this law? They knew that someone who ruled over them had to be a member of their ethnic nation. When the Israelites consecrated David as their king, they exclaimed: *"Behold, we are thy bone and thy flesh"* (2 Sam. 5:1; see also 1 Chr. 11:1). King David was an Israelite of the tribe of Judah, who was promised that the royal scepter would never depart from his tribe (Gen. 49:10). Christ is the archetypal ruler and is also a descendant of the tribe of Judah. One of Christ's prominent titles throughout the New Testament is "son of David." This shows that King David is an Old Testament type fulfilled in Christ. King David is presented as an archetypal ruler in the same way that Adam and Eve are presented as the archetypal marriage. Thus we can see that being of the same bone and flesh is precisely what Moses had in mind when he commanded that the Israelites take a king from among their brethren in Deut. 17:15.

Just as the marriage of Adam and Eve serves as our example of what constitutes marriage, King David provides us with a firm example of what constitutes biblical civil government. In the same way that Jesus appealed to the nature of the marriage between Adam and Eve in his dispute with the Pharisees to argue for the indissolubility of marriage, so too should we make a similar appeal in our disputes with the alienists. When Adam comments that Eve was of the same "bone and flesh," he is providing us with an aspect of what "helpmeet" means. God states that He will create a helpmeet for Adam, and presents him with a woman of his own bone and flesh; hence, of his own ethnicity. Therefore, we can be safe in concluding that this should be a normative aspect of all marriages. I am certainly not the first to employ this rationale. Many other Christians before me have arrived at this conclusion as well. R.J. Rushdoony writes:

> *Man was created in the image of God (Gen. 1:26), and woman in the reflected image of God in man, and from man (I Cor. 11:1-12; Gen. 2:18, 21-23). "Helpmeet" means a reflection or mirror, an image of man, indicating that a woman must have something religiously and culturally in common with her husband. The burden of the law is thus against inter-religious, inter-racial, and inter-cultural marriages, in that they normally go against the very community which marriage is designed to establish.*[25]

Conclusion

It should be apparent that the alienists of our time treat the issue of miscegenation in the same way that the Pharisees of Christ's time approached the issue of divorce. The Pharisees capitalized on the fact that there is no clear prohibition of divorce in the Mosaic law and affirmed that divorce was permissible on the basis of the case law in Deut. 24:1. Christ clearly reproved the Pharisees' tortured logic and rescued the true intention of God by turning their attention to the institution of marriage by God Himself in the Garden of Eden. Likewise, the kinist rescues the true intention of God for marriage by appealing to the same passage that discusses the institution of marriage. Just as God intended for marriage to be a lifelong union, God also intended for marriage to by practiced among those of the same ethnic background, seeing as this is how "bone and flesh" is used throughout the biblical narrative. The Pharisees dismissed Christ's defense of marriage by appealing to an accommodation to divorce in the Mosaic law and the alienist unwittingly follows suit. Christ clearly demonstrates how the Pharisees' appeal to an accommodation in the Mosaic law is problematic. In the next article, we will see

---

[25] Rushdoony, R.J. *The Institutes of Biblical Law*, p. 256f.

how the alienists' appeal to an accommodation in the Mosaic law is equally problematic.

Part 2
May 28, 2012

In the previous article, we saw demonstrated that kinists can easily defend the normative nature of intra-ethnic marriage in the same way that Christ defended the indissoluble nature of marriage. Both Christ and kinists appeal to the language used to describe the institution of marriage to defend our positions. Christ most reasonably infers that marriage is a lifelong covenant since God joins a couple together in matrimony, and kinists reasonably infer that marriage is to be between those who are of a similar ethnic background. This is because marriage is normatively between members of the same bone and flesh (Gen. 2:23), which phrase is used to denote common ethnic or national identity elsewhere in the Bible. Like the Pharisees' inadequate use of a Mosaic accommodation, the alienist's response is likewise inadequate.

The Alienist Appeal to a Mosaic Accommodation

The alienist often responds by suggesting that the argument elaborated in the previous article is irrelevant, and usually provides a couple of different rebuttals to the kinist position. The first is to suggest that many godly men in the Bible were involved in interracial marriages, but there are a couple of problems with this viewpoint. First of all, we cannot establish the morality of something simply by providing examples of godly people doing what we are defending. No traditional Christian advocates for practicing polygamy, for instance, simply because the godly patriarchs practiced it. Another way of alienists respond to kinists is to provide Deuteronomy 21:10-14 as a proof text:

> [10]*When thou goest forth to war against thine enemies, and the LORD thy God hath delivered them into thine hands, and thou hast taken them captive,*
>
> [11]*And seest among the captives a beautiful woman, and hast a desire unto her, that thou wouldest have her to thy wife;*
> [12]*Then thou shalt bring her home to thine house, and she shall shave her head, and pare her nails;*

13And she shall put the raiment of her captivity from off her, and shall remain in thine house, and bewail her father and her mother a full month: and after that thou shalt go in unto her, and be her husband, and she shall be thy wife.

14And it shall be, if thou have no delight in her, then thou shalt let her go whither she will; but thou shalt not sell her at all for money, thou shalt not make merchandise of her, because thou hast humbled her.

Notice how this alienist response mimics the response of the Pharisees to Jesus when they were discussing divorce. The Pharisees tried to use Deuteronomy 24:1 to justify their case for the permissibility of divorce, and the alienists try to use Deuteronomy 21:10-14 to justify their case for the permissibility of miscegenation. Like the Pharisees' argument, the alienist's argument is problematic. In the same way that the Pharisees argued that divorce was a matter of moral indifference based upon a concession in the Mosaic law, so too do alienists argue that miscegenation is a matter of moral indifference based upon an analogous concession in the Mosaic law. Like Jesus, kinists should refer the alienist back to God's original intention for marriage. Whatever concessions the Mosaic law provides because of the hardness of men's hearts, these concessions should never be allowed to replace what God intends for marriage. Ethnic homogeneity is clearly advocated based upon comparing the way that "bone and flesh" is used in the Bible with its use in Genesis 2:23.[26] Just as the Pharisees misapplied the concession in Deuteronomy 24:1, the alienists misapply the concession given in Deuteronomy 21:10-14.

---

[26] Some might demur at this point by observing the way that "bone and flesh" is used in Eph. 5:30: "*For we are members of his body, of his flesh, and of his bones.*" This is the only use of the bone-and-flesh idiom in the New Testament of which I am aware. Some argue that because all Christians, as members of the Church, are connected to Christ in a bone-and-flesh relationship, this nullifies the Old Testament's more physical use of the term. But context is critical, as with any other passage. We must be careful not to use this verse as a mere proof text. The Apostle Paul is speaking in a passage which metaphorically considers the relationship between Christ and the Church to be a marriage (Eph. 5:22-33). Just as Christ loves the Church, men ought to love their wives, and just as the Church ought to submit to Christ in all things, so too should wives submit to their husbands in all things. Paul is simply continuing this metaphor of marriage by referring back to the bone-and-flesh principle. This demonstrates that Paul considers this principle to have continuing validity for marriage today.

It is important not to carry metaphorical language beyond what is intended by the author. By comparing the relationship of Christ and the Church to marriage, Paul is highlighting an important pair of attributes in this relationship, namely the love of Christ for the Church and the Church's submission to Christ. That is all. It would be incorrect to try to apply other aspects of marriage to the identity of the Church. An example of this would be to say that because the Church is the bride of Christ, the Church is therefore essentially female in character. That would be a category fallacy, as metaphors or analogies are never intended to conceptually replace what is being compared. In other words, the marriage of Christ and the Church does not replace or do away with individual Christian marriages. It would be absurd to argue that because all Christians are members of the body of Christ, we therefore do not have physical bodies of our own. Thus, while all Christians have an important connection as members of the body and bride of Christ, this does not replace individual bodies or marriages. Paul's usage of the bone-and-flesh principle in his analogy to marriage clearly indicates that Paul considered this principle as an essential part of marriage even under the New Covenant.

It is true that Deuteronomy 21:10-14 provides us with an example of Israelites marrying foreigners. But like the Pharisees, the alienists make overgeneralizations. This passage in Deuteronomy is referring to women taken in battle, and thus, obviously, did not give anyone a blank check to marry any foreigner he wanted. The Israelites would not have been permitted to marry Canaanites, for instance, since these nations would be driven out by total war (Deut. 7:1-4). Moreover, this concession naturally would have presumed that the war in question would have been a just war, lest Israel be charged with wanton kidnapping and murder. These wars would have likely been fought against nations in their immediate vicinity, who were also descended from Shem. These would have been brother nations due to their close common ancestry.[27] Thus it is unlikely that Deuteronomy 21:10-14 is dealing with what we consider interracial marriage in the first place.

But even if it could be construed in such a way to include more distant non-Semitic nations, such marriages would have been rare and certainly non-normative. Another factor to consider is that the binding nature of these marriages was less than what was normally expected. An Israelite could divorce a foreign captive wife only if he had "no delight in her," whereas he would have only been allowed to divorce because of "uncleanness" under normal circumstances (where, again, "uncleanness" refers to sexual immorality).[28] This further demonstrates that this is a mere concession, and nothing should be generalized from this regarding God's will for marriage. This concession would not have allowed women to marry foreigners, especially when they stood to inherit property. In this case, they would have been required to marry someone within their father's tribe (Num. 36).

Finally, we should also note that this concession did not apply to priests. Levitical priests were required to set a good example for marriage, and so their standards were set higher than for Israelites in general (Lev. 21:14; Ezek. 44:22). All of this demonstrates that 99.9% of racially-mixed relationships and marriages do not fall under the concession given in Deut. 21:10-14. It is apparent that the majority of divorce cases today are not based upon a proper application of Deut. 24:1 or Matthew 19:1-9, in the same way that the majority of racially-mixed marriages do not fall under the concession given in Deut. 21:10-14. And even when this concession can be applied, it does not mean that it would not be better to marry under traditional circumstances according to the example that God has given us in Adam and Eve.

---

[27] See, for example, Numbers 20:14 and Deuteronomy 23:7.
[28] Compare Deut. 21:14 to Deut. 24:1.

Application of this Argument to Polygamy and Other Issues

This same logic is used frequently by Christians without their even realizing it. If we consider the question of whether it is permissible for a man to have more than one wife, we use a very similar argument to show that polygamy should generally not be practiced. Most Christians correctly point back to the monogamous marriage of Adam and Eve to indicate that God intends for Christian marriage to be monogamous. There is no Bible verse that explicitly prohibits a man from having more than one wife, and we could also find plenty of godly patriarchs who had more than one wife. Like divorce and miscegenation, the Mosaic law provides a concession to this as well (Deut. 21:15-17).[29] In spite of a concession given in the Bible and examples of godly men who practiced polygamy, virtually no one argues that polygamy should be permitted today on this basis. Would a pastor consider it legalism to insist that a man have only one wife? After all, with a possible exception for clergy (1 Tim. 3:2), there is no clear prohibition of polygamy in the Bible, and it seems that the law allows for it under some circumstances. The Church properly considers polygamy to be contrary to God's intention for marriage, and thus does not allow her members to practice it. In doing so, the Church appropriately applies Christ's logic that He used to confound the Pharisees.

We could apply this logic to other issues important to marriage as well. Should a couple who wants to marry be similar in age? Of course; that should not even be controversial. We should be able to say this without a Bible verse to tell us this. The fact that couples ought to be similar in age should simply make sense to us. This could also be justified by appealing to Adam and Eve: Adam and Eve were very similar in age, with Adam being slightly older than Eve. Can a man marry a woman who is younger than him? Of course: married couples do not have to have to be born on the same day. However, we should be able to extrapolate from this that married couples should be suitably similar, and age is included in this. Historically, most married couples have been within ten years of age.

Can a couple who is more than ten years apart marry each other? Absolutely they can, particularly if the couple is similar in other ways, including race and religion. However, we should be able to say that it is wrong for an eighty-four-year-old man to marry a nine-year-old girl! This clearly goes against the intent of marriage that God established in the example of Adam and Eve. Can a woman marry a younger man? Sure, but again, there must be other essential similarities that balance this out. It can certainly be more difficult for a woman to submit to a younger man, which is required of her (Num. 30; 1 Cor. 11:3, 14:34; Eph. 5:22-24;

---

[29] Interestingly enough, this concession appears right after the possible concession for miscegenation given in Deut. 21:10-14. It is strange how people do not seem to suggest that Deut. 21:15-17 constitutes a blank check for polygamy in the same way that many argue that Deut. 21:10-14 supposedly provides a blank check for miscegenation.

Col. 3:18). The order of creation was intrinsic to the roles of marriage itself (1 Cor. 11:8-9; 1 Tim. 2:13). This is why marriage gaps are even more critical when a woman is older than her husband. Historically, "cougar" marriages were completely anomalous, and are only promoted today in the entertainment industry as a means to further undermine Christian order.

Conclusions

After discerning that there are indeed similarities in the way that the Bible treats divorce, miscegenation, and polygamy, we can easily see that the way that the alienist approaches the question of miscegenation is clearly flawed. The alienist wants to remove any moral prohibition or taboo from the practice of miscegenation. Indeed, some alienists like John Piper argue that miscegenation actually glorifies God. Like divorce and polygamy, miscegenation should be prohibited in all but the most extraordinary circumstances. Divorce and polygamy might be permitted by the general equity of Deut. 24:1 and Deut. 21:15-17, respectively, but these would be considered exceptions to the rule that God has given us in the example of Adam and Eve. It is the Church's duty to ensure that these practices are not allowed to be considered acceptable under normal circumstances.

We can say the same thing about racial intermarriage. There may be rare circumstances in which intermarriage can be justified on the basis of the general equity of Deut. 21:10-14, but the Church should make sure that this too does not become the norm. Even when they might be justified due to extraordinary circumstances, mostly dealing with displacement due to war or crisis,[30] they should still be actively avoided. Acceptable circumstances are indeed rare, and especially so today. Demographically speaking, whites are staring down the barrel of a gun, and we cannot afford to allow these demographic trends to continue. What we should be able to conclude is that the modern church is certainly wrong to follow the pop-cultural trend in promoting racially mixed marriages. Mixed marriages clearly violate the standard that God provided for us in the marriage of our first parents, Adam and Eve, on the basis of the bone-and-flesh principle taught in Gen. 2:23. The sooner the Church wakes up to this fact, the better it will be for everyone.

---

[30] One historical example might be the Confederados of Brazil, who are descended from some Confederate expatriates that fled the South after the War Between the States in 1865.

Ten Christian Zionist Myths

Part 1

October 17, 2012

Introduction

Christian Zionism is a relatively recent political movement within evangelical Christianity, an attempt to harmonize evangelical theology with the political ideology called Zionism. Zionism as a political movement began in the nineteenth century as a Jewish-influenced effort to create a Jewish homeland in the Middle East. As dispensational theology began to gain traction among conservative Protestants, Zionism became a political goal affirmed in some dispensationalist circles. For the sake of clarity, we should distinguish between dispensationalism, which is a theological perspective, and Christian Zionism, which is a political paradigm. Not all dispensationalists are necessarily Christian Zionists, and not all Christian Zionists are necessarily dispensationalists. However, the overlap is significant enough that the two terms are commonly used interchangeably throughout these essays.

To begin, we should review the history of the creation of the modern state of Israel. Zionism was first coined in 1890 and with its goal *"to establish a home for the Jewish people in Eretz Israel."* Zionism emerged as a major political movement in the twentieth century, and the modern state of Israel was established as a result of the social and political circumstances that developed out of the two World Wars. What the First World War set into motion, the Second World War made a reality.

From the outset of World War I, Zionist Jews financed both the Allied Powers and the Central Powers, but generally favored Germany and the Central Powers against their Allied enemies. Many Jewish people in neutral America were from Germany and favored Kaiser Wilhelm against Czar Nicholas. The tide began to turn in 1916, as Zionist agents in Britain were able to secure the support for Zionism from certain British politicians like Arthur Balfour. With this show of support from Britain, Zionists switched sides and were able to secure American entry into the war on the side of the British and Allied Powers, despite the campaign promise by President Woodrow Wilson to remain neutral. With this change, the tide of the war changed dramatically as Germany faced defeat and unconditional surrender.

Zionists secured the Balfour Declaration, which pledged British imperial support for "a national home for the Jewish people" in the region of Palestine. This would not be realized, however, until the conclusion of World War II.

Just as in World War I, Zionist bankers managed to finance both sides of World War II, before throwing their ultimate support to the Allies against the Axis Powers. Specifically, Zionist bankers financed the National Socialists until their victory in 1933, when they promptly supported the cause of the Soviets and British Imperialists against National Socialist Germany. The putative measures of the Versailles Treaty, combined with the economic sanctions against Germany by Zionist bankers in the early 1930s, precipitated hostilities between National Socialist Germany and the Allied victors of World War I. The defeat of National Socialist Germany, ironically an early supporter of Zionist goals, led to the realization of the Zionist dream. The creation of the state of Israel occurred in 1948, only after displacing many of the original Palestinian residents who were already dwelling there. Gary Burge writes, "*According to U.N. records in June 1999, about 3.6 million Palestinian refugees are the victims of Israel's nationhood.*"[31] Many of the Palestinians displaced have been Christians, and many churches are in ruins as a result of the ruthless activities of the Israeli paramilitary. In the next few articles, we will investigate several popular Christian Zionist myths that wrongly justify this activity.

Are Modern Ethnic Jews Lineal Descendants of Ancient Israel?

The first myth of Christian Zionism is arguably the most important, because the entire theory of Zionism in general and Christian Zionism in particular hinges on the idea that modern Jewish people are the lineal descendants of the Biblical Jacob. If this theory can be disproved, or at least discredited, then we lose any grounds to believe that the modern Jews are God's chosen people with a divine right to the land in Palestine, and the foundation of the Christian Zionist theory is undermined.

One confounding issue in defining the Jewish identity is the meaning of the word "Jew." Many people consider "Jew" and "Israelite" or "Hebrew" to be synonymous. But the problem with this common misunderstanding is that "Jew" is a contraction of a couple of different words which have different meanings. Originally, "Jew" was simply intended as a contraction of "Judah," which was the dominant southern tribe that continued the Davidic line after the northern insurrection. Thus, all Jews in this sense would be Israelites, but not all Israelites were Jews. The word "Jew" eventually morphed into a contraction for "Judea," derived from the name of the Roman province in the region of Judah. During the revolt of Judas

---

[31] Burge, Gary M. *Whose Land? Whose Promise? What Christians Are Not Being Told About Israel and the Palestinians*, pp. 208-210.

Maccabeus, many Edomites and other non-Israelites were compelled to convert to Judaism. From this time forward, a Judean was more of a geographic identification, rather than an ethnic one. Thus, the contraction "Jew" underwent a substantive revision by the time period of the New Testament. An example of this revision is that the puppet king of Judea under Roman rule was Herod, who was considered Jewish even though he was ethnically an Edomite, not an Israelite.

After the destruction of the temple in Jerusalem by the Romans in A.D. 70, genealogical records could no longer establish a Levitical priesthood among the Jewish people. Patrilineal descent from the tribe of Levi was considered essential to membership in the priesthood. For example, families had to be able to establish their priestly lineage by genealogy during the rebuilding of Jerusalem under Ezra and Nehemiah (Ezra 2:59-62). The thorough destruction of the temple and the city of Jerusalem resulted in the loss of any records that could establish a Levitical priesthood. Since this time, practicing Jews have only had rabbis or teachers. No Jewish leader can legitimately be considered a priest, since they all lack the requisite genealogical records. This destruction of the temple and the ordinances of the Old Testament were predicted by the prophet Daniel in Dan. 9:27, when he wrote that Christ would cause the sacrifice and the oblations to cease until the consummation of the abomination of desolations. This was also what Christ was predicting in the Olivet Discourse, when he stated that "not one stone" of the temple would be left upon another (Matt. 24:1-2).

It is not impossible that someone who is considered to be Jewish would be descended from the original Israelites, but many are descended from non-Israelites who converted to Talmudic Judaism. Jewish people can be considered as broadly Caucasian, though not originally of Indo-European extraction. There are several ethnic divisions among modern Jews. The largest of these are the Ashkenazim, who historically have dwelt in Germany and Eastern Europe. Another large division is the Sephardim, who dwelt in Spain, Portugal, and some areas of North Africa. The Ashkenazim have an extensive history in Europe and comprise the majority of Jewish people whom we encounter here in the United States, as well as the majority of Jewish people who comprise the modern state of Israel.

Most Ashkenazi Jews descend from a Turkish-Mongolic tribe called the Khazars, who converted to Judaism in the late eighth and early ninth century. They do not originate from the ancient Israelites. The definitive work on the conversion of the Khazars to rabbinic Judaism is *The Thirteenth Tribe* by Arthur Koestler. Koestler himself is of Hungarian Jewish descent, and he wrote his *magnum opus* in order to refute both National Socialist and Zionist theories of the origin of Eastern European Jews. Why does this matter? This is crucial, because Zionist claims about an intrinsic, God-given Jewish right to Palestine hinge on theories that most or all Jews descend from the original tribes of Israel. Koestler's work, along with the works of other ethnologists, has demonstrated that most of the Jews in Palestine today have a decidedly weak claim to an ancestral tie to the land there.

The result of this is that Christian Zionists have based their entire paradigm upon a faulty premise: namely, that today's modern Jews are (or at least mostly are) descendants of the ancient European tribes. Many of the most hard-line supporters of Christian Zionists are whites. One can easily wonder if some of the staunch support that white Christians show to Israel is due to their own loss of racial and ethnic identity. In the wake of the overwhelming vilification of white ethnic interests, many white Christians have consequently turned to the more politically acceptable support for Jewish people and for Israel.

Ironically, most white Christians have as good as a claim on ancient Israel as anyone. I'm not invoking far-fetched theories derived from specifically Christian Identity or British/Anglo-Israel claims, either. It seems that, during the time of the Maccabean revolt against the Seleucid overlords of the Israelites, the Israelites established a pact with the Spartans based upon the fact that both the Israelites and the Spartans were descended from Abraham (1 Macc. 12:21). The Spartans (sometimes referred to as the Lacedemonians) are portrayed in the movie *300* for their heroic stand against the Persians at Thermopylae, and are a major pillar of European civilization. If the Spartans are descendants of Abraham, as the ancient Israelites believed, then it would seem logical that all Europeans are likewise descended from Abraham. This could explain at least in part how Japheth (the general ancestor of Europeans) dwells in the tents of Shem, according to Noah's prophecy in Gen. 9:27. It is a truly sad irony that European Christians expend so much energy on lobbying for a group of people with a less clear claim to descent from the ancient Israelites than they have themselves.

Regardless of where one believes that the ancient Israelites ended up, or where they were scattered, it should be clear from research done by ethnologists like Koestler that modern Jewish people do not have the kind of claim that Christian Zionists maintain. Interestingly enough, Christian Zionism is essentially a form a Jewish supremacy. It is contrary to Biblical teaching to assert that anyone has an intrinsic covenant with God based solely upon ethnicity. Unfortunately, in today's climate of consummate hypocrisy, many Christians do not bat an eye at overt Jewish supremacy, but consider any claim to white solidarity to be irredeemably "racist."

Was the Recognition of the Nation of Israel in 1948 a Fulfillment of Biblical Prophecy?

Dispensationalists and Christian Zionists will often suggest that the "rebirth" of the nation of Israel was a fulfillment of a prophecy that Christ gave in his famous Olivet Discourse (so called because Jesus was revealing these prophecies on the

Mount of Olives, according to Matt. 24:3). The primary text used by Christian Zionists to assert this is Christ's illustration using the fig tree in the Olivet Discourse. In the Olivet Discourse, Jesus is predicting the destruction of the temple and a period of great tribulation that would precede His coming in Judgment upon the ungodly. The passage of interest to Christian Zionists is Matthew 24:32-33, in which Jesus states: *"Now learn a parable of the fig tree; When his branch is yet tender, and putteth forth leaves, ye know that summer is nigh. So likewise ye, when ye shall see all these things, know that it is near, even at the doors."*

If you find it difficult to see how this passage relates to events in post-World War II Palestine, you are not alone. Very few theologians historically made the connection that Christian Zionists make regarding this passage. However, fairness dictates that we investigate the rationale behind the Christian Zionist usage of this passage as a proof for their position. Most dispensationalists and Christian Zionists assert that the image of the fig tree represents the nation of Israel herself. This is based upon a couple of passages in which figs or a fig tree seems to represent Israel or at least Judah. Let us examine these passages in turn. The first passage is Jeremiah 24, the second is Matthew 21:19-20, and the third is Luke 13:6-9.

In Jeremiah 24, the nation of Israel is symbolized as two baskets of figs. One of the baskets contains good figs and the other basket contains bad figs. God explains to Jeremiah that the good figs are the faithful of Israel whom He will return home from the Babylonian exile (vv. 5-7). God then explains that the bad figs are the faithless of Israel who will be scattered among the nations to be a reproach and a taunt (vv. 8-10). With this in mind, it should be noted that only the faithful among true Israel will return from exile. For reasons already established, I believe that it is incorrect to consider modern Jewry as equivalent to Israel in this passage, but even if this passage is referring to modern Jewish people, it should be obvious that they cannot qualify as the good figs in this prophecy. Modern Jews have not experienced the national repentance and conversion to Christianity that this passage requires for restoration.

It is significant that most dispensationalist commentaries written prior to 1948 believed that Jewish people would experience this national conversion prior to being restored for this very reason. The events of 1948 then became a *post hoc* explanation to dispensationalists that the fig tree "prophecy" in the Olivet Discourse had been fulfilled. As for the fulfillment of this prophecy, we can see that God did take care of the faithful Israelites among the captives. The book of Daniel is filled with information on God's provision for the faithful captives. God ultimately did restore this remnant to the land under the Persian King Cyrus, who allowed Ezra and Nehemiah to rebuild Jerusalem under David's descendant, Zerubbabel (2 Chronicles 36:22-23). An ultimate fulfillment can be perceived when the Israel of God, which includes all of the faithful, is restored to paradise in the New Heavens and the New Earth (Rev. 21-22). There simply is no concrete connection between what is predicted in Jeremiah 24 and in the Olivet Discourse.

The next two passages can be considered together because of their similarity. In Luke 13:6-9, Jesus gives a brief parable in which a man plants a fig tree in his vineyard and observes that it produces no fruit for three years. The vinedresser pleads with the Master to allow him one more year to tend to the fig tree, after which it would be cut down if it produced no more fruit. Matthew 21:19 (cf. Mark 11:12-14) is a similar story. Jesus is hungry and sees a fig tree from far off in the distance and approaches it in order to eat off of its branches. When Jesus and the disciples reach the tree, however, they discover that there is no fruit. Jesus curses the tree and says, "*Let no fruit grow on thee henceforward forever.*" It is certainly possible that Jesus is referring to the faithless and fruitless people in Judea who were rejecting him, but this does not help the Christian Zionist cause, since Jesus curses the tree and suggests that it will never be fruitful ever again. This is hardly congruous with a prediction that Israel as the fig tree would one day bud again. A much clearer symbol for Israel is the olive tree of Romans 11. In this passage, the Apostle Paul calls the tribes of Israel the "natural branches" that had been given the covenant but were cut off in unbelief. The Gentile nations are "wild branches" that have been grafted into the covenant (here illustrated as an olive tree) through their faith. Israelite believers can be re-grafted into the covenant by faith, and the Gentiles can be cut off in the future by disbelief. This is a far more concrete illustration than the tenuous connection that is drawn between the fig tree illustrations in the Olivet Discourse to the nation of Israel.

A couple of final considerations demonstrate that the creation of the state of Israel in the Middle East in 1948 was not a fulfillment of Biblical prophecy. The first is to notice the way that the fig tree image is used in the Olivet Discourse. Matthew's account of the Olivet Discourse is the most detailed, and we can recall that in Matthew 24:32-33, Jesus suggested that the budding of the leaves of the fig tree means that summer is drawing near, so, likewise, when the disciples see the signs that Jesus predicted, they should know that His coming was near. The reason that this allusion to the seasonal budding patterns of the fig tree cannot be taken as a prophecy of what occurred in 1948 are twofold. The first is that we can compare this statement to Luke's Gospel account of the Olivet Discourse and see that Jesus is not drawing a specific reference to the fig tree, but simply making an analogy based upon the budding patterns of trees in general. Luke's version of this statement in Luke 21:29-31 begins as follows: "*Behold the fig tree, and all the trees.*" As Ralph Woodrow points out, if the fig tree is supposed to represent Israel, then Luke's reference to all trees must be indicative of all nations! For this reason, even a strong dispensationalist commentary notes that among dispensationalists, "*the fig tree ... is universally interpreted to mean the Jewish nation, BUT THIS COULD NOT POSSIBLY BE THE MEANING."*[32]

The second of these final considerations is what immediately follows the fig tree illustration. Jesus says, *"This generation shall not pass, till all these things be fulfilled"* (Matt. 24:34; Mark 13:30; Luke 21:32). Jesus makes several references to "this generation" in the Gospels, and there is not a single one that isn't obviously referring to his contemporaries. Passages like Matthew 12:38-45, 16:3-4, 17:17, and 23:36 clearly bear this out. In all of these passages, Jesus obviously means to address those present at that time. There is no reason to interpret "this generation" in the Olivet Discourse any differently. Dispensationalist C.I. Scofield suggested that "generation" in the Olivet Discourse was a reference to the fact that the Jewish race would survive until the prophecies of the Olivet Discourse were fulfilled. But there are a couple of problems with this explanation. One is that the Greek word *genea* is best translated as "generation." If the Evangelists wanted to convey the idea of "race," they could have used Greek words such as *genos* or *ethnos* to confer this idea. A second problem is that this would make Jesus's response to the disciples' question of when this would take place nonsensical. Simply stating that there would always be Israelites does not answer the question of when these events would take place. By interpreting the phrase "this generation" naturally, we understand Jesus to be making a time frame reference and providing a reasonable answer to the disciples' question.

The idea that the prophecies in the Olivet Discourse were fulfilled in the past, as opposed to awaiting a future fulfillment, is termed *preterism*. There is not space to provide a comprehensive defense of the preterist viewpoint, but the basic premise can be defended easily enough. A preterist will contend that the prophecies of the Olivet Discourse have been fulfilled in the first century A.D. within the lifetime of Jesus's contemporaries. Those who oppose preterism, called *futurists*, argue that this is impossible because Jesus's prophecies were not fulfilled. Jesus predicted the destruction of the temple (Matt. 24:1-3), which futurists understand to be a future temple that has not yet been built. Jesus also predicted that the nations would see Him coming on the clouds in judgment (Matt. 24:29-31). Many futurists consider Matthew 24:40-41 to be a prediction of the rapture, in which they suggest that Jesus will gather all of His elect at the end of a future tribulation. They connect these verses to Paul's prediction in 1 Thessalonians 4:13-18. Have these prophecies been fulfilled, as preterists contend?

First, we should point out that the temple that Jesus predicted would be destroyed was not a future temple which has yet to be built, but rather the temple that existed during His own lifetime. Jesus makes it clear in the early verses of Matthew 24 that it was the current temple that He was predicting would be de-

---

[32] *Dake's Annotated Reference Bible*, p. 27. Emphasis in original.

stroyed. There is no warrant for assuming that this prophecy has some future temple in view. What are we to make of Jesus's prediction that the nations would see Him coming on the clouds in judgment? Christ repeats this prediction before Caiaphas prior to His crucifixion in Matthew 26:63-64. While modern readers might misunderstand Christ's imagery, Caiaphas and the Sanhedrin most certainly did not! They understood that Christ's reference to *"coming on the clouds of heaven"* was a reference to his divinity. Jesus is making a reference to the coronation of the Son of Man in Daniel's vision (Dan. 7:13-14). Jesus combined this imagery with David's proclamation in Psalm 110 that his Lord would sit on the Lord's right hand on high. It was precisely this claim to divinity that caused the Sanhedrin to condemn him (Mark 14:63-63). Moreover, when Jesus speaks of His coming on the clouds, He is simply using a common Old Testament symbol for divine judgment. Clouds are used as an image when discussing judgment in passages such as Ezekiel 30:3, Joel 2:1-2, and Isaiah 19:1. This same imagery is reiterated by John in Rev. 1:7: *"Behold, he cometh with clouds."* David Chilton concludes,

> *"The crucifiers would see Him coming in judgment — that is, they would experience and understand that His Coming would mean wrath on the Land. . . . In the destruction of their city, their civilization, their Temple, their entire worldorder, they would understand that Christ had ascended to His Throne as Lord of heaven and earth."*[33]

Finally, Matthew 24:40-41 is not a prediction of the rapture. It is apparent from the context of this prediction that it is actually the unjust that are swept away in judgment and the righteous that are left behind. There is neither any warrant for trying to connect the prediction made in Matthew 24:36-41 to 1 Thessalonians 4:13-18.[34] Thus, when we understand the proper meaning of the predictions that Jesus is making in the Olivet Discourse, it is easy to see that these were indeed fulfilled in the first century within the lifetime of his contemporaries. The temple and the city of Jerusalem were destroyed by Roman soldiers crushing a Jewish rebellion in the year of A.D. 70. This was indeed Christ's divine sentence upon the city of Jerusalem for her unbelief, as the unrighteous were swept away in judgment. Since this time, there has been no formal worship according to Old Testament precepts, no Levitical priesthood, and — most importantly — no temple. Christ's claims have indeed been verified quite vividly, and His divinity has thus been confirmed beyond a shadow of a doubt.

---

[33] Chilton, David. *Days of Vengeance*, p. 66.
[34] For more information on the subject of eschatology, I recommend Hank Hanegraaff, *The Apocalypse Code*.

Conclusions

In this first installment on Christian Zionism, we have investigated two of the more prevalent myths that are popular within Christian Zionist circles. The idea that the Jewish people have a divine right to most, if not all, of the land of the Middle East is rooted in two myths. One is that those whom we typically identify as Jewish today are predominantly the lineal descendants of the original tribes of Israel. This thesis has been formidably challenged by Arthur Koestler, himself an Eastern European Jew. Koestler neither deifies nor vilifies the Jewish people, and has no apparent axe to grind. His only goal is to challenge the more extravagant claims to Jewish origins proposed by National Socialists and Zionists.

The second myth is that the creation of a Jewish state in the Middle East was a fulfillment of Christ's fig tree illustration used in the Olivet Discourse. This makes current Jewish settlements seem as though they are a *fait accompli* from a prophetic perspective. The reason that this is untenable is because the connection of the fig tree illustration to the Israelite identity is tenuous at best. Within the context of the Olivet Discourse, it is implausible to draw such a conclusion from Jesus's illustration of the fig tree, since He couples this illustration to all trees as recorded in Luke's account. The fig tree cannot represent Israel, unless all trees represent all nations. This would of course reduce Jesus's words to absurdity and cannot possibly be the meaning of the passage. Jesus also did not defer the fulfillment of His predictions in the Olivet Discourse to some future generation, but rather insisted that His predictions would come to pass during the lifetime of His contemporaries. Finally, many who interpret the Olivet Discourse as containing a prediction of the creation of the modern state of Israel overlook the symbolism of Christ's prediction that He would come on the clouds. Clouds are a common symbol given in the Old Testament in conjunction with divine judgment. By invoking this symbol and appropriating it to Himself, Christ was claiming divinity and predicting His divine retribution on the wicked in Jerusalem. Caiaphas and the rest of the Sanhedrin understood Christ's intended meaning perfectly, which is why this pushed them past the brink and caused them to demand Christ's execution.

In the next article, we will investigate more Christian Zionist myths about the modern state of Israel. The next article will investigate Israel's supposed allegiance to American interests, and the idea that America has been blessed because of our support for Israel.

Part 2
February 19, 2013

In the previous article on Christian Zionist myths, we deconstructed two popular myths that prevail in modern evangelicalism. Many if not most evangelicals are firm believers that Jews are the descendants of the ancient Israelites and thus have an intrinsic right to the land of the Middle East. This claim is buttressed by the idea that the formation of the state of Israel in Palestine was a direct fulfillment of prophecy that must precede the second coming of Christ. But both of these myths have foundations of sand. Neither one can hold up to close scrutiny. In this installment on Christian Zionist myths, we'll investigate some additional Zionist claims in the realm of politics. Specifically, we will deconstruct the myths that America has been blessed by her historic support of Israel and that Israel has been a consistent ally of American interests.

Genesis 12 and Its Implications for Zionism

It is not uncommon for Christian Zionists or dispensationalists to argue that America is or has been blessed by God because of our historic support for the interests of Jews and Israel. Minnesota Congresswoman Michelle Bachmann has stated:

> "I am convinced in my heart and in my mind that if the United States fails to stand with Israel, that is the end of the United States. . . . [W]e have to show that we are inextricably entwined, that as a nation we have been blessed because of our relationship with Israel, and if we reject Israel, then there is a curse that comes into play. And my husband and I are both Christians, and we believe very strongly the verse from Genesis [Genesis 12:3], we believe very strongly that nations also receive blessings as they bless Israel. It is a strong and beautiful principle."[35]

The primary text that Christian Zionists appeal to in defense of this idea is Genesis 12:1-3:

> Now the LORD had said unto Abram, Get thee out of thy country, and from thy kindred, and from thy father's house, unto a land that I will shew thee. And I will make of thee a great nation, and I will bless thee, and make thy name great; and thou shalt be a blessing. And I will bless them that bless thee, and curse him that curseth thee: and in thee shall all families of the earth be blessed.

---

[35] Michelle Bachmann, as quoted by "Israpundit." In a 2008 interview.

In this passage, God is speaking to Abram (before he is renamed Abraham), commanding him to leave his homeland in Ur and to go to the land of Canaan, where God would bless him and his descendants. Christian Zionists interpret this passage to mean that the Jews, as Abraham's descendants, have a permanent covenant relationship with God, such that anyone who blesses the Jews under any circumstances will be blessed, and anyone who curses the Jews under any circumstances will be cursed. Many Christian Zionists imply that these principles apply regardless of whether the Jews in question are Christian believers, and regardless of the actions taken by the Israeli state against her enemies.

I see several problems with this interpretation of the passage in question. First of all, there is the question of Jewish descent from the tribes of Israel, which was addressed in the previous article. Since there is good reason to consider modern Jews to be descended from the Khazars, this would automatically nullify any argument that the state of Israel must be supported on the basis of Gen. 12 today. Secondly, it is true that God made this covenant with Abraham and his covenant seed, but this was made with Abraham's seed "according to the promise," and must be seen in the larger context of redemptive history. This is the whole message of the book of Galatians, which is summed up in Gal. 3:29: "*if ye be Christ's, then are ye Abraham's seed, and heirs according to the promise.*" Paul also makes this clear in Romans 9-11, where he remarks that not all are Israel (covenantal) that are of Israel (physical) in Rom. 9:6. Paul likens covenantal Israel to an olive tree (Rom. 11:15-24). The original branches were the tribes of Israel, who have been cut off due to their unbelief. The Gentile nations have been grafted into the covenant by belief, and remaining in the covenant is contingent upon faith. Since Israel today is a secular state that rejects Christianity, it is not a part of the covenant, and therefore the promises that God gave to Abraham in Genesis 12 would not apply to them.

Another approach that Christian Zionists take with Gen. 12 which some might argue is that God has a physical chosen people (modern Jews) and a spiritual chosen people (the Church). The promises made to Abraham would be accorded to his physical descendants, presumed to be modern Jews. Yet the problems with this are similar to the problems listed above. We have reason to doubt that modern Jews are synonymous with ancient Israelites; additionally, we lack reason to believe that God has two chosen peoples. There is one covenant made with covenantal Israel, who is the Church (Gal. 6:16). This covenantal Israel inherits the earth, not just some real estate in the Middle East (Matt 5:5; Rom. 4:13). Another problem with this view is that Abraham's physical offspring includes much more than Israelites. If this promise can be extended by physical descent alone to all of his descendants in perpetuity, then why could this promise not also be applied to most of the Near Eastern and Western world? Most of these nations are descended from Abraham, so why narrow it to one branch of Abraham's descendants? For example, if this is to be applied to the current Israeli-Palestinian conflict, why could we not argue that we are obligated to support the Palestinians, who are themselves likely descendants of Abraham (indeed, more likely than modern Israel)? If one appeals to the faith of the ancient Israelites, then we are right back where we started, since past faith would not trump current unbelief. The tribes of Israel would still be cut off and would not be members of the covenant any more than other groups of unbelievers.

Has America Been Blessed for Our Historic Support for Israel?

When weighing the implications of a particular interpretation of a passage of Scripture, we should ask how this interpretation fares in the development of actual history. If the Christian Zionist interpretation of Genesis 12 is accurate, then we should see strong historical evidence that America has been blessed because of our consistent support for Israeli interests. Is this what we see? A major difficulty with the idea that America's historic success and prosperity is derived from support for Israel is that America has existed as an independent political country since 1776, while Israel did not become a country until 1948. Can American prosperity be attributed to support for a country that did not exist until recently? The suggestion seems absurd! Furthermore, it seems that American prosperity has been steadily declining since the end of World War II when the Israeli state came into being, as evidenced by our enormous debt[36] and loss of world power.[37]

Perhaps some could argue that although modern Israel was not an organized country until recently, America has been blessed due to her historic support of Jewish interests. This is also difficult to affirm in light of the fact that during the colonial period of American history, religious test acts prevented Jews or other heretics from voting in elections or holding public office. Furthermore, when we realize that Jews have managed to find themselves disinvited from many European societies throughout history, we can establish a clear pattern: if we compare dates for Jewish expulsions with the general history of the regions involved,[38] we can see the noteworthy trend that countries have tended to prosper after Jewish influence has waned, exiting from the destructive money-lending and usury concomitant with the presence of large Jewish populations. A classic case is the expulsion of the Jews due to their alliance with the Moors from Spain by Ferdinand and Isabella. It was after this that Spain experienced her golden age and conquered half the planet.

---

[36] "US Debt Visualized: Stacked in 100 Dollar Bills." *Kleptocracy.us*, usdebt.kleptocracy.us/.
[37] Reynolds, Thorin. "2016 Projected End of 'Age of America.'" *Faith Heritage*. 25 Apr. 2011, faithandheritage.com/2011/04/2016-projected-end-of-age-of-america/.
[38] "Jewish Expulsions and Resettlement, 1100-1500." *A Teacher's Guide to the Holocaust*, Florida Center for Instructional Technology, College of Education, University of South Florida, fcit.usf.edu/holocaust/gallery/expuls.HTM.

How has this played out in American history? For most of American history after the revolution, Jews were largely ignored. Religious tests restricting their role in public life were removed, yet most Jews still lived lives that placed them outside of America's mainstream. Almost all American statesmen throughout our golden age have not been Jewish. However, as Jewish influence has advanced in politics, the media, and the entertainment industry, we have experienced a corresponding steep decline over the recent decades. Frankly, then, there is no basis for the belief that America's historic success has been the result of a supportive disposition towards Jews or Israel. America's greatest days came at a time when Americans had a strong sense of their own identity—when Americans self-consciously identified themselves as white and Christian.[39]

Has Israel Historically Been an Ally of American Interests?

Some contend that Israel is America's only or greatest ally in the Middle East. In the wake of consistent threats of terrorist attacks (which prove to be very useful to the emerging police state), we hear more and more about how support for Israel is essential for America's success in combating terrorism. Some politicians, such as former Republican Party vice-presidential nominee Sarah Palin, are so convinced of this that they opt to fly Israeli flags in their offices! Is this adulation of Israel merited? Has Israel been a consistent ally of American interests? Many people are deeply committed to the idea that Israel is America's strongest ally; however, a brief investigation of the history of Israeli/American interests shows that this idea is based upon misconceptions and propaganda rather than the truth.

Fr. John Sheehan sums up American/Israeli relations the best when he said, *"Every time anyone says that Israel is our only friend in the Middle East, I can't help but think that before Israel, we had no enemies in the Middle East."*[40] This is because America's historic alliance with Israel and commitment to backing up every act of Israeli aggression has earned her the opprobrium of the other nations in this region. John J. Mearsheimer of the University of Chicago and Stephen M. Walt of Harvard's John F. Kennedy School of Government have written an excellent book, *The Israel Lobby and U.S. Foreign Policy*, which deals with the topic of Israeli influence over American policy-making. The authors dutifully explain how Israel's influence in America has discredited her reputation with many nations abroad, and how this disproportionate influence, unjustifiable on moral or strategic grounds, hurts both

---

[39] Carlton, Davis. "Who Does America Belong To?" *Faith Heritage*, 20 Jan. 2011, faithandheritage.com/2011/01/who-does-america-belong-to/.
[40] Quote from Fr. John Sheehan, S.J. (a Jesuit priest). Qtd. in *The Journal of Historical Review*, vol. 21, no. 2, p. 34. I am unaware of the original source, but Sheehan's point does not depend on the fact that he himself said it, anyway.

Israel and America by making them targets of terrorism as retaliation for meddling in Middle-Eastern affairs.[41]

The influence of the Israel lobby over American policy is evident from the history of the ascendancy of AIPAC (the American-Israeli Political Action Committee). Since the inception of AIPAC in the early 1960s, there has been a concomitant increase in American support for Israeli interests. According to the aforementioned book, *The Israel Lobby*, Israel receives about $3 billion annually in direct aid. Unlike other countries receiving aid from the United States, Israel receives her entire foreign aid at the beginning of each fiscal year, which allows them to earn interest on the money that they are given. Also unlike other countries, Israel is the only one that doesn't have to account for how it spends the money, rendering it impossible to make sure that Israel doesn't spend money in ways that the United States might oppose. Israel has access to American intelligence that other NATO allies are denied, while the United States turns a blind eye toward Israel's development of nuclear weapons. Since 1982, the United States has vetoed 32 United Nations Security Council resolutions that were critical of Israel, a number greater than the combined total of vetoes cast by all the other Security Council members.

Former Ohio Congressman Jim Traficant confirms that Israel receives about $15 billion per annum from the United States. The Israel lobby's power over American policy has harmed both America's and Israel's credibility with other nations who seek to establish meaningful peace in the region of the Middle East. This double standard remains consistent throughout Israeli rhetoric. Many times Israeli politicians will shake their fists with indignation at anyone who presumes to judge them or their actions. Israeli Prime Minister Ariel Sharon said, "*Israel may have the right to put others on trial, but certainly no one has the right to put the Jewish people and the State of Israel on trial.*" Does this make sense? Is it just for Christians to defend or ally themselves to a state that does not consider itself to be morally accountable?

We should also ask whether Israel is a positive influence in America, seeing as America was founded as a Christian nation. Many evangelicals who offer unrelenting support for Israel suggest that Israel is an ally of Western civilization and can therefore help advance the cause of Christianity indirectly, even if they themselves do not believe in Christianity. This thinking is obviously wrongheaded. Israel consistently mocks and ridicules the Christian faith and commits absolutely damnable blasphemy on a routine basis. Many examples of these terrible blasphemies are documented and easily accessible. Christians in Israel are constantly harassed and are often abused and spit upon by Jewish rabbis, in addition to secular Jews. Rather than ignoring this anti-Christian hatred, we should apply the many biblical passages that condemn partnership and cooperation with the enemies of Christ. One of the most prominent is 2 Cor. 6:14, in which the apostle Paul tells us

---

[41] Terrorism is an unintended consequence of America's unrelenting support for Israeli interests. This is commonly referred to as "blowback" theory.

not to be unequally yoked with unbelievers. If ever there were a time when this principle should be applied with a vengeance, it is in regard to such blasphemous and anti-Christian behavior that we see displayed prominently in Israel.

Finally, there are examples of Israel specifically subverting American and Western interests, and in the case of the USS Liberty, even attacking a peaceful American vessel. The USS Liberty was an American navy vessel that was attacked by Israeli bombers during the Six-Day War in June 1967. Those Americans who survived the assault have insisted that they were deliberately attacked. Yet, despite the murder of several innocent American sailors in the attack, Israel to this day maintains that the bombing of the Liberty be written off as a "mistake."[42] With allies like Israel, who needs terrorists?

Conclusions

It should be apparent that Christian Zionists grossly misinterpret the meaning of Genesis 12:3 as it pertains to contemporary foreign policy issues. It is a grave misreading of this verse to think that it demands unconditional support for Jews regardless of their religion or the wickedness of modern Israel. Unvarying Christian teaching on the identity of Israel informs us that Israel in the covenantal sense is limited to God's elect, whom He has chosen from the foundation of the world (Eph. 1:4). Those who abide in Christ are Abraham's seed and heirs according to the promise (Gal. 3:29), and with Abraham, Christians will inherit the world (Rom. 4:13). In addition to explicitly being called the Israel of God (Gal. 6:16), the Church and Israel are described the same way throughout the Bible. Both Israel and the Church are described as a royal priesthood who offer acceptable sacrifices unto God (Ex. 19:6; 1 Pet. 2:9). With such clear biblical teaching on the issue of the identity of Israel, it is amazing that so many professed Christians get this important question wrong! It is a sad testament of Christians' ignorance on so many important issues.

The misapplication of Genesis 12:3 to the modern state of Israel is not an unimportant or abstract theological issue. This faulty Christian Zionist interpretation has deeply influenced our flawed foreign policy in the Middle East, convincing many Americans that our interests rest with unconditional support for the state of Israel in whatever conflict in which they embroil themselves. As a result, America has become inseparably hitched to a dubious ally who works behind our backs to control American policy through lobbies, campaign contributions, or even out-

---

[42] For more information on the USS Liberty, see the BBC documentary "Dead in the Water: The Attack on the USS Liberty." The beginning of a 9/11 video called "Missing Links" also mentions the history behind the attack on the USS Liberty.

right spying. There is also the bombing of the USS Liberty, which cannot be ignored or forgotten by genuine American patriots. Instead of being blessed for her unflagging support of Israel, America has rather experienced steady and progressive decline since Jews organized Israel and became a nation in 1948. I certainly do not mean to suggest that America's support for Israel is the sole or even the primary cause of American decline; there is plenty of blame to be placed elsewhere. I merely mention this to show that America's unwavering commitments to an anti-Christian state like Israel have unquestionably brought us harm rather than good. As Christians, we are not to be unequally yoked with unbelievers. America's continued allegiance to the blasphemous and anti-Christian state of Israel makes a mockery of all for which Christians are supposed to stand. Israel's continued sacrilege and derision of Christianity render her worthy of condemnation. We cannot expect God to continue to ignore the ongoing crimes of the Israelis against Palestinians, especially against Christian Palestinians, and we cannot possibly imagine that God will consider the American empire guiltless for financing and supporting a regime like Israel. For this reason, it is of utmost importance that Christians understand why Christian Zionism is false and reject it entirely, before Christ spits us out of his mouth (Rev. 3:16).

Part 3
March 13, 2013

In the previous article, we looked at some of the common political myths of Christian Zionism concerning contemporary political issues. We noted that Genesis 12:3 does not apply to contemporary unbelieving Jews or the state of Israel, but rather applies to the faithful Christian Church. We also demonstrated the problems that the Christian Zionist interpretation of Genesis 12:3 has created. America, under the influence of Zionists, Christian or otherwise, has become entangled in an alliance with Israel that has not proved to be to our benefit. In this edition, we will investigate Christian Zionist myths about Jewish people and religion. We will discuss whether the so-called "Star of David" is suitable for Christians. We'll also discuss the notion that the Old Testament saints practiced Judaism as we know it today, as well as the idea that Jews and Christians worship the same God.

Is the Star of David a Suitable Symbol for Christians?

The symbol referred to as the Star of David is the most consistently recognizable symbol of the Jewish identity, whether ethnic or religious. The Star of David is immediately identifiable to the general public as a familiar symbol for Jews in the same way that a cross or crucifix is a traditional symbol associated with Christianity. But most people, including most Christians, are entirely unaware of the symbolism and meaning of the Star of David. Today, many Christians actually have tried to adopt the Star of David as a Christian symbol, alleging that it identifies them with Jews, the "older brothers in the covenant" to Christians. In doing so, these Christians are betraying their own ignorance, both of the differences between Judaism and Christianity, and of the history of the symbol itself.

Far from being a symbol associated with the worship of the true God, this symbol can be argued to have origins with the Khazars. The historical association of the Star of David with religious Judaism likely derives from the symbol's usage by the Khazars prior to their conversion to Judaism *en masse*. Once the Khazars converted to Judaism, the Star of David naturally became associated with Judaism. The Star of David's Khazar origins seem to directly contradict the notion that the Star of David has any connection to the biblical David or any other prominent persons from Hebrew history.[43] Yet, even if the Star of David could be shown to have a connection to ancient Israel—though any such connection is dubious at best—it would still be an inappropriate symbol for Christians to use. The symbol is unmistakably associated with Judaism, a false and idolatrous religion. Because of the association of the Star of David with Judaism, it cannot be dissociated from the murder of Jesus and the other Talmudic blasphemies

It is certainly possible for a non-Christian symbolism to take on a Christian meaning once the symbol passes into Christian usage. An example of this is how the pagan Celtic sun wheel was converted into the Celtic cross when the people of the British Isles were converted to Christianity. This is not what is happening, however, with the Star of David. Those professed Christians who wear a Star of David on their person or wave a Star of David flag are doing so, not because the symbol has historically been associated with orthodox Christianity, but rather because of its association with rabbinical Judaism. This is the kind of religious syncretism that is expressly condemned in the New Testament (1 Cor. 10:21; 2 Cor. 6:14-18).

While the hexagram isn't necessarily a heathen symbol, its association with the Jewish Star of David definitely makes this symbol compromised. Unlike the sun wheel which was converted to the Celtic cross, the hexagram has not received

---

[43] Some believe that it is possible that the Star of David is actually the Star of Remphan mentioned in the Bible in connection with the idolatrous worship of Moloch (Amos 5:26 and Acts 7:40-43).

any kind of conversion from its older meaning. The meaning of the hexagram is significant to Christian Zionists precisely because it is *not* a Christian symbol. The popularity of the Star of David among Christian Zionists should indicate to orthodox Christians that the loyalty of Zionists is not in the right place. From the standpoint of religious orthodoxy, Zionists are demonstrating loyalty to a false religion, and from the standpoint of politics, Zionists demonstrate their loyalty to a foreign country over their own.

Did the Old Testament Israelites Practice Judaism?

Most people today, including many Christians, assume that the ancient Israelites practiced the religion of Judaism. Because of this misconception, many people assert that Christianity developed out of Judaism. Consequently, it is common to hear people talk about the "Judeo-Christian tradition" or "Judeo-Christian morality." But do Christianity and Judaism derive from a common source? Is it accurate to say that the Old Testament saints practiced Judaism? I believe that the answer to both of these questions is an emphatic *no*.

The common misconception of Judaism and Christianity is that both religions derive fundamentally from Old Testament revelation. The only divergence between the two faiths is their identification of the Messiah—Christians believing that the Messiah has already been revealed in the person of Jesus Christ, and Jews anticipating the coming of a future Messiah, yet to be revealed. This mistaken view is overly simplistic and lacks a historical basis, as both Jews and orthodox Christians know well. Jewish scholar Joshua Adler comments, *"The differences between Christianity and Judaism are much more than merely believing in whether the messiah already appeared or is still expected, as some like to say."*[44] The Universal Jewish Encyclopedia also confirms that Judaism is based much more on extra-biblical Pharisaic teaching than on Scripture: *"The Jewish religion as it is today traces its descent, without a break, through all the centuries, from the Pharisees. Their leading ideas and methods found expression in a literature of enormous extent, of which a very great deal is still in existence. The Talmud is the largest and most important single member of that literature."*[45] Finally, Rabbi Ben Zion Bokser frankly admits, *"Judaism is not the religion of the Bible."*[46] And Dr. Gordon Ginn, an American Christian scholar, makes a very valid point when he notes: *"It is most interesting, indeed, that rabbis as well as Jewish scholars such as Mamlak and White agree with orthodox, historical Christianity that 'Judeo-Christian' is a contradiction in terms, even though that truth is yet to be discovered by contemporary evangelical and fundamentalist Christians."*[47]

---

[44] Qtd. in "The Myth of a Judeo-Christian Tradition," *New Dawn Magazine*, No.23, Feb.-March 1994.
[45] Qtd. in *Ibid. The Universal Jewish Encyclopedia*, Vol. VIII, (1942) p. 474
[46] Qtd. in *Ibid. Judaism and the Christian Predicament*, 1966, p. 159
[47] Qtd. in *Ibid. Smyrna*, August, 1993

The reality is that the Israelites of the Old Testament practiced what could be called pre-Incarnation Christianity. The Hebrew faithful were studied in the many prophetic predictions of the coming Messiah, fulfilled in the person of Christ. The visible Church at that time was generally confined to the nation of Israel, but in a different sense, covenantal Israel is not at all distinct from the Church (cf. Romans 9:6). In fact, before being martyred, the deacon Stephen called Israel the "church in the wilderness" while recounting the history of God's dealings with His people (Acts 7:38). (He uses the word *ekklesia*, from which we derive words like "ecclesiastical.") To make the same point, Paul taught that baptism makes us Abraham's promised seed and heirs according to the promise (Galatians 3:29), and that ancient Israel shared in the sacraments of the Church (1 Corinthians 10:1-4). Paul also sent salutations to the Church as the "Israel of God" (Galatians 6:16). This is because the religion of the Old Testament is in full continuity with the religion of the New Testament, such that to reject Christ and the revelation of the New Testament is to reject the God revealed in the Old Testament.

The rituals of the Old Covenant clearly point to their future fulfillment in Christ. The Westminster Confession of Faith ably summarizes their close connection:

> *This covenant was differently administered in the time of the law, and in the time of the Gospel: under the law it was administered by promises, prophecies, sacrifices, circumcision, the paschal lamb, and other types and ordinances delivered to the people of the Jews, all foresignifying Christ to come; which were, for that time, sufficient and efficacious, through the operation of the Spirit, to instruct and build up the elect in faith in the promised Messiah, by whom they had full remission of sins, and eternal salvation; and is called the Old Testament.*[48]

Hebrews is thoroughly cited in the prooftexts to this passage of the confession, since the book so clearly shows forth Christ as the fulfillment of the Old Covenant's sacrificial system.[49] Christ Himself is not just the High Priest of the New Covenant, but is also the Paschal Lamb that has been sacrificed for the sins of His people (1 Corinthians 5:7). The Old Covenant with its precepts was a schoolmaster to point us to our need for Christ (Galatians 3:24-25), and Christ is the goal and fulfillment of the precepts of the Old Covenant (Romans 10:4). Those Jews who would look to Old Testament rituals to save them, not seeing their clear culmination in Christ, lack an understanding of what these elements represented (Galatians 4:9). And not only are these Old Covenant rituals deficient for salvation, but since they have served their purpose of pointing to Christ, they are now no more. Modern Judaism has no temple, no sacrifices, and no priesthood, for Christ has

---

[48] *Westminster Confession of Faith*, 7.5
[49] See Hebrews 2:17-9:25; 10:21; 13:11.

destroyed them all. The religion which does not see their fulfillment in Christ cannot be said to follow the Old Testament, since the true followers of the Old Testament inevitably accepted the teachings of Jesus. *"For had ye believed Moses, ye would have believed me; for he wrote of me"* (John 5:46).

Do Rabbinical Jews and Christians Worship the Same God?

Because of the belief that Jews and Christians have a common religious origin in what is called Judaism, many conclude that Christians and Jews worship the same God. Yet it should be reiterated that rabbinical Judaism is a distinct religion from the religion of the ancient Israelites. This being the case, it is important to recognize that the reason Jews and Christians practice different religions is because Jews and Christians worship different deities, which is a central aspect of Christ's message in the Gospels. The myth that Jews and Christians worship the same deity is typically one-sided, made only by Judeo-Christians desiring brownie points. Most Jewish people will readily acknowledge that Jews and Christians do not worship the same god, since this would mean that Jews would worship Christ as God, which they do not. Jewish scholar S. Levin comments:

> *'After all, we worship the same God', the Christian always says to the Jew and the Jew never to the Christian. The Jew knows that he does not worship the Christ-God but the Christian orphan needs to worship the God of Israel and so, his standard gambit rolls easily and thoughtlessly from his lips. It is a strictly unilateral affirmation, limited to making a claim on the God of Israel but never invoked with reference to other gods. A Christian never confronts a Moslem or a Hindu with 'After all, we worship the same God'.*[50]

Levin is correct that Jews and Christians do not worship the same god, and that the God worshiped by Christians is far different from the false deity worshiped in rabbinical Judaism. The true God of Christianity is one God who subsists in three persons: the Father, the Son, and the Holy Ghost. It is impossible for anyone, even a professed monotheist, to believe in the true God while denying the deity of one or more of the persons mentioned. Moreover, Christian theology unequivocally affirms that the second person of the Trinity, the Son, also became incarnate in the

---

[50] "The Myth of a Judeo-Christian Tradition," *New Dawn Magazine*, No.23, Feb.-March 1994.

person of Jesus Christ. Since Jesus is the Son of the Father, he is properly called the Son of God[51] while equally being affirmed as God manifest in the flesh.[52]

Jesus stated that He did not teach on His own authority, but that His authority was derived from His divine Father in heaven (John 5:30; 8:28; 8:38). Jesus insisted that His teachings were entirely in continuity with Old Testament revelation, and that those who rejected Him and His ministry necessarily rejected the Old Testament precepts revealed through Moses (Luke 16:29-31; John 5:45-47). Thus, to reject Christ is in essence to reject the same God revealed in the Old Testament. Now, some might argue that Jewish people have not rejected God the Father, since Judaism recognizes the revelation from God to the ancient Hebrews. But the problem with this view is that the rabbinical authority within Judaism has replaced the truth taught in the Old Testament with evil teachings and practices which void the word of God that they had received (Matthew 15:1-9; cf. Mark 7:1-13).

The New Testament consistently teaches that it is necessary to receive the Son in order to be received by the Father. Jesus said that He is the Way, the Truth, and the Life, and that no one can come to the Father except through Him (John 14:6). There are many passages in the Gospels, as well as the epistles, that clearly indicate that God the Father only receives those who have received the Son.[53] This teaching is especially emphasized by the Apostle John. In fact, the idea that one must be united in faith to the Son in order to receive the Father is so clearly expressed in the Bible that it is a wonder any professed Christian could ever mistakenly believe that someone could truly acknowledge and worship the Father apart from worshiping and acknowledging his Son Jesus Christ. The fact that so many Christians erroneously believe that Christians and Jews (and sometimes Muslims) actually worship the same God is manifest proof of the biblical illiteracy and failure to catechize that sadly typify the modern church.

Conclusion

In recent decades, much has been made of the mythical "Judeo-Christian" tradition as the basis for American morality. The idea that Jews and Christians share a common source of morality in the Bible is a recent innovation, and both Jews and discerning Christians know that this idea is a canard. Those who promote this

---

[51] Daniel 3:25; Matthew 8:29; 14:33; 16:16; 27:54; Mark 1:1; 3:11; 15:39; Luke 1:32-35; 4:41; 8:28; John 1:49; 3:18; 5:25; 6:69; 11:4; 11:27; 20:31; Acts 3:13, 26; 8:37; 9:20; Romans 1:4, 9; 5:10; 8:3; 1 Corinthians 1:9; 2 Corinthians 1:19; Galatians 2:20; 4:4-7; Ephesians 4:13; Hebrews 1:8; 4:14; 6:6; 10:29; 1 John 3:8; 4:9-15; 5:5-20; 2 John 3, 9; Rev. 2:18

[52] Exodus 3:14 (cf. John 8:24, 58; 14:6-7); Isaiah 7:14 (cf. Matthew 1:23); 9:6; 43:10-11 (cf. Revelation 1:17-18; 2:8); 44:6 (cf. 2 Peter 1:1), 24 (cf. John 1:3; Colossians 1:16); John 1:1-3; 5:17-18; 10:30-33; 14:9-11; 20:28; Acts 20:28 (cf. Revelation 1:5-6; 5:8-9); Philippians 2:5-7; Colossians 2:8-9; 1 Timothy 3:16; Titus 2:13; Hebrews 1:1-9; 2 John 7; Revelation 1:8, 22:13)

[53] Matthew 10:32-33; 11:25-27 (cf. Luke 10:21-22); John 6:37-65; 8:16-56; 10:15-38; 12:26-50; 13:1-3; 14:1-31; 15:1-26; 16:3-32; 17:1-25; 20:17-21; 1 John 2:22-24; 2 John 9

myth the most vehemently are evangelicals who seek to lend a greater degree of legitimacy to their quest to turn America back in a more traditional direction. Not realizing that Judaism is based upon an alternative system of morality presented in the Talmud and that Jewish people consistently support liberal policies that evangelicals claim to oppose,[54] evangelicals' appeal to a mythical and nonexistent "Judeo-Christian" tradition has hit a dead end.

The promotion of this pernicious myth of the "Judeo-Christian" tradition is the result of more than just wishful thinking. The desire to merge the Jewish and Christian religions together into one tradition or common source of morality demonstrates the profound, willful ignorance of modern Christians. It is essential to understand that Judaism and Christianity are different religions that worship different gods. The triune God of the Bible is nothing like the Unitarian false deity revealed in the Talmud. Worship of a false god inevitably yields false morality, so it is incorrect to assert that Jews and Christians have a common source of morality. Christianity is built on the foundation of the Apostles and Prophets with Christ Himself being the chief cornerstone (Ephesians 2:20). Judaism is built upon the foundation of the Pharisees, who rejected Abraham, Moses, and the Law and the Prophets. The two religions are diametrically opposed to one another and cannot be unequally yoked without destroying the unique truth and character of the Christian faith (2 Corinthians 6:14). In the next installment of this series, we will discuss the false idea of two-covenant theology, which teaches that God has a physical covenant with the Jewish people and a spiritual covenant with Christians. We will also be correcting the myth of Jews as perpetual victims of Christian violence throughout the history of Christendom. Finally, we will discuss the outlandish notion that Jews actually did not reject Christ as the Messiah or bear any corporate responsibility for the crucifixion of Christ.

Part 4
June 26, 2013

In this edition in the series on Christian Zionist myths, we will dissect the myth of Jews' perpetual suffering at the hands of Christians. We will have a brief overview of the history of Jewish people within Christendom and deconstruct the myth that Jews are the perpetual victims of Christian hatred. We will also discuss the role of the Jewish rabbis and Sanhedrin in the crucifixion of Christ.

---

[54] A classic example of this is the late Jerry Falwell inviting a pro-gay marriage Jewish rabbi to give a convocation at Liberty University in which said rabbi encouraged tolerance for gay unions

Have Jews Been the Victims of Perpetual Persecution?

It is becoming increasingly more popular to assert that Jewish people have been the perpetual victims of "anti-Semitism," perpetrated mostly by Christians out of anger for the crucifixion of Christ. This idea is used to justify the outright banning of certain "anti-Semitic" attitudes in the cases of Europe and Canada, or the ostracizing of "anti-Semitic" offenders in the case of the United States of America. Children are commonly taught in both public schools and religious schools that Christians have been terrible persecutors of Jews. What is often ignored is the history of Jewish antagonism towards Christians and the historical circumstances that precipitated Jewish banishment from Christian lands.

There is a long and sorrowful history of Christian persecution at the hands of Jewish authorities. Jewish and rabbinical authorities were at the forefront of persecution in the early Church. The book of Acts records constant harassment of the apostles and the faithful by the Jews in the towns in which they traveled and preached.[55] This persecution of Christians did not cease after the destruction of Jerusalem and the Temple in A.D. 70, but has continued throughout history. An additional example of Jewish violence against Christians occurred in Palestine in the seventh century A.D. The Jews aided Persians who were attempting to capture Roman-controlled Palestine. Once Jerusalem capitulated to the Persians, the Jews instigated a massive slaughter of the Christians that were there.[56] When Zionism was discussed earlier, it was mentioned that many Christian Palestinians continue to suffer under Jewish rule in the Middle East. Many are unjustly driven from their homes and settlements to make way for the encroaching secular Jewish state.

Recent research by a Jewish professor in Israel also paints a dramatically different picture of Christian/Jewish relations. Dr. Ariel Toaff is a son of the Rabbi of Rome and a professor at the Jewish University of Bar Ilan outside of Tel Aviv. As a professor, Dr. Toaff's specialty was medieval Jewry. Dr. Toaff discovered that Jews in medieval northern Italy were actually kidnapping and crucifying Christian babies, using their blood to invoke the spirit of vengeance against hated Christians. Of particular concern to Toaff was the case of Simon of Trent (later canonized as St. Simon of Trent). On the eve of Passover in 1475, Jewish kidnappers murdered two-year-old Simon. After many deliberations, Pope Sixtus IV appointed a panel of six cardinals to hear the case. They found the Jewish defendants guilty. In an amazing reversal, the Vatican overturned the conviction of the perpetrators in 1965

---

[55] See Acts 4:3-22, 5:17-42, 6:8-8:3, 9:23-24, 12:1-5, 13:44-51, 14:5-20, 16:16-24, 17:1-15, 18:12-17, 19:23-41, 20:19, 22:30-23:11, 23:12-14

[56] *"There is no doubt that the . . . Jews aided the Persians with all the men they could muster, and that the help they gave was considerable. Once Jerusalem was in Persian hands a terrible massacre of Christians took place, and the Jews are accused of having taken the lead in this massacre"* – James Parkes, *As The Agents of Persians: A History of Palestine from 135 AD to Modern Times*, p. 81. Oxford University Press, New York, 1909.

in order to kowtow to influential Jews. Many today will be inclined to think that such an accusation is so outrageous and intrinsically improbable that it cannot be true, dismissing it immediately in their minds, but the very fact that Toaff's work is so thoughtlessly dismissed, and that the exoneration of the perpetrators occurred as political correctness was gaining ground in 1965, should cause us to reconsider that opinion.

In addition to this case, Dr. Toaff lists several other incidents that took place over the span of some five hundred years. Upon publishing his findings in the Italian-language book called *Pasque di Sangue*, Dr. Toaff's academic career was threatened and his professional reputation was ruined. He even faced the prospect of serving jail time. Amidst these threats, Dr. Toaff withdrew the publication of his book, but it has since been independently translated into English.[57] Dr. Toaff's findings demonstrate the extreme hostility that Jews in Christendom could exhibit towards Christians. Until being sacked for publishing politically incorrect opinions, Dr. Toaff was considered a foremost medieval historian. Since there seems to be a sound foundation for the story of Simon of Trent as well as other cases, Christian hostility towards Jews is understandable, even if at times it overflowed into abuse.

Much is made of Christian anger directed at Jews throughout history for various reasons. It is certainly the case that there have been historical occurrences in which Jews have drawn the ire of Christians for one reason or another, and not always for just reasons. That being the case, one would be hard-pressed to find examples of Jews being summarily murdered by Christians the way that Christians were massacred by Jews after the Persian conquest of Jerusalem in the seventh century. Jews have been expelled in most European countries throughout history, but what typically precipitated their expulsion was their involvement in usury, or what is now called interest. The Church consistently denounced usury as a grave evil against humanity, and consequently prohibited Christians from participating in the practice.[58] Occasionally, Christian civil rulers would permit Jews in their kingdoms or territories to lend money on usury, giving them a monopoly on an illicit market.

Naturally, when usury brought about ruinous conditions—when the lower classes suffered misery, being bled by interest-based debt—Jews were looked upon disfavorably. Certainly, Jews were not the only people responsible for the introduction and mainstreaming of usury into Christendom. Far too many Christians were complicit in the practice. However, this is not to deny that there was

---

[57] The English edition is called *Passovers of Blood: The Jews of Europe and Ritual Murders*
[58] See *Usury: Destroyer of Nations* by S.C. Mooney and *Usury in Christendom: The Mortal Sin That Was and Was Not* by Michael Hoffman

appropriate criticism of Jews for their role in the practice which left so many impoverished. With his typical semi-sarcastic wit, Martin Luther quipped regarding the prevalence of usury among Jews:

> *Moreover, they are nothing but thieves and robbers who daily eat no morsel and wear no thread of clothing which they have not stolen and pilfered from us by means of their accursed usury. Thus they live from day to day, together with wife and child, by theft and robbery, as arch-thieves and robbers, in the most impenitent security.*[59]

It may be difficult for a modern thinker to understand the vitriol that people had in the past to usury. We have become ignorant of the ruin that usury causes in society, but it was not always so. Many Christians were understandably angry for the role that Jews played in draining society's wealth by means of usury. This does not mean that we can assign sole blame to Jews for their role in usury. It is likely that we ought to assign even more guilt to Christian rulers and officials who allowed usury to be practiced in their dominions. The most righteous rulers, such as Charlemagne, did not. From the understandable anger of Christians at the practice of usury to the frequent persecution of Christians by Jews, we can see that the idea of perpetual Jewish suffering at the hands of unscrupulous Christians is a myth.

Did the Jews Kill Jesus Christ?

The question of who murdered Jesus Christ is certainly a controversial one. The idea that the Jewish authorities are responsible in a unique way for the crucifixion scandalizes the modern Christian mind. Nevertheless, this is indeed the traditional Christian understanding of Christ's Passion. Today there are a couple of explanations that are offered to extricate the first-century Jewish authorities from the unique role that they played in the crucifixion of Christ. The first is to posit that "we all killed Jesus." This is given as a contemplative point to ponder. It is argued that since Christ died for the sins of the world, everyone shares in the culpability for Christ's death. The second explanation is given by some Calvinist theologians who are committed to the doctrine of Christ's particular redemption of the elect. These theologians assert that God Himself is responsible for the death of Christ, since He presided over Christ's execution in His sovereignty. Let's discuss both of these explanations, and why they are both inadequate to extricate first-century Jewish culpability.

First is the explanation that everyone shares responsibility for Christ's death on account of their personal sin. There may be a contemplative sense in which this

---

[59] Comment extracted from Rev. Martin Luther's much maligned work, *On the Jews and Their Lies*

is true. Jesus Christ would not have been required to take on human nature in the Incarnation and sacrifice Himself for our atonement if not for humanity's sinfulness. There is a real sense in which my personal sin was a cause for Christ's suffering. The problem is that this contemplative reality does not really address the question of who killed Jesus Christ. The reason for this answer's appeal in our society is not because we prefer to ponder contemplatively rather than seek concrete answers to historical issues. The reason for its appeal is rather that it allows us to avoid making uncomfortable assertions about the historical murder of Christ. It is extremely unfashionable in our place and time to admit the central role the Jewish authorities played in the crucifixion. Thus, opting for a contemplative approach which focuses on how our collective and personal guilt motivated Christ to die is preferred to answering the question of a particular party's historical culpability. Again, the issue is not that the contemplative approach to Christ's death has no validity. The issue is that it does not actually address the question being asked, which is historical.

Just because Christ died to save sinners, it does not follow that each individual sinner is responsible for the historical murder of Jesus. The historical murder of Jesus was perpetrated by the Jewish authorities and by the gathered mob who demanded Christ's death by the hands of their Roman overlords. This is clearly and unambiguously presented in the Passion narratives of the Gospels.[60] Jesus was condemned by the high priest and the scribes and elders, who then prompted the Romans to execute Him as an insurrectionist against Rome. In their treatment of Christ, the Jewish authorities swore allegiance to Caesar and his Roman interlopers. The Roman governor of the province of Judea, Pontius Pilate, asked these rabbis why they would want to kill their own king. In response, the mob answered: *"we have no king but Caesar"* (John 19:15). This was the ultimate treason against the nation whose interests they claimed to represent.

The reason for their professed allegiance to Caesar was simply because they feared Caesar rather than God. They viewed Caesar as a source of their continued power and authority, and were thus willing to see the Messiah murdered in order to preserve their own power and influence. However, the Jewish people in general were also fooled into endorsing the crucifixion. Just a week before being murdered, Christ was overwhelmingly welcomed by the masses during His triumphal entry into Jerusalem. Many of these same people would have been present during Christ's trial before the chief priests. Pilate offered to free either Christ or Barabbas to the crowd, and the crowd emphatically insisted that Christ be crucified, shouting: *"his blood be on us, and on our children"* (Matthew 27:24-25). The anger towards Christ and the disciples continued after the crucifixion. Many disciples remained in hiding "for fear of the Jews" (John 19:38, 20:19). The Apostle Paul also confirms the culpability of the Jews in the crucifixion when he writes that *"the Jews...killed*

---

[60] The Passion is recorded in Matthew 26:46-27:54; Mark 14:42-15:39; Luke 22:47-23:47; and John 18:1-19:37.

the Lord Jesus, and their own prophets, and have persecuted us; and they please not God, and are contrary to all men" (1 Thessalonians 2:14-15). While it is clear that not all Jews indiscriminately participated in the crucifixion, and that Gentiles there, such as Pontius Pilate, share guilt for their cooperation in the scheme of the Sanhedrin, there is simply no way around the fact Jewish culpability in the murder of Christ is the clear teaching of the New Testament.

The second explanation offered for the question of who murdered Christ is that "God did it," as offered by Reformed Baptist apologist James White. While there is some basis for this view, the explanation lacks biblical rigor. White cites Isaiah 53:6: "*Surely he hath borne our griefs, and carried our sorrows: yet we did esteem him stricken, smitten of God, and afflicted.*" He also cites the apostle Peter's statement in Acts 4:27-28: "*For of a truth against thy holy child Jesus, whom thou hast anointed, both Herod, and Pontius Pilate, with the Gentiles, and the people of Israel, were gathered together, for to do whatsoever thy hand and thy counsel determined before to be done.*" Both of these passages clearly demonstrate God's sovereignty over the death of Christ, but we must be careful to distinguish between God's providence by which He guides history and the morally culpable actions of humans who perpetrated murder.

F.J. De Angelis, a theologian affiliated with *Semper Reformanda*, explains that the eternal decrees of God, by which He controls whatsoever comes to pass in temporal reality, must always be distinguished from the created will of men and natural causation that are at work within the bounds of temporal reality. De Angelis writes:

> *God sovereignly decreeing that Christ should suffer and bear the sins of His people (as Rev. White correctly stated) does not mean that God murdered Jesus Christ, or in White's assessment, that 'God did it.' Christ was smitten of God by virtue of having the sins of His people laid upon Him; it was the sovereign decree of God that He would redeem His people. It was decreed that the events would transpire, but those that carried it out bear the guilt for their actions. . . . As such, the people that rejected Jesus Christ, the people that gave Him an illegal and corrupt trial based upon contradictory and deceitful testimony, the people that cried out for Him to be wrongly executed, the people that rejected Him as their Messiah, these are the people that 'did it.'*[61]

White did issue a rejoinder to De Angelis assuring his readers that he really does understand concepts like the Creator/creature distinction and ultimate vs. proximate causation. That is all well and good, but if he really does understand these

---

[61] Much of the information on the question of who murdered Christ is from S.C. Mooney on his blog *Crisis and Culture* under the entry "Who Killed Jesus Christ?"

concepts (which I believe he does), then he should have made this clear in his original answer to the question of who murdered Christ. It seems likely that White did not wish to speak of the proximate cause of Christ's death because of the social consequences for doing so. While it is true that there is a contemplative sense in which our personal sins made Christ's death necessary, and there is a providential sense in which God ordained the death of Christ on the cross, neither sense properly answers the question of who was responsible for Christ's murder. The scriptures are clear that the major culpability in the murder of Christ belongs to the Jewish authorities and the Jewish mob who insisted that Christ be crucified in place of Barabbas. This doesn't mean that individual Jews today are personally responsible for the murder of Christ, but the Jewish Talmud does acknowledge and celebrate the murder of Christ, besides blaspheming the Christian faith in many other ways.[62]

Does this mean that Jews cannot be converted and saved? Of course not: Jews can and should be encouraged to repent and embrace the saving truth of the Gospel. This will not happen, though, as long as Jews fail to grasp the harm that Pharisaical Judaism has done. Christians who try to answer the question of Christ's murder in ways that preclude or obscure Jewish culpability in the murder of Christ are doing far more harm than good. Our zeal for evangelism in keeping with the Great Commission should motivate us all the more to confront evil and preach the free offer of forgiveness through Christ. When preaching to Israelites gathered on the day of Pentecost and afterward, Peter did not obfuscate the facts of Christ's crucifixion. Instead, he boldly proclaimed the truth to the men of Israel that were listening to him.[63] Peter acknowledged that ignorance played a role in their actions (Acts 3:17), though this did not remove the guilt of their actions. Peter told them to repent and to be converted so that their sins would be blotted out (Acts 3:19). Just as the Jews of the first century called down a curse upon themselves and upon their children during the crucifixion (Matthew 27:25), forgiveness for them and their children is freely offered by repentance and belief (Acts 2:38-39). Those who refuse to address this issue forthrightly are not doing Jews any favors, but are rather downplaying any chance that Jews have of being forgiven for following the ways of the Pharisees and Sadducees.

---

[62] See *The Talmud Unmasked: The Secret Rabbinical Teachings Concerning Christians* by Rev. I.B. Pranaitis for good information on Talmudic teachings. Another good source is Michael Hoffman's *Judaism Discovered* and *Judaism's Strange Gods*.
[63] See Acts 2:14-23; 3:12-19; 4:26-28

Conclusions

The persecution of Christians by Jews and Jewish culpability in the murder of Christ are controversial issues, to be sure. It is not uncommon to hear from Christian Zionists or evangelicals how Jews suffered terrible persecution at the hands of Christians in ages past. By promoting this myth as genuine, these Christian Zionists find themselves siding with secularists, liberals, and other assorted anti-Christians in their assault on historic Christendom. This also downplays the persecution of Christians by Jews, which continues on to this day in Palestine.

The matter of the crucifixion is an issue from which everyone is currently fleeing. It seems that it is acceptable to assign blame to anyone except for the people that actually were responsible. The first-century Jews arranged for Christ's arrest, provided compromised testimony, and insisted upon Christ's execution. While not all Jews participated in the crucifixion, the New Testament assigns blame to the Jewish authorities and Jewish mob. Jews today continue to follow this religion, which is based upon the precepts of the Pharisees rather than the Bible.

In the final and concluding edition to this series on Christian Zionist myth, we will discuss the outlandish notion that Jews actually did not reject Christ as the Messiah, particularly the claim made by John Hagee that the Jews did not reject Christ as Messiah since Jesus was not, in actuality, the Messiah. While this myth is not general to most Christian Zionists, it is important to address because John Hagee is such a prominent promoter of Christian Zionism. We will wrap up by reviewing how Christian Zionism has hijacked the legitimate interests of white Christians. Instead of supporting a rogue, secularist, anti-Christian state in the Middle East, white Christians should be supporting the interests of their own families, tribes, and nations.

Part 5
July 25, 2013

In this final edition on Christian Zionist myths, we will investigate the claims made by Zionist pastor John Hagee. Hagee is an arch-Zionist who believes that Jesus was actually not the Messiah. After this, we will conclude the series on Christian Zionism. We will discuss how Christian Zionism continues to influence the contemporary political discourse and foreign policy. Finally, we will end with an appeal for Christians to return to traditional Christian beliefs and to turn their political energies away from Israel and back to their own people.

Was Jesus the Messiah?

It is unbelievable that this topic needs to be addressed. Throughout the history of the Christian Church, acceptance of the belief that Jesus was indeed the promised Messiah was considered a *sine qua non* of the faith. Even the vast majority of Christian Zionists in history would have accepted this article of faith without the least bit of hesitation. This has changed for megachurch apostate John Hagee. Hagee is a Zionist conman *par excellence* who has raised millions of dollars to be given to the state of Israel. He is the founder of Christians United for Israel (CUFI) and spends his time clamoring for war in support of the Zionist state. Israel has been known to support Zionists (Christian or otherwise) who do their bidding, and Hagee is certainly no exception. He has his own private Lear jet, as well as an 8,000-acre luxury ranch with his own mansion. The man lives in extravagance because he has sold his soul for the purpose of defending the anti-Christian state of Israel.

Hagee wrote a book in 2007 called *In Defense of Israel*. In this book, Hagee makes the audacious claim that Jesus Christ actually did *not* claim to be the Messiah that had been promised to Israel.[64] In order to support this appalling claim, he relentlessly twists the Scriptures to try to justify his apostate interpretations. Hagee tries to redefine the Messiah as a purely political deliverer. But the plain fact is that Jesus did claim to be the Messiah and defended this claim against the rabbinical authorities who persecuted Him.

The Gospels clearly present the fact that Jesus was the Messiah. When Andrew found Jesus, he ran to tell his brother Simon Peter: *"We have found the Messiah"* (John 1:41). Jesus is also identified as the Messiah when conversing with the woman at the well. *"The woman said to Him, 'I know that Messiah is coming (He who is called Christ); when that One comes, He will declare all things to us.' Jesus said to her, 'I who speak to you am He'"* (John 4:25-26). Both of these passages directly confirm the fact that Jesus was indeed the Messiah, and thus Jesus is identified with "Messiah the Prince" of Daniel 9. These passages also translate Jesus's common title, "Christ," from the Hebrew word for Messiah. Therefore, all references to Jesus as the Christ in the New Testament confirm that He is the Messiah. Simon Peter confesses: *"Thou art the Christ, the Son of the living God"* (Matthew 16:16). Jesus prayed that His people would know him as Jesus Christ (John 17:3). Jesus is also identified

---

[64] In the book Hagee makes the following claims. *"If God intended for Jesus to be the Messiah of Israel, why didn't he authorize Jesus to use supernatural signs to prove he was God's Messiah, just as Moses had done?"* (p. 137). *"Jesus refused to produce a sign . . . because it was not the Father's will, nor his, to be Messiah"* (p 138). *"If Jesus wanted to be Messiah, why did he repeatedly tell his disciples and followers to 'tell no one' about his supernatural accomplishments?"* (p. 139). *"The Jews were not rejecting Jesus as Messiah; it was Jesus who was refusing to be the Messiah to the Jews"* (p. 140). *"They wanted him to be their Messiah, but he flatly refused"* (p. 141). *"He refused to be their Messiah, choosing instead to be the Savior of the world"* (p. 143). *"Jesus rejected to the last detail the role of Messiah in word or deed"* (p. 145).

as the Christ during the Passion narrative (Luke 24:26, 46). All these fortify His status as the Messiah.

Contrary to Hagee's claim that Christ refused to confirm Himself as the Messiah, Christ directly affirmed His identity when challenged by His enemies. *"Again the high priest was questioning Him, and saying to Him, 'Are You the Christ, the Son of the Blessed One?' And Jesus said, 'I am; and you shall see the Son of Man sitting at the right hand of Power, and coming with the clouds of heaven'"* (Mark 14:61-62). Again, this is confirmed when the Jews were questioning Jesus. *"So the Jews gathered around him and said to him, 'How long will you keep us in suspense? If you are the Christ, tell us plainly.' Jesus answered them, 'I told you, and you do not believe. The works that I do in my Father's name bear witness about me, but you do not believe because you are not among my sheep"* (John 10:24-26).

The apostles continues to identify Jesus as the Christ after the Gospels record the resurrection. During Peter's address at Pentecost, he tells his audience, *"Let all the house of Israel therefore know for certain that God has made him both Lord and Christ, this Jesus whom you crucified"* (Acts 2:36). Likewise, the apostle John considers the question of Jesus's identity as the Christ come in the flesh as absolutely essential to the faith. He writes, *"Who is the liar but he who denies that Jesus is the Christ? This is the antichrist, he who denies the Father and the Son"* (1 John 2:22). The fact is that Jesus's identity as Messiah is among the clearest and most unambiguous messages conveyed by the New Testament. Its truth is absolutely essential to orthodox Christianity. If this belief is given up, Christianity itself becomes meaningless.

Given the clear testimony of Scriptures which clearly identify Christ as the Messiah, it is incredible that a supposed pastor like John Hagee could publicly deny this. After understanding John Hagee's corrupt character and Zionist idolatry of Israel, it becomes apparent that this idolatry blinds him to clear truths taught in the Bible. Hagee has made a reputation as a supporter of the state of Israel no matter the circumstances. By his unwavering support for a state that opposes Christian teaching and openly mocks Christ, Hagee demonstrates how steeped he has become in idolatry. While Hagee represents an extreme in the Zionist position, his popularity in evangelical circles demonstrates that this idolatry of the Israeli state is becoming ever more prevalent, which corresponds to the modern apostasy of Christians from the truth.

Conclusions on Christian Zionism

Many dispensationalists teach that Christ offered the people of Israel a physical, earthly kingdom and temporal deliverance from the Romans during His earthly ministry. They teach that because the people of Israel rejected this earthly kingdom, Christ died on the Cross and ushered in the church age as a "parenthesis" in history, unknown to the Old Testament prophets.[65] This view is directly contradicted by what we read of Christ's triumphal entry into Jerusalem. The crowd tries to make Jesus their king by force, but He hides to avoid such a coronation (John 6:15). The belief that the Jews are the physical people of God, the Church being only His "spiritual" people, has developed into the political system known as Christian Zionism. Many Christian Zionists even believe that the creation of the state of Israel in Palestine was a partial fulfillment of the Olivet Discourse! Christian support for the state of Israel is due to the fact that most Christians are ignorant of the Khazar origins of modern Jews and of the nature of the Abrahamic covenant.

The seed of Abraham spoken of in Genesis 12 are Abraham's spiritual seed by faith (Galatians 3:29). It is thus a serious error to conclude that the state of Israel (or any political state) must be supported because of the text. The seed of Abraham and the Church are one and the same. Yet because of this unwavering support for Israel, many people believe that Israel has been a consistent ally of American interests, rather than a country that cynically uses American foreign aid and military support to secure its own expansion while imperiling American interests. It is precisely because America supports illicit Israeli expansion that countries in the Middle East have grown to hate us. Americans are hated not because we are rich or free, but because we have provided weapons and money to a wicked state who has run various Middle-Eastern peoples out of their homes and burned their settlements (or at the very least, threatened to do so). The Israel lobby has successfully lobbied for unquestioned support from America for Israeli interests, while at the same time tarring those who want to secure American borders from foreign interests as "racists" or "extremists."

In addition to being a political liability, Zionism has also proved to lend itself towards religious syncretism. Many falsely assume that the religion of Judaism is simply in continuity with the teachings of the Old Testament. The reality is that Judaism arose out of a conscious rejection of the Old Testament prophets. Jesus stated unequivocally that to reject Him was to reject Moses and the prophets, since they spoke of Him. For this reason, the primary source of revelation in Judaism is not the Old Testament, but rather the rabbinical Talmud. Many Christian Zionist scholars are aware of the role of the Talmud within Judaism, but are either ignorant or possibly even apathetic about the blasphemies against Christ and the faith found therein.

We are in a dark period in the history of Christianity. The former Christian consensus on doctrine and morals has been shattered, and one of the only things

---

[65] The Gentiles coming into the Church was predicted by the Old Testament prophets via the New Covenant: see Jer. 31:31 (cf. Heb. 8:8-13; 12:24); 32:37-40; Ezek. 16:60-62; 37:26; Isa. 19:23-25; 55:3; 56:3-8. The New Covenant, including its central theme of Gentile salvation, was certainly not a "parenthesis" unknown to the Old Testament prophets.

on which many Christians do agree is the necessity of supporting Israeli or Jewish interests because they are "God's chosen people." I believe that God is judging the Church and Christendom for our religious syncretism by trying to artificially create concord between Christ and Belial (2 Cor. 6:14-18). We live in a period of unparalleled apostasy and immorality, and the only way out of this abyss is to rediscover the truth that we, as Christians, are God's chosen people, and that Judaism is consequentially a false religion based upon the rejection of Christ and His Church. We are not being genuinely caring when we obscure the truth in order to make people feel more comfortable. Although the traditional Christian teaching on the exclusivity of the Christian faith is unpopular, we are called by God to be faithful in season and out of season (Romans 3:4; 2 Timothy 4:2). To deny the truth so that our enemies won't hate us is an act of fear and cowardice. Christ has promised that the gates of Hell itself will eventually fall against the onslaught of the Church (Matthew 16:18). Having this hope, there is no reason why fear should rule the day. It is long past time for Christians to stop worrying about who we will offend and to preach the truth of Christ without fear.

In Defense of Privilege, White or Otherwise

October 8, 2016

It is fashionable these days to categorically denounce the concept of privilege. The #checkyourprivilege movement has been gaining traction over the past several years and has become the popular explanation of cultural Marxists and social justice warriors for why straight white men have it so easy in comparison to minorities. As a straight white Christian man, it might make sense to explain the fact that blacks and mestizos are arrested at higher rates than whites in light of the fact that these groups are more prone to committing crime. Likewise, it might seem reasonable to me to witness the unhealthy and antisocial behaviors rampant among homosexuals and transsexuals and infer that there must be something intrinsically wrong with these behaviors. But according to social justice warriors, this is but one example of my privilege blinding me to the harsh realities that are faced by non-Christians, homosexuals, non-whites, and women.

The general premise of opposition to privilege by social justice warriors is that virtually all negative experiences of non-whites, non-Christians, homosexuals, or women can be reduced to their lack of privilege. The Free Dictionary defines "privilege" as "a special advantage, immunity, permission, right, or benefit granted to or enjoyed by an individual, class, or caste." The argument is that straight white Christians are afforded special advantages that allow us to subsist without having to resort to a life of crime, as well as immunity from arrest and prosecution when we do commit crime. The same argument is used in regards to non-Christians and homosexuals and virtually every other minority group under the sun. Muslim terrorists who target innocent civilians are just acting out of a lack of privilege and opportunity. Likewise, anti-social and unhealthy trends among homosexuals are simply a manifestation of their lack of privilege.

The social justice warrior manages to find the lack of tolerance or acceptance, subconscious discrimination, "glass ceilings," and "microaggressions" everywhere he looks. In this "check your privilege" paradigm, the answers to society's problems are simple. We need affirmative action that favors minority groups at the expense of heterosexual able-bodied white men, dispensing with outdated standards of quality and excellence. We need a greater visibility of non-whites, women, homosexuals, disabled persons, and so on in places of prominence. We need to celebrate the real or imagined achievements of the "under-privileged" at every possible opportunity. Finally we need to protect the "under-privileged" from all forms of discrimination against them, and this means that free association must be abolished in favor of integration, just as equality has replaced quality in terms of hiring and promotions.

Most mainstream conservatives try to oppose the leftist narrative by challenging the perception that straight white able-bodied men are as privileged as they are made out to be, although this opposition from movement conservatives to the "check your privilege" movement has certainly lost gusto in recent years. This isn't necessarily a bad argument, though it fails to get to the heart of the issue. Many correctly point out that white privilege is often exaggerated by the left. The comments made by Bernie Sanders to the effect that white people don't know what it is like to be poor in a recent Democratic debate serve as a good example.[66] The truth is that white privilege is largely a leftist trope with little basis in reality. Leftists frequently cite cases of "white privilege" as though this implies that whites have an unjust advantage, while ignoring similar racial disparities that favor non-white racial or ethnic groups. The Left essentially attributes everything wrong with the non-white world to white privilege and colonialism.

One example is leftists' fixation on the fact that whites fare better economically than blacks or hispanics. What is conveniently ignored is that many Asians and Jews are typically wealthier than whites, and yet we never see the "check your privilege" crowd excoriating "Asian privilege" or "Jewish privilege." Likewise, a good deal of what is considered to be white privilege simply correlates with intact families. The very liberal Brookings Institute found that simply graduating high school, having a full-time job, and avoiding children before marrying around age 21 dramatically reduces poverty. Whites are more likely than blacks or hispanics to be raised in traditional two-parent families, and this accounts for much of the differences between the standard of living of whites and non-whites. This is obviously not an unjust privilege, but the natural consequences of healthy family life. Leftists also conveniently ignore that whites are often openly discriminated against in the form of affirmative action for diversities... I mean minorities. White privilege is largely a leftist excuse for non-white underachievement and the natural consequences of bad behavior.

The Left uses the concept of privilege to argue that the underachievement of non-whites and non-Christians is due to their "underprivileged" status which hinders them from achieving their full potential. Underlying this commitment is the belief that equal opportunities will yield equal results. If experience teaches us that all do not perform equally even under similar circumstances, this is interpreted as systemic favoritism benefiting the overachievers. The Left has been in ascendancy for the past several decades, and has succeeded in instituting many social programs aimed at advancing non-whites and non-Christians in Western society. The

---

[66] This argument also contradicts the SJW faux statistic that "whites are on welfare as much as nonwhites." You can't have it both ways.

strategy adopted by the mainstream Right has been to advocate for the idea of equal opportunity without guaranteeing equality of results. Occasionally the mainstream Right will even deconstruct leftist rhetoric about white privilege and reject leftist attempts to manufacture equality by means of affirmative action or government hiring and spending initiatives as "reverse racism," although even this strategy has diminished in recent years until the Trump campaign brought the issue back into the limelight, much to the chagrin of cuckservatives.

The mainstream establishment Right has been mostly ineffective in resisting the Left, and this is mostly due to the fact that Conservatism, Inc. has accepted the leftist belief in equality as well as the leftist rejection of privilege as a just social concept. Establishment conservatives have generally supported the concept of "equal opportunity" without the government as a guarantor of equal results. The Left is quick to pounce on this inconsistency. If everyone is truly equal, then equal results would naturally result from equal opportunities being made available to all. But it is painfully obvious that equal results are false when we compare the general success of whites to non-whites. The Left can easily explain this as the result of white privilege, but the Right has no good explanation, as those in the mainstream cannot bring themselves to oppose the principle of equality. The Left continues to win major battles because the Left has succeeded in having its foundational plank of equality accepted by all mainstream politicians and thinkers. It is my belief that the only path to victory for the Right is to challenge the Leftist concept of equality, and to defend the traditional concept of social hierarchy.

The principle of equality emerged from the French Revolution in the late eighteenth century, and conservatives such as Edmund Burke were wise and courageous enough to oppose equality and offer a robust defense of privilege. Christendom did not reject privilege or embrace false egalitarian ideas, but instead sought to place men of privilege who had used their gifts well into positions of power and influence in society. Historically, privilege was an important concept within Christendom, and privileges were carefully distinguished from rights. Rights were defined by the responsibilities established by the Second Table of the Ten Commandments, which establish our duties towards our fellow men. Just as we have a responsibility not to kill or steal, we also have a right to life and property which cannot be taken away by any authority without a just cause. These rights are truly universal in that they apply to everyone no matter what differences there might be in a person's external circumstances. By contrast, privileges vary between the social classes and the sexes, as well as among races and families and by individual circumstances. This is an undeniable fact of nature.

We are all different, and there is no question that someone born into a traditional, two-parent family that is financially secure and lives in a safe neighborhood is better off than someone raised by a single mom in Section 8 housing. Moreover people differ in their talents and abilities, and people with greater aptitudes will naturally be presented with more opportunities as well as the means of taking advantages of the opportunities that they encounter. An example of natural privilege is how physically attractive people tend to be more successful than people of average or below-average attractiveness. People are typically drawn to those who are physically attractive, and this translates to the good-looking enjoying many tangible benefits of their physical beauty. There is simply no avoiding the reality of differences among people and the concrete ways in which this translates into different opportunities and outcomes. In a very real sense privilege is not unearned, but rather the inherited benefits earned for good behavior from a collective group of people.

Jesus assumes that people are not equal in his parable of the talents (Matt. 25:14-30; cf. Luke 19:12-27), in which servants are given different amounts of talents to put to use for the benefit of their master and are judged by how well they did by what they are given. Aquinas also argues that inequality demonstrates the glory of God in nature: "the wisdom of God is the cause of the distinction of things, so the same wisdom is the cause of their inequality."[67] The traditional Christian understanding of hierarchy and privilege is explained well by the brothers Grimm in their story, "Eve's Unequal Children." In this story God is said to visit our first parents after they are driven out of the Garden of Eden and after Eve begins to bear children. Eve brings her attractive children before the Lord to be blessed, and God obliges by blessing them with titles of nobility of various ranks. Eve then decides that she will bring her unattractive children to the Lord to receive His blessing. When she does, these children are blessed with various vocations of manual labor.

Eve is disappointed, because she believes that the Lord should treat her children with equality—while failing to note that she had treated them unequally in the first place by hiding the ugly ones. Eve protests, "Lord, how unequally you divide your blessings. All of them are my children, whom I have brought into the world. You should favor them all equally." The Lord responds:

> *Eve, you do not understand. It is right and necessary that the entire world should be served by your children. If they were all princes and lords, who would plant grain, thresh it, grind and bake it? Who would forge iron, weave cloth, build houses, plant crops, dig ditches, and cut out and sew clothing? Each shall stay in his own place, so that one shall support the other, and all shall be fed like the parts of a body.*

To this Eve replies, "Oh, Lord, forgive me, I spoke too quickly to you. Let your divine will be done with my children as well."

---

[67] Aquinas, Thomas. *Summa Theologica*, Part 1, Question 47: The Distinctions of Things in General. Article 2: "Whether Inequality of Things Is from God?" Aquinas cites Sirach (Ecclesiasticus) 33:7-13 to argue that inequality is built into God's design and not necessarily the result of sin.

Christendom accepted the existence and goodness of inequality in this world, and sought to make the best use of people's talents and abilities as possible. Edmund Burke in his famed protest against the egalitarian thought of the French Revolution wrote:

> *From hence they thought themselves obliged to dispose their citizens into such classes, and to place them in such situations in the state, as their peculiar habits might qualify them to fill, and to allot to them such appropriated privileges as might secure to them what their specific occasions required, and which might furnish to each description such force as might protect it in the conflict caused by the diversity of interests that must exist and must contend in all complex society; for the legislator would have been ashamed that the coarse husbandman should well know how to assort and to use his sheep, horses, and oxen, and should have enough of common sense not to abstract and equalize them all into animals without providing for each kind an appropriate food, care, and employment, whilst he, the economist, disposer, and shepherd of his own kindred, subliming himself into an airy metaphysician, was resolved to know nothing of his flocks but as men in general.*[68]

To Christian traditionalists who defended Christendom like Edmund Burke, it is paramount that we understand and recognize people's different talents and abilities and order society accordingly. The lesson that Eve learned in this tale of the Grimm brothers—understood well by luminaries such as Burke—is something that has been forgotten today. Today we seek to make all equal, and in doing so we fail to see the purpose of inequality in the world as it exists today. Jesus taught that all will be judged in light of what they have been given, for "to whom much was given, of him much will be required" (Luke 12:48). The impetus behind the push for equality is the West's faithlessness. Our Christian ancestors understood that biological and social differences and inequality had a purpose in the divine plan, even if this purpose was not always apparent to us in this world. Our Christian ancestors did not share our modern concern for "social justice" which seeks to level society and eliminate all distinctions and differences, since inequality is not an unjust accident of history, and those who are given advantages by God will be judged according to how they use these gifts. Lacking this foundational belief in divine providence, the modern West has been powerless to resist the rhetoric of the egalitarian Left. The only path to succeed in our existential battle with the liberal cancer that is rotting the soul of Europa is to reject unnatural equality and reaffirm the proper place of privilege in society, and embracing the doctrines of the Christian faith is the only way this is going to happen.

---

[68] Burke, Edmund. *Reflections on the Revolution in France*, p. 152.

Nil Desperandum

> Nil Desperandum is of European descent and resides in the States, eagerly awaiting the re-Christianization of the West. He enjoys studying theology and philosophy, especially epistemology and ethics.

Hate the Sin and Hate the Sinner

June 16, 2011

Introduction

Most Christians today, in seeking to follow after our Savior's injunction to love our enemies (Matt. 5:44), tend to deeply emphasize love. Unfortunately, they do so to the point of maudlin sentimentalism. This is reflected by the modern praise bands with their sappy Jesus-is-my-boyfriend songs, the effeminacy of Christian men in refusing to stand up for truth, and the sick pacifism which would obligate a man to watch the rape of his wife and daughters rather than fight back. It is tragically pervasive in the church today.

Usually fueling this idea is the phrase often quoted by Christians, "Hate the sin and love the sinner." It would be permissible for Christians to accept a qualified form of the phrase, but the modern advocacy of it is unqualified and radical. It is of no help to such Christians that the phrase cannot be located in Scripture, but it is especially problematic when we understand that the originator of the commandment was not even a Christian, but the pagan Mahatma Gandhi. This is usually, though irrationally, justified by the supposition that Gandhi was a "good" unbeliever, but even that idea is mere propaganda. As such, it would behoove us to see the implications of this command and, more importantly, to apprehend the biblical doctrine on love and hatred.

Unconditional Love

Tied with the idea of "hate the sin and love the sinner" is unconditional love. This follows necessarily because, in making such a chasm between the person and his actions, the phrase demands that we love someone no matter what he does: we must love him unconditionally. In some respects, this can be a noble Christian goal. For instance, even when it comes to very evil unbelievers, we should still hope that they repent and believe in Christ. After all, St. Paul himself was "breathing threats and murder against the disciples of the Lord" (Acts 9:1), consumed in unregeneracy, and he was nevertheless brought to spiritual life. Even then, however, such a loving desire for repentance would not be genuinely *unconditional*, since there is an unforgivable sin (Mark 3:28-40; cf. Heb. 10:26-27). This should be clearer when we recognize that there is not a clear sense in which we are supposed to love Satan or his angels, or even the damned. They all have incorrigibly opted for perdition, and have therefore fulfilled a condition which requires a significant withholding of love.

We can also speak of love in the sense of supreme adoration, that kind of love due to God alone. It might be this kind of love that Jesus had in mind when He explicitly said, "If anyone comes to Me and does not hate his father and mother, wife and children, brothers and sisters, yes, and his own life also, he cannot be My disciple" (Luke 14:26; cf. Matt. 10:37). Yet, Jesus's statement goes even further than the modest claim that we ought not to worship our family members. He is also claiming that disharmony and bitterness can occur for His followers, even in that wonderful sphere of familial affection and solidarity. "For I have come to 'set a man against his father, a daughter against her mother, and a daughter-in-law against her mother-in-law'; and 'a man's enemies will be those of his own household'" (Matt. 10:35-36).

While it is obvious that we should not unconditionally love anyone in the sense of worshiping him — in fact, given that definition, there are no circumstances when we should "love" someone besides God — our Savior's language in Luke 14:26 also states something else about unconditional love. He explicitly denies that we are to unconditionally love our own family members, and *a fortiori* He denies that we are to unconditionally love anyone. There always comes a point — there is always a certain condition to be fulfilled — when allegiance to our God requires some sort of strife, some breach of peace and harmony. "Those who forsake the law praise the wicked, but such as keep the law contend with them" (Prov. 28:4).

This is where we can see the evils of "hate the sin and love the sinner." It results in an odious doctrine of unconditional love, a doctrine which stresses not a longsuffering desire for the repentance of evildoers — the only acceptable meaning of "unconditional love," even though it is not strictly unconditional — but an alluring impulse for false amicability in the face of wickedness. It is against this false understanding of unconditional love that theologian R.J. Rushdoony wrote:

> *Unconditional love is a more revolutionary concept than any other doctrine of revolution. Unconditional love means the end of discrimination between good and evil, right and wrong, better and worse, friend and enemy, and all things else. Whenever anyone asks you to love unconditionally, they are asking you to surrender unconditionally to the enemy.*[69]

Rushdoony's wisdom here ties together two notions from above — the vast disconnect between persons and actions which such a view of "love" requires, and the disobedience to God displayed by loving His enemies. That is, if we claim to unconditionally love a person — to treat him cordially, amiably, and peacefully, no

---

[69] Rushdoony, R.J. *Roots of Reconstruction*, p. 625. Qtd. in "The Fallacy of Unconditional Love."

matter what he does—then that means we do not care if he commits sinful atrocities; we do not see any relation between his own actions and how we ought to treat him. This is metaphysical and ethical insanity, not to mention inconsistent with Scripture (1 Cor. 5:11; Matt. 18:17). As Rushdoony notes, to unconditionally love our enemies in this fashion is *surrender*; it is to allow the baneful influences of demons to go unfettered throughout society. Such an outlook is neglect of and disobedience to our King. It is a feigned love of sinners which is an actual love of sin: it is not biblical love. But this is what happens when we sever a man from his actions, as "hate the sin and love the sinner" requires. A different way of stating this is that such a view of love is in reality an *indiscriminate niceness*. Like animals, we make no discrimination between good and evil, but simply act as people-pleasers in order to maintain false unity and peace. God abhors this (Jer. 6:14; Gal. 1:10).

The connection between a sinner and his sin should be obvious when we consider that God punishes *sinners* in hell for their sin, not sin itself. Scripture expressly states that God hates sinners (e.g., Ps. 5:5; 7:11; 11:5), and accordingly He pours out His wrath upon them: sin and sinner are connected.[70] Our dispositions should be geared in the same way; we should not believe in such a gaping divide between sinners and sin. This is why David, as an inspired psalmist, can proclaim, "Do I not hate them, O LORD, who hate You? And do I not loathe those who rise up against You? I hate them with perfect hatred; I count them my enemies" (Ps. 139:21-22). We are supposed to love our enemies (Matt. 5:44), but hate God's enemies.[71] Hence the usual assertion of "hate the sin and love the sinner," with its

---

[70] No doubt, the doctrine of unconditional election would remind us that God does unconditionally love His elect, and that He loves them regardless of what sins they commit. In that sense, God *does* separate the sinner from his sins. But to discourse on this would be to veer from the subject matter. Suffice it to say that God's unconditionally benevolent treatment of His elect is due to the righteousness and finished work of Christ imputed to their account. Or, it is one thing to say that God will treat a nefarious and hell-bound reprobate as if his sins were *irrelevant*, and it is another thing to say that God will treat an elect sinner, cleansed by the sacrificial blood of Christ, as if his sins were *covered*.

[71] Correction: I now believe it is false that the proper harmonization of such verses as Matthew 5:44 and Psalm 139:21-22 is to "love our enemies but hate God's enemies." Please see my article "Biblical Love and Hatred Harmonized," answer #7 of which has been reproduced here:

"7. We are to love our own enemies, but we are to hate God's enemies.

This might be the most common answer presented, and it was likewise the answer which I promoted in my previous article on biblical hate. Its force is clearest when the two passages cited at the beginning of this article are juxtaposed, Matthew 5:44 and Psalm 139:21-22. Yet the latter passage includes a phrase which immediately disproves the view: "I count them mine enemies." David, as the inspired psalmist, here writes that his shared hatred of God's enemies makes them to be shared enemies as well. God's enemies become his enemies. But it inevitably follows, then, that it is permissible, even righteous in certain circumstances, to hate certain individuals as personal enemies, i.e. as enemies to one's own person. This principle is made much more obvious in other psalms, which explicitly refer to personal enemies of the psalmist (e.g. Ps. 6:10; 35:4-8; 109:29).

Irrespective of these citations, however, this explanation is inherently implausible. The reason why God's enemies deserve our hatred is because of the grievous sin involved in opposing God. But this same grounds for holy hatred—sin—exists when people unlawfully oppose us as well. Obviously, there is a very relevant distinction here, for those who oppose God ipso facto commit sin, whereas other men can oppose us righteously and thus not deserve any indignation of ours in response. Moreover, it is a far graver sin to oppose God than to (wrongfully) oppose men. Nevertheless, the just cause for hatred is

unqualified and unclarified meaning, is a cowardly denial of our obligation to hate God's enemies. It necessitates total societal surrender to antichrists. It is a venomous exhortation.

Our obligation to hate God's enemies while loving our own enemies tends to result in a more complicated ethic, since these two categories can overlap and apply to the same people, requiring us to love people in some senses and hate the same people in different senses. In contrast, the ethical code of the sentimentalist will be that in all circumstances (unconditionally), we ought to be nice to others; in no circumstances should we refuse to be a doormat. But, of course, we can understand that ethical codes need to be neither simple nor simplistic. The ethical complexity introduced by a biblical conception of conditional love should help us to realize the splendor of God's law, our feeble inability and unwillingness to keep it, and the perfection of our Savior to fulfill it in our stead. May His Spirit grant us the practical wisdom to discern how to manifest each disposition appropriately.

The Centrality of Love in Christianity

While it is clear that a sentimentalist conception of love is pestilential, it is nonetheless clear that love is central to Christianity. After all, if there were not biblical passages which emphasized love, then what would the sentimentalists twist to support their own perversions? We must therefore understand what it means to love the Lord and love our neighbor in light of our mandate to hate God's enemies.

In the first place, it is crucial to understand that to love someone includes the fulfillment of our moral obligations, as defined in God's law, with respect to him (Rom. 13:8-10). Some might object to this, arguing that love involves acting from the heart, rather than from some cold or mechanical sense of duty; but this poses a false dilemma. Part of God's law regulates our emotional temperaments, or, in other words, it is our *duty* to act from the *heart*. When a husband displays sincere and tender affection for his wife, loving her as Christ loves His Church, he is also fulfilling his duty to do the same (Eph. 5:25). What would the alternative to this be—that it is *not* our duty to act with a spirit of love? This understanding of love as being the fulfillment of law is helpful, because then we know that we do not need some extra, unrevealed component to transform law-keeping into genuine love: God's law-word is sufficient to instruct us in our duties of love.

One of the favored passages by sentimentalists is Matthew 5:38-42, where Jesus seems to denounce the *lex talionis* while telling us to turn the other cheek, walk

---

found in both God-hatred and man-hatred, and thus we can hate personal enemies qua personal enemies, so long as these personal enemies wrongfully oppose us, hating us "without a cause" (Ps. 35:19; 69:4)."

the extra mile, etc. At first glance, our Lord looks to be ordering total concession in just about every action we experience or undertake. But in fact, Christ is condemning only personal vengeance and unrighteous retaliation. Rather than correcting the *lax talionis* itself, He is correcting a misapplication of it to the personal sphere. In the civil sphere, it is a splendid law of proportionate justice, as Jesus Himself revealed earlier in history (Deut. 19:21), but here, He is commanding that although we may be personally humiliated or mocked (e.g., slapped in the face), we may not use violence, or even hatred, for the sake of self-glory. We ought to be self-abasing in a Christ-exalting way, caring not at all about our glory but only about His glory. "He must increase, but I must decrease" (John 3:30). Moreover, Jesus is here speaking of smaller injuries we endure, the bearing of which for peace's sake is a greater act than causing unnecessary strife. It is important to note that this interpretation is consistent with the vengeance to be pursued in the judicial sphere (Rom. 13:4), as well as with the right of a man to defend his own and others' lives. To protect ourselves from harm, and even to protect our reputation from slander, is not necessarily to glorify oneself, and consequently these are not forbidden by Jesus in the passage. They are different from hating or attacking someone else *just because* your ego has been hurt—rather than because, say, you are in mortal danger.

The biblical mandate of love extends elsewhere. All over Scripture, and especially the New Testament, we are taught to be humble, gentle, longsuffering, meek, tender, and gracious (1 Cor. 13:4-5; Eph. 4:2, 29; Phil. 4:5; Col. 3:12; 4:6; 1 Tim. 6:11; 2 Tim. 2:24; 1 Pet. 3:15; James 1:19-20). These passages lucidly teach that we are not supposed to be hotheads, easily angered at the least bit of sin in others. Our Father is infinitely longsuffering towards us (Rom. 2:4), and we should imitate Him. Yet, while these passages teach such gentleness and patience, it does not follow that the modern, womanish meaning and application of those terms is requisite, nor does it follow that warmness is the normative pattern of behavior in all circumstances and towards all men. We are indeed to be gracious and kind in ordinary circumstances and towards most people, but this does not entail that we are to be indiscriminately nice. A doctrine of indiscriminate niceness would contradict all the biblically approved examples of harsh language (e.g., 1 Kings 18:27; Hosea 1:2; Gal. 5:12; Phil. 3:2; 1 Tim. 4:1; Jude 8-15; Rev. 2:9; 22:15). One of the best instances of this is Jesus Himself in Matthew 23, when He verbally eviscerates the Pharisees. This aligns with His forceful example of driving out evil money changers from the temple (Matt. 21:12-13). Note, the overt enemies of God—the prophets of Baal, the Judaizers, the Pharisees, the false teachers—were the ones who received such verbal devastation. This should be kept in mind when we discern when to be gentle and when to be harsh, a practice we should approach with caution and prayer (Prov. 15:1).[72]

Thoughts into Action

We already covered part of Matthew 5, but there is another important principle to be gleaned from that same passage. In vv. 27-28, Jesus condemns heart-adultery. What He shows here is a strong connection between the outward act and the incipient disposition. There is an adamant connection between thoughts, words, and actions (cf. Mark 7:20-23).[73] What is salient is that this connection is upheld when it comes to our duties. In the same way that a prohibition of an outward sin entails a prohibition of an inward sin, so also a command of an outward duty entails a command of an inward duty, and vice versa. This is particularly relevant when we must understand the aforementioned command to hate God's enemies.

Before moving on, I want to slow down a bit to cover some more biblical material concerning the hatred of sinners. Besides the overt and explicit example of David's hatred in Psalm 139:21-22, we also see many other injunctions in the psalms expressing the same heart attitude: the desire for the destruction of the wicked. For instance, Psalm 35:26 says, "Let them be ashamed and brought to mutual confusion who rejoice at my hurt; let them be clothed with shame and dishonor who exalt themselves against me." These imprecations are very similar to David's example in Psalm 139:21-22. They express a desire for the destruction of sinners—and what is a hatred of God's enemies but a desire for their pain and destruction? Remarkably, these maledictions can be found quite frequently (Ps. 7:14-16; 35:4-8; 55:9, 15, 19, 23; 58:6-11; 69:22-28; 79:6-7, 10, 12; 83:13-18; 109:6-20, 29; 137:7-9), and the same imprecatory outlook of the biblical author can be found in the New Testament as well (Gal. 1:8-9; 1 Cor. 16:22; 2 Tim. 4:14). Such New Testament citations should be superfluous, because moral principles do not change across time, yet they show the importance and continuity of this doctrine nevertheless.

The practical import of this arrives, as I said, when we see that inward duties are linked with outward duties. Our obedience is deficient if we limit it to obedient thoughts; if we are called to a balanced hatred, it ought to manifest itself in manfully resisting evildoers in society.

---

[72] It would be important to note that our attitudes of harshness or gentleness can also vary as we talk with the same person over a longer period of time. For instance, there might be a man promoting doctrines of demons in one's church: it would probably not be right for an elder to immediately denounce him. He should be patient in correcting him. Later, if it turns out that such a man is incorrigible and proud, then to that degree harsh language becomes more appropriate. I would contend that this understanding makes better sense of such verses as 2 Tim. 2:24.

[73] This is why the Ten Commandments, by implication, forbid a lot more than what they expressly command or forbid.

Conclusion

Rather than embrace the simplistic sentimentalist ethic of indiscriminate niceness, we ought to affirm the majesty and perfection of God's law. It might seem complex to us, but it is perfect. "How sweet are Your words to my taste, sweeter than honey to my mouth! Through Your precepts I get understanding; therefore I hate every false way" (Ps. 119:103-104). "[T]he law is holy, and the commandment holy and just and good" (Rom. 7:12).

Assuredly, God's law is difficult to follow. It is hard enough to do what we know we ought to do (Rom. 7:19), and it is increasingly arduous when we do not know when exactly to display biblical hatred. Regardless, God still promises to sanctify us (Ezek. 36:27), improving both our understandings and our wills. As sinners, we will probably choose at times to be passive when we ought to be wrathful, or we might be scornful when we ought to be gracious. When these times come, we must repent and seek forgiveness, all the while being reminded of God's promises, Jesus's example, and His atoning sacrifice. As we learn how we ought to behave when confronted with evil in society, we must not neglect these portions of hatred displayed in God's perfect law-word. We must know when we ought to hate the sin and hate the sinner.

False Sins

September 23, 2011

Introduction

One of the major sources of strife and disarray in this world is moral disagreement. Though anger emerges for many reasons, virtually always caused by or in response to sin, one of these ways is when people disagree as to the identification of moral and immoral actions. Even when actions viewed by a man to be immoral are not performed by anyone else, it is common and normal for him to be angry when others merely profess the morality of those actions. As an overt and shocking example, imagine how you would respond if some man told you that he saw nothing wrong with the rape of children. Even if he also claimed that he would never do it, any conscience not entirely burnt out would still express moral outrage at his beliefs.

The ancient Greek philosopher Plato echoes these thoughts in his dialogue *Euthyphro*. In it, the character Socrates states:

> *What subject of difference would make us angry and hostile to each other if we were unable to come to a decision? Perhaps you [i.e., Euthyphro] do not have an answer ready, but examine as I tell you whether these subjects are the just and the unjust, the beautiful and the ugly, the good and the bad. Are these not the subjects of difference about which, when we are unable to come to a satisfactory decision, you and I and other men become hostile to each other whenever we do?*[74]

God constituted us, as creatures in His image, to have a powerful moral disposition. When we apprehend immorality, we are designed to generate moral indignation. Though we are to be forbearing with others' frailties, we are yet required to defend the law of God and hate all unrighteousness. Therefore, when others espouse a different morality—when they declare a contrary set of duties and sins—it is proper and natural (and obligatory!) for us to oppose them, instituting God's law as supreme. And since any rationalization of sin necessarily involves the supplanting of divine law with some instantiation of man-made law, we should understand that opposing false law-systems is not uncommon. Sinners in rebellion to God love to concoct their own lists of false sins.

---

[74] Plato, *Five Dialogues*, trans. G.M.A. Grube, p. 9

The Nature of Morality

As Scripture makes clear, morality is well understood in terms of law. Just consider the definition of sin as lawlessness (1 John 3:4), and the primacy of the Ten Commandments. We are required to do certain actions and to refrain from other actions. Even more fundamentally, however, it would be accurate to make a threefold distinction in understanding how morality applies to actions. Given any particular action whatsoever, we can say that it has one of three classifications: obligatory, prohibited, or permissible. Since the three categories are mutually exclusive[75] and jointly exhaustive, you can select any action that a moral agent might be faced with, and it can be categorized according to one of these three categories, necessarily. For instance, consider the actions of taking a walk at night, or selecting pepperoni rather than cheese pizza, or going to church on Sunday mornings.

Now, there are a couple of qualifications I should add to help clarify this. First, although every action will necessarily be placed in one of the three categories, we may not know which category. That is just to say that certain things are morally fuzzy, or that sometimes we will be faced with moral dilemmas. This is not problematic, so long as we understand the necessity of the categories in themselves.

Second, there are levels of generality in which these actions can be understood. This should be easier to grasp when we understand that sometimes we might respond to the question, "Is X obligatory, prohibited, or permissible?" with the answer, "X is sometimes obligatory, sometimes prohibited, and sometimes permissible." Consider my previous example of attending church on Sunday mornings. We might say that we are ordinarily obligated to attend corporate worship on the Lord's Day, but there can always be extenuating circumstances which make it permissible not to attend. What is crucial, again, is understanding that, when dealing with any *particular* action, where we can analyze the relevant, morality-determining circumstances sitting before a particular moral agent, an action will always fall in one, and only one, of the three moral categories. If I were to ask you whether it was obligatory for you to attend your particular church service on August 21, 2011, then the answer could not be, "it is sometimes one or the other." And therefore it is still the case that the three moral categories necessarily apply to any particular action.

---

[75] Someone might object that obligatory actions are also permissible — if I am obligated to love my neighbor, then certainly I am also permitted to love him — and therefore that the two are not mutually exclusive. However, when I use the term "permissible," I refer to those actions which are *merely* permissible. They are permissible but non-obligatory by definition.

The Inescapability of Moral Law

Moral philosophizing aside, the significance of this tripartite moral categorization is how it points to the inescapability of moral law. Everyone must necessarily have a view of the moral law. Everyone must classify various actions according to one of the three categories, and therefore everyone must have some systematic understanding of morality. Even if someone were to claim not to know the moral status of various actions, he would still be forced to treat them, in practice, as obligatory, prohibited, or permissible. For example, after seeing the historic view on the subject, a man might say: "I do not know if miscegenation is moral or not, so in the meantime I'll not take any risks, but just marry within my race." In instances where we may not know the moral status of an action, but are still forced to treat it as belonging to one of the three categories, our *modus operandi* ought to be that whatever is not done in faith is sin (Rom. 14:23). God's law governs with clarity even those instances where our moral choices are initially unclear.

Given that everyone has a certain set of beliefs concerning what is obligatory, prohibited, and permissible, it follows that some people are incorrect, and that there is but one true view. Specifically, God's law is the full set of all correct categorizations of moral obligation, prohibition, and permissibility; and man's law will deviate from this set in some fashion. Everyone has a certain view of moral law, inescapably, and everyone must try to adhere to the true law as much as possible. It is not a matter of neutrality, but a religious question which everyone is forced to answer—either God's law, or some perversion thereof. To oppose God's law is to oppose Him as King and Lawgiver (Isaiah 33:22), and therefore to be His enemy, garnering His and His people's hatred and wrath (Ps. 5:5; 139:21-22).

A crucial doctrine emanating from the inescapability of this religious question is how antinomianism and legalism—two false views concerning the content of God's law[76]—are intertwined. Being a moral creature, designed to obey God's law in all its particulars, man will usually be uncomfortable and dissatisfied when he merely omits moral obligations. Instead, he will want to replace the divinely imprinted obligations he dislikes with his own set. If man dislikes God's law, he tends not only to remove parts of God's law, but to replace it with his own law, displaying a dialectical relationship between antinomianism and legalism. If rejecting total nihilism, man must have law; but sinners hate God's law. Man will therefore create false duties and false sins, the most prominent of which today belong to the dogmas of cultural Marxism and political correctness.

---

[76] There are other ways that "antinomianism" and "legalism" are employed besides with reference to the *content* of God's law. For example, one form of legalism is viewing law-keeping as salvific: this is a false view of the purpose of the law, not its content. But, as a matter of fact, I am employing the terms to refer to those errors respecting the content of God's law, not some other feature.

The Bankruptcy of Marxist Morality

There is a slew of new vocabulary that has arisen in discussions concerning Western ethics. Whereas terms like "fornication," "miscegenation," "bastard," and "infidel" have all but disappeared, a new list of sins has appeared, the most prevalent of which are racism, sexism, homophobia, anti-Semitism, xenophobia, and Islamophobia. Much ink could be and has been spilled in showing the vacuousness of these terms, which are often utilized in ways that reduce to self-contradiction, irrationality, and name-calling. For instance, Craig Bodeker in his "A Conversation About Race" shows how "racism," when defined as belief in racial superiority, is not consistently espoused, but is merely used as a hammer to manipulate and guilt-trip whites. Further, any promotion of biblical and hierarchical gender roles is deemed as "sexist," since hierarchy implies inequality; and any moral condemnation of sodomy is deemed "homophobic." The idea that American men should not be sacrificed to fight wars for Israel is "anti-Semitic." The examples could be multiplied.

The vitality of these false sins is grounded in obfuscation and propaganda. The media and government schools muddy the issue by never providing a definition of these terms which is analyzed or consistently professed, including in the scope of these terms both real and false sins. For example, after impressing upon spectators the idea that racism involves mindless hatred of and violence toward other races—always non-white—the propagandist will then include a number of sinless actions in the scope of the term. To prefer one's children to marry white is then seen as racist, as is citing statistics which do not remove the warts of other races. Before you know it, any white making any racial claim whatsoever (besides groveling) receives the reactionary accusation of "Racist!"

This bears repeating: true sins can be properly encapsulated by every one of the false Marxist sins listed. A murder of a Muslim, just because he is Muslim, could accurately be called "Islamophobia." Yet it does not follow that these terms ought to be used, for they are associated with outlawing what God does not outlaw and requiring what He does not require. They are constructs produced expressly for the propagation of a false law-system, and therefore Christians should repudiate them.

What is so dangerous about these labels is that they impress in people's minds a new set of duties and sins, a new categorization of obligatory, prohibited, and permissible actions. Even though various Marxist-infiltrated institutions might profess a decent-sounding principle that might not, in itself, require deviation from the tripartite moral categorization of God's law—e.g., that we ought to treat all races with respect—they *in practice* promote a set of obligations, prohibitions, and permissibilities that completely assaults true law. Masquerading as angels of light, these men of darkness subvert godly order and morality.

Conclusion

Given the great degree and intensity of false guilt which results from the proliferation of false sins, we can see how fighting for the supremacy of Christ's law is fighting for liberty. False guilt enslaves populations, but a free population is one based on true morality, Christian morality, understanding the guilt that was appropriated by Christ. When we truly believe and apply Christian doctrine and law to our lives and society, liberty will necessarily increase.

Only Christianity can lay claim to a true expression of divine law. Our modern religious milieu of cultural Marxism has a different system of moral law which necessarily wages war on competing systems, and Christians need to be in battle for the true King of kings, upholding God's law and tearing down this idol and false morality.

The Case for Postmillennialism

Part 1

October 12, 2011

Introduction

It should be obvious that an accurate view of how God orders history will be exceedingly practical in the life of Christians. (If it were not obvious, witness the paralytic obsession of dispensationalists over Zionism and rapture-longing.) Eschatology, literally the study of the last things, is immensely important, and serves as a converging pinnacle of the other fields of systematic theology:

> *In theology it is the question, how God is finally perfectly glorified in the work of His hands, and how the counsel of God is fully realized; in anthropology, the question, how the disrupting influence of sin is completely overcome; in christology, the question, how the work of Christ is crowned with perfect victory; in soteriology, the question, how the work of the Holy Spirit at last issues in the complete redemption and glorification of the people of God; and in ecclesiology, the question of the final apotheosis of the Church.*[77]

Eschatology includes a philosophy of history, providing us with a foundational understanding of history's trajectory, serving as a backdrop against which we can interpret historical events. A Christian eschatology views history as guided by God's sovereign providence, including all the actions of men; and all these events have a specific purpose, the glory of God. This implies a distinctly linear view of history, culminating with the fullness of God's glory, and it can be contrasted both with the cyclical pagan view and with the utterly purposeless secularist view. The Christian view also involves God's own intrusions into history, especially the Incarnation: we are not left alone in our sin and in this fallen world.

However, beyond the application of these indisputable Christian doctrines to the study of history, there still is an important doctrine which must be settled, the doctrine of millennialism. In this series, I hope to provide a good construction of the separate views, including reasons why the postmillennialist view is superior.

---

[77] Berkhof, Louis. *Systematic Theology*, p. 665.

Preliminary Considerations

There are four views one can take on the subject of millennialism: dispensational premillennialism, historic premillennialism, amillennialism, and postmillennialism. All of these terms are some variant of the term "millennialism," and this is due to the prominence of Revelation 20:1-6 in determining people's eschatological opinions. I find the prominence of this passage unfortunate, but nevertheless, the terms are now rooted and in place.

Of the four views, three of them are pessimistic and one is optimistic. All are optimistic, of course, in the sense of believing that Christ will ultimately be victorious, but three are pessimistic since they doubt that Christian victory will occur on earth in any substantial sense before Christ's return.

Now, I do not intend to poison the well by calling all non-postmillennialist views pessimistic: we ought to believe what Scripture teaches on the subject, period, irrespective of any optimism we might desire. However, it is still helpful and vital to understand the importance of divergence on this issue. When Christians believe in victory and triumph for the gospel over idolatry, then they are given the motivation to actually go out and seek to redeem souls and culture. Conversely, when they believe that Jesus will not be victorious on earth until He physically returns, it can lead to social irresponsibility and lethargy. If the church does not believe that she will be successful on earth prior to Christ's return, then she will not anticipate or labor towards such an end. In short, people are motivated by results, and therefore a debate over what God has decreed the results to be is crucial.

Other Distinctions Among the Views

There are a number of miscellaneous observations one can make in distinguishing the four views. In the first place, observe the prefixes of each word. Defining the "millennium" generally as a golden age, the premillennialists believe that Christ will return prior to the millennium, whereas postmillennialists believe that Christ will return after the millennium. Amillennialists simply deny that any earthly or overtly visible manifestation of the millennium will occur (i.e. that it will not be a golden age). Another way of saying this is that premillennialists believe the millennium is currently unrealized, while postmillennialists and amillennialists believe that it is presently realized.

Dispensational premillennialism is distinct from historic premillennialism in that the former is (obviously) dispensational. It holds to a strictly literal hermeneutic; maintains that the millennium will be distinctly Jewish, with Christ physically sitting in David's throne in Israel and with the temple-sacrificial system reinstituted; and believes in the rapture, that believers will be transported from the earth prior to (or in the middle of) the great tribulation, after which Christ will return to usher in the millennium. Historic premillennialism differs in that it does not hold to a reinstitution of Old Covenant ceremonies, nor does it hold to the rapture. It maintains that there will be only one second coming, and that believers will go through the tribulation before Christ returns.

Both forms of premillennialism are based on a literal interpretation of Rev. 20:1-6. The passage says that the souls of dead saints will reign with Christ for one thousand years. On the surface, this appears to be saying quite plainly that Christ will first return, and then the millennium will be ushered in (premillennialism), at which point He will reign with His saints. Premillennialism can truly claim to be the literal interpretation of Rev. 20:1-6. Yet, I would contend that this interpretation is unjustified, given that Revelation is far and away one of the most symbolic books in the Bible, and given that other clearer passages of Scripture would guide us to a separate interpretation. We always ought to let clear passages shed light upon unclear ones, and Rev. 20 is quite a figurative and unclear passage. (This will be covered more in a subsequent article.)

Amillennialists hold that the 1000 years of Rev. 20 represent the entire interadvental period (i.e. the time between Christ's first and second comings) and that the deceased saints in that passage are presently ruling with Christ in heaven. The binding of Satan occurred at His first advent, permitting the gospel to spread beyond Israel unto the entire world. Amillennialists also believe that Scripture teaches that Christ's second coming and the final judgment are simultaneous, which would forbid a millennium from existing between the two, as the premillennialist timeline dictates. Amillennialists would maintain that there will be no rapture, nor will Christ reign bodily on earth. The cosmic events we can foretell, biblically speaking, are the second coming of Christ, one general resurrection of believers and unbelievers, and the final judgment, which will immediately send believers to glory and unbelievers to perdition.

The timelines of amillennialism and postmillennialism are actually quite similar with respect to the main events. The fundamental difference, as mentioned above, is the optimism of postmillennialism. Amillennialists generally believe that the amount of good and evil in the world will stay about the same until Christ returns, though some believe that evil will eventually triumph on earth. Amillennialists deny that the world will be heavily Christianized when Christ comes back, while postmillennialists affirm it. (There are also "optimistic amillennialists" who might believe in a moderate amount of Christianization.)

Conclusion

I do not intend to convey that this series is about eschatology in general. There are a vast number of eschatological elements which could be mined from Scripture, such as the identity of the man of sin of 2 Thessalonians 2, whether Matthew 24 is future or fulfilled, who the various characters of Revelation are, and other things. I am concerning myself chiefly with these four broad millennial views, or more properly, these four historical-framework views.

In future posts in this series, I intend to show the deficiencies in the premillennial timeline, vindicating the amillennial and postmillennial timeline. After establishing that, I plan to show the incredible optimism which Scripture warrants us to believe concerning the spread of the gospel and world Christianization.

Part 2
November 16, 2011

Introduction

Many Christians have a different understanding of how history will progress, holding different views on millennialism. After having previously discussed the four different millennial views, distinguishing dispensational premillennialism, historic premillennialism, and amillennialism from postmillennialism, I now wish to progress in making a case for the latter. This will involve a demonstration of the general timeline followed by both amillennialists and postmillennialists, thereby refuting the two variants of premillennialism. This will also include an alternative interpretation of Revelation 20.

A Refutation of the Premillennial Timeline

The general timeline followed by premillennialists is that Christ will return at some point in the future, which we can expect at any time — and they usually believe it is very soon — at which point He will usher in a 1000-year kingdom. He will reign visibly on earth with His saints for that millennium, in accord with the literal interpretation of Revelation 20:4. Following this millennium will be the resurrection of all who were not already resurrected to reign with Christ (Rev. 20:5), a final satanic rebellion (vv. 7-10), and the final judgment of all (vv. 11-15). Therefore premillennialists contend that Christ's second coming is not simultaneous with the final resurrection of all or with the final judgment, instead positing a full thousand years between those two great cosmic events. Amillennialists and postmillennialists, on the other hand, assert that Christ's second coming *is* simultaneous with those events.

Scripture denies the premillennialist view, teaching that Christ's second coming and the final judgment occur at the exact same time, or at least very near one another (Matt. 16:27; 25:31-33; Jude 14-15; 2 Thess. 1:7-8; Rev. 22:12). The only way for the premillennialist to avoid the perspicuous import of these passages is to say that Christ is merely mentioning these two events with each other, not implying anything of their chronological relation. But this explanation fails. Just consider, for example, the first verse I listed, Matthew 16:27:

> *For the Son of Man will come in the glory of His Father with His angels, and then He will reward each according to his works.*

The premillennialist must take the phrase "and then" to permit the interpretation of "and after a very long time," but it is obvious that such an interpretation is impermissible. The passage teaches a near simultaneity of Christ's return and judgment. This is even more clearly stated in Matthew 25:31-33:

> *When the Son of Man comes in His glory, and all the holy angels with Him, then He will sit on the throne of His glory. All the nations will be gathered before Him, and He will separate them one from another, as a shepherd divides his sheep from the goats. And He will set the sheep on His right hand, but the goats on the left.*

Such a passage hardly needs commentary. When Christ returns is when He will separate the sheep from the goats for eternity. The only way to escape the force of these passages is to state that this is referring to some third coming of Christ, as if He departed after the millennium and then returned again—but that is just not what premillennialists say, as it is not supported by a literal reading of Revelation 20. The passage does not speak of a departure of Christ and a subsequent return. Hence these passages must be referring to Christ's second coming, demanding the amillennial and postmillennial timeline.

Proof of One General Resurrection

Revelation 20:4-6 speaks of a "first resurrection" and implies a second resurrection, and so premillennialists take this to mean that there are two significantly different cosmic events, two different resurrections punctuated by 1,000 years. The passage reads:

> *And I saw thrones, and they sat on them, and judgment was committed to them. Then I saw the souls of those who had been beheaded for their witness to Jesus and for the word of God, who had not worshiped the beast or his image, and had not received his mark on their foreheads or on their hands. And they lived and reigned with Christ for a thousand years. But the rest of the dead did not live again until the thousand years were finished. This is the first resurrection. Blessed and holy is he who has part in the first resurrection. Over such the second death has no power, but they shall be priests of God and of Christ, and shall reign with Him a thousand years.*

It, again, is clear how a literal understanding of this passage leads to the premillennial view. Two resurrections are implicitly stated, leading premillennialists to believe in an initial resurrection of the righteous and a later resurrection of the wicked.[78] But what does the rest of Scripture say? Do other Scriptures militate against a literal interpretation of this passage? First, the passages concerning the simultaneity of Christ's second advent already imply that two resurrections cannot be future events of history, since those events' close occurrence outlaws any thousand-year gap from existing between two resurrections. Therefore, even if the Bible did not say anything outside of Revelation 20 regarding whether there will be one or two large-scale resurrections, we still would have great reason to reject the literal rendering of Revelation 20. However, in addition to this, a good case can be made from Scripture that one general resurrection of the righteous and the wicked is taught. Though it is not as evident as the biblical teaching on the simultaneity of Christ's second advent and the final judgment, Scripture still shows that there is only one general resurrection.

There are three passages I wish to address that teach a general resurrection of the righteous and the wicked: Acts 24:15; John 5:28-29; and 1 Cor. 15:22-26, 51-54. Acts 24:15 is the least clear of the three. In it St. Paul says the following:

> *I have hope in God, which they themselves also accept, that there will be a resurrection of the dead, both of the just and the unjust.*

This passage is not particularly powerful in refuting the two-resurrection view, since Paul is making this statement in passing, and it would not be unreasonable

---

[78] Premillennialists generally make this distinction between the two resurrections, holding that the first is for the saints and the second is for the damned, but Revelation 20 could reasonably allow that some saints are also raised in the second resurrection, with only certain kinds of saints raised in the first resurrection (namely, those saints who had been martyred). Whatever the particular interpretation is, the salient point is that premillennialists will hold to two resurrections separated by the millennium.

to take his phrase "a resurrection of the dead" as referring to the fact that everyone will be resurrected rather than to one corporate resurrection-event. For example, in a different context, someone might say, "I have hope that there will be a punishment for the wicked"; in saying that, he could be referring to the fact that each unbeliever, immediately after death, experiences hell torments. In this case, he would mention "a punishment" which would actually involve several separate events at different times. Similarly, it could be that Paul is referring to the fact that all will be resurrected, even though it might occur at different points in time. Thus, the passage is generally underdeterminative, although it would still lend *prima facie* weight to the one-resurrection view. Although "a resurrection" *can* be taken to refer to refer to a chronologically separated plurality of events, its default or initial meaning is clearly that there is only one resurrection. This interpretation is strengthened when we view another main passage, John 5:28-29, wherein Jesus says:

> *Do not marvel at this; for the hour is coming in which all who are in the graves will hear His voice and come forth — those who have done good, to the resurrection of life, and those who have done evil, to the resurrection of condemnation.*

Our Savior's words here carry more weight than Paul's, since He is actually addressing the resurrection and final judgment in context (thereby additionally evidencing that those two events are simultaneous), and since He here speaks of an event occurring in a short period of time when all men, both workers of righteousness and workers of evil, will be resurrected. He actually speaks of two different resurrections in a sense, one of life and one of condemnation; but He makes it clear that this is one event, not two split apart by an entire millennium. It is not problematic to speak of one general resurrection as being two, since the point in dispute is the amount of time separating the events, not how many events into which the overall event might be subdivided. (For instance, if there were one billion elect persons who were raised in the resurrection of the righteous, then it would not be incorrect to speak of the event in which they are all raised as either one resurrection or one billion resurrections.) At any rate, the text is clear: "the hour is coming" when "all who are in the graves" will be resurrected and judged. There will be one general resurrection.

The third passage in consideration involves Paul's discourse on the resurrection in 1 Corinthians 15, verses 22-26 and 51-54 in particular:

> *22 For as in Adam all die, even so in Christ all shall be made alive. 23 But each one in his own order: Christ the firstfruits, afterward those who are Christ's at His coming. 24 Then comes the end, when He delivers the kingdom to God the Father, when He puts an end to all rule and all authority and power. 25 For He*

must reign till He has put all enemies under His feet. ²⁶ *The last enemy that will be destroyed is death.*

⁵¹ *Behold, I tell you a mystery: We shall not all sleep, but we shall all be changed –* ⁵² *in a moment, in the twinkling of an eye, at the last trumpet. For the trumpet will sound, and the dead will be raised incorruptible, and we shall be changed.* ⁵³ *For this corruptible must put on incorruption, and this mortal must put on immortality.* ⁵⁴ *So when this corruptible has put on incorruption, and this mortal has put on immortality, then shall be brought to pass the saying that is written: "Death is swallowed up in victory."*

This passage is perspicuous. According to vv. 23-24, "the end" comes following the resurrection of the righteous, and according to vv. 51-52, the elect shall receive resurrection bodies "at the last trumpet." There is no room for an entire millennium between the resurrection of Christians and the final judgment. The premillennial timeline is false.

An Alternative Understanding of Revelation 20

Given that Scripture itself forbids a literal interpretation of Revelation 20, it might be asked what an appropriate interpretation of the passage is. Though a complete justification for a particular figurative interpretation of this passage would require a fuller and broader look at the book of Revelation as a whole — for figurative interpretations need to be responsibly grounded in the meaning of the text, and cannot be conjured out of thin air — we will have space here only for rather preliminary observations. First, there is much in the passage to suggest a figurative interpretation: 1,000 is a round number; Satan is depicted as a dragon and bound with a chain, even though he is a spirit; the souls of slain saints are still visible to be seen by John; etc. It is a vision (v. 1), and therefore it is very reasonable, not a stretch, to interpret it figuratively.[79]

A plausible and meaningful interpretation sees the millennium as encompassing the whole span from Christ's exaltation to His second advent. The binding of Satan in vv. 1-3 refers to the disarming of Satan in the first century to enable the spreading of the gospel outward from Israel and unto the entire world (cf. Matt. 12:29; Col. 2:15), while the saints reigning with Christ are in heaven and in the intermediate state; the "first resurrection" is therefore the event in which the saints die to achieve a disembodied presence with the Lord (cf. 2 Cor. 5:8). The two res-

---

[79] Information on this is taken in part from *A Defense of (Reformed) Amillennialism* by David Engelsma

urrections, therefore, might be stated as a resurrection of the soul and a resurrection of the body, which both correspond to the first death and second death experienced by reprobates who die before the final judgment.[80]

More could certainly be stated in trying to further clarify the chapter, but it is not necessary. The basic point I wish to establish is the falsity of the premillennial timeline: the clarification of Revelation 20 is consequently secondary, included only to provide further (though not strictly necessary) warrant for rejecting the literal and premillennial interpretation of the passage. So long as a figurative interpretation is justified, the literal interpretation cannot be foisted upon non-premillennialists as a legitimate objection.

Conclusion

The first step in proving postmillennialism, establishing its general timeline, is complete. There still is the very fundamental dispute between amillennialists and postmillennialists—indeed, between postmillennialists and all their opponents—over the success of Christianity in sanctifying and consecrating the world. A future article will address this essential question, demonstrating from Scripture that success on earth and in time should be the Christian's expectation.

Part 3
December 19, 2011

Introduction

Many Christians have a different understanding of how history will progress, holding different views on millennialism. The previous article sought to disprove the two variants of premillennialism, leaving only amillennialism and postmillennialism as viable candidates. This article will involve a basis for the great optimism characteristic of postmillennial eschatology, as opposed to the pessimism or mild optimism belonging to historical amillennial thought.[81]

---

[80] Some postmillennialists disagree with this interpretation of the first resurrection, but I do not think it is essential to postmillennialism anyway

[81] For the following information I owe a great debt both to Ken Gentry's book on postmillennialism, *He Shall Have Dominion*, 2nd ed., and to the following mp3 lectures by Greg Bahnsen: "Chronology and History," "The Nature of Christ's Kingdom," and "Christ's Expectation of His Earthly Kingdom."

Redemption by the Second Adam

Historic covenant theology informs us that God made a covenant of works with Adam upon his creation, promising him everlasting life conditional upon his meritorious obedience. One part of Adam's obligations to the Lord included the "cultural mandate," or the drive to take dominion over all the earth: "Be fruitful and multiply; fill the earth and subdue it; have dominion over the fish of the sea, over the birds of the air, and over every living thing that moves on the earth" (Gen. 1:28; cf. Ps. 8:6-8). This command was not negated by Adam's fall into sin, but reaffirmed with Noah (Gen. 9:1-3). The mandate refers specifically to plants and animals, but it is clear that it involves a full dominion of every task that man takes up with creation, whether technological, cultural, political, entrepreneurial, or anything else. Even after the fall, Adam and all his descendants quickly obeyed God in this, with culture developing at a rapid rate: men were raising livestock, creating music and instruments, and crafting tools (Gen. 4:20-22). Civil government was also instituted later (Gen. 9:6). Orienting all aspects of culture to display the glory of God was the intention of the people of God at that time, and it is likewise our obligation to do so today (2 Cor. 10:5; Col. 3:23). This should be obvious apart from verses like Genesis 1:28, but Scripture also makes it clear. God is glorified not merely in the salvation of individual souls, but in the Christianization of the institutions and kingdoms of this world (cf. Rev. 11:15).

This mandate is the foundation on which we understand the work of redemption which the Father has decreed, the Son has executed, and the Spirit has applied (and is applying). Christ will not only fulfill the covenant of works in the elect's stead, but will also redeem what Adam ruined vis-à-vis the cultural mandate. He will redeem His bride, the church, and also creation as a whole (Rom. 8:20-21). This comports with the fact that God created everything good in His sovereign act of creation (Gen. 1:31), and will not abandon His own purposes by merely seeking to save some souls here and there. In the end, God will be greatly glorified as the world will shine forth in redemption.

This idea is very consistent with the tenor of Scripture. Psalm 110, the most cited psalm in the New Testament, speaks of *all* enemies being made Christ's footstool as He sits down following His accomplished work of redemption. After defeating the powers of wickedness, triumphing over them on the cross (Col. 2:15), Christ has sat down next to the Father to watch as all His enemies are destroyed (1 Cor. 15:24-26; see also Ps. 2; Matt. 28:18-20), not just to spectate as a small number of souls invisibly change their dispositions towards Him. The entire world will become the kingdom of the King of kings.

Vast Salvation Promised

Even the most pessimistic of Christians would grant that Christ will eventually conquer all aspects of creation, since they affirm the sinlessness of heaven. The crucial point to establish, therefore, is whether God promises in His Word vast salvation prior to Christ's second coming. The question to be settled is whether He promises great success for His church on earth and in history. As it turns out, this is prophesied a number of times in Scripture.

Very early in redemptive history, yet following the *protoevangelium* of Genesis 3:15, God promised innumerable descendants to Abraham over and over again (Gen. 12:2-3; 13:14-16; 15:5; 18:18; 26:4; 28:14). While this has a physical component, St. Paul elsewhere teaches that these "descendants" also have a spiritual signification, referring to fellow believers in Christ the Messiah (Rom. 4, esp. vv. 11, 16-18). The great number of spiritual sons of Abraham prophesied here should serve as *prima facie* warrant to be increasingly optimistic at the prospect of world Christianization. True, amillennialists could claim an enormous cumulative number of Christians in history without needing to affirm that a large percentage of the world's population at any given point is Christian, but the prospect of such uncountable spiritual children gives preliminary evidence for postmillennialism.

Many other passages speak of widespread belief. They might refer to a large number of believers, or to the conversion of entire nations to the true religion, or something else. More significantly, there are many passages which refer to widespread biblical religion, but which also must be fulfilled before Christ returns again. These passages have indicators in the text which require them to refer to a period before Christ's final coming. I will list several examples of this.

First are all the postmillennial assertions in the book of Psalms. Psalm 2 speaks of how the "nations" and "ends of the earth" (v. 8) are Christ's, and calls kings of nations to worship Christ (vv. 10-12). This is referring to the present age, for sin is involved (vv. 1-2). Psalm 22:27-31 refers to vast conversion (v. 27), which cannot take place in the eternal state—believers exist in the eternal state, but not conversions from unbelief to belief—in addition to death (v. 29) and posterity (v. 30). Psalm 72 speaks of widespread belief and prosperity (vv. 3-5, 7-8, 11, 17) though it also mentions sin and pain (vv. 4, 9, 12-14) in addition to the cycle of the sun and moon (vv. 5, 7, 15, 17), which will not persist in the eternal state (Rev. 21:23; 22:5). As mentioned above, Psalm 110 speaks of how Christ is still sitting as His enemies are His footstool—He is not arising and returning to earth; He rules from heaven.

Second are many passages in the book of Isaiah. Isaiah 2:1-4 (along with Micah 4:1-3) speaks of how Christianity will be exalted and followed by all nations (v. 2), which will result in world peace (v. 4). Yet, there also will be sin to rebuke (v. 4), showing that this is not a description of the eternal state. Isaiah 9:1-7 shows how conversion (v. 2), the end of warfare (v. 5), and ever-increasing peace and justice (v. 7) will be wrought by Christ (v. 6), called the "prince of peace." Such an increase of His kingdom will be fueled by the zeal of the Lord of hosts (v. 7). Isaiah 11 speaks of widespread prosperity, even mentioning how the knowledge of Christ shall be as plenteous as the ocean (v. 9). The passage elsewhere speaks of punishment and violence (vv. 4, 13-15), showing that it cannot be referring to the eternal state. Isaiah 65:17-25 also speaks of prosperity, and even of great longevity. Yet, death is still present (v. 20), showing that this is before Christ's return.

Also worth noting, even though it is cited earlier, are Paul's words in 1 Corinthians 15, specifically vv. 22-26:

> [22] *For as in Adam all die, even so in Christ all shall be made alive.* [23] *But each one in his own order: Christ the firstfruits, afterward those who are Christ's at His coming.* [24] *Then comes the end, when He delivers the kingdom to God the Father, when He puts an end to all rule and all authority and power.* [25] *For He must reign till He has put all enemies under His feet.* [26] *The last enemy that will be destroyed is death.*

St. Paul states here that the final resurrection of the dead will occur immediately before "the end," but also states in v. 25 that this end of history will occur after the subjection of all of Christ's enemies. Christ will reign *in heaven* and at the Father's right hand "till He has put all enemies under His feet." The vanquishing of all of Christ's enemies must be comprehensive in scope, or otherwise "all" would not be a fitting description. Paul, therefore, makes reference to great success by the church, the body of Christ, prior to the eternal state.

These passages give a fuller meaning to Christ's words in the Great Commission (Matt. 28:18-20). His command to "make disciples of all the nations" is with the expectation of eventual but widespread success. This expectation is preceded with the basis for such success: "All authority has been given to Me in heaven and on earth." We can have assurance that all the nations of this world—the whole nations, not just a few elect scattered in every nation—will be discipled and taught Christ's law. This is in accord with the power Isaiah ascribes to the Godhead over all peoples:

> *Behold, the nations are as a drop in a bucket, And are counted as the small dust on the scales; Look, He lifts up the isles as a very little thing. . . . All nations before Him are as nothing, And they are counted by Him less than nothing and worthless (Isa. 40:15, 17).*

Conclusion

Despite this predicted success, some might still reject the label of "postmillennialist," instead describing themselves as "optimistic amillennialists." Though these optimistic Christians might disagree with postmillennialists on the degree of optimism we ought to hold, it is not important to utilize the particular label of "postmillennialism," nor is it important to locate the precise line of distinction between optimistic amillennialism and postmillennialism. What is important is that we have great optimism to trust God's sovereign grace in regenerating His world.

Because the King of kings has promised vast salvation, we ought therefore to take up the torch of Christendom. We ought to seek to fulfill the cultural mandate by the grace and Spirit of Christ, applying God's law to every sphere of life. Nonetheless, there still might be some important considerations to clarify for a proper comprehension of biblical postmillennialism. These will be covered in a future article.

Part 4
January 10, 2012

Introduction

The doctrine of postmillennialism supplies us with great hope for the future of our world, a promise of vast redemption. After having laid some basic foundations for the optimistic doctrine in previous posts, I wish here to further clarify the nature of this vast redemption, rather than leaving it amid such unclarity. Dissenters have made many biblical and theological objections against the doctrine based largely on a misunderstanding of it, and so I desire to explicate the doctrine in such a way as to clear the reader's minds of potential objections.[82]

---

[82] As with part 3 of the series, for the following information I owe a great debt to Ken Gentry's book on postmillennialism, *He Shall Have Dominion*, 2nd ed., and to the following mp3 lectures by Greg Bahnsen: "Chronology and History," "The Nature of Christ's Kingdom," and "Christ's Expectation of His Earthly Kingdom."

In God's Timing

Inasmuch as postmillennialists affirm that "salvation is of the LORD" (Jonah 2:9), we will likewise maintain the monergistic essence of world Christianization. Plenteous redemption will come by the bountiful grace of God, not by some inherent goodness in man, nor by some social gospel, nor by any other fanciful conjuration. Postmillennialism stresses the ultimate power of Christ, not man, over sin.

Consequently, just as everything else executed in time and history is by the counsel of God's predestinating will (Eph. 1:11), so also the progress of His plan of salvation will be entirely according to God's timing. Although God could, if He wanted, convert every single soul in an instant, He has decreed for the progression of His kingdom on earth to be gradual and steady, just as the creation of the world, the unveiling of special revelation, the nature of sanctification, and the history of redemption are (or were) similarly gradual. While Jesus taught that unregenerate sinners would always exist before His return (Matt. 13:24-30), He nonetheless instructed us concerning the gradual development (Matt. 13:31-32; Mark 4:26-29) and the ultimate outcome of the kingdom, namely, that the kingdom would thoroughly permeate the earth (Matt. 13:33; Dan. 2:44-45).

Our Savior also has ordained a particular means by which widespread conversion will ordinarily come to fruition, the preaching of the gospel — contrary, e.g., to the manner of Bolshevik Jews with their violent revolution and upheaval. Christ's church will save souls through the proclamation of the Word (Rom. 10:14), and hell's own gates will collapse (Matt. 16:18) by the sword of the Spirit.

Therefore, the "picture" of the victory of Christ's kingdom on earth is one where Christ presently reigns from heaven (Matt. 28:18-20) as His enemies are made His footstool (1 Cor. 15:24-26). Rather than anti-Christian revolutions, Christian dominion is essentially spiritual, not essentially political — though it has manifold political implications.[83] Christ rules by His spiritual representatives on earth, the church, just as Satan attempts to rule on earth through unbelievers; and by and through them His kingdom progresses. This progression can take a very long time, perhaps many millennia: whatever God has willed.

Optimism and Occupation

The fundamental optimism which characterizes postmillennialism has very practical implications for us. We can be confident that our endeavors on earth will be worthwhile in the long run, for God has promised worldwide Christianization.

---

[83] Carlton, Davis. "A Christian Perspective on Legitimate Civil Authority, Part 1." *Faith Heritage*, 8 June 2011, faithandheritage.com/2011/06/a-christian-perspective-on-legitimate-civil-authority-part-1/.

This stands in contrast with other Christian eschatological systems, which, with their emphasis on the imminent return of Jesus, argue that "one shouldn't polish the brass on a sinking ship," thereby abandoning society to Satan's designs. Contrary to such pessimism, the Lord Jesus Christ commands us to occupy until He returns (Luke 19:13).

Interestingly, adherents of pessimistic eschatological views will usually accuse postmillennialists of undermining a constant watchfulness, since we hold that Christ's coming is in the distant future—yet they do not realize the terrible practical implications of their pessimism. Scripture teaches that we do not know the date of Christ's return (Matt. 24:36, 42; Acts 1:7), and even seems to note that it will be a long time (Matt. 25:5, 14, 19), but it never teaches that His return is ever-imminent.

The practical utility of an optimistic eschatology can actually be ascertained from a cult with which we are all familiar, Mormonism. Not only do Mormons have a workable model of missions—sending unmarried men to work in foreign lands before bringing them back home to settle down, keeping their family and societal roots safe—but they also have an incredibly optimistic eschatology, one which manifests itself in exorbitant evangelistic energy for their own religion. Irrespective of what they might believe regarding the eventual success of Mormon conversions, they believe that with sufficiently righteous obedience on earth and participation in the church, one may become a god and gain sovereignty over his *own planet* following death. This feature of Mormon personal eschatology undoubtedly motivates many of its adherents to righteous living and impassioned evangelism. This is not to say their views have any merit, of course—only that eschatological beliefs have very practical consequences. Having understood the promises of Scripture that the saving knowledge of Christ will be as the waters covering the sea, and being energized and sanctified by the true God, the Holy Spirit, Christians ought to surpass Mormons in postmillennial fervor.

The Bruising of Christ's Heel

While Christ's kingdom will, in the long run, progress towards a full Christianization of the world, there will always be brief, anomalous downward trends (cf. John 15:6). Yet, we can still rest on the promises of God, realizing that He will nevertheless be victorious on earth and in history. Just as we can be confident that our personal sanctification will progressively increase in holiness despite anomalous breaches here and there, so also we can be confident that the world's corporate sanctification will do the same. These "anomalous breaches" in the scope of world history might last a very long time, and might involve the decadence of a large society into full-blown degeneracy; but nevertheless we cannot engage in what Greg Bahnsen has termed "newspaper exegesis." Despite the downward trends in our modern Western civilization, we can still be ultimately confident of Christ's victory.

Since the church will sometimes experience backwardness (and even comatoseness) at certain points in time, we should hesitate to condemn postmillennialism when we read passages speaking of small numbers of the redeemed at a given point in time (e.g., Matt. 7:13-14; 22:14). Such verses are examples of previous circumstances which served to spur Christ's servants on to greater obedience, not predictions of how things will always be in the future. Descriptions of certain periods in history do not constitute predictions of how history will always be. Tertullian's observation that "the blood of martyrs is the seed of the church" was not intended to extend through all of history.

Moreover, the fact that the church will be victorious on earth and in history does not imply that she will experience no pain or suffering in the process. Anti-postmillennialists sometimes appeal to Scriptures dealing with persecution (e.g. 2 Cor. 4:7-9; Phil. 3:10; Rom. 8:17), but these do not imply defeat for the church. Warriors usually exit battle with scars and wounds, and the war between Christ and Satan will be no different. But what we can be assured of is that, in our war, we will be victorious through Christ, the Conqueror of the nations by the sword of the gospel (Rev. 19:11-16). Though Satan will bruise Christ's heel, Christ shall yet crush his head (Gen. 3:15).

Kinistic Postmillennialism

As I outlined in part 3 of this series, God's plan of salvation involves more than the invisible modification of scattered souls. Seeking to glorify Himself above all, the Lord will transform the whole world, redeeming all of creation (Rom. 8:20-21). This will no doubt involve a prodigious number of individual conversions, but neither will it be so circumscribed: salvation will apply to all the kingdoms of this world. Only with sporadic exceptions, all institutions, all cultures, all nations, all peoples will be turned to the Lord.

In a similar vein, the Great Commission of Matthew 28:18-20 shows our Savior commanding His disciples to "make disciples of all the *nations*." The nations, as nations, are the proper objects of evangelization and discipleship; and due to this, the obligations attendant to the Great Commission and to the cultural mandate give the gospel-transformation of the world a theonomic and kinistic character. There will be an organic redemption of all the institutions and cultures of this world.

Rejecting the principles of kinism, many Christians will unfortunately retain a utopian vision of world Christianization. They may generally hold that it will be theonomic, but will still fantasize about a world where biology is erased rather than redeemed. They might fantasize that nations like Liberia and Guatemala would, post-redemption, be unaffected by their lower average IQ or their native propensity to sins of violence, and so be as prosperous and righteous as we would expect a European Christian nation to be. While such a view is to be commended for its high view of divine efficacy, it can be criticized for its deficient understanding of the faculties with which God has endowed other peoples, in addition to its implicit affirmation that God will wipe out these characteristics to create utterly "new" spiritual beings, rather than redeem them as they are. Certainly, the redemption of such nations will be for their people's great benefit, not only eternally but temporally, yet it would be foolish and unrealistic of us to expect them to act in ways impossibly different from how they behave currently.

For example, though this is not a fact in which we glory, it is a frank matter of fact that blacks behave more violently than whites, as well as that they have a lower IQ. Though blacks can be steadily improved by multi-generational Christian instruction, it is fanciful to suppose these deficiencies would ever be entirely erased; and consequently, if we multiply these differences in characteristics to the scope of entire nations, the nations will be very visibly different. It is at a time like this when we realize that "the poor you have with you always" (John 12:8).

This is certainly no reason for anyone to boast. Whatever good characteristics a people may possess, they possess them by the plentiful grace of God; and even the best possible race anyone can imagine would be nothing compared to the superlative power, wisdom, and glory of God. More to the point, the differing characteristics of the races, including the various superiorities and inferiorities among them, should drive the nations to aid each other. Having separated into ethnostates, each race can collectively work to minimize their weaknesses while maximizing their God-given strengths. The gospel, serving as the balm of the nations (cf. Rev. 22:2), will bring each of them into a harmonious and perichoretic interrelation.

However, given the kinistic doctrine that the nations will be unequal with respect not only to neutral features (such as cuisine), but also to various value-laden characteristics (such as intelligence and industriousness), it follows that certain races will likely be more among the helpers, and others more among the helped. This conclusion might remind the reader of the older practice of colonialism; and indeed, I would affirm that in many ways, worldwide Christian victory might consist in and be caused by practices resembling white colonialism. White Christian nations certainly should not favor foreign evangelism to the point of altruistic suicide, as is occurring today, but we should nevertheless apprehend our grand responsibility. For practical purposes, however, I contend that, in the present, we ought to focus our attention and efforts exclusively towards our own. The West needs to survive before she can consider how much she ought to aid others.

Conclusion

The biblical doctrine of postmillennialism is one of which all Christians need to be more mindful. Though the promise of salvation and God's general sovereignty over all things ought to serve as a firm basis in spurring Christians unto holy action, the larger scope of worldwide gospel success, divinely authorized and guaranteed, ought to serve as even further motivation in the hearts of believers. Jesus Christ is Lord over all, the one "bringing many sons to glory" (Heb. 2:10), and we may therefore joyfully anticipate the ever-increasing of His government and peace, of which there will be no end (Isa. 9:6).

Our Familial and Racial Existence in Heaven

December 22, 2011

Introduction

Many Christians today fundamentally misunderstand the nature of our existence in glory. They see themselves as being deracinated and materially indistinguishable from other people-groups. They view Galatians 3:28 as, in effect, having a physical and outward fulfillment in heaven, rather than restricting it to the spiritual unity St. Paul intended to convey. This inevitably leads to a depreciation of racial and ethnic identity in our daily lives prior to eternity, and is a fit subject for inquiry. I will defend the thesis that in glory we maintain meaningful relations with those of our family and ethnic and racial groups, not abandoning such covenantal realities for some pretension of atomistic and hollow holiness.

Neither Marrying nor Being Given in Marriage

It is hardly necessary to confute the alienist interpretation of passages like Galatians 3:28. Interpreting those to refer to physical unity is clearly destructive of all of God's predestined distinctions, permitting not only miscegenation but feminism and sodomy. Those falsely relying on "there is neither Jew nor Greek" passages inevitably undermine basic tenets of Scripture and common sense.

A more formidable opponent contending for the deracinated view of heaven is based on Jesus's response to an objection from the Sadducees, found in Matthew 22:23-30:

> 23 *The same day the Sadducees, who say there is no resurrection, came to Him and asked Him,* 24 *saying: "Teacher, Moses said that if a man dies, having no children, his brother shall marry his wife and raise up offspring for his brother.* 25 *Now there were with us seven brothers. The first died after he had married, and having no offspring, left his wife to his brother.* 26 *Likewise the second also, and the third, even to the seventh.* 27 *Last of all the woman died also.* 28 *Therefore, in the resurrection, whose wife of the seven will she be? For they all had her."* 29 *Jesus answered and said to them, "You are mistaken, not knowing the Scriptures nor the power of God.* 30 *For in the resurrection* **they**

neither marry nor are given in marriage, *but are like angels of God in heaven.*"

The argument goes that if there is no marriage in heaven, then the lack of married couples extinguishes families, which likewise causes tribes, nations, and races to vanish. Or, if it does not cause all these corporate groupings to vanish, it still shows them to be of no consequence: if the marital union is itself without significance, then so are relatively less important groupings. Perhaps there are certain superficial or physical distinctions in heaven, but, as with marriage, groups based on such distinctions will be effectively nonexistent.

If it were not obvious enough from the implications of this interpretation, Jesus's statement can be shocking if not understood properly. To say that families and married couples do not exist in heaven grates strongly against our affections and intuitions, seemingly telling us that what we find so important and dear to us is actually worthless. Therefore it is important to have a proper understanding of this passage.

In the first place, we should note that the passage (as well as its parallel in Mark) is a rather isolated instance of the principle in dispute. If it means what the alienists think it means, then it would be the only passage in Scripture teaching it. God need only speak once in order to bind our hearts and minds to a particular doctrine or practice, but the isolation of the passage should lead us to be cautious in ensuring that we do not deceive ourselves.

Second, it is also important to note that Jesus is here dealing with a strictly legal question. He is not concerning Himself with some statement about the importance of our material existence in glory, but is confounding the gainsaying Sadducees who are trying to trap Him. They ask Him a legal question, trying to find a contradiction in biblical law and doctrine, and He provides a legal answer to absolve the contradiction. The context does not extend beyond this legal dispute, in which case we should be careful not to take implications too far. It still could be that the content of His legal answer logically entails that family and race will not persist in heaven, but the nature and the context of the discussion still help us to focus on the meaning of our Savior's claims. Yet, before elaborating on the true meaning of Christ's words, I wish to make some statements about our personal identity.

Personal Identity and Corporate Relations

When we reflect on the initially abstract question of our identity, of who we are, we inevitably are led to define ourselves according to various outward relations with others. A mother cannot define herself without reference to her particular children and husband, nor can people living in a closely-knit community define themselves apart from the others. We cannot accurately apprehend our personal constitution apart from our particular sex, and neither can we try to define ourselves satisfactorily without including our cultural and genetic inheritance from our ancestors, which is inextricably tied in with our specific ethnic and racial group. A proper view of identity is corporately and covenantally grounded.

The nature of our identity even provides certain restrictions on how we can hypothetically conceive of ourselves. For example, consider a white male living in some small twenty-first century American town named John Doe. Someone could ask the question, "What would John Doe be like if he were born a woman in Africa in 1450?", but the question would be purposeless, as it would be speaking of a different person altogether. Part of who *He* is includes his identity as God has rooted it in a particular sex, race, time, and place—not to mention other factors. Our identity cannot be separated from these factors, not even hypothetically. There is a certain sense in which we can hypothetically discuss how we might have been had different things occurred in our lives, but this is within limits. I might be able to discuss how I would be different if I went to a different school when I was younger, but I would be speaking of a different person if I posited too many hypothetical alterations.[84]

This fundamental premise of human nature leads to a significant conclusion: if *we* are truly resurrected in glory, then *we* will not be stripped of these various relations. If a man is resurrected and sees his father, it will not be as if both of them acknowledge the mere biological-paternal relation and forget everything else about how they interacted with one another on earth. On the contrary, the deepness of the father-son relation will be amplified and sanctified in glory. They will certainly be ecstatic to see each other again after having fought the good fight. They will be overjoyed in such a way that presupposes the reality of their familial unity. To think that their relation would not exist in the new heaven and new earth is morally monstrous, a denial that *they* will genuinely be subjects in heaven. If they are stripped of this father-son relation, or if the relation is reduced to a bare acknowledgment of biological begetting, then the two men are not the father and son they were on earth. The two men might bear certain physical, mental, and behavioral similarities to the father and son, but they are fundamentally different people.

Yet, if we grant this for fathers and sons, why would we deny it for the deepest of all human unions—marriage? Why would we say that those who have become

---

[84] Moreover, we can in one sense discuss how "we" might have been if *substantially* different things occurred in our lives, but it is probably more accurate to discuss how such substantial differences would affect *someone like us* at an earlier point in our history. For example, it does not make sense, strictly speaking, to ask how John Doe would be if he were born to different parents in a different country, but it does make sense to ask what someone with such a genetic endowment would be like if born to such parents in such a country.

one flesh must abandon all the deep affections that we know are now part of their identity? It is madness to say that marriage terminates on earth in the sense that those deep relations do not persist in eternity.

But what does Jesus mean when He says that in heaven "they neither marry nor are given in marriage"? It would be folly to accuse the Son of God of being incorrect, and His answer really seems conceptually necessary to avoid the paradoxes that emerge from the prospect of legitimate re-marriage. The only way to avoid the conclusion that something like polyandry can exist in heaven is to substantially alter or abolish the institution of marriage as a whole. Yet, that very answer reveals how we can still love our spouses in eternity: there is a difference between the *institution* of marriage, and the various deep relations stemming from it. The official structure of the family, by which God has delegated authority to the patriarch, entails that the rest of the family is bound to obey the patriarch (within limits), just by the nature of his office as husband and father. This office is part of a formal structure or institution of the family, a structure that will no longer exist in heaven; the obligations bound up with that structure last only "till death do us part." There will still be deep, abiding affections and relations among family members, but it will not be the case that the family as an authoritative institution will subsist. God has reasons for the institutions of marriage and family (and civil government, etc.) in our life here on earth, but He may no longer have reasons for such institutions when we are in glory.

To directly answer the alienist contention from this passage, then, we say the following: if a woman is legitimately re-married on earth, and she and her multiple husbands achieve eternal life, then they will maintain the deep relationships fostered on earth, and those relations can exist in eternity without envy. The formal institution or marital structure will not be present, but the deep bonds formed will, and all without sinful competition. The spouses will have plenty of time to spend with each other and to love each other, and there will be neither sin nor pain.

A Continental Divide

Even though this passage in certain senses is inconsequential, one's chosen interpretation of it is a continental divide. As the aforementioned alienist argument goes, an unqualified dissolution of the marital bond *a fortiori* undermines every other meaningful bond we have with other humans. It leads to an impoverished view of man, disconnecting him from his social identity and abstracting him from his divinely ordained context. It is ultimately anti-Christian. A proper view of this passage, qualifying the abrogation of marriage as only the abrogation of the institution or formal structure, preserves the materiality and corporate identity of man. It allows us to still be ourselves when we are resurrected.

Because of this continental divide, it does not take much of Scripture to give us a proper view of heaven. Even though common sense and reason dictate that we will not, for example, forget our bonds with our parents in heaven, Scripture actually provides further corroboratory evidence that the kinist interpretation is correct. In particular, God's Word explicitly says that various tribes, nations, and peoples will be present to worship the Lord in heaven (Rev. 7:9). Given the fact that nations and tribes are composed of families (Gen. 10:5, 20, 31-32), it follows that all these corporate groupings will also exist in heaven. Scripture affirms a tenet belonging to the kinist side of the continental divide, by implication affirming the entire kinist outlook.

An objection usually launched against the kinist view of heaven, trying to move the biblical position to the other side of the continental divide, involves the practice of segregation. Race-denying Christians might formulate the argument this way: In heaven, we will have racial integration. It will not be as if all the races will not talk to or associate with one another; instead, we will all worship together. Therefore the kinist premise that racial segregation is valued by God is false, and race is effectively negligible. Race will be inconsequential in heaven, and so it should be inconsequential now.

The problem with this argument is that it fails to understand that segregation comes in varying gradations. It is not an all-or-nothing concept. Just consider how families segregate one from another in different houses, or how men of different racial groups might generally spend time with their own although occasionally interacting with others. Interaction (to some degree) is not logically incompatible with segregation (to some degree), and therefore the broad existence of racial interaction in heaven does not negate the overall kinist view. In heaven, we will certainly seek out those whom we know well in this life, such as our family members, and likely will spend more time with them than with others. Such a practice of familial segregation is consistent with the general fellowship to be enjoyed by all the elect families with each other. Likewise, the practice of ethnic or racial segregation could also occur to a certain degree. The numerous redeemed ethnic and racial groups will especially enjoy the company of the elect of their own kin, as is natural; and this is consistent with other interethnic and interracial interaction.

A separate type of objection is that this is all too speculative. Since we should not speak where God has not spoken (Deut. 29:29), conjecture on the nature of our fellowship and identity in heaven can only be dangerous. To require God to conform to our sentiments on an issue is blasphemous; if it were really that important, He would have made it obvious to us in His Word—and so the objection goes. Ironically, this objection turns out to be quite presumptuous itself. To say that God needs to have made a doctrine like this one obvious is to say that He is forbidden from stating doctrines implicitly in His Word. It cannot be seriously argued that some particular degree of explicitness is required for us to believe a doctrine. We either can reason about it on the basis of general and special revelation, or we cannot.

The question ultimately comes down to the chain of reasoning provided above. Given the premises that we will not at the resurrection somehow forget all our deep bonds, and that part of who we are is corporately grounded, it follows that we will maintain our familial and racial identity in heaven. The reasoning is inexorable: a mere argument that Scripture does not explicitly state my conclusion—even though it essentially does in Revelation 7:9—is irresponsible.

Conclusion

The modern church's view of heaven is disgusting, teaching in essence that we will be un-sexed, un-raced, un-familied, and un-married aberrations when we reach the pinnacle of human existence and the joy of man's desiring. This view is satanic in its denial of our humanity and in its death-wish to be removed from our worldly ties, better befitting eastern paganism than biblical Christianity. A healthy view of the resurrection therefore needs to be stated, that the modern church may truly grasp the goodness of the material here and now. More than likely, the church falsely sees our disembodied existence in the intermediate state (between our deaths and Christ's return: 2 Cor. 5:8; Col. 1:22-24; Heb. 12:22-23)[85] as ideal, even though the intermediate state is to be understood as deficient and unnatural, just as death itself is unnatural. Following Paul, we should desire to be "further clothed" with our resurrection bodies (2 Cor. 5:4; cf. 1 Cor. 15:51-54), embracing the full material reality with which God has so graciously endowed us. The modern church denies that *we* will be resurrected, but Job (ch. 19) says the opposite:

[26] *And after my skin is destroyed, this I know,*
That in my flesh I shall see God,

[27] *Whom I shall see for myself,*
And my eyes shall behold, and not another.
How my heart yearns within me!

---

[85] The doctrine of the intermediate state also logically follows from the biblical data that we will remain conscious after death but before we receive a resurrection body (1 Thess. 4:14-17; Luke 16:19-31; 1 Pet. 3:18-20). This requires that we retain some disembodied existence prior to Christ's second advent.

Christianity as a Necessary Foundation for White Nationalism

Part 1: Morality

August 9, 2013

Introduction

Many today in opposition to worldwide white dispossession have become quite disenchanted with the modern Christian church, and understandably so. The church has become a vestige of what it once was—siding entirely with antichrists, affirming views on race identical to MTV's and Hollywood's. Having witnessed this mass apostasy, it can be very tempting to think that a religion which abets such inordinate injustice is simply false; it can be very tempting to dispense with Christianity altogether. If one is well aware that resistance to Zionism and racial egalitarianism is the unpardonable sin according to the zeitgeist, then the prospect of non-Christian white nationalism, whether of the pagan or the atheist/agnostic variety, appears viable and even necessary.

But this is indeed only an appearance and a temptation. While the Christian church's opposition to today's wicked milieu is entirely embarrassing, Christian principles are still fundamental to ultimately overthrow it. The condition of biblical religion has been the direct target of attack in our nations, in which case rejecting it would be complicit with the aims of our intruders. It is important to realize just how indispensable the Christian religion is for supporting our peoples.

Moral Universalism

One Christian tenet thought to have wreaked havoc on whites might be called "moral universalism." Certain non-Christian white nationalists contend that whites' exclusive insistence on their moral obligations to aid other racial groups has degenerated into a suicidal impulse, an ugly branch which spawns from the problematic root of moral universalism. Some might even appeal to the example of Jewish people, whose ethical deliberation predicates itself upon one fundamental question of moral particularism: "How does this help our people?" They are a clear example of a people who will not suffer extinction, since they do not allow themselves to place alien interests above their own. Some non-Christian white nationalists maintain that whites ought to do likewise, rather than care so much about moral abstractions.

Such a description grossly distorts the issue. It is one thing to affirm the universality of moral obligations, and it is another to affirm that the content of those moral obligations requires ethnomasochism and the exaltation of foreign interests. It is one thing to claim that moral principles apply universally; another to claim that these principles apply without regard for any distinction between "us" and "them." One of the crucial points taught in Faith and Heritage is that we—and not just we, but all people—have augmented obligations to our own families, tribes, nations, and races. This principle of concentric loyalties entails the increased investment of time, energy, and capital in our own people's interests—and that for everyone, universally. If whites adhered to these principles of fundamental morality, then we would not face the problems we currently do. The problem therefore lies not in a misconception of morality as universal, but in the misconstrual of the content of morality to omit our obvious obligations towards our own (1 Timothy 5:8).

In fact, arguing in the opposite direction, just what are moral obligations, if not universal? To say that someone is morally obligated to a particular course of action is to imply that anyone else in the same circumstances ought to do the same thing; otherwise moral advice and moral reasoning would be nonsensical. To reject moral "universalism" is therefore to reject morality itself, undermining our own moral objections to the dispossession and suicide of European-derived peoples. And if we reject moral universalism, we not only forfeit our moral objections to our dispossession and make complete nonsense out of morality, but also mock and trample upon God and His universally binding law.

Even further, given that a central problem for our people is not merely the attack from without, but the ethical decay from within, the idea that we ought to reject morality in order to save white people from their incredible moral degradation is, frankly, insane. Moral excellence is required in any pro-white movement that would successfully resist the established power and propaganda of our adversaries, but derogating moral universalism is a surefire way to make a movement care nothing for morality, and so utterly fail at achieving moral excellence. If we cannot win when white nationalists are dissolute or promiscuous in their personal lives, then we also cannot win when we employ a quasi-Jewish moral particularist framework. A firm commitment to Christian moral universality is, consequently, a necessary foundation.

Shifting Moral Standards

An unbelieving white nationalist might concede the universality of moral obligations while nevertheless denying that Christianity can consistently claim them. In Gregory Hood's recent article[86], he laments Christianity's modern role both in promoting human rights, egalitarianism, and nonjudgmentalism and in rejecting the "'unchosen' loyalties of kin and country." He is certainly correct to lament this. The visible church, those who profess Christ and form institutions in His name, has largely apostatized and bowed the knee before Equality within the last century. We have rejected the historic Christian virtues of patriotism, chastity, and dignity, denouncing them as racist, sexist, homophobic, and the like. This apostasy from the heights of Western Christian civilization to the cesspool where we now reside knows no precursor of equal magnitude in church history.

But apostasy presupposes an original position of honor and principle from which one has fallen. It presupposes that the religious principles of our former civilization have been denied, rather than carried to their full fruition. Mr. Hood can claim that the devolution from our civilizational zenith to our multicultural sewer is a "natural" one, given the principles of Christianity, but that is an entirely separate argument to make and cannot depend solely on the historical fact that the formerly Christian West has embraced cultural Marxism. (Nor can it depend on Mr. Hood's vague rhetoric regarding justification by faith and other Christian doctrines, which rhetoric betrays an awful misunderstanding of the faith.) Besides, Matt Parrott has already identified Mr. Hood's foolish contradiction: claiming simultaneously that "Christianity properly understood does not demand egalitarianism" and that the Eastern Orthodox, upon reading their Bibles, will finally apprehend its true teachings of equality and multiracial suicide. He wishes to claim both that true Christianity teaches against the zeitgeist (perhaps because this shields him from pro-Christian criticisms among white nationalists) and that true Christianity supports it.

Mr. Hood thus has no grounds to claim that the previous century's apostasy from biblical truth is due to a Christian God whose character "smoothly modifies itself to fit modern moral standards." His claim requires far more argument and a much more informed understanding of Christian ethics. Such a claim must upend, not only Mr. Hood's own claim that the Bible opposes egalitarianism, but also all the ink spilled in Christendom defending the hierarchical implications of a Christian social order. We at Faith and Heritage are glad to have added to that collection, and we encourage Mr. Hood to learn more here about the national and racial implications of true Christianity.

---

[86] Hood, Gregory. "Why Christianity Can't Save Us." *Counter Currents*, 31 July 2013, counter-currents.com/2013/07/why-christianity-cant-save-us/.

God as Moral Lawgiver

Leaving aside for now the misconstruals of particular Christian moral teachings, it is important to consider the nature of morality in a more abstract way. Above, I discussed and established morality's universality. But when I mention the union between morality and Christianity, I do not intend to posit a merely accidental connection. It is not only the case that moral universality is a tenet which Christians affirm, but even further, morality itself requires Christianity. The very notion of a moral obligation presupposes a moral authority who can dispense commands unto subjects (and impose penalties). For instance, to say that I ought not murder presupposes that someone else has bound me unto that course of action. Of course, someone might object that this is entirely arbitrary and unproven. He might even give a counterexample: "If I want to be good at this sport, then I ought to practice it often"—and this sense of "ought" clearly does not presuppose an authoritative lawgiver. But moral obligations involve a different kind of ought-statement than this sports one; moral obligations involve what might be called unqualified or unconditional obligations. The sports example carries the introductory phrase, "if I want to be good at this sport..."; and the "obligation" or "oughtness" to practice the sport often is seen as the means to fulfill the end marked out by the introductory phrase, namely, to be good at the sport. Many types of non-moral ought-statements can be made along these lines: if I want to do X, then I ought to do Y—since X is the end and Y is the means.

What is so different about morality, however, is that it involves this unqualified or unconditional feature: our moral obligation not to murder can be expressed in the statement, "We ought not to murder, period." It is true that our refusal to murder others can have certain purposes to it—for example, we can choose not to murder because not doing so alleviates human suffering, or because not doing so glorifies God—but nonetheless, the obligation persists irrespective of the agent's aim for those purposes. It is not as if "I ought not to murder" is true only if I value a certain purpose which can be achieved by my not-murdering. Rather, "I ought not to murder" is true without any qualification or conditionality. These obligations just exist for us as rational and moral beings; a plain fact of our existence is that we ought to do certain actions and refrain from certain actions. And it is this type of obligation which requires an authoritative Lawgiver. Without such a Lawgiver, there could be no real, binding obligations, only a fleeting sense of them.[87]

It is because of this unique quality of moral duties that certain atheistic philosophers flatly reject them as exceedingly strange. J.L. Mackie, for example, even

---

[87] It does not follow either, that the inference from obligation to Obliger requires us to see all moral laws as instituted solely by the positive will of God, as if His command were the metaphysical basis, or *ratio essendi*, of moral distinctions. Such would be a confusion of moral law and positive law.

argues that because moral obligations are so bizarre, we therefore lack sufficient reason to believe they exist. According to him, "If there were objective [ethical] values, then they would be entities or qualities or relations of a very strange sort, utterly different from anything else in the universe."[88] Many other atheists also argue that morality is relative and ultimately a matter of preference, rather than affirming any genuine obligations to certain courses of action. Contra Mackie and the consistent atheist, the Christian—along with any other sensible and honest mind—affirms that morality is real, and that there really is an objective moral transgression when, say, a black man rapes and slays a white girl.

But if objective morality is granted, then these "odd" unqualified obligations exist and thereby stand in need of explanation. The most plausible explanation, if not the only possible one, is that they emerge from the commands of an authoritative Lawgiver. Other theories might explain our sense of moral duty (e.g. that we have evolved with these feelings in order to better propagate offspring), but no other explanation can ground the reality of duty. There must be an original, uncreated moral Authority who binds us unto the moral law which we, as to its basic principles, clearly apprehend by conscience. The Lord, of course, is this moral Lawgiver (Isaiah 33:22).

One might object that the nature of moral obligations entails only theism, not Christianity as a whole; but I am not presently interested in providing a comprehensive Christian apologetic. Suffice it to say that the nature of morality leaves us only with the revealed monotheistic religions and deism as our candidates, among which Christianity is clearly the superior. Pre-Christian European paganism and full-bore atheism or agnosticism are capable neither to defend morality nor to defend our people. Besides Christ, all other ground is sinking sand.

Conclusion

Although the altruism which characterizes the white race has been perverted into anti-white suicidal tendencies—and not without Jewish influence—it would be wrongheaded to transfer the blame to the nature of morality itself. Such an accusation is in practice leveled at the Giver of that law, which is immoral and even blasphemous.

Equally blasphemous are the plans of white nationalists who deny God as the uncreated moral authority but still believe the well-being of white people to be their ultimate purpose. Any non-theistic or non-universalist conception of morality requires one to view some lesser created entity—in this case, white people—as ultimate, and so practically as God. This conception of morality is monstrous to reason, to conscience, and to faith. I would certainly not desire these men to be

---

[88] Mackie, John (1977). Pg. 38. *Ethics: inventing right and wrong*. London.

consistently nihilistic in their rejection of moral universality, but rather pray that they see their error and repent for their sins. White nationalists need to affirm the only morality there is: universal morality, with the Christian God back of it.

Part 2: The Glory of God
August 12, 2013

Introduction

Due to the large numbers of unbelieving white nationalists and the widespread apostasy of the modern multicultist church, it is crucial to establish the Christian religion as the *sine qua non* of a robust white nationalist movement. I have already argued that morality, obviously necessary for the moral foundations of white nationalism, requires God as Lawgiver. Yet another consideration is in order. I contend here that the theocentric nature of reality is the only framework in which a love of one's own people can properly and reasonably be embedded. To elevate race to an ultimate level brings about nihilism by implication, contrary to the purposeful and meaningful struggles of white nationalists. But before I flesh out this conclusion, I need to spend some time explaining particular objections to Christianity vis-à-vis the Christian doctrine of the glory of God.

God's Glory, Our End

After reading about God's existence and the nature of morality, some might remain unconvinced of their obligation to worship God. They might still be unsure in their minds as to whether God really exists and, even if He does, why they should be so committed to His worship. Going to church every Sunday to sing songs and give money seems less worthy than opposing the dispossession of possible destruction of European-derived peoples. The commitment to the ostensibly frivolous practices and extraneous doctrines of Christianity just seems to be a commitment to irrelevance. Even if God existed, would He really care if I expended my energy in saving my people rather than in being a Christian? Is He concerned more with my sitting in a pew weekly than with my noble actions to prevent my own ethnic dispossession and death?

Such questioning misunderstands the Christian and commonsense conception of God, or at least fails to draw proper applications therefrom. The living God is omnipotent, omniscient, omnipresent, and in possession of all other superlative attributes. He is utterly perfect in every way. He is the instantiation and the source of all good, the repository of all gifts, and the fount of all excellence. The consequence of this is that He is utterly and intrinsically worthy of all rational creatures' worship and obedience: deity's image-bearers have a primitive (and unqualified) moral obligation to glorify Him in everything, reflecting all praise vertically. All is to be focused on Him.

Along with racial orthodoxy, this doctrine of God is generally neglected by the modern church, which views salvation as primarily meeting a human need. Churchgoers choose to ask Jesus in their hearts because they have a "God-shaped hole" in that organ, or because they need a personal relationship with the Lord, or just because they are told they need to be saved. They might have the motivation to obtain "fire insurance" by turning to Christ, believing in Him primarily to get to heaven. Whatever the variation, salvation becomes on this view the way to get as much happiness out of life as possible, and the preaching of the gospel becomes an appeal to self-interest. Its ultimate end or purpose is therefore human well-being.

Without denying that salvific union with Christ leads to a joyous personal relationship and the fulfillment of a psychological need, neither of those can be one's ultimate motive in seeking such a union. Our fundamental reason to repent must be *ad maiorem Dei gloriam*: for the greater glory of God.[89] Obedience to God and to His gospel must be motivated within our souls by the apprehension that He is completely worthy of our obedience, an obedience we have completely failed to give Him. We ought to obey Him — even if *hell* is our destination (cf. Rom. 9:3) — simply because He is worthy to be obeyed and glorified in our obedience, not because we expect future reward. His glory ought to be an end rather than a mere means; human happiness ought to be strictly subsidiary.

This preeminent aim for God's glory ought to characterize all our actions, not merely our pursuit of salvation. For instance, our motivation to help a neighbor in need should not be that our neighbor is our highest end, for God is. Likewise, our motive to support our family through material gain should not be that our family is our highest end, for God is. And the same goes with the extended families that our ethnic and racial groups are. We have obligations to love and benefit our people, our "kinsmen according to the flesh," yet these obligations, to be morally situated, must be subordinated to our love for God, as He is our *summum bonum*. There will sometimes be conflicts between these lesser goods and the Good Himself, such as when family members entice us to sin, but ordinarily we serve God precisely through our service unto the natural relations He has given us. At times we must oppose father and mother for Jesus's sake, since they are lesser loves than God Himself (Matt. 10:34-37), but in the natural course of events, where family

---

[89] Do not interpret the inclusion of this phrase as an endorsement of the Jesuits.

members have not sinfully disrupted God's order by making familial allegiance supersede God's claims upon us, we show our love for God primarily through our love for family. Jesus Himself castigated the Pharisees for encouraging children to "serve God" by denying provisions for their own fathers and mothers; He rightly saw such a moral imbalance as a denial of the fifth commandment (Matt. 15:3-6). We likewise need to strike this balance concerning race, seeing it as an important moral end, yet not the highest one.

Such a balanced kinist view of race and God's glory is entirely lost on unbelieving white nationalists, who interpret this exaltation of God's glory as egalitarian. Witness, again, Gregory Hood's article on the subject:

> *And of course, that divine order is, at its heart, egalitarian. Though Christianity properly understood does not demand egalitarianism, racial suicide, or messianic liberalism, the central doctrines of the cult of the cross make this evolution natural. Like acid, Christianity burns through ties of kinship and blood – as Christ states "He that loves father or mother more than me is not worthy of me: and he that loves son or daughter more than me is not worthy of me."*

God did not create the family and command us to honor it only to then deny the propriety of all familial allegiances. Our family is an ever-important moral good, and so long as, in God's providence, family members do not sinfully cause others to choose between family and God, our choice to love God necessarily results in love for our families. Because family is a natural institution created by God, it is a means by which we ordinarily can demonstrate our love for Him. Conflicts between the lesser good of family and the greater good of God emerge only if sin has driven a wedge into this natural order. But the same occurs with race: it is a divine creation of God to provide national and societal harmony, peace, and stability, and consequently it is a real and important moral end, just not the highest one. Christianity is so far from "burning through ties of kinship and blood" that it actually establishes them, for God has designed us to especially love our blood relations.

God's Glory, His End

On the anthropocentric view, not only does man, in salvation, act ultimately for man's good, but God does as well. The presumed motive for God to create the universe in the first place was to enter into a "love relationship" with humans, and the only reason any suffering occurs in the world is for the future benefit of the sufferers, rather than any satisfaction of retributive justice. According to modern philosophical literature on the "problem of evil," any painful events that occur in the world require a justification on God's behalf located in His love rather than

His justice, since God loves everyone equally and bears no other disposition towards them. This type of theology is thus overtly man-centered, viewing man's joy as God's highest goal. As these humanists conceive of the issue, what else could He value?

Against this egalitarian error of the modern church, Scripture clearly states, again and again, that God acts for His own glory, or "for His name's sake" (e.g. 1 Sam. 12:22; 2 Sam. 7:23; Ps. 23:3; 31:3; Jer. 14:7; Isa. 63:12; Ezek. 20:9). The Puritan philosopher and theologian, Jonathan Edwards, likewise wrote that the end for which God created the world was His own glory, the manifestation of "a supreme and ultimate regard to himself in all his works." Sheer logic even demands it: man is a contingent rather than necessary being, and therefore it is absurd that God, as a necessary being, should hold us contingent creatures as His ultimate end. Such a conception would involve a great deficiency in the self-existent Trinity apart from the creation of the universe; the three blessed Persons would not be persisting in self-sufficient intra-trinitarian love and indwelling, but would rather be unfulfilled and lacking until the creation of man. Worse, after creation, this man-worshiping God would not even fulfill His purposes, as a substantial mass of mankind would eventually enter perdition! This is neither a reasonable nor a biblical conception of the God of Scripture and of nature, all of whose plans will certainly come to pass (Ps. 115:3; Job 42:2).

The centrality of God's glory is a cardinal truth of the Christian faith. Normatively speaking, all our actions ought to strive towards the effulgence of His everlasting fame (1 Cor. 10:31), and positively speaking, all being converges and will converge on the resplendent glory of God.

Consequent Obligations for Unbelievers and Agnostics

What should be obvious from this doctrine of God is the comprehensive transformation it ought to effect in a believer's life, even apart from direct supernatural influence. Even if God does not exist, it is true that *if He does*, He would clearly be the focal point of all that is and of all human thought; and therefore those who believe in His existence would grasp the immorality of denying Him the total and complete reverence, worship, and obedience which He intrinsically deserves. Even if believers were completely wrong, it is lucid that they, to be consistent, ought to act in an overtly theocentric way, ordering their lives with Him at the center.

What this implies, in turn, is that unbelievers, if *they* are wrong, are also committing great sin by denying God the worship and obedience He deserves. And unless they think that the issue is fully settled, that atheism has been stringently and fully demonstrated, it therefore follows that they could be very, very wrong about the way they are living their lives, and consequently ought to heavily investigate the question. Even the hypothetical proposition that God *might* exist, given His existence's behavioral and noetic implications, obliges unbelievers (and believers, for that matter) to seek out the question and follow the true religion. The weightiness of this conditional proposition—if God exists, then He deserves our full obedience—should oblige anyone skeptical of the question to seek out the answer with all his heart and mind. In other words, obeying the first commandment, which prohibits idolatry and mandates the worship of the true God, is an obvious obligation we can perceive from the created order (cf. Rom. 1:18-21).

Unfortunately, many unbelievers, not apprehending the vital importance of the life of the mind, fail to act in accord with their obligation to seek out the question of God's existence and how to obey Him properly. The vast majority of people frankly lack any interest in truth, selfishly concerned more with the various mundane events and tasks of their own lives than with anything to do with God. Certainly, many will be (more or less selflessly) preoccupied with rather important responsibilities, such as supporting a family or even striving to resist anti-white forces; but to disregard the pursuit of God, who is Himself Truth, is heinously foolish (cf. Ps. 14:1). Yet even with that qualification, frivolities such as television, idle chatter, and video games, as well as the sin of fornication, are the predominant idols of the modern pantheon. Engrossed with these gods which are no gods, most unbelievers today, including the vast preponderance of professing believers, practice a mindless atheism. They are not studied atheists or studied agnostics, but just religious *apathists*. Their desert will be just.[90]

This silences the objection of the apathist who sees no good reason to even pursue the God-question. It is not as if one must choose between boring church banalities and determined white nationalism. The inquiry of the true worship and obedience of God is the most important investigation one could undertake.

Theocentrism the Alternative to Nihilism

While I have answered the objection that becoming a Christian and worshiping God through His Son seems like a purposeless superfluity in contrast with the purposefulness of irreligious white nationalism, I additionally contend that any pursuit, white nationalism included, becomes meaningless when divorced from a God-glorifying and theocentric outlook. Christian worship and practice is not only compatible with the purposefulness of white nationalism, but necessary unto it.

---

[90] I should qualify this by also noting that people are differently equipped in their intellects to properly wade through all the evidence for the true religion. Christ's righteous judgment will certainly take this into account.

While atheism in several ways entails the objective lack of meaning, value, or purpose in life, there is additionally a significant sense in which idolatry—elevating a lesser entity to the place of God—by implication reduces life to absurdity. On the Christian view, the glory of God is the end or *telos* by which every subsidiary purpose gains its significance. Every other human pursuit attains meaningfulness inasmuch as it relates to the everlasting glory of God. (On a similar note, consider how theology is the "queen of the sciences.") This overarching purpose to life is also inexhaustible; even 10,000 years in glory will not work to complete this end.

By contrast, every subsidiary end is necessarily finite and exhaustible. God Himself can suffuse these various ends with meaning, but on their own they can have meaning only through the subjective intention of human agents. Without God, existentialism surfaces, and so does the existentialist maxim that meaning is whatever you make of something. Do you love your family and seek to help them? Do you love yourself and seek to live a life of gratuitous hedonism? Both of these are equally legitimate options, so long as *you* find them meaningful. The worthless and destructive love of fornication and television becomes as objectively meaningful as the most ostensibly important white nationalist movement. All that is important is that you "stick to your values," whatever values you so choose to have. This problem of existentialist worthlessness springs up in any godless worldview. The only answer is Christian theism.

It is true that we intuitively recognize certain purposes as possessing objective goodness, and certain purposes as having substantially more objective goodness than others; but this recognition on unbelieving presuppositions must be explained as just what we feel due to cultural consensus. Society just happens to agree that certain purposes (say, raising money for the poor) garner more outward esteem. However, to be consistent, no unbeliever could affirm that any purposes have greater objective goodness.

This reduction of goodness-recognition to subjective consensus is worthless and inadequate; the true doctrine is that we correctly recognize various ends as better than others. A life of hedonism is objectively worse and less meaningful than a life devoted to one's family. But if we can clearly recognize objective meaning in its varying degrees, then God's existence, and the entire theocentric worldview associated with Him, becomes a necessity.[91]

---

[91] As with the article on morality, one could again object that this proves only generic theism, and not Christianity specifically; but again, I am not concerned with a cumulative-case apologetic in this singular article. If the options are reduced to deism, Islam, Judaism, and Christianity, then, especially given the white demographics of historic Christendom, I doubt that atheistic white nationalists will see the other three options to be as prima facie acceptable as biblical religion.

Conclusion

God's glory must be central in everything we do, the (temporal and eternal) salvation of our people included. Yet, the motive to obey God is not that we may attain heaven, nor that it will benefit white people, nor that it will bring about world Christianization. The fundamental reason we all ought to repent and believe in God is because He irreducibly and intrinsically *deserves* our obedience; He is glorified in and by it. We ought to see God as worthy of our obedience and love even if we can expect hell as our ultimate destination. Contrary to anthropocentric theologies, everything we do needs to converge on God's glory.

Furthermore, since everything gains meaning inasmuch as it reflects its own glorification unto the Creator-King, a proper view of race, and a love of for European-derived peoples in particular, must be embedded in a more comprehensive worldview which values the glory of God above all else. Without such an inexhaustible end of our existence, all degenerates into nihilism. Religion in principle must trump race, lest race decay into meaningless existentialist drivel. Although motivated by a righteous desire to see white people increase and prosper, unbelieving white nationalists, whether pagan or humanist, need to affirm the God of the Bible as the Savior of Europe.

Part 3: Design, Order, and Kinds
August 14, 2013

Introduction

White nationalists ought to be commended for their courageous willingness to oppose the modern multicultural zeitgeist. Most people today, and especially much of the modern Christian church, have utterly fallen for the lies and deceit spewed forth with the influx of egalitarian propaganda. This has led many white nationalists to reject the Christian religion itself as untrue, specious, and crippling. While this diagnosis would be accurate if aimed toward the modern institutional church, the same cannot be said about the true religion. As I will argue, Christianity provides us with the necessary foundation to view the world as including various "kinds," metaphysical categories which carry with themselves various normative obligations. Unbelief obliterates prescription and reduces these kinds to random concatenations of descriptive characteristics; it thereby gives us no reason to regard our people as a unit we ought to acknowledge, benefit, or champion.

God-Created Categories

A view held antithetically to Christian physics and metaphysics is the materialistic doctrine of evolution. On this view, all life arose from a common ancestor (perhaps taking the principle of "one blood" to the extreme), and so all the biological distinctions we see today have arisen over an enormously prolonged and painstaking series of mutations differentiating one group from another. While the biblical view sees our Creator God as designing everything according to its kind (Gen. 1:11-12, 21, 24-25), from and within which all posterity is generated, the evolutionary theory posits no strict or intentional distinctions in the realm of biology. The Darwinist claims that the interminable biological past of our people includes an unordered progression through many other inferior forms of life, positing a grand and inevitable interrelatedness for all of life.

Using "kinds" to refer broadly to any taxonomic classification at all, rather than to some particular level in the taxonomic hierarchy, the Christian need not posit that the kinds listed in Genesis 1 are the only kinds which exist, for God can still supernaturally intervene at any point in history, and could even bring about new kinds through natural causes (e.g. humans' crossbreeding animals, or microevolution): what is important is that His intelligence is the ultimate driving force behind biological demarcation, stamping organisms' creation with His authority, rather than their arising entirely by some purely natural and immanent engine of differentiation. The God-createdness of the various categories of organisms, as revealed in Genesis 1, gives us a different idea of their distinctiveness and taxonomy than does the materialistic-evolutionary outlook, which denies any God back of the biological diversity we currently observe. The teleology provided by our divine Author turns out to be very important.

Egalitarianism and Stereotypes

Because unbelievers must take biological distinctions as lacking the imprint of the God who created them—or, one might say, as lacking the fixedness or determinacy which accompanies divine sanction—atheists must view different biological categories as, at most, a series of statistical generalities. The reader can understand this well by considering the egalitarian promotion of female pastors. Scripture expressly forbids that women are to teach or possess positions of authority (1 Tim. 2:12). Defenders of biblical patriarchy will sometimes support this principle[92] by indicating that women are generally worse as pastors: they do not handle positions of authority as well, and they tend to embrace more sentimentalist ideas which compromise biblical doctrine. In other words, they would offer these statistical generalities as the *ratio essendi* for God's prohibition of female pastors, the reason in the nature of things motivating His moral commandment on the subject. But the egalitarians would quickly respond that a general pattern does not justify this type of absolute rule. (Many egalitarians today would further say that any difference of skill between men and women is due to historical patriarchal oppression, but that is a separate point.) It could be that some women can handle positions of authority well, and it could be that some women would not compromise their theology with sentimentalism—those are bare possibilities, at the very least—so why is there a wholesale prohibition on all women? Why couldn't there just be *bona fide* requirements for becoming a pastor, with no mention of gender? Perhaps, given these *bona fide* requirements, few (or no) women would eventually become pastors; but there is no reason to forbid a woman from the pastorate at the outset just because of her gender.

The Christian, believing in a God-ordained natural order of things, can answer this feminist contention by seeing gender as not merely the ground of a number of descriptive generalities (e.g., that men are more aggressive, and women more sentimental), but as a natural kind with intrinsically concomitant *obligations*. There is a certain purpose, function, or end (*telos*) for the different categories which God has created, including an environment for which God has designed His creatures and tasks which He has fitted them to perform. There is, in a word, an *essence* to the biological kinds God has created, including a certain design plan for which members of a kind ought to strive. Thus, against the egalitarian, the Christian could say, "Perhaps a woman can possibly wield authority ably, and perhaps a woman can avoid the sentimentalist temptation characteristic of many women — but nonetheless, she cannot be a pastor, as that would be unnatural and unbecoming of her gender; it would contradict the divine design of femaleness, and thus not serve to cultivate her femininity." Another way of stating this is that a *properly functioning* female will not serve in a position of authority: that there is a way which females as females ought to behave, an end or purpose intrinsic to femininity as such, the fulfillment of which is a moral duty.[93] Such an answer presupposes

---

[92] I do not mean to insinuate that God's Word needs any human support to be considered valid or worth following. We ought to believe that a verse such as 1 Tim. 2:12 is just and wise, simply because God commanded it. Nonetheless, while we do not need any other reason to know why we ought to obey that command, it still can be fruitful to understand the basis upon which God makes the commandment in the first place. God's prohibition of female pastors is not arbitrary.

[93] The notion of proper function is one clear to us in many fields of science, both hard sciences like biology and soft sciences like psychology. For instance, we understand that there is a way a human heart ought to behave, and how our cognitive faculties ought to behave, if functioning properly. What is remarkable is that this rather common-sense notion completely presupposes an intelligent Designer in order to ac-

a divinely sanctioned basis for the category of gender, one which provides further obligations for us than whatever obligations arise from our empirical knowledge of how the sexes tend to behave. There is a certain nature and purpose to gender which is the ground of, but which nonetheless exceeds, the various statistical generalities that describe the characteristics, behaviors, and tendencies of males and females.

If one does not accept this line of argumentation in defending patriarchy, he inevitably falls prey to the egalitarian's accusation of "stereotyping."[94] One of the actually legitimate (but rarely applicable) accusations of stereotyping is when the accused person acts as if everyone in a group possessed the average or typical characteristics of that group. It would be wrong and irrational to turn a generality into an unqualified absolutization, neglecting that averages often result from a degree of diversity in a population, rather than from strict uniformity. But if one defends the scriptural prohibition of female pastors merely on the grounds that women are generally inferior in fulfilling pastoral duties, then one would be turning a generalization (with respect to all those women unfit to be pastors) into an absolutization (with respect to all women entirely). The prohibition's rationale, to be justified, must make some statement about femaleness or femininity, including the ideal for which women ought to strive—but such an essence, with ends intrinsic to femininity, could be situated only within a theistic worldview. Divinely ordained teleology is requisite unto the idea that females, as females, ought to function a certain way. (And note, this applies not merely to a prohibition on female pastors, but also to any conception of femininity as a female ideal whatsoever.)

Not Positive Law, but Design

Do not mistake this explanation as a mere reliance upon positive law. (Recall the distinction between moral law and positive law, the former being grounded in the nature of things and the latter being grounded solely in an authority's command.) It is not as if the metaphysical basis for the morality of gender roles is solely God's command: as though the nature of the sexes themselves were insufficient to ground moral obligations, requiring an additional positive law to make them into truly universal duties. This would be the same mistake many Christians make when explaining the immorality of various sexual sins. If sexual sins like sodomy and fornication were wrong solely because God authoritatively

---

count for a "design plan" according to which such entities function properly. In fact, the Christian philosopher Alvin Plantinga shows how the notion of proper functionality is required for us to understand how humans have knowledge; see his *Warrant and Proper Function*.

[94] It is ridiculous, of course, that the modern usage of "stereotype" gives the word a negative meaning. Just as an archetype (or prototype) is a first instance or progenitor of a series or kind, so also a stereotype is a typical or average instance of that series or kind. But stereotyping today is viewed as some ill-defined sin involving the stereotyper's generalizing about cherished minority groups.

forbade them, and not due to any immorality the actions possess by their nature, then God could simply rescind the commandments and make those actions completely morally permissible. But we recognize that they are wrong by nature — even "against nature" (Rom. 1:26) — because they contradict the *design* with which God has created us. Thus the commandments cannot be rescinded merely by God's say-so, since their immorality is based upon our very constitution as humans. Such actions would not have been sinful had God constituted us vastly differently, but given the ends He has embedded within His design of human nature, they are indeed sinful, and their sinfulness, therefore, cannot be undone by a rescission of positive law. They are actions contrary to the *moral* law, rather than intrinsically permissible acts prohibited only by God's sole authority. It is the same with gender roles, and as we will see, it is the same with our moral obligations to our "kinsmen according to the flesh."

The basis for these sins' immorality, though not dependent solely on God's authoritative command, still is dependent upon Him, for they require His *design* as a coherent explanation. Women are morally forbidden from ecclesiastical positions of authority because such positions are contrary to the ends God has built into femininity. Femaleness has a teleology, a set of ends which women, as women, are designed to fulfill in the whole scope of domestic life and human society. God designed women to have particular tasks for their social existence, and He related this design to the rest of His design for human society, indeed for the whole universe. Because there is a teleology intrinsic to femininity as such, we can thus make moral claims about females as such (and the same for masculinity and males); we do not need to restrict our moral premises to the statistical differences between men and women. Yet this is the crux of the issue: teleology cannot be asserted where there is no universal design plan, and thus no universal Designer. The embedding of ends within human nature and the rest of the created order requires the intentions of an omnipotent, omniscient, all-wise God, our Creator. While divine positive laws are not a necessary (or sufficient) explanation for the morality of gender roles, a divine design for a gendered teleology — of a design plan for the sexes and for all human society — is. Materialistic unbelief cannot possibly attribute purpose, order, and design to natural categories like gender, and neither can it do so for race.

Metaphysics Versus Pragmatism

Properly cognizing gender in this way aids us in our understanding of race. Race is more than the ground of several statistical generalities. While we can easily prove the reality of race through statistics — we can point to all the behavioral, moral, intellectual, physiological, and other differences among varying groups of mankind, as demonstrated by the scientific and statistical evidence—we understand that there is more to racial differences than the bundling of those statistics. A real and important category subsists in order to ground or "bundle" those statistical generalities, and that category, race, is one which carries various intrinsic obligations with it, just like gender. Undoubtedly, the way in which gender carries intrinsic obligations is different from the way in which race carries intrinsic obligations. We do not pursue ideal whiteness or blackness in the same way that we pursue masculinity and femininity; the obligations accorded to race are not necessarily with respect to the type of people we ought to be, as if white and black virtues were different in the same way that masculine and feminine virtues are. But there still are other obligations intrinsically connected to race, particularly as they bear on our social relations, duties, and commitments. A notable example of this, and an obvious one, is our obligation to love our own ethnic or racial group just because it is ours (Rom. 9:3)—not necessarily because it is statistically superior to other groups in some merit-based category, but simply because it is *our own*. If we cherished our people merely because of their achievements and characteristics— i.e. if we apportioned our love for our people solely due to their meritorious deeds, not simply because they belonged to us and we to them—then we could equally value a multiracial utopia where the best characteristics, regardless of one's particular race, are eugenically emphasized, distributed, and sustained. We could even reject humanity altogether: a society of artificially intelligent machines could as well accomplish this end. But we acknowledge that, just as with family, we have obligations to love and have pride in the ethnic and racial group in which God has placed us. Moreover, we are designed to live among our people, to have our political and societal arrangements informed by our ethnic constitution. These are moral obligations concomitant with racial distinctions and not reducible merely to the categories' statistical generalities. And they are moral because they are part of God's design, which no unbelieving nationalist could ever claim.

Unless suppressing the truth in unrighteousness, we naturally recognize these metaphysical categories and their attendant duties, because God has constituted us to do so. When we study the world and notice the large differences between men and women, we not only identify statistical generalities, but garner conceptions of masculinity and femininity, which conceptions contain their own intrinsic obligations: either to act masculinely or to act femininely. Or, perhaps as a more obvious example, we understand that gender is not merely statistical when we apprehend by conscience that any sex (or "marriage") between two people of the same gender is sin, irrespective of whatever harms consequentially follow from the consensual act. Our recognition of the statistical generalities among men and women directs us to a metaphysical category back of those statistics, gender, with only insane egalitarians pretending that there is no natural (and thus moral) design to which male and female behavior ought to conform. Besides gender, another example of this metaphysical recognition, albeit abstract, is our knowledge of other people's existence. In a purely empirical way, we cannot know if the other human-looking bipeds with whom we daily interact possess individual minds, since that is not empirically observable by its nature—yet we clearly know that we are interacting with other minds, and we apprehend moral duties from this as well. God has made us to recognize a certain metaphysical category, personality, upon our empirical interaction with humans. He likewise has constituted us to recognize other metaphysical categories upon the recognition of the statistical generalities marking them out: race and gender. It is these ever-important metaphysical categories, containing their own essence and intrinsic moral obligations, which only a theistic worldview can undergird.

Against this, unbelief has no intellectual arsenal to mark out these categories as having intrinsic obligations. To the evolutionist, these categories consist of generalities that arose merely by chance, and therefore can only provide packets of guidance in telling us how to further survive and propagate the species—that is, if we happen to desire to propagate: we have no teleological obligation to do so. The unbeliever cannot explain why it is intrinsically morally obligatory to honor one's parents or ancestors, nor can he explain why sodomy is contrary to nature (Rom. 1:26); at most he can condemn those things only insofar as they result in harm, but not intrinsically. Gender and race (as a super-extended family) can have no intrinsic obligations for the atheist, because all they are is the merely physical concatenation of statistical generalities and characteristics. Such categories can give us pragmatic guidance in how to go about life, but they cannot bind us to any real courses of action. They cannot explain why we ought not try to transcend these lowly categories, obliterate boundaries, and become transhumanists. White nationalists intuitively understand that we ought to love our own by marrying among our own and seeking our nation's benefit—they truly apprehend these objective moral obligations—but these obligations can be grounded only in a robust conception of racial distinctions with metaphysical (theistic) support, not in the pragmatist foundations which unbelief lays.

After all, one of the great intellectual sins of our age, so characteristic of egalitarianism, is rebellion against and hatred of the metaphysical. Gender, race, and nationality are treated as man-made constructs, lacking any metaphysical or God-created character, and sinners consequently see no reason to obey the roles naturally associated with them. The upholding of race-related obligations is "racist," just as the upholding of gender-related obligations is "sexist" and the upholding of sexual ethics is "homophobic." Since these God-created categories have distinct natures, they have various statistical expressions in nature; but when people reduce these categories to their statistical expressions, viewing them merely as social constructs, not God-ordained essences, they then blind themselves from perceiving the divinely-sanctioned obligations we have back of those generalities. One of those vital tasks, so vivid to our ancestors and so well-expressed in Scripture, is our obligation to love and defend our own (1 Tim. 5:8).

Salvation as the Fulfillment of Our Design

The grace of God in salvation not only grants us full absolution from the penalty of our sins, but is designed to produce an inner holiness within the redeemed. This holiness, being intimately linked with righteousness, comprehends all our moral dispositions and relations, and thus takes into account our divine design, improving our concordance with it. True, God created mankind to live in a state of glory that exceeds its natural happiness and aims, but this is to say that His grace restores and exalts nature; it does not negate it. Horribly false, then, is the modern mutilation of Galatians 3:28, which teaches that nature is itself destroyed by grace, as if God sought to redeem us from His own creation. The true interpretation is that no particular category of nature restricts the openness of salvation; a person of any gender, nationality, or social stratum may obey the gospel and attain life everlasting—at which point he is bound to become sanctified with God's moral law, including as the law bears upon his ethnic and racial identity and its station within God's social design. The Christian view, then, wishes all men, as a consequence of this universally applicable redemption, to honor "the bounds of their habitation," precisely as God designed the nations to reside.

Gregory Hood, in arguing for the inefficacy of Christianity, disagrees. When writing that the true faith "burns through ties of kinship and blood," he cites Galatians 3:28 to show how this egalitarian monstrosity is "natural" from the text. He likewise criticizes Christianity's "universalist message of salvation and overall moral and metaphysical outlook," as well as its doctrine of justification *sola fide*:

> *For any who accept "justification by faith," salvation or damnation is conferred by an abstract individual choice as to whether one accepts Jesus Christ as his savior. Such a creed renders family, kin, and nation irrelevant. . . . The most Bible-believing Christians, modern evangelical Protestants, are gradually transforming Christianity into its true form, a cult of egalitarian true believers, with the special "Chosen People" serving as the sole exception.*

These contentions are far from the truth. Justification by faith renders family, kin, and nation "irrelevant" only in the sense that one does not strictly need to belong to any particular family, kin group, or nation in order to be among the redeemed, not in the sense that no moral duties emanate from them. Fanatical Anabaptist "Protestants" who hate nature and see personal salvation as the sole moral objective within this world are the ones transforming Christianity into its false, Equality-worshiping form, for they atrociously misunderstand the role of our ethnic identity within God's design (and thus His moral law), seeing nature as a barrier for redemption to overcome and vanquish. Why Mr. Hood agrees with their absurd interpretations is the question I would pose to him.

Mr. Hood expands upon his disdain for Christianity's "overall moral and metaphysical outlook":

> As de Benoist describes, Christianity and monotheism generally paves the way for atheism by desacralizing the world. The result is plagued with a hatred for the world as it is, a world-denying impulse that naturally lends itself to messianic liberalism to make the fallen world fit with the divine order.

Christianity does not "desacralize" the world any more than pronouncing it to be created and non-divine. A denial of this distinction actually leads to a world that is itself divine which, by blurring the Creator-creature distinction, marches toward pantheism and then atheism. More importantly, Christianity alone recognizes that the way in which our fallen world must "fit with the divine order" is by restoring it to its Edenic condition, that is, fulfilling the original design which God intended. The moral renewal of our world and of all our relations is predicated upon a fundamental love for what God primordially pronounced as "very good," including its holy and intricate design, rather than upon a demented, unbelieving view of the world where death is normal and natural, and where all can be fully reduced to physico-chemical processes. Contrary to Mr. Hood, then, Christian metaphysics, fully equipped with its robust teleology and the resultant ethical implications, supplies us with a powerful foundation for a healthy nationalism.

Conclusion

The white nationalist movement needs to acknowledge God in order to properly establish and conceptualize our intuitive obligations to save our people. Some white nationalists attempt to justify their view based ultimately on freedom of association: roughly, we ought to be allowed to choose our own company; we should not be deemed racist for preferring the company of our own people and teaching our children the same. While I would not dispute with this position, especially in its rhetorical and tactical utility, I contend that we should go further. We *ought* to love our own people and marry among them. We are *sinning* if we "prefer" to abandon our racial group and spurn our people, exercising our freedom of association against their well-being. If we allow freedom of association as our highest good, then we cannot decry the propaganda encouraging miscegenation, since we would have already abandoned normativity in race relations to the unimpeachable preferences of the individual. If we stand ultimately with freedom of association, then we must suppress sound moral intuition. Without understanding the deepness of our racial identity, without seeing it as carrying intrinsic obligations, white nationalism becomes pragmatic and depends upon whites' not abandoning their natural affections. It loses its moral dimension, so vital to our cause.

Therefore, in conclusion: Scripture teaches that God has created the various categories or "kinds" which we see today. Whether or not the scriptural usage of "kind" refers to a particular level in the taxonomic hierarchy of biology, it is crucial to acknowledge the God-createdness or divine sanctioning behind the world's biological diversity. If we do not acknowledge it, the categories we clearly perceive, such as race and gender, are evacuated of normative significance and reduced to groupings of statistical generalities. Since white nationalism so heavily relies upon whites' moral obligations to defend their own, it is cardinal that this normativity not be abandoned. The answer lies in God and His Son, Jesus Christ.

Part 4: Anti-Judaism
August 16, 2013

Introduction

A multitude of white nationalists today, in seeking to increase their people's birthrate and the overall influence and autonomy of European peoples in the world today, grasp that one of the clear and present dangers to our racial group stems from Jewish hegemony in the West. It is not a coincidence, they realize, that names like Bernanke, Blankfein, Goldstein, Ovitz, Rosenberg, Sulzberger, Weinstein, and Zuckerman belong to men in positions of power and authority, and that the country is startlingly pro-Israel and morally decadent. None other than a Stein even admits that his people run Hollywood. Naturally, white nationalists find this problematic, as should anyone else who understands the curse and effects of foreign usurpation and domination (Deut. 28:43).

But these same white nationalists fall into error when they suppose that Christianity — rather than Judeo-Christianity, as is the current mutilated title — is a Jewish deception, used for the same ends of psychological and sociological coercion as other ideologies the media and public schools disseminate. They might take the otherwise mindless anti-racist retort, "Jesus was a Jew," holding it as genuine grounds to reject Christianity. Or they might have a more sophisticated articulation of how the universality of Christian love logically leads to the same egalitarian and suicidal altruism which is accepted by whites and promulgated, albeit hypocritically, by Jewish-controlled and Jewish-influenced institutions. Whatever their peculiar reasoning, it would be helpful for them to understand the historic anti-Judaism of the Christian Church and follow the King of kings as "he treadeth the winepress of the fierceness and wrath of Almighty God" (Rev. 19:15).

Preliminary Considerations

This article will be different from the other three guiding white nationalists to Christ. The other three are about broader theological or philosophical principles, seeking to demonstrate the truthfulness of theism as well as its necessity unto the meaningfulness of white nationalist goals. They aim to demonstrate and support theism, which indirectly supports Christianity as the rational option given the theistic alternatives. This article, by contrast, will concern itself chiefly with historical data and specifics of the Christian religion. While the other three should lend support to Christianity by supporting theism, this one directly and explicitly supports Christianity from the premise of anti-Judaism.

Second, any comprehensive discussions of Jewish people would need to include not only their religion, but also their ethnic composition. Jewishness is generally emphasized as an ethno-religious identity, and therefore understanding the competing claims to true Hebrew identity and identifying the genuine descendants of Jacob are vital areas of study. However, since I lack the time, space, and acumen to dissect that matter appropriately, and since the topic has been covered elsewhere,[95] I will simply refer to those whom we commonly identify as Jews today, including their support for Judaism and/or Israel and their self-identification as a definitively demarcated and cohesive ethnic group.

Modern Senselessness Notwithstanding

The central impetus driving unbelieving white nationalists to identify Christianity as foundationally Jewish, no doubt, is the asininity of the modern Christian "church" with its worship of Israel and its betrayal of white Gentile interests. Too many Christians are mindless zombies in their obedience to a falsely constructed anti-biblical ethic of egalitarianism and pietism. Genuflecting toward all other racial groups, but having no pride in their own people, modern believers are an embarrassment to anyone with a modicum of awareness of the zeitgeist. These Christians, rather than perceiving anti-Judaism in Christ's censure of the Pharisees, treat any Christians who are willing to pray imprecatory prayers, or who care about

---

[95] See Davis Carlton's series on "Ten Christian Zionist Myths"

stringently following God's law and believing His doctrine, or who are just plain meanies, as the *real* Pharisees. Further sanctified Christians ought to be patient and loving in correcting these errant believers, to be sure, but nonetheless one can understand the moral ire which racial realists harbor towards them.

In any case, it should be evident to the honest non-Christian nationalist that these aberrations of biblical religion do not serve to refute the proper expression of it. If we apprehend the enormous extent to which so much of our society has been corrupted, we should not be surprised to learn that our churches are corrupt as well. But truth is eternal, and we should seek to identify those timeless principles which are themselves immune to corruption. Though the purification of the church is a tall order we Christians must undertake, for now we must realize that the present corruption of the church does not have evidentiary value in refuting Christianity. In sum: we are as indignant about the church as you are.

Old Testament Objections

The response that corrupted institutions do not nullify true religion might not convince the unbelieving nationalist who finds in Scripture principles which inevitably justify Jewish supremacy. He might cite the Old Testament passages permitting the Israelites to commit genocide in obliterating the nations of Canaan (e.g. Deut. 7:1-5; 20:16-18). Giving such a clear privilege to one nation, so clearly exalting them to the point that there apparently is no golden rule between them and other nations, is a perfect recipe for Jewish domination and ascendancy. If Jewish people are allowed to destroy nations which seem to be opposed to them, and if they do so backed by the authority of God Himself, then they are seemingly justified in doing whatever they want. Passages permitting genocide remove any barriers and inhibitions from any goal the Jewish people may seek for themselves, it is argued. If a Gentile gets in the way of these plans, so much the worse for him. Of course, the Bible-believer might try to say that genocide was permissible only in that context, but how can the universal and eternal principles of morality be so egregiously modified?

The true answer is that such a circumstance-specific qualification would not be contrary to fundamental principles of morality. All proper minds can concede the basic premise that God, being Lord and Owner of all, can righteously take life entirely as He pleases. He is not obliged to preserve the lives of sinners, but could justly destroy every single man, woman, and child at any moment. In fact, for those without the covering of Christ's righteousness, perdition is imminent and looming. But if we concede this premise, then we can also concede that, if He wanted, God could employ *human means* in bringing about any punishments He wanted. It is God's prerogative to take life as He pleases, and it is likewise His prerogative to use humans to accomplish whatever ends He so pleases. This entails not that humans are ever permitted to murder, but merely that certain acts, which would be murderous in ordinary circumstances, are not murderous if one has supernaturally received extraordinary authority from God Himself. In other words, the moral law teaches that, by default (i.e. without having received any authority from God), a man may not kill another apart from self-defense or the execution of justice. Yet God can dispense authority to slay. This is what He did with Abraham when He commanded him to sacrifice Isaac, even though that was revoked in time to save Isaac's life. This is also what God does in granting certain political rulers the authority to bear the sword for the punishment of evildoers (Rom. 13:4), as well as in granting citizens the right to rebel against tyrants.[96] The delegation of authority to act in ways forbidden to those without authority is a perfectly intelligible concept; and it is easy to see that such authority-delegation is clearly limited for certain people to certain times and certain places. The same would apply to ancient Israel: they were given extraordinary authority to serve as instruments of God's wrath in punishing Canaanites, but this assuredly does not entail some *carte blanche* for Jewish supremacy today over just any Gentile ethnic or racial group. God's Word provides nothing resembling warrant for such a heresy.

Covenant Theology

Objections aside, a proper biblical understanding of Israel positively forbids any possibility of Jewish preeminence. St. Paul makes it clear that all men, Jew and Gentile alike, are under sin (Rom. 3:9ff.), emphasizing the need for "the righteousness of God, through faith in Jesus Christ, to all and on all who believe" (Rom. 3:22). Even though he mentions his affinity for his Israelite kinsmen (Rom. 9:3), Paul nevertheless states this in the context of their status as unregenerate. Far from being especially privileged by God, Jews will be damned and trampled underfoot if they do not repent.

After concluding in Romans 9 that salvation comes not by blood but by God's sovereign choice, and in Romans 10 that the *sine qua non* of salvation is the profession of Christ, Paul makes a bold comment in Romans 11 that "all Israel will be saved" (v. 26). Many Christians, including many great, orthodox Christians, have held that this passage foresees a great conversion of Jewish people to true biblical religion in the future. I dissent from this opinion, partly because I think there is great confusion on the true identity of the genetic descendants of Jacob, but mostly because I doubt the text supports the ethnic-Israel interpretation. Yet, whatever

---

[96] These political delegations would be moral and not positive like Abraham's, but the point remains.

one believes about the fulfillment of Romans 11:26, Paul makes a key point in Romans 11 that is a bane to Jews: Israel was "cut off" from God's covenant due to her unbelief (vv. 19-22). The grand fulfillment of this covenantal divorce came in A.D. 70, when Jesus Christ poured judgment upon Jerusalem, utilizing the pagan Roman army as His instrument.

Paul wrote at length of how he, as a Jewish man himself, should understand that God has apparently cut off the nation to whom He has made promises of everlasting love (e.g., Psalm 94:14). But in answering this objection, he at no point asserts that Jews retain any special privilege over Gentiles in God's electing love. He asserts that Israel was indeed blessed by God as recipients of the ancient oracles of God and as the source of Jesus the Messiah (Romans 9:4-5), but he now affirms that the members of the church, a multinational (because worldwide) entity composed of all those who bend the knee of Lord Jesus, are, as those circumcised in heart and not necessarily in the flesh, the *true* Israel (Romans 2:28-29), that is, the true object of God's affection and love. Modern-day Israel is not this true Israel, especially insofar as it continues to resist Jesus's lordly claims, and as such it, on rudimentary Christian principles, Israel carries no special claim to God's favor or privilege. On the contrary, while impenitent, they abide under His wrath.

Further Biblical Testimony

A proper understanding of covenant theology helps one to understand that the Jews have no special privilege before God, but need to repent and believe as all the rest. Yet a further perusal of Holy Writ can help us to see that, as a people, Jews are also to be viewed as especially dangerous and cruel. As mentioned earlier, Jesus's words against the Pharisees are exceptionally well-known. He reserved nothing but the harshest of words for them; His verbal castigations fill Matthew 23 to the brim. In addition, we read in Matthew 27:25 that the Jews, in pursuing the Messiah's murder, were even willing to affirm the guilt of their deed for their posterity. And from these preliminary passages, it must be asked: how ought Christians to deal with those who accept a religion which has amplified and multiplied its blasphemies since the time of Christ? How ought we to treat those who revere the Pharisees as their spiritual forefathers and who obey the rabbinic tradition of the wicked Talmud? Even if there were no genetic link between Jews in Christ's time and those who call themselves Jews today, their affirmation of the same repulsive tradition is enough to generate substantial moral skepticism.

Going even further, the apostle John records Jesus's excoriation of the Jews in chapter 8 of his gospel, where Christ calls them sons of Satan. This parallels His words for Jews in Revelation 2:9 and 3:9, where He calls their places of worship "synagogues of Satan." And in addition to the excruciating words of the Lord, St.

Paul speaks of those "of the circumcision" as ones who subvert households and attempt to acquire filthy lucre (Titus 1:10-11). He similarly unleashes sweepingly condemnatory words for them in his first epistle to the Thessalonian church:

> 14 *For you, brethren, became imitators of the churches of God which are in Judea in Christ Jesus. For you also suffered the same things from your own countrymen, just as they did from the Judeans,* 15 *who killed both the Lord Jesus and their own prophets, and have persecuted us; and they do not please God and are contrary to all men,* 16 *forbidding us to speak to the Gentiles that they may be saved, so as always to fill up the measure of their sins; but wrath has come upon them to the uttermost (2:14-16).*

It is because of language like this that the New Testament can be openly denounced as anti-Semitic; and it is because of open accusations of anti-Semitism that Christianity clearly is anti-Judaic. Scripture presents the Jewish people as a dangerous population, conspiring to kill Jesus (e.g. Mark 11:18) and plotting to incite violence and murder throughout the book of Acts (4:15-17; 5:33; 6:11; 9:23-24; 17:5; 20:3, 19; 23:12-13). Christianity therefore must be utterly perverted to become what it is today. But if one is looking for good reasons to oppose corrosive, Jewish-inspired culture-destruction, Christianity certainly provides the proper and true basis.

The Testimony of Past Saints

The accusations of anti-Semitism extend also to the practices and statements of Christians throughout church history, of which I will provide some cursory examples. It would first be profitable to view some statements of the early church fathers. Ignatius of Antioch (A.D. 35-108), for example, stated, "For if we still live according to the Jewish law, we acknowledge that we have not received grace. . . . It is absurd to profess Christ Jesus, and to Judaize. For Christianity did not embrace Judaism, but Judaism Christianity."[97] Similarly, Justin Martyr (A.D. 103-165) wrote a dialogue with a Jewish man named Trypho, in which he said the following:

> *For the circumcision according to the flesh, which is from Abraham, was given for a sign; that you may be separated from other nations, and from us; and that you alone may suffer that which you now justly suffer; and that your land may be desolate, and your cities burned with fire; and that strangers may eat your*

---

[97] Ignatius, *The Epistle of Ignatius to the Magnesians*, chs. 8, 10.

fruit in your presence, and not one of you may go up to Jerusalem. . . . Accordingly, these things have happened to you in fairness and justice, for you have slain the Just One, and His prophets before Him; and now you reject those who hope in Him, and in Him who sent Him – God the Almighty and Maker of all things – cursing in your synagogues those that believe in Christ. . . .

For other nations have not inflicted on us and on Christ this wrong to such an extent as you have, who in very deed are the authors of the wicked prejudice against the Just One, and us who hold by Him. For after that you had crucified Him, the only blameless and righteous Man – through whose stripes those who approach the Father by Him are healed – when you knew that He had risen from the dead and ascended to heaven, as the prophets foretold He would, you not only did not repent of the wickedness which you had committed, but at that time you selected and sent out from Jerusalem chosen men through all the land to tell that the godless heresy of the Christians had sprung up, and to publish those things which all they who knew us not speak against us. So that you are the cause not only of your own unrighteousness, but in fact of that of all other men.[98]

Augustine (A.D. 354-430) also speaks of the Jewish people as accursed:

[T]he voice of God in the Holy Scriptures accuses the Jews. For the blood of Christ has a loud voice on the earth, when the responsive Amen of those who believe in Him comes from all nations. . . .

So the unbelieving people of the Jews is cursed from the earth, that is, from the Church, which in the confession of sins has opened its mouth to receive the blood shed for the remission of sins by the hand of the people that would not be under grace, but under the law. . . . [T]he Church admits and avows the Jewish people to be cursed.[99]

Perhaps the most emphatic and forceful father to oppose Judaism was John Chrysostom (A.D. 347-407):

But the synagogue is not only a brothel and a theater; it also is a den of robbers and a lodging for wild beasts. . . . Indeed the synagogue is less deserving of honor than any inn. It is not merely a lodging place for robbers and cheats but also for demons. This is true not only of the synagogues but also of the souls of the Jews. . . . Here the slayers of Christ gather together, here the cross is driven out, here God is blasphemed, here the Father is ignored, here the Son is outraged, here the grace of the Spirit is rejected. Does not greater harm come from this place since the Jews themselves are demons? . . .

---

[98] Justin Martyr, *Dialogue with Trypho*, chs. 16-17.
[99] Augustine, *Contra Faustum*, Book 12, §§ 10-11.

> *The Jews [are] the most miserable and wretched of all men. . . . The difference between the Jews and us [is] not a small one, is it? Is the dispute between us over ordinary, everyday matters, so that you think the two religions are really one and the same? Why are you mixing what cannot be mixed? They crucified the Christ whom you adore as God. Do you see how great the difference is? . . .*
>
> *But after [Christ] died on the cross, he then destroyed your city; it was then that he dispersed your people; it was then that he scattered your nation over the face of the earth. In doing this, he teaches us that he is risen, alive, and in heaven. . . . For God did not threaten that he will forgive the sins of the Jews but that he will execute vengeance upon [them].*[100]

Other church fathers provide similar attestation, but I think such a sample is sufficient. It would also be beneficial to note an influential medieval thinker. Thomas Aquinas, in a letter to Margaret of Flanders, asserted that the Jews possessed "nothing except what they acquired through the depravity of usury," in which case their stolen property should be expropriated and distributed to the robbed Gentiles. Many popes could also be cited for their edicts and behavior, as they reflected the disposition of the Catholic Church in general. Last but not least would be Martin Luther's famous treatise, *On the Jews and Their Lies*:

> *No human reason nor any human heart will ever grant [Christian doctrines], much less the embittered, venomous, blind heart of the Jews. As has already been said, what God cannot reform with such cruel blows, we will be unable to change with words and works. Moses was unable to reform the Pharaoh by means of plagues, miracles, pleas, or threats; he had to let him drown in the sea. . . .*
>
> *[T]he Jews will not give up their pride and boasting about their nobility and lineage. As was said above, their hearts are hardened. Our people, however, must be on their guard against them, lest they be misled by this impenitent, accursed people who give God the lie and haughtily despise all the world. . . .*
>
> *By virtue of such futile, arrogant circumcision in the flesh they presume to be God's only people, until the foreskin of their heart has become thicker than an iron mountain and they can no longer hear, see, or feel their own clear Scripture, which they read daily with blind eyes overgrown with a pelt thicker than the bark of an oak tree. . . .*
>
> *Alas, it cannot be anything but the terrible wrath of God which permits anyone to sink into such abysmal, devilish, hellish, insane baseness, and arrogance. If I were to avenge myself on the devil himself I should be unable to wish him such evil and misfortune as God's wrath inflicts on the Jews, compelling*

---

[100] Chrysostom, John. *Eight Homilies Against the Jews*, Homilies 1, 4, and 5.

them to lie and to blaspheme so monstrously, in violation of their own conscience. Anyway, they have their reward for constantly giving God the lie.[101]

The presence of anti-Jewish art in church history, such as *Ecclesia et Synagoga*, nicely supplements the testimony of these prominent Christian figures. If the church has so consistently opposed Jewish influence and their devastating religion from the early church onward, certainly it is not the case that Christianity is in principle a religion that promotes Jewish supremacy. On the contrary, Christ's religion stands as the most formidable and potent opponent of today's Jewish influence. White nationalists should know that if the church triumphant is clearly and uniformly this way, so also should the church militant be.

Conclusion

As befits the history of Christian-Jewish relations, Christianity is not an ideology constructed for the worship of the Jewish nation, but has only today been perverted into that monstrosity known as Judeo-Christianity. Though always tempering our interactions with love and a desire for the conversion of Jewish people, Christians ought to desire to resist Jewish influence and harbor moral skepticism towards confessions of Judaism. This perfectly makes sense of the Jewish corrosion of Western culture in recent times; white nationalists therefore have every reason to follow Christ in His plan for dominion. In this last installment of the series, I hope to have made that abundantly clear.

What is more, it would be foolish of white nationalists to deny Christianity if they wish to combat Jewish hegemony. Paganism has been shown to be weak and contrived,[102] and all attempts to bring white nationalism into secularism would encounter thoroughgoing Jewish ideology: any endeavor to secularize society would thus require some sort of acceptance of Jewish influence. White nationalists therefore must either join Jewish activists in de-Christianizing the West, or follow Christ. Before such a King all should tremble, and to such a King all must repent.

---

[101] Luther, *On the Jews and Their Lies*. The first two quotes are from chapter 1, the third is from chapter 2, and the fourth is from chapter 10.
[102] Carlton, Davis. "The Proper Place of Pagan Mythology in the European Identity." *Faith and Heritage*. 14 March 2011. https://faithandheritage.com/2011/03/the-proper-place-of-pagan-mythology-in-the-european-identity/

ADAM GREY

> *Adam Grey is a white American who loves God and his neighbor, and is therefore a dissident in a dystopian society.*

Fear Eve, Lose Eden

October 6, 2017

Is it uncomfortable to talk about gender relations? Often times it is, even for traditionally-minded Christian men and women. I remember my adolescent days when the liberal pastors I sat under would spout off feminist talking points during sermons touching on gender relations. Somehow even the very clear scriptural gender roles described in passages such as Ephesians 5:22-33 became arguments for misandry. They'd read verse 21 back into the subsequent 12 verses like it was a magic decoder ring from a box of Cracker Jacks. The mutual submission referred to in verse 21, by the way, regards the female submission Paul went on to describe — not the man's submission to the wife within the household. If verse 21 was an instruction for husbands to submit to their wives, Paul would be uttering nonsense in verses 22-33. This is akin to abolitionist hermeneutics.

Twenty years later while sitting under "conservative" pastors, I heard that same nonsense, proving the late, great Robert Lewis Dabney right again.[103] Socially acceptable conservatism really is just liberalism a few years later.

For traditionalists, we know that the Bible has spoken clearly on gender roles. We may dispute whether women need to wear head coverings in church or in the home, and the place of jewelry and makeup. We may debate whether or when it is appropriate for women to work outside of the home. However, we do not debate whether the husband or wife is head of their household. We do not dispute the impropriety of women competing for elected office or ordained ministry.

These divisions on the attire and income-earning role of women are secondary to the unanimity we express on the submission of women to men in the family, church, society, and nation. This unanimous view among members of the Alt Right and traditionalist Christians puts us completely at odds with polite society, aka the devil's culture.

Recently I came across a rhetorical question posed by a blogger that intersected our Alt Right views on race with our views on gender roles. It caused me to rethink the priority I had hitherto given to male-female relations in my own life, and in my views of helping the pro-white, Alt Right movement make progress.

---

[103] Carlton, Davis. "Robert Lewis Dabney: A Forgotten Visionary." *Faith and Heritage.* 19 Feb. 2011. https://faithandheritage.com/2011/02/robert-lewis-dabney-a-forgotten-visionary/

Essentially the question was this: if we can't rule our own women in our households, what makes us think we'll be able to deliver our country from hordes of non-white men?

This is an important question to ask ourselves. It is an argument from the lesser to the greater. If you or I can't handle an individual who is ethnically and religiously identical to you, and who (if married) has wedded herself to you and owes you spiritual and legal duties, how could you possibly overcome the objections of an individual (or masses) who is nothing like you, owes you nothing, and is physically far more dangerous than that lone woman?

The degree of social risk, legal risk, and physical danger that a white man faces in simply defending himself from a non-white assailant is far greater than what he faces in nonviolently asserting his will with his wife regarding things like budgeting, child rearing, or conjugal relations. And yet not a few white men, their traditionalist views notwithstanding, would rather face the aforementioned risks of self-defense in our anti-white society as opposed to having to confront the women they live with! Is it because the legal system gives our wives leverage that many strangers don't have? Or is it because we're simply afraid to end up with the woman Proverbs 21:9 and 25:24 describes?

"Better to live on a corner of the roof than share a house with a quarrelsome wife."

If you can't even handle one woman, how will you ever get your country back?

It is akin to the argument that if you're not willing to get in the pro-white fight now, while the First Amendment still legally protects us and the government isn't jailing us for memes and tweets like in the U.K., what makes you think that you'll be fighting in the streets and risking jobs and homes when legal persecution begins in earnest?

At its heart the question asked about the willingness of individual white males to see their will through to fruition. It asked about our willingness to confront unhappy, hostile people and overcome their objections instead of reaching a compromise solution or avoiding the confrontation in the first place.

We can neither demand things of our women and ignore their feelings, nor abdicate our responsibility to command them in favor of a wishy-washy "niceness." The truth is that God made women less capable when it comes to the traits that make good leaders. If we don't do our job, everybody suffers, including our women. They can be wrong sometimes, and they need us to show them the way when their female blinders prevent them from seeing it. It's not in fallen Eve's nature to submit to male leadership, though, which is why Paul had to explicitly instruct the women of the early church to do so. Similarly, it's not in fallen Adam's nature to be tactful or attentive to his female subjects, which is why Paul had to explicitly instruct the men of the early church to do so. They're women, not infantrymen, and have to be commanded and cared for accordingly.

For the purposes of this article, the important thing is that if we don't assertively lead our women, we won't develop the nerve and skill needed to fight bigger and far less pretty foes. If we can't lead our women with the steely, absolute, back-against-the-wall confidence of Aragorn fighting before the Black Gate of Mordor, there's no way we will be able to change the world.

On the other hand, if you can handle your wife, what's to stop you from handling more difficult problems? That is a very encouraging thought.

A Time for Choosing in the Church

October 26, 2017

The dividing lines have been drawn. On the one side are the churches willing to sell out white people to a Jewish globalist regime dedicated to crushing what remains of Christendom. These wolves in shepherds' clothing will get their thirty shekels of silver, sell out their own people, and still end up hanging from the white genocide tree. Blessing the act of miscegenation will not make them any less white, or any less racist, in the eyes of their anti-white beholders.

On the other side are we dissident faithful who adhere to Christ and the way of life He, the apostles and prophets, and our forefathers preached for millennia. We stand with faces towards the future in opposition to the anti-whites who want to drag us into the superstitious, self-contradicting, Third-World past. We believe that there is such a thing as logic, truth, and righteousness. For merely defending the old truths we are castigated as the scum of the earth by the leadership of every major denomination in Christendom.

The plain teachings of Scripture, the traditions of our fathers, and the light of reason show that we, not they, are the confessors of the orthodox, catholic, evangelical faith. They are the heretics.

So let's be done with it. Protestant,[104] Catholic,[105] and Orthodox,[106] alike have issued their bulls against us. Let us treat their decrees with the contempt they deserve, as did our ancestors before us in the days of the great Reformation.

We believe in one God, the Father Almighty, Who designed and preserves the races of man, distinct and separate, for our benefit and His glory.

We believe that God made man, male and female, distinct in their minds, bodies, and souls, and that their persons, duties, and rights are not interchangeable.

We believe in one Lord, Jesus Christ, the only-begotten Son of the Father, through faith in Whom alone all men may be saved and made members of His Body the Church in their distinct social stations, without abolishing those distinctions.

---

[104] Carter, Joe. "What Christians should know about the alt-right." *The Ethics and Religious Liberty Commission of the Southern Baptist Convention.* 14 June 2017. https://erlc.com/resource-library/articles/what-christians-should-know-about-the-alt-right/

[105] Bishop James D. Conley. "Our response to Charlottesville." *Catholic News Agency.* 17 Aug. 2017. https://www.catholicnewsagency.com/column/our-response-to-charlottesville-3808

[106] Orthodox Church in America. "Holy Synod of Bishops issues statement on recent tragic events in Charlottesville, VA." 16 Aug 2017. https://www.oca.org/news/headline-news/holy-synod-of-bishops-issues-statement-on-recent-tragic-events-in-charlotte

We believe in the Holy Spirit, the giver of life, Who calls every ethnic group to repentance and faith in Christ, and therefore gives every race, nation, tribe, and tongue the right to exist as a distinct body, forever.

We believe in one holy, catholic, and apostolic Church, which is composed of men from every nation, and therefore has no power to punish them for loving their families, nations, tongues, and races above those of others.

In other words, we say to the wayward leaders of our fathers' churches that they are wrong to impose false, collective guilt on innocent people. They are wrong to harm a people group through false guilt, through shaming, through destroying its history, and through outlawing its culture. They are wrong to impede and oppose that people group's continued existence as itself, free and independent from the manipulation or oppression of others.

White Christians have the God-given right to live as White Christians, forever.

The Alt Right Won't Win with Atheism

November 14, 2017

Fault lines have cut across the Alt Right for years.

For several years at least, those in the Alt Right/pro-white/kinist world have struggled over a definition of its core tenets. The 2016-17 split between the Alt Right and the Alt Lite was one manifestation of this, as those two camps divided over whether ethnic solidarity, or civic patriotism, defined American nationalism. On the one hand were those such as us at FaithandHeritage.com, and on the other hand were the likes of Milo, Mike Cernovich, and Paul Joseph Watson.

Prior to this was the divide over whether Jews ought to be defined as potential allies of whites, or identified as our archnemesis. On the one side stood people and organizations like Jared Taylor and the Council of Conservative Citizens. On the other side stood those such as Dr. David Duke and Counter-Currents.

At present the division over the Jewish Question has faded in significance, as members of both factions have allied against the common Leftist foe (and that foe is obviously Jewish). As for the division over ethnonationalism versus civic nationalism, that debate was settled before it even started.

There's another fault line that runs through the pro-white movement that stretches back millennia. It is the question of religion. Lately I've been looking at whether or not any major religious tradition has organizations that accept and embrace us. The answer is no, and the solution to that seeming problem is spiritual entrepreneurship, in my opinion.

But I don't want to compare religions in this article. I want to talk about no religion. Atheism—whether intentional and ideologically rigorous, or unintentional and rooted in indifference towards spiritual matters—permeates much of the Alt Right.

Influential Alt Right figures such as Mike Enoch, Richard Spencer, and those in their immediate circles prefer atheism over Christianity for well thought-out reasons. Their embrace of atheism is a willful choice. Their atheism includes an active disdain for traditional, orthodox Christianity. They may embrace the cultural benefits of Christianity, but they abhor its actual beliefs and morals. Sometimes they intentionally deride the Faith and at other times it seeps out. Either way, it's clear to anyone who's listening that to these and similar leaders of the Alt Right, Christianity is at best a silly idea to tolerate, and perhaps a devious Jewish plot to destroy Western man.

As a Christian who wants to see his nation and posterity thrive in a free, prosperous future, I value the work and hardships that these atheists have contributed towards our collective survival, notwithstanding their rejection of the God whom I love and who made Western civilization great. God's common grace yields benefits through all His creatures, including those who deny and deride Him. This article is not a direct criticism of these individuals (though they are emblematic and thus relevant to this discussion), but is instead a direct criticism of the atheistic worldview.

My criticism of atheism and its influence in the Alt Right has been consistent. In podcasts here, here, and elsewhere, I have publicly discussed the fact that atheism is a cancer to our race, to the success of our cause, and to the souls of our loved ones.

For the record, the major irreligious organizations reject pro-white people and their views as much as the insane or cucked religious organizations.

I do not automatically discount atheists' claims or disregard their grievances. I am familiar with atheists' claims about evolution, religious wars, supernaturalism, the Jewishness of Jesus, the Christian doctrines of forgiveness, self-control, sin, judgment, and servant leadership, i.e. "slave morality." As a white man who has suffered in the same sick societal waters that they tread to stay afloat, and experienced the letdowns that accompany a spiritual life, I sympathize with their complaints on an experiential level.

I know what it is to have loved ones die too soon, to see God "not answer" my prayers, to not understand God's will for my life or my world. I know what it is to be rejected by my church community, to see the Church hijacked by cucks and perverts, and to see the Bible that inspires me twisted to condemn me. I know the temptation to reject it all out of hand, or at least to redefine it in order to fit my experience.

I know what it is to feel alone, poor, helpless, and to desire nothing more than the means to never again let myself and my loved ones be vulnerable. To seek and attain power, as Spencer openly says he believes he should do, in order to create a better society from the top down.

The temptation to unbelief and self-will are as old as Eden. Like millions of souls before us, we in the Alt Right suffer and struggle with our sinfulness, the degeneracy of the world around us, and the seeming illogic of the lives we live. It's not my place to condemn anyone for feeling these temptations or even taking strides in those directions, as I have felt those feelings and done things that I regret. But the answer to life's seeming injustices and God's seeming illogic is not to close oneself off from one's Creator, or choose a life of radical independence from and rebellion against Him. That is literally the path of Satan. It is the path of all degeneracy and all evil. We will not aid ourselves, our families, or our people if we reject the source of all life, hope, and peace simply because life hurts and we don't understand why.

The hero's path—the Christian's path—is a combination of hard work, experience, wisdom, exercises in judgment, and faith in a God who saves us. A God who is the Hero that all other heroes merely imitate. A God whose grace, mercy, patience, knowledge, and power are unbearably strong. Therefore, the Christian lives by walking, falling, getting up again, and continuing to move forward—all by the mercy and grace of Almighty God.

Atheism does not do this. It walks away, walks backwards, and walks contrary to one's own self-good and the good of others. Atheism defies one's own Maker and Judge, and as such is supremely foolish. It is noteworthy that the Bible calls the atheist a fool.

Thousands of years ago David penned the words of Psalm 14:1, "The fool says in his heart, 'There is no God.'" Today atheistic fools still mock God in their books, movies, TED Talks, and podcasts. Sadly for them, the verdict has stayed the same, and their arguments have been refuted by able Christian apologists since the days of the early Church. This biblical verdict speaks to their true nature and their competence as leaders. If faithlessness blinds us to important realities, how can a person effectively lead others with no awareness of those realities? If our movement is led by and for atheists, I do not believe that this movement will succeed any more than the movement of atheist fools in Russia did from 1917-1991, or than the humanists in power across Europe and America succeed today.

Also, I do not believe that an atheistic movement is a desirable political vehicle for my children or my people. An atheistic, secular ethnostate is not something for which I will ever fight.

In our Anglo-American tradition, the concept of decentralized government depends on our rights coming from God. God is the possessor of all power, which He grants to individuals and families, who then delegate some of that power to form governments for certain ends. If this sounds familiar, it's because it's exactly what Thomas Jefferson wrote in the Declaration of Independence. Spencer's concept of totalitarian state power to create or deny rights based on nothing but its own power is fundamentally identical to the Soviet/postmodern American police state concept of taking and granting privileges. Atheistic ideas have consequences, and those continental European-style consequences are nothing that my English-speaking kin and I have, or will ever, fight for.

If, like pawns on Satan's chess board, one anti-God multicultural regime were sacrificed to make way for another, racially homogenous one, the net result for our race, children, and honor would be negative.

Practically speaking, it's unclear to me how atheists such as the Alt Right Politics panel expect to build a movement that is attractive to white men by espousing the personas and views of Beltway nabobs who look down their pointy noses at us guns-and-Bible-toting "bitter clingers." An honest appraisal must conclude that they simply may not care for us any more than their colorblind liberal colleagues.

That's their right, and it may be a true expression of their philosophy. However, it's not one people like me will ever embrace.

Atheism denies and defiles the most important essence of man. Take for example Mike Enoch and the Death Panel's dismissal of traditional Christianity in favor of Gnosticism and Marcionism on The Daily Shoah Episode 117 last year at Christmas. The fact that dissecting Christianity and praising heresy was the subject of their Christmas podcast spoke volumes. Nowhere was there praise of the Christ Child, of the wondrous miracle of the Virgin Birth, or of the meaning of Christ's Incarnation and the inauguration of His first advent. Nowhere was there a look forward to the hope of Easter and the amazing grace of Good Friday. Instead, there was an autopsy of what they believed was a dead and false religion. Their reasons for journeying to that intellectual and spiritual desert were their own, but the net result of every desert is lifelessness.

A movement that finds Christmas inspiration for atheistic and heretical diatribe instead of wonder, joy, and grace is not a movement that has—or offers—hope to the human soul. Given that white man and his civilization is essentially spiritual, that is a big practical problem, and will be a death knell to the willingness of men like me to subscribe to that movement if unchecked.

I value these men and their efforts, and I happen to think God has better things in store for them than s—posting about Gnosticism at Christmas time, or praising authoritarianism while being persecuted by a near-totalitarian State and society. But those blessings require turning to Christ with faith and repenting of sin and unbelief.

We here at Faith and Heritage believe that Christ, not Nietzsche, is the most relevant philosopher for the success of the Alt Right. The Cross is the symbol of our people. Atheism is as diametrically anti-white as is Judaism. The hero's path is the straight and narrow path Christ commanded us to walk. The future of the white race is tied up in the Faith. Atheists should remember that the only time they've subjugated Christians was as failing Roman imperialists, and as Jew-dominated Bolsheviks. Both times, they fell. We're still here. And we won't send our boys to be cannon fodder for a godless cause.

Thorin Reynolds

Thorin Reynolds grew up in South Carolina and now resides in Texas. He holds an MBA as well as an undergraduate degree in political science. A native southerner, he has ancestors who fought with the patriots in the American Revolution, with the Texans at the Alamo, and with the Confederacy in the War for Southern Independence.

There Is No Male and Female

May 24, 2011

There is neither Jew nor Greek, there is neither slave nor free, there is no male and female, for you are all one in Christ Jesus.

> Galatians 3:28 (ESV),
> currently one of the most abused verses in the Bible

Unlike the revolutionary branch of Marxism, which believed that its dream of utopian equality should be pursued from the top down via the overthrow of the existing order and the creation of a new order, the cultural branch of Marxism held that utopian equality should be pursued from the bottom up through the gradual eroding of the prevailing culture and the co-opting of the existing order. The revolutionary method was tried and largely failed in the USSR and Communist Bloc, while the cultural method is currently ongoing in the USA, UK, and the rest of the West with great success. The cultural Marxists have managed to co-opt almost all of our institutions, including the government, the media, the education system, and even the church. Yes, even the church has bought into the cultural Marxist ideology, with its ungodly goal of complete earthly equality and its scorning of God's sovereignty and particular gifts. Rejecting God, the Marxist seeks to create his own twisted version of heaven on earth. No barriers, no boundaries, no borders, no distinctions, no discrimination — we are all one and the same. No sin, no sinners, no judgments — well, except for those heretics who don't embrace the true gospel of equality. Salvation can be obtained without God through devotion to the social gospel, equality, and tolerance.

The liberal wing of the church has embraced this ideology so thoroughly that they cannot even be termed "Christian" any more, while the more conservative (i.e. slightly less liberal) wing of the church thinks that it can embrace the older, more accepted parts of the Marxist ideology to ingratiate themselves with the pagan culture while not embracing other newer, less accepted parts. For example, the conservative church thinks that it can embrace miscegenation, but not homosexuality, "civil rights" for non-whites, but not feminism, and racial Marxism, but not gender Marxism. Thus, when a Kinist like myself starts talking about the reality and importance of race, they will throw out "there is neither Jew nor Greek" as proof that racial/ethnic differences are irrelevant and that discussing them is unchristian (unless it's whites groveling before minorities). However, they hypocritically refuse to follow through and apply the rest of the verse in the same way. If this verse is saying that Christ erases all physical racial differences, then the verse *must* also mean that Christ erases all physical gender differences too. If "skin color" is accidental and meaningless, then why should "genitalia" be any different? There is no logically or morally consistent way to oppose homosexuality or feminism while supporting miscegenation or racial egalitarianism.

This couple in California has taken cultural Marxism to its logical end by attempting to raise a genderless baby.

> *"If you really want to get to know someone, you don't ask what's between their legs,"* says [the father].
>
> When Storm was born, the couple sent an email to friends and family: "We've decided not to share Storm's sex for now – a tribute to freedom and choice in place of limitation, a stand up to what the world could become in Storm's lifetime (a more progressive place? …)." …
>
> Witterick and Stocker believe they are giving their children the freedom to choose who they want to be, unconstrained by social norms about males and females. …
>
> "What we noticed is that parents make so many choices for their children. It's obnoxious," says Stocker.[107]

This is, of course, grossly unnatural and anti-Christian. God sovereignly grants us our gender as a blessing, with each having its own special roles. Far from being "obnoxious," parents who raise their sons as boys and daughters as girls are doing their Christian duty to prepare their children for their unique roles. Witterick and Stocker are not only in open rebellion against God, but are seriously screwing up their children.

With all that being understood, the modern church, both liberal and conservative, due to their own Marxist interpretation of Galatians 3:28, *cannot* consistently condemn this couple. The church sees the verse as erasing physical distinctions, rather than interpreting it as a statement of spiritual unity among Christians, as it was intended. If it is sinfully "racist" and hateful to raise white children as whites, teaching them to be proud of being white and to fulfill their role as whites, as many Christians have told me that it is, then it is likewise sinfully "sexist" and hateful to raise children as boys or girls, teaching them to be proud of being boys or girls and to fulfill their respective gender roles. In fact, this twisted interpretation of Galatians 3:28 would make a genderless upbringing to be the *truly Christian way* to raise

---

[107] Poisson, Jayme. "Parents keep child's gender secret." *The Toronto Star*. 21 May 2011. Updated 15 Nov 2013. https://www.thestar.com/life/parent/2011/05/21/parents_keep_childs_gender_secret.html

children. After all, there is no male and female—only Christians and non-Christians—so why would you want to set up artificial distinctions like "gender"? The church's acceptance of Marxist presuppositions puts them in the position of having to call good evil and evil good to remain consistent (Isaiah 5:20). Of course, the conservative wing of the church will be hypocritical and condemn this couple anyway while still holding onto their racial egalitarianism, but that does not change the fact that they really don't have a leg to stand on. You must fully reject Marxism and glory in the God-made distinctions of mankind, or you will be forced to incrementally embrace more and more of the Marxist positions as the pagan culture pressures you to be consistent with the presuppositions that you have already conceded.

To further prove my point that this couple holds the same Marxist presuppositions as the modern church, try reading the article again, but this time replace the word "gender" or "sex" with "race," "boy/girl" or "male/female" with "European/African/Asian," "genitalia" with "skin color," etc. You'll swear the article was written by your Sunday School teacher talking about racial equality.

A Christian View on Segregation

September 11, 2013

The Presbyterian Church in the United States (PCUS) sprang from the Southern branch of the American Presbyterian church resulting from the North-South break in 1861. Its two spiritual fathers are considered to be Rev. James H. Thornwell and Rev. Robert L. Dabney, even though both died relatively soon after it was created, with their defense of conservative Christian social order and Southern slavery firmly rooting the denomination in biblical traditionalism and conservatism until the mid-twentieth century, when the nationwide slide into liberal Marxism began to take hold. One man who stood against this slide into perdition as a true heir to Thornwell and Dabney was Rev. Guy T. Gillespie, D.D. Gillespie was a pastor in the PCUS and president of the denomination's school of Belhaven College in Jackson, Mississippi. Thus he can definitely be considered one of the leading men of the denomination at the time, at least of the conservative wing, and not just some fringe member. Two weeks ago, I posted excerpts from a sermon given by the eminent fundamentalist preacher Bob Jones, Sr., entitled "Is Segregation Scriptural?" While his scriptural reasoning is primarily sound, Jones relies primarily on a single Bible verse to make his point. Now that verse is more than sufficient to prove Jones's point, yet being a Presbyterian myself, I prefer exhaustive systematic preaching to the more Baptist-esque "pick a single verse and make an entire sermon out of it." Rev. Gillespie provides this in an address given to the Synod of Mississippi of the PCUS on November 4th, 1954, entitled "A Christian View on Segregation." The full address is too long to post here, but it covers not only scriptural proofs, but also logic, history, and experience. Gillespie makes six main points:

1. *Segregation Is Not the Child of Race Prejudice*
2. *Segregation Is One of Nature's Universal Laws*
3. *Segregation Tends to Promote Progress*
4. *Segregation Does Not Necessarily Involve Discrimination*
5. *The Principle of Segregation May Be Defended on Biblical Grounds and Is Not "Unchristian"*
6. *Segregation Is a Well-Considered and Time-Tested American Policy*

As we are most interested in the direct biblical arguments, while in no way discounting the value of the others, we will only post the fifth section in full. However, I highly recommend that you read the entire address.

The Principle of Segregation May Be Defended on Biblical Grounds and Is Not "Unchristian"

While the Bible contains no clear mandate for or against segregation as between white and negro races, it does furnish considerable data from which valid inferences may be drawn in support of the general principle of segregation as an important feature of the Divine purpose and Providence throughout the ages.

Concerning matters of this kind, which in the inscrutable wisdom of God have been left for mankind to work out in the light of reason and experience without the full light of revelation, we dare not be dogmatic, but we do well to examine with open mind some of the more pertinent references.

(1) The First Separation (Gen. 4:11-26).

A mark is placed upon Cain, and he is separated from the other branch of the human family, represented by Seth and his descendants. From Cain were descended men of great vigor and inventive genius, from Seth were descended men who began to call upon the name of the Lord, and were evidently those elsewhere referred to as "The Sons of God."

(2) The Demoralization Resulting from Intermarriage (Gen. 6:1-7).

The promiscuous intermarriage of the Sons of God, that is, the descendants of Seth, with the "Daughters of Men," who were apparently the descendants of Cain, resulted in the complete breakdown of family life and such widespread immorality and wickedness as to provoke the Lord to destroy the earth with the flood. A possible though not necessary inference from this tragic story is that the intermarriage of dissimilar groups, whether the differences be moral, cultural, or physical, is not conducive to the preservation of wholesome family life or to morality, and therefore is contrary to the purpose and will of God.

(3) New Divisions After the Flood Stemming From Sons of Noah (Gen. 9:18-29).

After the flood the three sons of Noah, Shem, Ham and Japheth, became the progenitors of three distinct racial groups, which were to repeople and overspread the earth. The descendants of Shem migrated eastward and occupied most of Asia; the descendants of Japheth migrated westward and ultimately occupied the continent of Europe, while the children of Ham moved generally southward toward the tropics and occupied the continent of Africa, and possibly southern Asia and the islands of the Pacific.

This brief record, the accuracy of which has not been successfully disputed by the anthropologists and ethnologists, while affirming the unity of the [human] race, also implies that an all-wise Providence has "determined the timed before appointed, and the bounds of their habitation." Which same Providence by determining the climatic and other physical conditions under which many successive generations of the several racial groups should live, is thereby equally responsible for the distinct racial characteristics which seem to have become fixed in prehistoric times, and which are chiefly responsible for the segregation of racial groups across the centuries and in our time.

(4) *Origin of Linguistic Differences (Gen. 11:19).*

This indicates that the Confusion of Tongues, which took place at Babel, with the consequent scattering of the peoples was an act of special Divine Providence to frustrate the mistaken efforts of godless men to assure the permanent integration of the peoples of the earth. Incidentally it indicates that the development of different languages was not merely natural or accidental, but served a Divine purpose, in becoming one of the most effective means of preserving the separate existence of the several racial groups.

(5) *Abraham Called to a Separated Life (Gen. Chapters 12-25).*

Abram, later changed to Abraham, was called to separate himself from his home and his kindred in Ur of the Chaldees and to live as a "stranger in a strange land." Under Divine guidance and blessing he and his household lived peaceably with the inhabitants without mingling with them socially or intermarrying with them. The Covenant of Circumcision instituted by God provided a sign or seal which was to distinguish and set apart in a most significant way the "Seed of Abraham," or the Hebrew people from all the other peoples of the earth throughout all generations. Many incidental circumstances, such as the refusal of God to allow the son of Hagar, the Egyptian bondwoman, to become heir of the covenant promise, the great care exercised by Abraham to secure a wife for his son Isaac from among his own kindred rather than from among the Canaanites [Gen. 24:1-4], and a similar concern manifested by Isaac and Rebekah concerning wives for their sons, all emphasize the importance which is attached to the principle of segregation, and doubtless paved the way for the emphasis given to it in the Mosaic economy and in the subsequent history of Israel.

(6) *Prohibitions Against the Mingling of Diverse Things (Lev. 19:19).*

According to the law delivered to Moses, the crossbreeding of diverse strains of cattle, the planting of mixed seeds, and the mixing of wool and linen in a garment were forbidden. We are not told the reasons for this curious law, but it seems impossible to escape the conclusion that if such intermixture of diverse elements in the lower orders of animal and plant life were unseemly and contrary to the Divine purpose, the same principle would apply with even greater force with respect to human relations.

(7) The Warnings of Moses Against Intermarriage With Other Peoples (Deut. 7:3).

Moses strictly warned the Israelites against allowing their sons and daughters to intermarry with the pagan peoples with whom they came in contact, under the penalty of bringing upon themselves the Divine wrath and judgment. This warning was emphasized repeatedly, and was specially burned into the consciousness of the nation by the terrible penalties which were inflicted upon those who committed whoredom with the daughters of Moab at Baal-Peor (Numbers 25:1-8).

(8) Ezra's Condemnation of Mixed Marriages (Ezra, Chapters 9-10).

After the return of the Jews from Babylonish captivity, it was discovered that great numbers of the prominent Jews had taken wives from among the heathen people of the land. This caused Ezra to rend his clothes and tear his hair, and cry unto God for mercy upon the sinning nation. The drastic steps which were taken to purge out this evil practice emphasized anew the vital importance which was attached to the preservation of the purity and integrity of the racial stock by the leaders of the nation and by their Divine ruler.

(9) The Attitude and Teachings of Our Lord—The Four Gospels.

There is no question but that the emphasis placed by Our Lord upon the love of God for the whole world (John 3:16, and other passages) was intended in part at least, as a rebuke to the bigotry and intolerance of the Jewish leaders, and to counteract the attitude of contempt and indifference which the Jewish people as a whole manifested toward the other peoples of the world. Likewise his declaration as to the supreme worth of the human soul (Matt. 16:26) and His last great command to His followers to go into all the world and make disciples of all nations (Matt. 28:19-20) make it abundantly clear that the redeeming love of Christ knows no limitations of class or condition or nationality or race, but like a mighty river sweeps across every national or artificial barrier to bring the water of life to the thirsty souls of men. He used the story of the Good Samaritan to rebuke the smug complacency and narrow-minded prejudice of the Jews, but he did not ignore or denounce racial distinctions, nor did he set plans on foot to abolish them and to bring about amalgamation of the Jews and the Samaritans, or of any other races. As a matter of fact, in sending out the twelve on their first Gospel missions he directed them to go "only to the lost sheep of the house of Israel" (Matt. 10:5-6) and in dealing with the Syro-Phoenician woman he takes particular care to emphasize the different status of the two races, before granting the request. The Golden Rule, as proclaimed by Our Lord, must unquestionably be applied to the field of race relations as well as to all other human relationships; at the same time no reasonable interpretation of this great principle requires to do unto or for, the individual or the race, for the sake of some fancied benefit or *momentary satisfaction, that which we have reason to believe will in the end imperil the stability of the social order and the future welfare of the race.*

(10) The Attitude and Teachings of the Apostles—The Acts and the Epistles.

The Gift of Tongues at Pentecost was undoubtedly a prophecy that the Gospel should be preached to all nations and that every people should hear the Gospel in their own languages, but it gives no hint that all linguistic, nation, or racial differences are to be wiped out in the Gospel Dispensation.

Peter's Vision on the housetop in Joppa, his subsequent visit to the home of Cornelius, the Roman Centurion, his baptism of the household after they had received the Holy Ghost, and his statement that "God is no respector of persons," marks the removal of the Jewish traditions and prejudices which barred the entrance of the Gentiles into the household of the faith, and sets the pattern for Christianity as the new religion for all nations and all the peoples of the earth.

Paul, the Apostle to the Gentiles, naturally had more to say concerning this question than any of the other New Testament writers. In his notable speech to the Greeks at Athens he said: "God . . . hath made of one blood all nations of men, for to dwell on all the face of the earth; and hath determined the times before appointed and the bounds of their habitations" (Acts 17:24-26). Writing to the Colossians he said: "And have put on the new man, which is renewed in knowledge after the image of Him that created him; where there is neither Greek nor Jew, circumcision or uncircumcision, Barbarian, Scythian, bond nor free, but Christ is all in all."

In the first passage Paul affirms the unity of the race based upon a common origin, concerning which there can be no difference of opinion among those who accept the authority of the Bible. In the second passage Paul asserts the unity of all believers in Christ, regardless of their racial differences, but this unity is a spiritual relationship resulting from the mystical union of each believer with Christ Himself, in which all enjoy the same spiritual privileges and benefits. That Paul had in mind the absolute uniformity of believers in external relations and the wiping out of all distinctions of race, nationality, social status, sex or cultural heritage, is disproven by the fact that Paul never ceased to identify himself as a member of the Jewish race, and he made very practical use of his right to Roman citizenship. He recognized the master-slave relationship prevalent in Greek and Roman society, and enjoined obedience to the reciprocal duties arising therefrom. He also clearly recognized the status assigned to women by social custom, and denied to women some of the privileges and functions exercised by men in the churches under his supervision.

(11) Preview of The Church Triumphant (Rev., Chapters 4-7).

The Seer of Patmos was permitted to behold in wonderful symbolism a preview of the Church Triumphant, the grand consummation of redemptive purpose through the ages. Before the rainbow circled throne set in the midst of the heavens, he beheld "a great multitude which no men could number, of all nations, and kindreds, and peoples and tongues," uniting in a mighty chorus of praise to God and to the Lamb upon the throne. It would be presumptuous indeed to say exactly what this symbolism means, or to rest the validity of any conclusions upon such interpretation; nevertheless it accords well with the whole scheme of creation, Providence and redemption to see in the rainbow which circled the throne a fitting symbol of the spectrum of redeemed humanity made up of the peoples of every nation, kindred, race, and language blended into a beautiful and harmonious unity, and yet each preserving its own distinctive genius and virtues, the better to show forth the infinite riches and diversity of the Divine glory and grace throughout the ages to come.

(12) Summary of Bible References.

There are doubtless many other parts of Scripture which may have some bearing upon this question, but which we cannot undertake to deal with in this discussion. But to summarize the interpretations of the passages above considered, the following conclusions would seem to be warranted: (a) Since for two thousand years the practice of segregation was imposed upon the Hebrew people by Divine authority and express command, and infractions of the command were punished with extreme severity, there is certainly no ground for the charge that racial segregation is displeasing to God, unjust to man, or inherently wrong; (b) Since Christ and the Apostles taught the love of God for all mankind, the oneness of believers in Christ, and demonstrated that the principles of Christian brotherhood and charity could be made operative in all relations of life, without demanding revolutionary changes in the natural or social order, there would appear to be no reason for concluding that segregation is in conflict with the spirit and the teachings of Christ and the Apostles, and therefore un-Christian.

And thus the movements of "civil rights," "social justice," and alienism are damned. As I said in my posting of Bob Jones, Sr.'s sermon, I'm posting these older sermons on race-related topics to show that both our views and our proofs match those of our forefathers by blood and the faith. We are the true heirs of the Christian faith, and our views are the ones holding continuity with the past. Do not flinch when we are named heretics by moral and intellectual midgets who have adopted the morality of the pagan culture in place of true Christian principles, for we stand with Christ and our fathers.

GIC SERRY

Gic is a writer who seeks to glorify God by bringing his people to repentance and contributing to their future.

From Higher Criticism to Marxism:
The Treasonous Behavior of the South African Dutch Reformed Churches Towards the Afrikaner People

November 14, 2012

Theological liberalism, as we know it, is generally thought to have begun in Germany in the nineteenth century, with its most notable proponent being Friedrich Schleiermacher. This is true in the sense that the ideas of higher and lower biblical criticism had not been openly professed and propagated before the likes of Schleiermacher, Westcott, and Hort at that time. However, liberalism's historical roots in Protestantism lie a little deeper, most notably in Reformed orthodoxy, where, for example, one Christoph Wittich was the first Calvinist theologian to propagate the so-called *Akkomodationstheorie*. Descartes arrived at this theory after concluding from his second meditation that, while God is not an absolute malicious deceiver, He still at times might have spoken falsely in the Scripture; accordingly, reason alone can liberate man from any possible error of an omnipotent God.[108] Wittich was first among the Reformed scholastics to incorporate this into his understanding of the authority of special revelation.

These developments never had a particularly significant impact on the Reformed Churches in South Africa until they were propagated by John Du Plessis (1868-1935), a former lecturer in theology at the University of Stellenbosch. Du Plessis was heavily influenced by the Wesleyanism of Rev. Andrew Murray and the biblical criticism of the liberal Dutch theologians Doedes and Van Oosterzee. During a class-sermon in 1892 on II Cor. 4:7 at Stellenbosch, where Du Plessis studied, he noted: "our faith rests on no external authority: it rests upon neither errorless Bible nor infallible Church." This statement is one of the earliest indications of Du Plessis's alliance with modernism. He was not indoctrinated in this historical-critical exegetical method by his mentors, but came under its influence by his own studies, as evidenced from the commentary of his professor Hofmeyr on the above statement: "This must be modified." In 1905, he became editor of *Die Kerkbode*, which is also today one of the most deceptive and anti-Christian Afrikaans publications around. J.D. Du Toit, being of the more conservative *Gereformeerde*

---

[108] Goudriaan, A., 1999. *Philosophiesche Gotteskentnis bei Suarez und Descartes – im Zusammenhang mit der niederländischen reformierten Theologie und Philosophie des 17 Jahrhunderts*. Leiden. p. 177

Maandblad, opposed Du Plessis.[109] Du Toit also argued in favor of using the Textus Receptus, rather than the lower-critical text of Westcott and Hort, for the translation of the New Testament into Afrikaans a few decades later, due to the providential preservation of these mostly Byzantine-type texts. However, Du Toit's excessive love for the Jews (inherited from his father's idolization of the tribe), unfortunately, led him to also support the use of the corrupted, Talmudic Hebrew text for the translation of the Old Testament in favor of the Septuagint. One of the resultant errors was his rejection of the explicit prophecy of Christ in Isaiah 7:14.[110] Du Plessis consistently applied his erroneous epistemology when he also opposed the first apartheid legislation implemented in 1913.

When a friend of Du Plessis, Rev. Meiring, became editor of *Die Kerkbode* in 1923, it once again gave Du Plessis a platform with which to propagate his ideas. One of Du Plessis's major opponents would turn out to be Dwight Snyman, who studied in the United States and was heavily influenced by J. Gresham Machen. Snyman accepted a call to a congregation in Stellenbosch in 1927, and in February 1928, he helped to formulate the official complaints against Du Plessis's heresies on behalf of the church curatorium. The heresies included the *Akkommodationstheorie* (i.e. the doctrine that Scripture's historical narratives can be erroneous) and an implicit denial of the divinity of Christ by overriding His claims regarding the historicity of the tale of Jonah (Matt. 12:40) and the Mosaic authorship of the Pentateuch (Mark 10:3-8). The synod found Du Plessis guilty, but the presbytery of Stellenbosch supported him and, unfortunately, so did the civil court when the matter was eventually taken up there. Du Plessis, however, was not to continue lecturing in Stellenbosch after 1930, but he had a loyal following among many students. His ideas sent the Dutch Reformed Church on an irreversible course.[111]

Higher criticism gradually took over the Dutch Reformed theological faculties in all of South Africa, which led to its eventual treason against the Boer people. Before getting there, however, it should first be noted that the denomination which mainly opposed higher criticism in South African theological circles, the Reformed Churches in South Africa, also officially announced its hatred for the Boer people in 1991, albeit through a different path. The Reformed Churches in South Africa followed Totius's Judeo-Christian pietism and the sociological errors of his tutor, Abraham Kuyper, and thus ended up committing the very same treason, officially announcing its support for South Africa's Marxist government at its 2006 synod.

By his application of higher criticism and consequent spurning of the historicity of the creation and fall of man, Du Plessis paved the way for the church's rejection of the doctrines of creation and original sin, a heresy that logically denies

---

[109] Olivier, AR. 2006. Die Lewe en Werk van Johannes Du Plessis – 'n Kort Oorsig. (lecture with the inauguration of the Du Plessis statue at the University of Stellenbosch)
[110] *Het Kerkblad*, December 20, 1915
[111] Olivier, AR. 2006. Die Lewe en Werk van Johannes Du Plessis – 'n Kort Oorsig. (lecture with the inauguration of the Du Plessis statue at the University of Stellenbosch)

the mediatorship of Christ and, in the long run, also enabled Marxism to take over the church. When I started my theological studies at the university as a nineteen-year-old in 2008, one of the first heresies I was taught was that the first eleven chapters of Genesis are mythological; and once these historical narratives, from the seven-day creation of man to the tower of Babel, were rejected as premises, the professors could basically sell any Marxist dream to the students. First and foremost, a historical Redeemer is not necessary to redeem man from a mythological fall, so the resurrection of Christ can be doubted—as can all the Old Testament prophecies of Him as the Messiah, since the first one (Gen. 3:15) is mythologized as well. This heresy, in turn, paves the way for Arianism and antinomianism, since it maintains a complete discontinuity between the two testaments. And furthermore, the cultural and revolutionary Marxism taught in the Belhar confession also rests almost solely on the rejection of the doctrines derived from the narratives of creation, the fall, and Babel (Acts 17:26-27), in favor of a narrative fostering white guilt. David Heleniak's observations regarding the Episcopal Church in the United States during the 60s are just as applicable to the Reformed Churches in South Africa in the 90s:

> [I]n the 60s, Nietzsche's death of God caught up to the Episcopalians who made up the American ruling class. They could no longer believe the old mythologies: Adam and Eve, original sin, blood atonement, all that medieval bs. But they couldn't give up the religion that they grew up in, with the community fellowship, the memories of church hayrides, etc. So they looked in the mirror and said: "What can I feel guilty about, now that I've rejected the reality of Adam's sin, so I can keep being a Christian. Aha. I'm white, male, and Christian. I will feel guilty for being white, male, and Christian."

This false confession of sin is what drives a great deal of the Reformed ecclesiastical world in South Africa, as it does in many other parts of the West. By accepting this confession, church leaders have openly declared their opposition to the real and personal edification and sanctification of the nations, which Christ commanded His church to accomplish (Matt. 28:19), and they stand opposed to any real progress to be made by the white race, to whom a particular task was endowed by God in having dominion over creation (Gen. 9:27).

And so the church has bowed the knee to both gender and racial egalitarianism, such that it is virtually impossible to become an ordained minister in the Dutch Reformed Church today without verbally embracing homosexuality, female ordination, and alienism. Today, following in the footsteps of its leaders from the early 90s, Heyns and Jonker, the family of Dutch Reformed Churches in South Africa are essentially unmatched in their prideful, presumptuous hatred for the white race in general and the Afrikaner people in particular. Recently, even the most conservative professor from my school's theological faculty apologized on behalf of the Afrikaner people for what happened at Bloedrivier and during apartheid—publicly humiliating the very people God has providentially entrusted to carry the gospel into Southern Africa for the sanctification of the peoples there for over 300 years. This is merely one of countless contemporary examples of how the church actively opposes not only Afrikanerdom, but, by shamelessly siding with Marxism, all of Christendom.

A few voices have been raised against the Marxism of the mainline Dutch Reformed Church, such as the formation of the Afrikaans Protestant Church in 1987, a church for conservative Afrikaners. No real, effective alternatives or praiseworthy polemics have been offered by the APC, unfortunately, which itself (though not nearly as bad as the DRC) has been greatly corrupted by the heresies of gospel-sanctification, radical two-kingdom theology, and biblical criticism. However, in another very recent—and positive—development, a number of congregations associated with a theologically conservative movement known as the *SteedsHervormers* (StillReformers) disaffiliated from the Dutch Reformed (*Hervormde*) Church, due to the denomination's theological liberalism and postmodernism. Yet, even though the authority of Scripture is rightly the primary reason for their secession, it remains to be seen whether they can rid themselves of all the distortions that accompany the amillenial eschatology which is so characteristic of the South African Reformed Churches in the Dutch tradition, such as the ridiculous yet common idea that it is wrong to "preach politics."

The Reformed Churches in South Africa are largely apostate, and, while some congregations are better than others and contain some true regenerates, it would make perfect sense for any Reformed, theonomic, Bible-believing Afrikaner not to attend an institutional church and submit his family to its church discipline. As it is a biblical command to regularly gather for worship and fellowship on the Lord's Day, however (I Cor. 16:1-2; Heb. 10:25), we cannot be content with merely practicing our religion within our respective private residences. The remnant must actively seek out one another and continually pray to God to raise up legitimate and godly ministers and elders, so that the true church might once again become visible among the Boer people of today—so that we, as a nation, may be sanctified to His glory and be a light unto the world.

Kinism in the Early Church

February 12, 2014

Introduction

An accusation which Christians advocating for the doctrine of ethnonationalism often face is that we have embraced modernism and evolutionary materialism. It is argued that "racism," the heresy of kinists (or Christian ethnonationalists), is a nineteenth-century development that emerged as the revolutionary Enlightenment infiltrated the West following the French Revolution. Alienist authors assert that the "spirit of racism" took hold of the West during the nineteenth and twentieth centuries. No matter the denomination, most conservative Christians today who claim to oppose the spirit of self-deification in modernism vehemently assail the biblical doctrine of ethnonationalism as heretical. My purpose with this piece is to show that this accusation is false and historically illiterate, as a belief in God-ordained racial realism, including the moral corollary that we ought to love our own people over foreigners, is present far earlier in church history.

Before any analysis of the traditional Christian position on this issue can proceed, it is vital to note that although the development of the nation-state in nineteenth-century Europe was partially a development of modernism, it was far more a reaction to Napoleonic imperialism than a continuation of the spirit of Rousseau and Voltaire. Furthermore, it is also true that some Darwinists are, to this day, race-realists, for any deep interest in the science of biological change will tend to bring evidence for racial distinctions to the fore. However, it cannot be overlooked that multiculturalism and Marxism are far more prevalent philosophies of modernism, to the extent that the race-realist camp within modernist circles forms a rather insignificant minority. In fact, it is clear that for modernism as a whole, the destruction of the family, tribe, guild, nation, and church is a primary objective; this should be evident to all students of philosophy. Another noteworthy historical factor is that prior to the era of European exploration and colonialism, Europeans had very little contact with other races, Jews and Turks being the rare exceptions. The context in which they found themselves, by implication, meant that the church has had little need to formulate a comprehensive, systematic understanding of the orthodox doctrine of race and nationhood prior to the twentieth and twenty-first centuries, just as the need to formulate the orthodox doctrine of grace did not arise until Augustine refuted Pelagius's heresies in the fifth century, and just as the doctrine of justification by faith alone was not articulated until the sixteenth century against Rome's grievous errors. Ironically, kinists today face similar opposition from mainstream Christianity as the first Protestant Reformers did from the Roman Catholic Church.

By analysing some of the kinist statements by the early church fathers, I intend to show that, although it is true that the doctrine of race and nationhood (rightly) received little attention in the early church, the church fathers aren't completely silent on the issue, which further proves that it is the traditionalist position.

The First Century

Arguably the strongest argument for kinist beliefs within the early church comes from the Acts of the Apostles, wherein Paul addresses our pagan ancestors in Athens and beautifully explains to them the value of the providential creation and preservation of the *ethne* for the glory of God (Acts 17:26-27). In the same apostle's letters to the first-century church, he explicitly expresses his love for his own kinsmen (Romans 9:3) and encourages Philemon to embrace Onesimus with the love that is due to kinsmen (Philemon 16). He also makes it clear that the naturalness of love towards one's own people or nation is so evident, that even depraved pagans know it to be good and normative (I Tim. 5:8).

Another text which "Christian" Marxists love to quote, Galatians 2:11-14, ironically further proves the reality of ethnonationalism in St. Paul's thought. While Peter tried to force Gentile Christians to integrate into Jewish culture and accept its customs in order to be accepted into the covenant, Paul counters that one does not have to surrender his ethnic identity to become a Christian, for Christianity effectuates the sanctification of nations (Matt. 28:19-20), not their destruction. That this was the view of the first-century church is also confirmed by the Christian Reconstructionist R.J. Rushdoony, whose historical analysis of the matter ought to be considered authoritative, particularly in light of the groundbreaking and thorough research he has done with regard to how the theological views of the early church laid the foundations for Western social order.[112]

Finally, the apostle John's apocalyptic visions, concluding the canon of special revelation during the first century, further prove that races and nations were received as a real and integral part of God's redemptive plan with creation. John witnessed a multitude of peoples whose ethnic and racial identity was to subsist eternally (Rev. 7:9), thereby showing their importance within God's design.

---

[112] Rushdoony, R.J. *Foundations of Social Order: Studies in the Creeds and Councils of the Early Church.* 1 Apr 1998.

Tertullian (A.D. 160 – 225)

The church father Tertullian in his *Ad Nationes* responds to a number of miscellaneous objections that had been made against Christians. Included among these objections is the contention from a man named Psammetichus that Christians are to be denigrated as a *tertium genus* (third race), evidently some sort of degenerated group of men. Included in Psammetichus's cavil is the story of how he determined the first race of men to be Phrygians: a number of infants were removed from all human society except to be raised by a nurse whose tongue had been surgically removed, so that their language would form purely from nature and not from any learning; Psammetichus then reasoned that the language to naturally emerge among the infants would be the language of the first race of men, and since the infants (it is alleged) spoke of *Bekkos* (Phrygian for "bread"), Psammetichus concluded that the Phrygians were the first race. Tertullian responds:

> *We are indeed said to be the "third race" of men. What, a dog-faced race? Or broadly shadow-footed? Or some subterranean Antipodes? If you attach any meaning to these names, pray tell us what are the first and the second race, that so we may know something of this "third."... Granted, then, that the Phrygians were the earliest race, it does not follow that the Christians are the third. For how many other nations come regularly after the Phrygians? Take care, however, lest those whom you call the third race should obtain the first rank, since there is no nation indeed which is not Christian. Whatever nation, therefore, was the first, is nevertheless Christian now. It is ridiculous folly which makes you say we are the latest race, and then specifically call us the third. But it is in respect of our religion, not of our nation, that we are supposed to be the third; the series being the Romans, the Jews, and the Christians after them.*[113]

The crucial element of Tertullian's quote here is his contention that all nations can (and presumably will) become Christian, as Christianity is fundamentally a religious category, not a racial one. This requires a clear distinction between the material and the spiritual, a conception that national identity is not removed but maintained and sanctified by conversion. Tertullian had a concept of race or nation as something distinct from religion yet narrower than humanity. Hence Rev. McAtee notes:

> *Tertullian sees race and nationhood as something physical rather than spiritual, thus he mentions the corporeal appellations like "dog-faced," and "shadow-footed" to describe different races. Tertullian also clearly connects the concepts*

---

[113] Tertullian, *Ad Nationes*, Book 1, Chapter 8.

of race and nationhood contra the alienist idea of propositional nationhood. . . . To insist that the Christian is a race, Tertullian seems to be telling us, is to slip into Gnostic categories. Christians are not a race but a religion and when races convert to Christianity, as they all will someday do, this will not negate the races or nations they already belong to. It will simply cause those races and nations to glorify God as one body with many parts glorifies God.

Cyprian (A.D. 200–258)

In a previous post, I already touched on Cyprian's use of race as a theological analogy.[114] Yet we can go even further in-depth. In St. Cyprian's tenth treatise, entitled *On Jealousy and Envy*, he argues that "nothing should be more guarded against by the Christian, nothing more carefully watched, than being taken captive by envy and malice, that none, entangled in the blind snares of a deceitful enemy, in that the brother is turned by envy to hatred of his brother, should himself be unwittingly destroyed by his own sword" (par. 3). He continues to describe jealousy as "the root of all evils, the fountain of disasters, the nursery of crimes, the material of transgressions" (par. 6). After explaining from various examples and commands from Scripture that Christians are to fight against all forms of envy, Cyprian goes on to admonish Christians to live Spirit-led lives and thereby "bear the image of Him who is in heaven" (par. 14). In paragraph 15, he continues to say that this change of heart should occur in Christians so that "the divine birth can shine forth" in us. Cyprian then makes the statement relevant for the current study:

> *If it is a source of joy and glory to men to have children like unto themselves — and it is more agreeable to have begotten an offspring then when the remaining progeny responds to the parent with like lineaments — how much greater is the gladness of God the Father, when any one is so spiritually born that in his acts and praises the divine eminence of race [genus] is announced!*[115]

As alienists are prone to misconstrue kinism to be some self-evidently false hatred of others for having the wrong skin color, this quotation merits a fuller explanation. When Cyprian here argues that men glory in having physically and behaviorally similar children — that such is more "agreeable" — he is not simply stating a matter of near-universal human preference, as if the joy which we take in our offspring's similitude was as subjective as a preferred flavor of ice cream. Instead,

---

[114] Serry, Gic. "Making a Virtue out of Envy: How "Christian" Marxism Destroys Orthodoxy." 3 Sept 2013. https://faithandheritage.com/2013/09/making-a-virtue-out-of-envy-how-christian-marxism-destroys-orthodoxy/
[115] *The Treatises of Cyprian*, p 1012.

Cyprian's argument presupposes that it is *proper* and *fitting* for men to take such joy, and hence that it is *improper* and *unfitting* for men to neglect the value of lineal similitude or, worse, to positively value dissimilitude. This joy in similitude is proper and fitting in the same way that God properly takes joy in His children's Spirit-led love, free of jealousy and envy. The entire force of this statement depends on the fact that we *ought* to value children who are similar to us, not merely behaviorally but also physically.

Hence, though it is here in seed form, Cyprian is nevertheless articulating a crucial element of God's social design of man: that we are designed to have children with people who look like us and act like us, and hence that we are to marry and live among people who look like us and act like us, including all the inarticulable and perspectival subtleties which are so integral to calling a people "our own." This principle, in other words, is ethnonationalist, even if only incipiently. Cyprian's purpose with this passage is to use the reality and value of race and the joy to be found in racial contentment as an analogy for explaining how God finds joy in remaking us in His image through His Spirit.

Peter of Alexandria (A.D. c. 200s – 311)

In his *Canonical Epistle*, Peter describes evil with reference to black skin, showing a connection in his mind between that race of men and evil in general:

> *To those who are altogether reprobate, and unrepentant, who possess the Ethiopian's unchanging skin, and the leopard's spots, it shall be said, as it was spoken to another fig-tree, "Let no fruit grow on you henceforward for ever; and it presently withered away." [Matthew 21:19] For in them is fulfilled what was spoken by the Preacher: That which is crooked cannot be made straight; and that which is wanting cannot be numbered. [Ecclesiastes 1:15] For unless that which is crooked shall first be made straight, it is impossible for it to be adorned; and unless that which is wanting shall first be made up, it cannot be numbered. . . . Against those whom, from desperation or depraved opinion, are impenitent, and carry about with them perpetually the inherent and indelible blackness of sin, as of an Ethiopian's skin, or the leopard's spots, he brings forward the cursing of another fig-tree.*[116]

It is of course proper to note that Peter does not speak of blacks as themselves evil; he merely describes their black skin as some sort of symbol of evil. Yet that very connection is far, far from what any modern alienist would dare to do: assert that racial distinctions can themselves carry moral-symbolic meaning, whiteness being

---
[116] Peter of Alexandria, *Canonical Epistle*, canon 4.

associated with moral purity and blackness with moral evil. Furthermore, it would be unreasonable to surmise that Peter would make this connection without believing there is any peculiar moral deficiency with the black race as such.

Gregory of Nazianzus (A.D. c. 329 – 389)

As with Peter, Gregory of Nazianzus likewise sees the black man as a symbol of moral evil. In an oration on baptism, he applies this symbolism to the narrative of the Ethiopian eunuch in Acts:

> *Do you also say, "See, here is water, what does hinder me to be baptized?" Seize the opportunity; rejoice greatly in the blessing; and having spoken be baptized; and having been baptized be saved; and though you be an Ethiopian body, be made white in soul.*[117]

Jerome (A.D. 347 – 420)

Jerome, in his *Against Helvidius*, writes a reply to Helvidius's assertion that Mary did not perpetually remain a virgin. As Helvidius argues that Scripture speaks of "brothers" of Jesus, implying that Mary was no longer a virgin after giving birth to Jesus, Jerome counters by specifying the different way in which that term can be taken. Hence in paragraph 16, we see Jerome giving a definition of "brethren" which affirms the kinist doctrine of race and nationhood:

> *How then, says Helvidius, do you make out that they were called the Lord's brethren who were not his brethren? I will show how that is. In Holy Scripture there are four kinds of brethren — by nature, race, kindred, love. . . . As to race, all Jews are called brethren of one another, as in Deuteronomy, Deuteronomy 15:12: "If your brother, an Hebrew man, or an Hebrew woman, be sold unto you, and serve you six years; then in the seventh year you shall let him go free from you." And in the same book, Deuteronomy 17:15: "You shall in anywise set him king over you, whom the Lord your God shall choose: one from among your brethren shall you set king over you; you may not put a foreigner over you, which is not your brother." And again, Deuteronomy 22:1: "You shall not see your brother's ox or his sheep go astray, and hide yourself from them: you shall surely bring them again unto your brother. And if your brother be not near unto you, or if you know him not, then you shall bring it home to your house, and it shall be with you until your brother seek after it, and you shall restore it to him again."*

---

[117] Gregory of Nazianzus, Oration 40, paragraph XXVI.

And the Apostle Paul says, Romans 9:3-4: "I could wish that I myself were anathema from Christ for my brethren's sake, my kinsmen according to the flesh: who are Israelites." Moreover they are called brethren by kindred who are of one family, that is πατρία, which corresponds to the Latin paternitas, because from a single root a numerous progeny proceeds. In Genesis 13:8, 11 we read: "And Abram said unto Lot, Let there be no strife, I pray you, between me and you, and between my herdmen and your herdmen; for we are brethren. And again, So Lot chose him all the plain of Jordan, and Lot journeyed east: and they separated each from his brother." Certainly Lot was not Abraham's brother, but the son of Abraham's brother Aram. For Terah begot Abraham and Nahor and Aram: and Aram begot Lot. Again we read, Genesis 12:4: "And Abram was seventy and five years old when he departed out of Haran. And Abram took Sarai his wife, and Lot his brother's son." But if you still doubt whether a nephew can be called a son, let me give you an instance. Genesis 14:14: "And when Abram heard that his brother was taken captive, he led forth his trained men, born in his house, three hundred and eighteen." And after describing the night attack and the slaughter, he adds: "And he brought back all the goods, and also brought again his brother Lot." Let this suffice by way of proof of my assertion.[118]

I should note that whereas I do not agree with Jerome's arguments for Mary's perpetual virginity (despite its being upheld by Roman Catholic, Eastern Orthodox, and even Protestant leaders), nevertheless his argumentation for the biblical support of racial brotherhood is very much orthodox. While alienists may not have an issue with the use of the word "brother" to denote membership in an extended family (such as Lot and Abraham), it is but a natural extension of this same principle to say that national and racial kinsmen are likewise "brothers": that they are part of a real, hereditary, biological grouping, and that it is fitting to assign moral duties of nearness unto these groupings—that we ought to love our kinsmen with a higher love than foreigners. If one wishes to quibble that Jerome does not specifically use the word "race" to refer to the continental racial classifications of today—white, black, oriental, etc.—it still stands true that the principle he cites would apply to such categories as well. Jerome therefore—once again, implicitly—provides support for ethnonationalism.

Augustine (A.D. 354–430)

Augustine writes in his sixteenth book of *The City of God* on the progress of the two cities in the period from Noah to Abraham. In the second chapter, he

---

[118] Jerome, *Against Helvidius*, paragraph 16.

writes the following concerning what was prophetically prefigured in the sons of Noah:

> *Shem, of whom Christ was born in the flesh, means "named." And what is of greater name than Christ, the fragrance of whose name is now everywhere perceived, so that even prophecy sings of it beforehand, comparing it in the Song of Songs [1:3] to ointment poured forth? Is it not also in the houses of Christ, that is, in the churches, that the "enlargement" of the nations dwells? For Japheth means "enlargement." And Ham (i.e., hot), who was the middle son of Noah, and, as it were, separated himself from both, and remained between them, neither belonging to the first-fruits of Israel nor to the fullness of the Gentiles, what does he signify but the tribe of heretics, hot with the spirit, not of patience, but of impatience, with which the breasts of heretics are wont to blaze, and with which they disturb the peace of the saints? But even the heretics yield an advantage to those that make proficiency, according to the apostle's saying, "There must also be heresies, that they which are approved may be made manifest among you." [1 Corinthians 11:19] Whence, too, it is elsewhere said, "The son that receives instruction will be wise, and he uses the foolish as his servant." For while the hot restlessness of heretics stirs questions about many articles of the Catholic faith, the necessity of defending them forces us both to investigate them more accurately, to understand them more clearly, and to proclaim them more earnestly; and the question mooted by an adversary becomes the occasion of instruction. However, not only those who are openly separated from the church, but also all who glory in the Christian name, and at the same time lead abandoned lives, may without absurdity seem to be figured by Noah's middle son: for the passion of Christ, which was signified by that man's nakedness, is at once proclaimed by their profession, and dishonored by their wicked conduct. Of such, therefore, it has been said, "By their fruits you shall know them." [Matthew 7:20] And therefore was Ham cursed in his son, he being, as it were, his fruit. So, too, this son of his, Canaan, is fitly interpreted "their movement," which is nothing else than their work. But Shem and Japheth, that is to say, the circumcision and uncircumcision, or, as the apostle otherwise calls them, the Jews and Greeks, but called and justified, having somehow discovered the nakedness of their father (which signifies the Saviour's passion), took a garment and laid it upon their backs, and entered backwards and covered their father's nakedness, without their seeing what their reverence hid. For we both honor the passion of Christ as accomplished for us, and we hate the crime of the Jews who crucified Him. The garment signifies the sacrament, their backs the memory of things past: for the church celebrates the passion of Christ as already accomplished, and no longer to be looked forward to, now that Japheth already dwells in the habitations of Shem, and their wicked brother between them.*

This great church father is here referring not simply to spiritual distinctions within mankind (followers of Christ versus heretics), but to physical races descending from the three sons of Noah. Only those blinded by Gnosticism would deny the physical dimension of the prophetical prefiguration as explained by Augustine. The Semitic race, as an *ethnos* in the form of ancient Israel, was reformed and their fallen nature restored so that they would be the carriers of the Old Covenant. Likewise in the New Covenant, by the spreading of the gospel to the white race and its consequent sanctification, Augustine explains, the prophecy concerning Japheth was fulfilled. It is therefore clear that among the real and valuable physical objects in which the Holy Spirit infuses grace, race is one such feature, along with individuals, couples, families, ethnicities, and countries.

Moreover, besides the basic fact that Augustine sees physical races as real categories having redemptive-historical significance, it is important to note how he sees the Noahic prophecy of Genesis 9 as teaching the primacy of the Japhethites (i.e. Europeans) in being the New Covenant standard-bearers of Christ, following the Shemites (including the Israelites) as the Old Covenant standard-bearers. All the while, Augustine deems the Hamites (most specifically including blacks) as mostly wicked heretics who hardly partake of this prophesied blessing. This is not a small detail, as the view that blacks are plagued by "the curse of Ham" is quite prominent throughout church history, so much so that this theory is automatically dismissed today as a racist conjecture.

This generally low view of Africans can also be confirmed in another statement he makes elsewhere. Commenting on the wide, universal reaches of God's grace through His church as prophesied in Psalm 72, Augustine says:

> [T]he Catholic Church has been foretold, not as to be in any particular quarter of the world, as certain schisms are, but in the whole universe by bearing fruit and growing so as to attain even unto the very Ethiopians, to wit, the remotest and foulest of mankind.[119]

Though we do not have a desire to mock blacks, it is nonetheless appropriate to have a sober look into the truth of Africans' historic behavior, including the assessment which our fathers have made of their behavior and seen fit to publish. Augustine generally agrees with our conclusion that Africans are innately more prone to various evils, on which grounds he deems Ethiopians "the remotest and foulest of mankind."[120]

---

[119] Augustine, "Exposition on Psalm 72."
[120] Again, it is important to emphasize that the moral differences among the races, and particularly between blacks and nonblacks, should not give any a pretense for hatred or cruelty. African savagery should, in addition to inspiring righteous anger in certain circumstances, also evoke our pity when we consider their deplorable condition. Yet none of this ever justifies glossing over these differences, as if it were too "mean" to even mention that blacks have certain moral problems as a race.

Proper Inferences

The temptation of the skeptic is, no doubt, to see these quotes as underdeterminative—to believe that we kinists are latching onto a handful of random quotes and proceeding to eisegete our own principles into the text. However, as this is precisely the same misinterpretation which alienists make of R.J. Rushdoony's kinism, it would be appropriate for us to articulate some of the differences between kinism and alienism, that the patristic support for kinism can be duly clarified.

As Nil Desperandum points out in the above post about Rushdoony, kinism is essentially the Christian belief in race and its importance. Kinism is *not* simply a belief in the intrinsic sinfulness of interracial marriage, as if the debate over whether miscegenation is unwise or sinful constituted the entire issue. Consequently, alienism is the ideology of those who deny the reality of race, who believe that race is a social construct, who hold that Galatians 3:28 proves the biological equality of all races, who (claiming to follow 1 Peter 2:9) contend for the removal of all national boundaries to establish a one-world Christian empire, and who accuse you of denying the image of God in nonwhites if you declare them to be different.[121] Anti-kinists, in other words, are not people who grant the reality of race, understand the prerogative of fathers to forbid their daughters to miscegenate, and see the importance of acting off racial considerations when, say, choosing where to live, but then deny that miscegenation is a sin. Those are not anti-kinists at all, as they would actually agree with us on the fundamentals. Hence, the purpose of the foregoing quotes is not to prove the historic backing of the very specific strong-kinist claim that interracial marriage is intrinsically sinful (a point we only expect to be discussed more recently in history), but to show in a general and broad way that the early church fathers believed in the existence of ethnonational and racial distinctions and saw them, in some sense, as significant—that they did not flatly deny all such distinctions, as alienists do. The fact that the fathers' quotations might seem very ordinary (e.g. Jerome's appeal to the fact that all ethnic Israelites were, in some sense, brothers) does not establish that the quotes are underdeterminative, but only underscores the fact that kinism is a very normal and commonsense doctrine.

This becomes even more evident when we apprehend how modern alienists would respond to quotes like this. Imagine if a white American said that other white Americans are his brothers, but not nonwhites, which is one reason (among many) why Barack Obama ought not to be president. This is a straightforward application of the ethnic brotherhood of the biblical Israelites, yet it would beckon

---

[121] This is made especially clear when we see Joe Morecraft preaching in a recent sermon that kinism evilly denies that nonwhites bear the image of God, much to the applause of conservative Protestants everywhere. That such a momentously slanderous argument would be convincing to so many "conservatives" indicates that these are truly their racial beliefs.

cries of racism and blasphemy from even the most conservative wings of the visible church. Similarly, imagine what screams of anguish would emanate from alienists today if any dared to say that children ought to physically resemble their parents! The modern church today either attributes zero value to ethnically homogeneous marriages or positively values miscegenous unions, and it would not take long for them to catch the scent of racism if anyone were heard promoting Cyprian's principle of lineal similitude. Again, if any were to speak of blacks as cursed in some sense or evil, or if any were to use black skin as a symbol for sin, the totality of the egalitarian "church's" wrath would be poured upon that individual, excommunicating him for his unconscionable racism. This should make it all the more obvious that the early church tacitly supported the views which we explicitly advocate.

Conclusion

The above quotes from the early church deal with the concepts of race and ethnonationalism at a time when those concepts were not centrally challenged by contemporary unbelief. Consequently it needs to be mentioned once again that, considering their context, no need arose in their time to form a comprehensive and explicit doctrine concerning this issue. Nonetheless, it was presupposed throughout as a tacit and generally accepted set of principles. Indeed, this becomes more evident when we consider how, once these issues were explicitly pressed by the unbelieving zeitgeist in the past few centuries, it was the conservative Christians who monolithically upheld our views and the liberals and unbelievers who opposed them. The explicit racialism of the church in recent times attests to the implicit racial views our fathers held prior to that point.

Thus it becomes clear that the kinist position is not only the biblical one, but also confirmed by its historical reception in the church throughout the centuries. Building upon these foundational proclamations of the early church concerning the role of race and nationhood in the Christian worldview, later Christian theologians like Thomas Aquinas, Martin Luther, Robert Lewis Dabney, Geerhardus Vos, and Rousas John Rushdoony could further develop this important doctrine. We at *Faith and Heritage* seek to stand in continuation of this tradition in the twenty-first century, as it is indeed due time for the church of Christ to proclaim and systematically set out the orthodox doctrine of race and nationhood clearly and unambiguously.

The Ethnoconfessional Nature of Culture

July 2, 2018

It is ironic that we use the term Cultural Marxism to describe the enemies of the cause of Western Christendom. These people, are of course, fundamentally antagonistic towards culture—that is, culture, traditionally understood. Much like neo-orthodoxy strategically redefines theological concepts to mean often nearly the exact opposite of what they traditionally did, neo-Marxism's redefinition of concepts like 'culture' serves a similar strategic purpose in the broader aim of destroying all traditional culture. The word itself is derived from the Latin passive participle of *colo*, namely *cultus*. The stem-word literally means to nurture or cultivate, but in a figurative sense denotes worship or honor. *Cultus*, strictly speaking, is therefore something that has been cultivated and/or worshiped.

'Culture' therefore denotes both something physical and spiritual, something natural and something religious. If applied to the human species, the most natural physical bond is the family and by extension the tribe, i.e. the *ethnos*, while any spiritual-religious manifestation in society comes about through this tribe's public confession of a belief or belief-system. Hence, the ethnoconfessional (or ethnoreligious) character of any culture.

The ethnoconfessional nature of culture is presupposed throughout the Bible. The Israelites are warned time and time again that mixed marriages with other nations would have serious religious repercussions. The intrinsic ethnic and racial dimension of covenantal religiosity was widely understood in ancient times prior to the ideological inroads made by modern globalism.

The critical reader would respond that ancient civilizations were indeed characterized by an ethnoconfessionally shaped culture, but modern civilization has advanced beyond this paradigm. In this regard it is interesting to note that narratives of secularization that proponents of globalism have historically used in justification for their endeavours, are, even in liberal academia, increasingly being challenged.[122]

It is increasingly being recognized that the public confession of a belief-system is an inescapable part of every functioning society. The term *de-confessionalization* is

---

[122] Harrison, Peter. "Narratives of Secularization." *Taylor & Francis*, 16 Jan. 2017, www.tandfonline.com/doi/abs/10.1080/17496977.2016.1255463.

therefore increasingly preferred over secularization. But even here, it must be recognized that any process of *de-confessionalization* is simultaneously a process of *re-confessionalization*, since the public domain is never a vacuum.

In this regard it is interesting to note the thoughts of professor Robert Faurisson from the University of Lyon in France with regard to public confession of Western society post-WWII:

> *The Six Million constitute a lay religion with its own dogma, commandments, decrees, prophets, high priests and Saints: Saint Anne (Frank), Saint Simon (Wiesenthal), Saint Elie (Wiesel). It has its holy places, its rituals and its pilgrimages. It has its temples and its relics (bars of soap, piles of shoes, etc.), its martyrs, heroes, miracles and miraculous survivors (millions of them), its golden legend and its righteous people. Auschwitz is its Golgotha, Hitler is its Satan. It dictates its law to the nations. Its heart beats in Jerusalem, at the Yad Veshem monument. . . .*
>
> *Although it is largely an avatar of the Hebraic religion, the new religion is quite recent and has exhibited meteoric growth. . . .*
>
> *Paradoxically, the only religion to prosper today is the "Holocaust" religion, ruling, so to speak, supreme and having those sceptics who are openly active cast out from the rest of mankind: it labels them "deniers", whilst they call themselves "revisionists."*[123]

For all the liberal talk of pluralism, Christianity in the West has simply been replaced by another religion. What is interesting about this new religion or *cultus*, however, is its unique stance against the physical dimension of culture, which, seen as a threat, it seeks to absorb and collapse into the spiritual.

Historically, Christianity did not see cultural diversity as a threat. Christianity never sought the complete destruction of the local culture, but the sanctification of it by the application of the truth of the gospel. Marxism, however, has always seen the spiritual and physical as antithetical, thereby failing to grasp or constructively contribute to the cultural development of any nation. Culture itself is such a threat to its agenda, that some Marxist university professors nowadays even claim that the very notion of culture itself is a myth. When, however, any culture expresses itself in a unique way, this is decried as racism—thereby neutralizing opponents of their theory of culture, strategically depriving them of the right of using concrete examples against this silly notion.

Even despite this assault, cultural differences remain evident throughout the world, including the West. The failure of multiculturalism everywhere proves this fact—the ethnoconfessional structure of culture remains inevitably present.

---

[123] Faurisson, Robert. "The secular religion of "the Holocaust", a tainted product of consumer society." 31 July 2008. http://www.zundelsite.org/assets/080907_secular.html.

Effectively engaging in the culture war in the public domain requires the Christian, especially in such dire times, to explicitly advocate for this ethnoconfessional nature of culture. Strategically, the culture war can also only be fought along ethnoconfessional lines, as Scripture and reality testify.

This does not exclude the necessity of alliances between Christians across racial and denominational lines, but an integral part of reshaping Western culture as an ethnoconfessional macro unit is the (institutional) cultivation of micro-identities such as, e.g., White Anglo-Saxon Protestantism or Southern Presbyterianism. These "kin, kith, and kirk" allegiances formed the solid basis through which our civilization was kept intact for centuries. These roots need to be nurtured if the tree is to flourish.

Ehud Would

Ehud Would is a Conservative Presbyterian of Scandian-Germano-Celtic background and a refugee from the reconquista state of Southern California, who having recently followed the Northwest Imperative, resettled his family in Coeur d'Alene, Idaho where he pursues writing, illustration, medical administration, and presides as an elected official.

Alienism: Bramble Path to Oblivion

March 14, 2012

The Reverend Bret McAtee has written of Alienism's dualistic Marxian-Gnostic ideology:

So, we have two opposite extremes kissing. It is the mirror phenomenon of ancient Gnosticism where you had the same worldview shared by people who were two opposite extremes.

In a brass-tacks sense, Alienism espouses the distinctly Marxian principle of leveling in its demand of absolute material/social equality; the Alienist brashly denounces any and all distinctions racial, national, ethnic, and even familial. And from this vantage point, the Alienist mounts his argument for the abolition of distinction on the material unity of mankind's descent from the first man, Adam.

But, despite their materialistic rhetoric and conclusions, Alienists deny any alliance with Marxism, specifically on the grounds of Marxism's ultimate and inescapable belief in materialism (atheism). Strange, I know.

This is where Gnosticism comes in: they argue that material and social leveling are a Christian mandate precisely because of the supremacy of things spiritual over things physical. Since men of all sorts may enjoy a unity of spiritual identity as citizens of Christ's Kingdom, all other distinctions are unimportant, imaginary, and/or outright impediments to Christendom—so they allege. Thus, they justify their Marxian materialism upon their premise of Gnosticism, an infamously anti-materialist view of reality.

This fusion of two antithetical ideologies in Alienism represents a truly irreconcilable tension. Laying aside for a moment the heterodoxy of their Gnostic presuppositions, their contending for materialism on anti-materialistic premises requires an absolute embracing of irrationalism. They see themselves not so much as servants under the universal dominion of the King, but as actors with God in an irrationally divided multiverse where the denigration and abolition of the material is essential to the realization of a coming homogenized universe, comprised purely, it would seem, of indistinguishable glorified souls. Our fathers pegged these Gnostic utopians with the French term *Deracines*, which is indeed the only title these individuals seem to respect—a testament to their own deracinated abandonment of the created world. Theirs is a variant of postmillennialism which, in spite of its claims to the contrary, knows nothing of Calvinism. Realize: they insist that material and social leveling is indispensably important—because material and social distinctions are completely unimportant. As they tell it, God created the distinctions amongst men in order to forbid any acknowledgement of them, and in time to purge them utterly, and banish to hell any who dares remember. There is, according to the Alienist, more than a hint of "Fake It Till You Make It-ism" in the divine mind, and the god of Alienism openly enjoins his followers to lie, deceive, and obscure in all matters pertaining to the clear distinctions of the created order. All of this underlies their insistence that, while on one hand, race does not exist, on the other, the White race must perish from the earth. Worse still, they inexplicably insist that the former actually justifies the latter. In their eyes, our (declared) non-existence necessitates our destruction. The Christian religion for them becomes little else than one big square circle—inherently illogical. It is a knowing embrace of irrationality as the highest good. Once the ultimate grounds of reality prove self-contradictory, truth itself becomes fallacy. The Faith once for all delivered to the Saints cannot truly be understood by anyone, because it has been declared by its own priests to be unintelligible. This is the heart of Christian* Alienism: irrationalism is its precondition.

But if Christianity, which is the study of reality itself, be unintelligible, then coherence is rendered not only imaginary, but heretical. Indeed, madness abhors understanding.

By this necessary movement from the dualism of Marxian Gnosticism through irrationalism, Alienism must, due to its inescapable commitment to incoherence, eventually find full expression in solipsism, which is the pure skepticism of intelligibility. The more consistent they become, the faster they will march down the bramble road to oblivion. But along that well-worn trail, they will shuffle in the company of many fellow travelers—pietists, radical two-kingdomists, Cathars, and docetists. They all trudge the same bleak path, because they share the same presuppositions. It is the orthodoxy of the mad.

When we say that they are passing into madness, it is no tongue-in-cheek *ad hominem*, but rather the unavoidable appraisal of their actual worldview. We can see the full expression of that destination in them even now: if one asks them to justify their ideology in light of Scripture and historic Christianity, then one is met with little else than mockery, threats of censure and violence, slander, and phone calls in the night to intimidate our employers into divesting us of our livelihoods, earthly possessions, and the means to raise our families. Certain Reformed writers have even publicly called for us traditionalists to be killed! Resorting to every expression of arbitrary power, they avoid explanation, discussion, and debate at all costs. They truly seem to feel no compulsion whatsoever to justify their position, let alone their Red Guard tactics, because their position, by its very nature, rejects internal coherence; and all that remains is arbitrary force to impose the whim of their personal ideology. Given their preferences, it seems that if they achieved their ambitions of social hegemony, they would follow the Marxian prerogative faithfully by genociding us outright, just as the Soviets did the Kulaks.

The rare instances in which they have ventured into dialogue with us are littered with statements like, "Your facts are irrelevant!", "Statistics and history are meaningless!", "I don't care what Christians have always believed!", "I don't care how that text has been understood by the Reformers and the Church Fathers!", "Your love of family proves that you are a Pagan!", "Since you're a racist anything you have to say is irrelevant!", "The text can't mean what you say it means because you're a racist!", and more of the like. Of course, these exchanges do not really represent dialogues in the sense of actual conversation, because the Alienist seems entirely uninterested in true interaction with any subject at issue, only in issuing wicked judgments on us. Condemning us to hell for daring to ask for biblical validation of their incoherent dogmas, they simply dismiss our arguments without consideration. Even Alienism's most charitable moments amount to a "will to power" for their irrational worldview.

The White Alienist feels no compulsion to justify his beliefs in absolute equality and fraternity with the brutish members of humanity, and even less so to justify his inverse denial of special relation with and duty to the children of his own people. And therein he spurns the prime lesson Burke succinctly drew from the French Revolution, namely, that equality destroys fraternity. "If every man be my brother, I have no brothers." If, through such leveling, a man is divested of the conception of near kinship, he has lost the very foundation needed to speak of the Alien as his brother as well. Truly, straining out the gnat, he swallows the camel.

The modern resolve to suppress the truths of natural hierarchy, clearly revealed racial, ethnic, and familial distinctions, and their proximate and limited obligations is an absolute declaration of ontological rebellion and the clear rejection of teleology. For the Alienist, providence is a slur, and design a hate crime. Understand: their doctrine demands absolute skepticism towards all intelligibility. Or, as Richard Weaver stated it:

> With ignorance virtually institutionalized, how can we get man to see? Bewildered by his curious alienation from reality, he is unable to prescribe for himself, for he imagines that what he needs is more of the disease. . . . Thus present day reformers combat dilution by diluting further, dispersion by a more vigorous dispersing. . . . The modern world is calling for madder music and for stronger wine, is craving some delirium which will take it completely away from reality.[124]

They revile the testimony of their own eyes. They scoff at hermeneutics as a construct of men. They sneer at logic for its carnal mediation. And on these same bases, they distrust the Scripture wherever it presupposes Kinism, which is virtually

---

[124] Weaver, Richard M. *Ideas Have Consequences*. 1948. p.184-185.

everywhere. While they cite their Christian* faith as justification for their skepticism, that skepticism fatally undermines that justification, as well as their means of knowing it or interacting with it in any way. Once committed to the notion that creation is illusion, and in the same measure evil for its lie, all certitude is forfeited.

This complete disregard for facts, dismissal of reality, and disavowal of logic itself which we have and are continuing to witness in the modern churches is Alienist solipsism congealing before our very eyes. The Orthodoxy of the Mad is coming into its own.

Kinism: The Only Theonomy

June 20, 2012

"We have now sunk to a depth at which restatement of the obvious is the first duty of intelligent men."
—George Orwell

Kinism is a term of admittedly recent manufacture, but the principles thereof have been with mankind from the beginning. The same continuum of concept has alternately been called familism, tribal theocracy, theonomic nationalism, or simply, traditional Christianity. For Kinism's antique pedigree as the orthodox Christian social order is attested to in the warp and woof of the writings of all the greatest thinkers in Church history—often explicitly, if briefly, and implicitly everywhere else.

Of course, the neo-churchmen (alienists) reject all of this out of hand, insisting that if Kinism were the true Christian social order, it would have found its way overtly into all of the creeds, confessions, and rulings of the councils—which is simply to say that they ignore the actual character of creedalism as it has expressed itself in time: as predominantly a consortium of reactionary rulings. Confessions have always arose in response to errors of their age. They define the Christian faith always so as to distinguish biblical orthodoxy from the vacillations of the zeitgeist.

But, as with subjects such as pedophilia or so-called "gay marriage," dedicated apologetics contra miscegenation, racial and social egalitarianism, or borderless one-worldism were not deemed as needing to be addressed simply because none could foresee a day in which churches would en masse begin promoting such moral aberrations. The fathers of the Faith simply could not think like our neo-churchmen, who now use every scriptural passage overtly communicating the reality of meaningful distinctions among genders, peoples, and classes as an occasion to excoriate as bigots and heretics any who might yet dare accept the perspicuous meaning of the text as our forebears did. Remember, if St. Paul says that "all Cretans are liars, evil beasts and lazy gluttons," or if Isaiah says that Hammites are "a people terrible from their beginning onward," you are worse than all of those things for accepting as meaningful their scathing critiques of ethnic groups as such. If a Christian dared speak like Paul or Isaiah today, he would be met with excommunication, loss of livelihood, and possible imprisonment.

As has been conclusively argued by many before this writer, racism, like sexism, homophobia, xenophobia, provincialism, and political incorrectness in general, is a fictitious sin very recently minted in the fires of cultural Marxism (which was merely a weaponization of earlier Jacobin principles), outlining a replacement for Christian penology, and thereby (and to that end) a counterfeit ethical system meant to supplant Christendom. In fact, each one of these "new sins" corresponds precisely to a previously cherished Christian virtue. Racism, for example, used to be known as patriotism, a love of the patria—an honoring of one's fathers and identification with their descendants.

And thus, by the necessity of distinguishing the historic Faith from the genderless, classless, raceless, and borderless religion masquerading as Christianity today, arises the reactionary doctrine of Kinism. It represents nothing new, only a reassertion of orthodox Christian penology, sociology, and axiology as they were accepted by virtually every saint passed on, and thus opposed venomously by every antichrist living today.

But the most recent phase of the cultural Marxist revolution is particularly galling: many of those claiming to be theonomists today have suddenly begun defining their postmillennial ambitions in these same unmistakably utopian terms and according to Marxian ideals propagated by the antichrist Left. This ain't your granddad's cultural mandate; that's for sure.

Of course, theirs is a truly impossible vision of theonomy, because God's Law presupposes the very thing which they claim it to prohibit—identity, age, gender, class, region, affiliation, family, culture, nation, and race—all necessary distinctions in God's Law, without which the Law cannot function or essentially even exist. If we prohibit the acknowledgement of the differentiable existence of things such as neighbors, fathers, mothers, foreigners, lineal inheritance, and others, the Law is rendered unintelligible. All must recognize that as much as the first table of the Ten Commandments assumes vertical separation and distinction between Creator and creature, so does the second table assume distinctions laterally between men. Even speaking of the first as distinct from the second, and seeing that both were entrusted to the esteemed prophet, Moses, we see this metaphysical necessity of identity impose itself upon us. More than lawful, such distinctions are lawfully necessary. Aside from these hierarchical, relational, and axiological distinctions between men and things, there can be no duties one toward another, as all would exist on an eternally zero balance, without variation; a society without debt or due is a society without charity or grace—a society without interrelation. An anti-society.

Distinctions are an indispensable precondition to theonomy. And to prohibit needful distinctions is to violate the Law which depends upon their existence.

Discrimination is seen then as a hallowed duty under every jot and tittle of God's Law, aside from which all jurisprudence in every sphere is relegated to fantasy. If we cannot discriminate between persons with their proximate duties and rights in their various relations and resulting associations, the Law strips everyone of everything, even their being. No Pharisee ever dreamt of a more thorough means of using the Law unlawfully than have those who have declared themselves the de facto magisterium of post-Rushdoonian theonomy.

Yet neo-theonomists continue to grouse, "God is no respecter of persons," "There is neither Jew, nor Greek, male nor female," "We are all 'one blood,'" "We are commanded to have special love for Christians, not our kin," mingled with leftist slogans like "No race but the human race," as if such citations refuted the existence of fathers, mothers, brothers, and others. But here we see that even their argumentation for the supremacy of church over family itself presupposes a certain discrimination and limiting of relational priorities—an inescapable feature of identification and belonging which Kinism, and Kinism alone, can account for. After all, calling God our Father, fellow Christians our brothers, and the Church our mother means that we rely upon the concepts of kinship, gender, and hierarchy as the framework for understanding our interaction with God and man. If my physical brother is seen as no special relation to myself, then the concept of spiritual brotherhood loses all significance. In order to deny Kinism, they must first presuppose it.

Clearly, if they love Christians or their pastor or denomination in a unique way, their assertion that Christ has abolished all preference, hierarchy, and honors is undone. Such discrimination of creed, membership, and testimony hollows out every invocation of categorical equality, as well as their insistence that we judge not upon appearance. After all, accepting the testimony of another is judging on appearance too, as none but God can truly know the heart of a man. In the name of anti-prejudice, they become the most prejudiced of all—and in the most profoundly hypocritical way possible.

So we turn now to the question of the feasibility of their propositional-nation theory: is a creedal nation even possible? By this, we do not mean to ask whether a creedal or propositional nation fits the definition of a nation. Historically, lexically, and biblically, such arrangements are generically known as empires, not nations. No: setting aside the definition, we are asking rather if a purely propositional Christian society can be coherent or viable. Is the idea even practicable?

Ferdinand Tonnies famously explicated the subject by the terms gemeinschaft and gesselschaft, the former referring to traditional identity and kinship-based societies and the latter referring to those based upon abstract individual, economic, or contractual (propositional) expediencies. Under the Wikipedia entry for the former, we find this excerpt:

> *Gemeinschaften are characterized by a moderate division of labor, strong personal relationships, strong families, and relatively simple social institutions. In such societies there is seldom a need to enforce social control externally due to a collective sense of loyalty individuals feel for society.*

Now compare that with the Wiki excerpt on the latter:

> *Gesselschaften emphasize secondary relationships rather than familial or community ties and there is generally less individual loyalty to society. . . . [S]uch societies are considered more susceptible to class conflict as well as racial and ethnic conflicts.*

The historical witness is quite clear—propositional societies are proven only to erode the family and incite ethnic as well as class strife. The ballyhooed tolerance of the open international-nation is really just a demand that a people yield to invasion, overthrow, and displacement. No matter their sweet language, it amounts to blatant aggression. Multicultural tolerance then evidences itself as nothing but a euphemism for suicide. Of course, following the historic Christian ethic on the matter, Americans long since passed judgment on the issue with the old chestnut, "Good fences make good neighbors." True international and interracial peace is only possible when "every man know[s] his own and abide[s] therein"[125] and therewith. And anyone who demands for one group to yield to the needless aggressions of another (or all others, as is the case in every European-stock country, and only European-stock countries) in the name of 'peace' either does not know the definition of the word, or is simply lying to cover ulterior motives—motives which, due to the observable fruit, must be an extreme antipathy toward the European race.

Yet, the neo-theonomists still make chesty boasts of a burgeoning multicult millennium. "This is the twenty-first century. The open international society is inevitable and irreversible." Not surprisingly, this "it's inevitable" argument is precisely the apologetic outlined by Karl Marx for one-world internationalism as the eschatological fulfillment of communism. Same argument, same objective, same system. The millennium envisioned by the neo-theonomists is one and the same with the golden age envisioned by Marx.

And if the history of propositional nations (empires) has been the source of the most historical strife between people-groups and individuals, the neo-theonomists maintain it is merely because none of those other propositional escapades were organized under the correct propositions. Laying aside the fact that this too is a classic Marxist deflection, we turn to examine just what the re-imagined and re-appropriated one-world multicult "nation" described by the neo-theos would ultimately look like. Again we ask, is it possible? Is it even coherent?

Their proposal generally breaks down into two hemispheres—the primary one which ingratiates them to leftist secular society, and the one they switch to when cross-examined by Kinists. In the first, they describe theonomy as necessi-

---

[125] Calvin's commentary on Acts 17:26

tating a pluralistic, open-borders society in terms of race, culture, and even religion. This description comports perfectly with NWO communism as expressed by every radical leftist group in existence.

Enter the Kinist, however, and the neo-theonomists' story takes quite a detour, because the essence of their disagreement with Kinism is their maintaining that the basis for camaraderie and nationhood is spiritual only, not physical or cultural in any way. So, as the horror dawns on them that allowing citizenship to anyone not overtly (confessionally) Christian forfeits their argument contra Kinism, they jump to the only alternative—a Reformed, Trinitarian confessional orthodoxy as definitive of citizenship.

But this raises many questions.

If unbelievers and heretics were declared illegal aliens, to what country exactly would they be deported? If an unbeliever were an expatriate of no previous country, you would have no lawful jurisdiction to dump American problems on other countries. And if you did it anyway, those countries would rightly consider it an overt act of unjustifiable aggression. Oh, wait, we're talking about a multicult millennium in which all countries are Christian and there are no borders (Borders keep people apart. That's sin, say the neo-theos.) Maybe unbelievers would be deported to a terraformed moon? Who knows? Not the neo-theos, that's for sure.

Or suppose they opt instead for regarding unbelievers as "resident aliens," creating a second class throng of Morlocks, forever disenfranchised and wholly barred from political representation, much like in the Muslim practice of Dhimmitude. Is this the neo-theonomist recipe for millennial peace? Again, they are silent on the issue.

It should also be noted that such a system would bear no small resemblance to the "halfway covenant" theory (an essentially Baptistic concept) to church and community membership—the very experiment which notoriously destroyed Puritan reign in New England.[126] But the proposal of such a Baptist type of church membership as the standard for the theonomic "nation" is at loggerheads with its basic and foundational covenantalism.

It goes without saying that there would be significant lateral movement back and forth between these classes, as some children of Christian homes would, as experience tells us, never come to a credible profession of faith. Others who had at one time been sound in doctrine, suffering head injury, stroke, or senility, might awake spouting heresy. All such people would be stripped of citizenship in such a system.

And then of course there's the problem of people lying about their beliefs simply to get citizenship. What immigrant or adolescent would want to disavow Christianity if such a move resulted in deportation or loss of rights? And thus any system constructed in this manner would necessarily contain a large and growing

---

[126] "Half-Way Covenant." *Wikipedia*, 13 Dec. 2020, en.wikipedia.org/wiki/Half-Way_Covenant.

group of false professers. This would be simply unavoidable and would, just as in New England, quickly undermine and then destroy the system.

We also must contemplate the magnitude of such an all pervasive government: Just how many INS agents would it require to keep everyone accurately categorized, distinguishing citizens from creedal foreigners? Just how frequently would the ecclesiastically certified selectmen have to run their white-gloved fingers across everyone's doctrinal banisters? And once divested of citizenship, whom would the national ex-communicant have to petition for the paperwork to be re-examined for citizenship? Just how long would that line be? Would the functionaries of such a bureaucracy be church or state officials? Is there a difference between them in the neo-theonomist's system? If not, then they have alloyed not only church, nation, and family, but government as well, into one chimeric, maximal state institution: a New World Order Leviathan. Babel revisited.

Most significant perhaps is the question, "Where on earth do the neo-theonomists find any of this stuff in the text of Scripture?" That one I can answer: nowhere.

The Kinist, however, can defer, as Christians have throughout history, to the archetype of the theonomic nation—the Israelite republic. We even have a straightforward and objective means of one-time-only documentation to determine citizenship in the standard divinely set by Ezra and Nehemiah—genealogies proving racial descent.

Speaking of Kinists, it is especially interesting to note that the neo-theonomists acknowledge one exception in their citizenship policy; they say their creedal standard would not apply to one category of persons—Kinists. Though we would more thoroughly meet the bar of confessional Reformed Trinitarianism than anyone (and they acknowledge this), they say we would never be granted citizenship, regardless, because they claim us to be murderers, even if we have never harmed a soul. On the contrary, they have resolved that upon seizing the reigns of power they would execute us outright, our orthodox confession be damned. Several of their supposed luminaries have boasted as much.

We used to call that hypocrisy, lawless, and murder. Real murder, not the ginned-up accusation of such. But in the wake of Rushdoony's passing it is being pawned off as theonomy. Though I suppose these are but trifles to them who consider genocide of the white race to be the manifestation of God's Law and Grace in society.

These spinmeisters even issue the same arbitrary ex cathedra rulings against anyone who dares to remind them that Rushdoony and all of his theological predecessors held to a distinctly Kinist reading of Scripture. They will declare you an honorary Kinist, whether or not you personally embrace the term. Anyone who happens to have a memory stretching back before the 1980s or who has ever read a history book, beware: they consign you to the same unmarked mass grave reserved for Kinists. They mean to entomb all their embarrassments in the potter's field, and to strike from the books all memory thereof.

To clarify, the neo-theonomists maintain at once that...

- The Christian nation is spiritual, not physical. Anyone demurring from this is a racist, and thereby, a murderer, and should be executed without delay.
- There are no such things as Christian nations, only the one monolithic Christian nation. Any demurring, see bullet point above.
- The Christian nation is composed of all peoples—who aren't actually peoples. Any demurring, see bullet point above.
- Nonbelievers and any incapable of credible profession of faith are non-citizens. This would logically include mental deficients, children, and the senile. Any demurring, see bullet point above.
- All Christian children are your children, and must be treated as your own. Therefore, all children are interchangeable and you are prohibited from having any preference for your own or denying all other Christians equal access to your children. Any demurring, see bullet point above.
- In the millennium all countries are Christian, and their populations interchangeable; therefore Christians must welcome invasion. Any demurring, see bullet point above.
- Segregation, whether racial, cultural, linguistic, or social, is murder. Therefore borders are abolished. Any demurring, see bullet point above.

The result is a borderless, universal empire under a one-world-government police state. And in such a world, it seems there is no longer anywhere to deport your "foreigners" (unbelievers) but to the moon, or, more likely, to the grave. It is nothing if not a baptized Babel—a New World Order police state—which they propose. It entails unimaginable bureaucracy, absolute tyranny, and perpetual forced social revolution. Any objecting to the universal leveling of race, nation, class, and family are resolved as guilty of capital offenses. If you hold your children to be yours, and not your neighbor's, that your race is yours and separate from the African's, or any other such acts of virtuous discernment, you are bound for liquidation. Their age of peace would by all indication be the bloodiest reign of terror and tumult in the history of mankind.

But, as is also apparent, the practical impossibility of their ideology is God's built-in fail-safe to prevent their ascendancy. Their worldview cannot work for its incoherency. There is no fruition possible for it in the real world because it is but a fevered dream of square circles inspired by the opiate of cultural Marxism and the fear of men.

A hundred years from now, alienism and the cultural Marxism of the neo-theonomists will be formally anathematized. In spite of the last sixty years of government and antichrist indoctrination to the contrary, the Church will, and is already in some quarters, awakening to the reality that Kinism is the only brand of theonomy possible, as it is the only understanding of God's Law which allows for the existence of things presupposed in the Law and on which the Law itself depends.

Kinism is the only theonomy.

A Kinist Commentary on the Ten Commandments

July 12, 2016

> ³ *And Moses went up unto God, and the Lord called unto him out of the mountain, saying, Thus shalt thou say to the house of Jacob, and tell the children of Israel;*
> ⁴ *Ye have seen what I did unto the Egyptians, and how I bare you on eagles' wings, and brought you unto Myself.*
> ⁵ *Now therefore, if ye will obey my voice indeed, and keep my covenant, then ye shall be a peculiar treasure unto me above all people: for all the earth is mine:*
> ⁶ *And ye shall be unto me a kingdom of priests, and an holy nation. These are the words which thou shalt speak to the children of Israel.* . . .
> ²⁵ *So Moses went down unto the people, and spake unto them.*
> ¹ *And God spake all these words, saying,*
> ² *I am the Lord thy God which have brought you out of Egypt, out of the house of bondage.*
>
> Exodus 19:3-6, 25–20:2

This preamble to the Decalogue is, if noted at all today, generally treated perfunctorily and cast as a rhetorical pretext for abolitionism and liberationism. "Because God liberated Israel from Egyptian slavery, He has ostensibly condemned all forms of slavery, and mandated universal equality." So runs the argument. And that in complete disregard of the fact that God's law goes on to establish and regulate many forms of just slaveholding inside the Covenant.[127]

But often, too, do moderns shuffle past this preface to the Law as if it were some sort of doxological formality rather than dare treat it for what it emphatically presents itself to be — an announcement of a distinctly familist/nationalist relation of God to men. As John Calvin says, "God neither forbids nor commands anything here, but only comes forth before them in His dignity, to devote the people to Himself. . . . [B]ut He adds, that He is the peculiar God of the Israelites."[128]

This preface to the Law announcing the *berith* (covenant) has been identified by Kline with the ancient framework of a suzerain treaty — the contract between

---

[127] Carlton, Davis. "Slavery: Its Morality, History, And Implications For Race Relations In America, Part 1." 30 Apr 2012. https://faithandheritage.com/2012/04/slavery-its-morality-history-and-implications-for-race-relations-in-america-part-1/
[128] Calvin's commentary on Exodus 20:1-2

monarch and nation common to the near East. Whatever else Kline may extrapolate from that point, his observation thus far holds true, for the *berith* is presented by God in distinctly nationalist terms. For God covenanted with Israel as an ethnic group—the Hebrew lineage of Jacob—and dictated the terms of His covenant to them unmistakably in the context of that ethnicity. Or as Calvin elaborates:

> He had said that by unusual favor this nation was taken from the midst of another; and he now adds that this was done on no other account but because God had embraced Abraham, Isaac, and Jacob with His love, and persevered in the same love towards their posterity. . . [A]nd it is pretty plain from the context here, wherein he attributes the election of the people to the love with which God had honored their fathers."[129]

Inasmuch as Israel was a peculiar nation to God, the footnotes of the Geneva Reformation Study Bible for Exodus 20:1-17 affirm the normativity of this relation of God to all nations under the aegis of Christ's Kingdom:

> The Commandments, or 'Ten Words' of the covenant. These expressions are the eternal law of God that transcend the Old and New Testaments. As God had created order in the heavens and earth with ten words (Gen. 1:3-29), so He creates order in society with ten words.

Yes, the Covenant transcends the Old Testament and grants order in society now just as in the time of the Sinai Treaty. It is eternal. As such, it maintains its context as hallowing the distinct peoples to whom it is applied. This means that all nations encounter the law as the terms of God's treaty of conquest and sovereignty over our respective nations, as nations: *goyim* in Old Testament Hebrew, as much as *ethne* in New Testament Greek—ethnicities.

Thus we find the Great Commission concluding the Gospel of Matthew (28:18-20) acts as a recapitulation of the *berith*—the national Covenant—and frames the character of Christian missions not as consonant with individualism or equalitarianism, but as an announcement of the national Covenant appropriated now to each converted people: "Go ye therefore, and teach all nations, baptizing them in the name of the Father, and of the Son, and of the Holy Ghost: Teaching them to observe all things whatsoever I have commanded you." Of which Calvin says, "So that He is not now the God of one people only, but of all nations, whom He has called into His Church by general adoption."[130]

The Westminster Larger Catechism confirms the same—"that he is a God in covenant, as with Israel of old, so with all his people."[131] Or as Rushdoony states

---

[129] Calvin's commentary on Deuteronomy 4:32-40
[130] Calvin's commentary on Exodus 20:1-2
[131] WLC, question 101

it, God's covenant with Israel announced that "God's order is absolute and absolutely binding on men and *nations*."[132]

All of which Calvin classically elaborated in his commentary on Genesis 35:11:

> *"I am God Almighty." God here, as elsewhere, proclaims his own might, in order that Jacob may the more certainly rely on his faithfulness. He then promises that he will cause Jacob to increase and multiply,* not only into one nation, but into a multitude of nations. *When he speaks of "a nation," he no doubt means that the offspring of Jacob should become sufficiently numerous to acquire the body and the name of one great people. But that follows concerning 'nations' may appear absurd; for if we wish it to refer to the nations which, by gratuitous adoption, are inserted into the race of Abraham, the form of expression is improper: but if it be understood of sons by natural descent, then it would be a curse rather than a blessing, that the Church, the safety of which depends on its unity, should be divided into many distinct nations. But to me it appears that* the Lord, in these words, comprehended both these benefits; *for when, under Joshua, the people was apportioned into tribes, as if the seed of Abraham was propagated into so many distinct nations; yet the body was not thereby divided; it is called* an assembly of nations, *for this reason, because in connection with that distinction a sacred unity yet flourished. The language also is not improperly extended to the Gentiles, who, having been before dispersed, are collected into one congregation by the bond of faith; and although they were not born of Jacob according to the flesh; yet, because faith was to them the commencement of a new birth, and the covenant of salvation, which is the seed of spiritual birth, flowed from Jacob, all believers are rightly reckoned among his sons, according to the declaration, "I have constituted thee a father of* many nations.*"*[133]

Stephen C. Perks has well reprised this issue:

> *Due to the pietistic theological consensus that has come to dominate the Church's understanding of the faith, it [the Great Commission] has been overwhelmingly taken to mean something else; namely, 'make disciples from among the nations.' This is a perfectly reasonable and correct understanding of the English, but it is an incorrect rendering of the Greek. The Greek says we are to 'Go and disciple the nations,' not make disciples of the nations, that is, from among the nations. . . . Many people misunderstand the Great Commission as a command to make disciples from among all the nations, but this is not what Jesus commanded us to do.* Rather, He commanded us to disciple the nations as nations, to make Christian nations.[134]

---

[132] Rushdoony, R.J. *The Institutes of Biblical Law*, p. 17. 1973. emphasis added
[133] Calvin's commentary on Genesis 35:1-29, emphasis mine
[134] Perks, Stephen C. "The Great Decommission." Audiobook. 2014. emphasis added

But the Liberationist interpretation of the Exodus and the Sinai Covenant gives way at the slightest inquiry to a degree of greater radicalism still. If questioned, the Marxist anti-colonial narrative of the manumission of a slave race from bondage unto imperialism transitions (in complete self-contradiction) to the rhetoric of Boasian anthropology alleging that the Covenant with Israel of old had no inkling of ethnic identity in the first place. Set aside the fact that this secondary position undercuts the first; granting the secondary position that it wasn't the people of Israel liberated from Egyptians, but generic people liberated from other people, it nullifies the Great Commission no less than the Sinai Covenant. Rather than Israel being delivered out of the Egyptians' hands, the Alienist imposes upon the text an assumption fundamentally irreconcilable with the words themselves: rather than Israelites, those whom God delivered in the Exodus were but a menagerie of atomized individuals delivered not from Egyptians, but from a broader mass of distinctionless humanity. The egalitarian view then makes nonsense not only of the terms 'Hebrews' and 'Egyptians,' but also of the 'mixed multitude' mentioned as having been liberated alongside Israel. This Alienist eisegesis thereby forfeits God's promise to Abraham that He would bless his physical descendants no less than His promise to make of him "many nations." The Alienist interpretation would here preclude, then, all semblance of covenantalism.

That is *if* we may even call what Alienists do with the text here 'interpretation,' because interpretation actually requires interaction with the words of the text. That isn't what they are doing. And there is no way to construe matters otherwise. They are simply *imposing* the zeitgeist upon the text. So too do they with every one of the commands which follow.

The First Word

Thou shalt have no other gods before me.
Exodus 20:3

While this is a foundational command to monotheism, it also means more than this. More than a command to generic monotheism, in context of its preamble, it conclusively identifies the one true God. By the terms there used, it implies much about the definition of gods, generally. For the word appearing here as 'gods' is Elohim, which means, in the general sense, 'judges.' Which is to say, then, that we shall brook no judicial systems contrary to the judgments of The Judge. And this was understood, because amongst the heathen of the ancient world, men of juridical-civil power were considered divinity. Even if secularism has lately studied to sterilize the language around politics of all religious overtones, the concept of divine right has resurged in entirely unattenuated form all across the Western world. Modern devotion to the arbitrary and ever more frequently lawless rule of 'officials' (in state, church, and academy) is the essence of Baalism and typified the god-states of the old Orient.

So we see the commandment precludes any claim to legitimate authority apart from obedience to the one true Judge, God Almighty. This, then, is a mandate of theonomy precluding even ecclesiocracy.

Question 104 of the Westminster Larger Catechism includes the following as a description of the duties required in this commandment: "yielding all obedience and submission to him with the whole man." This would clearly include all social aspects of our existence, which is to say that the first commandment cannot be alienated from its context—national Covenant. Moreover, question 101 further states, "He is a God in covenant, as with Israel of old, so with all his people; who, as he brought them out of their bondage in Egypt, so he delivereth us from our spiritual thraldom." This is rightly understood as a deliverance not only from personal sin, but from the sin of false social orders. This is all the more confirmed by question 105, which enumerates things forbidden in the first commandment as "carnal security, tempting of God; using unlawful means," etc.; and #106 charges us to do "as in his sight, whatever we do in his service."

All taken into account, any social-civil orders not founded upon God's law in the context of national covenant are but humanist fictions. Thus all the 'judges' propounding vanities such as political correctness, equality, civil rights, human rights, etc.—be they scientists, sociologists, psychologists, heads of state, or jurists—are the very 'other gods before me' denounced by the first Word. Aside from absolute theonomy for covenanted nations under the one ultimate Judge, all else violates His command. Propositional nation theory, known biblically as 'empire,' comprised as it has ever been of statist and/or individualist utopian schemes, is strictly prohibited. Those claiming authority apart from, or contrary to, the one true God's national covenant and law, are, irrespective even of professions of Christianity, 'other gods,' preaching a functional pantheism.

The Second Word
July 13, 2016

⁴*Thou shalt not make unto thee any graven image, or any likeness of any thing that is in heaven above, or that is in the earth beneath, or that is in the water under the earth.*
⁵*Thou shalt not bow down thyself to them, nor serve them: for I the Lord thy God am a jealous God, visiting the iniquity of the fathers upon the children unto the third and fourth generation of them that hate me;*
⁶*And shewing mercy unto thousands of them that love me, and keep my commandments.*

Exodus 20:4-6

Here is a clear command to iconoclasm. Though the first commandment principally dealt with the subject of other gods already, the second commandment is an immediate implication of the first. Barring first idols to other gods, it also forbids 'the sin of Jeroboam' — idols erected to the true God. In essence, even if wrought by Christian hands, any image of God conceived by men is necessarily false, and therefore a false doctrine. This understanding was not long ago so universally accepted that even MGM's epic films such as *The Robe* and *Ben Hur* concealed the face of Christ on screen in acknowledgement of the second commandment. An idol was an idol, whether it be stone, wood, or celluloid. That is to say that in the mid-twentieth century, even Jewish-run Hollywood was reluctant to trespass against the law on account of their American Christian audiences.

So was Iconoclasm generally taken for granted even in the Byzantine and Roman churches for the first few centuries, and was repudiated by them only as of the seventh ecumenical council, when syncretism was officially settled upon as a compromise, expanding the definition of Christianity to include icons as 'aids to the ignorant' — the new converts still clinging to the habit of idols. That was in A.D. 787, ninety-two years after Emperor Justinian II had, in advance of the Church, sanctioned iconography by minting gold coinage with an icon of Christ on it. Since the church, East and West, depended upon that very gold as well as a largely idol-habituated people, the magisterium came to see it as sufficiently expedient to finally canonize the practice. Thus did icons become established on account of finance, imperial multiculturalism, and the god-state — matters quite familiar to us in the multitudinous warnings of Scripture, as well as our contemporary experience.

Today, in fact, Protestants themselves have come through the aforementioned pressures to repudiate iconoclasm, so that any retaining this mega-majority opinion of Protestantism past are now viewed as an extraterrestrial species. Such antiquated views, though only fallen from prominence a couple decades, are now invariably met in the churches with accusations of legalism and Pharisaism — the same reaction come of the Roman church in the Reformation era. It is a near total inversion on the subject in less than a fifty-year span.

But this shift has not occurred in a vacuum. Rather, the rejection of iconoclasm for iconodulism has moved precisely apace with the paradigm shift in Protestantism and Christendom generally, toward antinomianism, egalitarianism, Marxism, and all the Gnostic -isms which have congealed into the perspective known today as Alienism. The first reason for this is the same as obtained under the paradigm shift of the seventh ecumenical council: rapid integration of pagan groups into an empire. Mestizos (the most rapidly growing ethnic group in America) are a people steeped in quasi-Romanism, and their expression of Romanism is really more accurately called Santería—a blend of Catholicism, voodoo, and indigenous heathenism. If Romanism was already plagued by superstition in Europe, its appropriation among non-European peoples exacerbated the issue a hundredfold. Whether we are speaking of Africa, the Caribbean, or America, Hamitic peoples, even if Christianized for centuries, virtually never seem to cast off the heavy influences of their hereditary faith—voodoo. As the saying goes, "Haiti is 70% Catholic and 30% Protestant, but 100% voodoo." But this description proves apropos of all Black and Mestizo communities everywhere. So as all our once White Christian nations have been flooded with non-White claimants of Christianity, idols in tow, the churches have found it expedient to disregard the iconoclasm which had been such a resolute fixture of our faith over the previous five centuries, especially. Yes, the quiet embrace of overt idolatry parallels the browning of America. Iconoclasm fell in America concurrent with and inextricable from the effects of the 1964 Civil Rights Act and the 1965 Immigration Act, among others.

Inasmuch as forced integration with 'People of Color' has compelled Protestantism in America toward a position of laxity on the question of idols, the aliens have themselves even come to be held up as idols. If secular Enlightenment thought venerated the abstraction of the 'Noble Savage,' American Christendom has lately reprised the idea with a vengeance. Sad to say, it is taken for granted now, even in what are regarded as 'conservative' churches, that the American Indian was the moral superior to the White Christian settler, the Black slave superior to his White Christian master, and Santa Ana superior to the White heroes of the Alamo who resisted Mexican encroachment to their last breath.

More's the pity, Protestants have even come to laud Black communist, plagiarist, adulterer, whoremonger, woman-beater, miscegenator, and heretic, Martin Luther King, Jr., as the greatest of Christian martyrs. I dare say their late veneration of the 'civil rights' pantheon bears all the hallmarks of worship. By use of the word 'worship' in this case one may think it hyperbole, but it isn't. For they have been programmed by the concerted efforts of Marxist-subverted institutions (including the denominational governments) to identify MLK reflexively as a universal symbol of all that is good; and to the extent that any dares to remind us of King's denials of the virgin birth, the Trinity, and other core Christian doctrines, he is himself denounced as a heretic. Yes, to point out King's heresy is to incur reflexive accusations of blasphemy, heresy, apostasy, and, of course, 'racism' — which, in the minds of Alienists, is the zenith of evil.

Albeit, MLK is but one manifestation of this new Brahman-esque cultural Marxist pantheon; the Black, in general, has become an archetype and what can only be described as a *theophany* of the new age divinity. For the interests of the Black hold unquestioned power in the churches now — even to the point of profaning holy worship with libidinous jungle rhythms and the crass gyrations and bravado of the ghetto. His whim is seen as every White man's duty under God; his religious inclinations, celestial. Because he isn't seen for what he is, but for what he represents — revolution, the overthrow of the White Man, and the transformation of Christianity into Liberationism — all of which are taken for the fulfillment of the Alienist eschaton. The Black has become a totem in the minds of White men. So too have Jews, the American Indians, Mestizos, and every other outlier group. Though discordant in their own narratives, all these idols of political correctness are united in a godhead of 'all is one' mass-Man. This new orthodoxy holds each of these categories and their reconciliation to one another in a monad of Mankind as the Kingdom Come, and therefore, above reproach.

Ever insightful, Rudyard Kipling identified this exaltation of the stranger-alien as beings of superior spirituality as 'the rule of En-dor':

But they are so deep in their new eclipse
Nothing they can say can reach,
Unless it be uttered by alien lips
And framed in a stranger's speech.
The son must send word to the mother that bore,
Through an hireling's mouth. 'Tis the rule of En-dor.[135]

This is the very scenario in the modern churches, where the faith is validated only by the presence of non-Whites, and where God is seen as genuinely accessible only by the mediatorial presence of aliens. All the diversity-obsessed outreach, multicult sentimentalism, and denouncements of White homogeneity from our pulpits and in our seminaries are a testament to the fact that the continued existence of the White race or White nations is now regarded tantamount to damnation. So deep is this conviction in contrast to all others, in fact, that while the pews may be brimming with impenitent sodomites, philanderers, whores, blasphemers, pedophiles, and every historic heresy under the sun, there is no public outcry to purify the churches of these fecund elements, but the slightest suspicion of 'racism' is met

---

[135] Kipling, Rudyard. "En-dor"

with red-faced overtures, charges of heresy, secret calls to employers and CPS, death threats, defamation across the blogosphere, opinion pieces in the local paper, and, in some cases, television news reports. Speaking from experience, one of the elders who presided over my own case confided in me that an allegation of 'racism' was regarded as "worse than anything else; even worse than pedophilia, or being a serial killer." Really.

Without the slightest sense of irony, or curiosity about how the Church's priorities could align so precisely with the secular and heathen world, they cleave all the more tenaciously to these idols held in common with all the non-Christian worldviews about them.

All pietistic self-flagellation on the part of Whites and liberationist slogans on the part of non-Whites, these idols of the multicult churches are oracles of an alien law system, and they announce the transplantation of God's Law in favor of tolerance, equality, unity, niceness, etc. These are the baals of our age. A doctrine of demons.

But the law goes on to annex reasons—promises and curses—to the second commandment:

> [5]*Thou shalt not bow down thyself to them, nor serve them: for I the Lord thy God am a jealous God, visiting the iniquity of the fathers upon the children unto the third and fourth generation of them that hate me;*
> [6]*And shewing mercy unto thousands of them that love me, and keep my commandments.*
>
> Exodus 20:5-6

Catechism question 110 describes these counterfactuals as reason 'more to enforce it.' Which is to say that hereditary blessing is a profound consolation and double inducement to keep the Word contra idols. Abstinence from idols is health to your lineage after you, and in the context of the national covenant in which it is given, grace to your folk corporately. Clearly, if the law tenders this inducement, the trustee family or clan model is directly vindicated, as is, by connotation, ethnonationalism. On this toledoth framework of the covenant, the Puritans were univocal:

> *Hereby you become grossly unfaithfull, yea, treacherous to your God, to your Ancestours, to Parents, to posterity, to the whole Church. God made you His Trustees, and so did Ancestours and Parents make you their spirituall Trustees, under God, to hold up Religion, Truth, the Worship, Wais, and Government of Christ, when they should be gathered to their Fathers; they look at and leave you their Children to be a seed of the Church, to be as plants, to hold up God's Orchards.*[136]

---

[136] Cobbett, Thomas. "Frutifull and Usefull Discourse," 1656

> *Consider and remember always, that the Books that shall be opened at the last day will contain Genealogies in them. . . . How shall we many of us hold up our faces then, when there shall be a solemn rehearsal of our descent as well as our degeneracies?*[137]

> *Some well Observed, God has so cast the Line of Election that for the most part it runs through the Loins of Godly Parents. . . . Doubtless, if an account of it were taken, it would be found that the greatest part of such as belong to God have descended from Godly Parents.*[138]

The antithesis — Marinov's revolutionary theory[139] of an atomized family and radical individualism[140] artificially severing us from previous generations — is here refuted. After all, if any teaching concerned for lineage and extended family is 'paganism,' he winds up leveling this charge flatly against the second commandment itself, because the law assures lineal covenant to 'thousands of generations' of those who keep His law. Inveighing against the law itself, he doubly violates it. More than revealing him insensate to the concerns of the law or the blessings of the covenant, it shows in him an intractable opposition to the law.

Through our fetishizing the alien in every way possible, he is very much an idol; and Alienists do not even shrink from sacrificing their children to the Other. Because the Other has become the definition of Goodness to them. For they displace affection due to the holy Creator God who is, in a profound sense, alien to us, and they lay that affection on all things alien in the created world. They seem, as it were, to isolate that distinguishing quality of God — His otherness and His alien righteousness — and superimpose divinity on all things alien. All of which otherwise happen to be part of the creation as opposed to the Creator. That displacement allows the Alienist to believe he is worshiping God when he is in fact only worshiping a characteristic of God — otherness. He will worship otherness wherever it is found. This makes the Alienist a pantheist idolater. Or, as Paul said it in Romans 1:

> *[22]Professing themselves to be wise, they became fools,*
> *[23]And changed the glory of the uncorruptible God into an image made like to corruptible man, and to birds, and fourfooted beasts, and creeping things.*
> *[24]Wherefore God also gave them up to uncleanness through the lusts of their*

---

[137] Stroughton, William. "New England's True Interest, Not a Lie," p. 33, 1670
[138] Mather, Increase. "Advice to the Children of Godly Ancestours, A Course of Sermons on Early Piety," pp. 5-6, 1721
[139] Carlton, Davis. "A Defense Of Kirk And Kin: A Response To Bojidar Marinov, Part 1" 21 Dec 2012. https://faithandheritage.com/2012/12/a-defense-of-kirk-and-kin-a-response-to-bojidar-marinov-part-1/
[140] Carlton, Davis. "More Folly from Marinov" 4 Sept 2013. https://faithandheritage.com/2013/09/more-folly-from-marinov/

own hearts, to dishonour their own bodies between themselves:
25Who changed the truth of God into a lie, and worshipped and served the creature more than the Creator, who is blessed for ever. Amen.

Romans 1:22-25

The apostle goes on to describe the behavioral sins flowing from such idolatrous theology: "Without understanding, covenantbreakers, without natural affection, implacable, unmerciful" (Rom. 1:31). Covenant-breakers without natural affections. Yes, that is Alienism, precisely.

Thus bowing to a pantheon of weirdling gods, the Alienist cannot tolerate the second commandment as it is. Even if he cites it, he does so only by infusing it with assumptions alien and irreconcilable to the words themselves.

The Third Word
July 14, 2016

Thou shalt not take the name of the Lord thy God in vain; for the Lord will not hold him guiltless that taketh His name in vain.

Exodus 20:7

The implications of this law are vast. Among them, the Catechism includes:

> *perjury; all sinful cursings, oaths, vows, and lots; . . . misapplying of God's decrees and providences; . . . abusing [the Word], the creatures, or anything contained under the name of God, to charms, or sinful lusts and practices; the maligning, scorning, reviling, or any wise opposing of God's truth, grace, and ways; making profession of religion in hypocrisy, or for sinister ends, [etc.]*[141]

In America the oath of office has traditionally been conducted with one hand on the Bible accompanied by the words, "I do hereby solemnly swear to uphold and defend the Constitution from all enemies foreign and domestic." This oath is violated radically by virtually all who swear it today: the soldier consents, in complete contradiction to his oath, to take part in an unconstitutional military complex following unconstitutional and ungodly orders dispensed by an unconstitutional foreign government which epitomizes the very enemies he swore to defend against; and the jurist who, by participation in the positivist paradigm now taken for

---

[141] Westminster Larger Catechism, question #113

granted by the entire legal system and tacit consent to the foreign occupation, does no less. In fact, be they soldiers or Supreme Court justices, virtually everyone who swears this oath now violates it by their initial consent to the oath itself, because the institutions into which the foresworn are inducted are completely at odds with the oath itself. Swearing the oath in this context renders it a perjurious mockery, doubly grave for its ubiquity. Ours now is, top to bottom, a system based upon violation of the third commandment. Defending the status quo in these matters only compounds the sin.

Granted, the taboo connected to this subject has grown strong even amongst Christians because of the invocation of God's Word in the oath, and secondarily, that of the Constitution also, which they understand for a thoroughly covenantal constraint on government. But the reflexive deference to these good words as a 'charm' (also forbidden by question #113) to hallow a system which is, in reality, their antithesis (the Leviathan anti-Christ state) is akin to Israel's fetishization of the Ark of the Covenant, or the Song of Lamech (Gen. 4). The turning of true revelation into a charm to hallow false premises, or to pursue that which is untrue and evil, is the common thread between everything from Talmudism to Wicca. Such word-magic, invoking some aspect of true revelation as a source of power by which to conjure into existence things contrary to that revelation, is part and parcel of witchcraft.

While taboo is an inescapable aspect of all worldviews, the taboos surrounding the oath of office and American militarism are of the same species which is pervasive in regard to all social matters today — political correctness. It is devotion to transparent lies in the name of truth.

We usually know political correctness by its more conspicuous forms, in matters race- and gender-oriented. These appertain to the penological categories introduced to Western society by cultural Marxism — racism and sexism. And these categories have, hydra-like, multi-cephalized into so many subcategories that I will not treat them here. Suffice it to say that the simultaneous insistence that race is imaginary and that we therefore must celebrate, congratulate, or support interracial marriage is, by way of self-contradiction, to knowingly embrace lies as virtue. Those who do so, generally take these principles as the *highest* virtues. As bad as it may be when unbelievers seem to universally reason this way, it is that much worse that claimants of Christ have been turning in recent years to cite the unigenesis of the human species as rendering all the nationalities and races (which are incidentally presupposed everywhere in text) as heretical fictions; because it sets revelation at odds with itself in pursuit of their imagined higher good — the vindication of Babel. Citing critical theory in place of biblical penology and declaring it the self-same as biblical law is to append Marxism to the very name of God. Alienism pursues the most notorious evils listed in Scripture while claiming to do so in the name of God. This is the epitome — in the words of the catechism — of "abusing it . . . to charms, . . . or any wise opposing of God's truth . . . ; making profession of religion . . . for sinister ends," and therefore, it is a most grievous violation of the third law. The Alienist's invocation of God and aspects of His word as a pretext toward Marxian-Babelite goals is blasphemy and treason against the Truth itself.

The Fourth Word
July 18, 2016

8Remember the sabbath day, to keep it holy.
9Six days shalt thou labor, and do all thy work:
10But the seventh day is the sabbath of the Lord thy God: in it thou shalt not do any work, thou, nor thy son, nor thy daughter, thy manservant, nor thy maidservant, nor thy cattle, nor thy stranger that is within thy gates:
11For in six days the Lord made heaven and earth, the sea, and all that in them is, and rested the seventh day: wherefore the Lord blessed the sabbath day, and hallowed it.
Exodus 20:8-11

The fourth law is addressed to the federal heads of household, and thereby presupposes a more limited context of authority inside the national body—that of clan and house. It is to this federal-familial authority structure that the sabbath is most immediately entrusted, albeit inside the national framework.

It refutes the equalitarian myth promulgated in the churches today that there is no separation nor distinction between covenant families. For it charges the federal head of every house foremost with domestic responsibility over his own clan, not his neighbor's. This was the onus of limited responsibility expressed by Joshua: "but as for me and my house, we will serve the Lord" (Josh. 24:15). This same priority of close kin is emphasized by Paul—that a man should "provide for his own, and specially for those of his own house" (1 Tim. 5:8). In place of the term 'his own' (Greek: idion[142]) which has in recent years become an archaic idiom, many modern translations have, for clarity's sake, opted for the word 'relatives,' which communicates the idea well enough. But Matthew Poole is emphatic: "By his own he means his relations, all of a man's family or stock."[143] 'Stock,' of course, being a preferred synonym for 'race.'

If this principle were not clear enough, Isaiah dispels all question of intent, saying, "hide not thyself from thine own flesh" (Isa. 58:7), which, in context, clearly

---

[142] ídios (a primitive word, NAS dictionary) - properly, uniquely one's own, peculiar to the individual.
[143] Matthew Poole's commentary on 1 Timothy 5

signifies one's provision for one's blood relations. Augustine's commentary on this passage doubly affirms that Moses, Joshua, Paul, and Isaiah had the same principle in view:

> *For the examination of a number of texts has often thrown light upon some of the more obscure passages; for example, in that passage of the prophet Isaiah, one translator reads: "And do not despise the domestics of thy seed;" another reads: "And do not despise thine own flesh." Each of these in turn confirms the other. For the one is explained by the other; because "flesh" may be taken in its literal sense, so that a man may understand that he is admonished not to despise his own body; and "the domestics of thy seed" may be understood figuratively of Christians, because they are spiritually born of the same seed as ourselves, namely, the Word. When now the meaning of the two translators is compared, a more likely sense of the words suggests itself, viz., that the command is not to despise our kinsmen, because when one brings the expression 'domestics of thy seed' into relation with 'flesh,' kinsmen most naturally occurs to one's mind.*[144]

The onus of responsibility in biblical law, therefore, prioritizes kinship, first with respect to immediate family, and then, proceeding outward by concentric circles, to tribe, ethnicity, race, and at length, men generically.

Albert Barnes's commentary expounds on this subject with chilling poignancy:

> *The words "his own," refer to those who are naturally dependent on him, whether living in his own immediate family or not. There may be many distant relatives naturally dependent on our aid, besides those who live in our own house.*
>
> *And specially for those of his own house* — *Margin, "kindred." The word "house," or "household," better expresses the sense than the word "kindred." The meaning is, those who live in his own family. They would naturally have higher claims on him than those who did not. They would commonly be his nearer relatives, and the fact, from whatever cause, that they constituted his own family, would lay the foundation for a strong claim upon him. He who neglected his own immediate family would be more guilty than he who neglected a more remote relative.*
>
> *He hath denied the faith* — *By his conduct, perhaps, not openly. He may be still a professor of religion and do this; but he will show that he is imbued with none of the spirit of religion, and is a stranger to its real nature. The meaning is, that he would, by such an act, have practically renounced Christianity, since it enjoins this duty on all.*[145]

---

[144] Augustine, *On Christian Doctrine*, book 2, chapter 12
[145] Albert Barnes's commentary on 1 Timothy 5

As orthodox Christians we take Paul's prioritization of kinship as harmonious with, and indeed founded upon, the law itself. So we see just how serious a matter lies before us, for those who refuse to accept the ethical priority established by God of kinship would seem to be rejecting not only the fifth law, but God's covenant of which it is such an integral part. We are therefore warned that egalitarianism is a forfeiture of the Christian faith. In regards of our modern egalitarian world, this should make our blood run cold.

The severity of this principle was likewise underscored by the Church fathers such as Tertullian:

> *Do we believe it lawful for a human oath to be superadded to one divine, for a man to come under promise to another master after Christ, and to abjure father, mother, and all nearest kinsfolk, whom even the law has commanded us to honour and love* next to God Himself, *to whom the gospel, too, holding them* only *of less account than Christ, has in like manner rendered honour?*[146]

Though viewed as scandalous amongst the churches in recent decades, the priority of kinship was always understood of Christendom past as penultimate beside devotion to God, and, as Tertullian intimated, entwined inextricably with the Gospel itself. Yes, prior to the last few decades, Bengel's maxim was the patent summary of the Christian view: "Faith does not set aside natural duties, but perfects and strengthens them."[147]

None of which is to discount or dismiss the onus we have toward Christians of all breeds. In deed, they are near relation as it pertains to the household of faith (Gal. 6:10), but that household is made intelligible only by its countervailing analogy, which is the kin-based household (1 Tim. 5:8) established in law as the undergirding social order of covenant Christianity. Apart from the Kinist understanding here, not only do we forfeit exclusive claims to our own physical wives and children, but we also lose the God-ordained analogy by which spiritual relations are made intelligible. And directly refuting the Alienist claim, we know the law forbids confusion of anything that is our neighbor's for ours (Ex. 20:17).

The fourth law also affirms the propriety of domestic slavery. No amount of wrangling will undo it. This principle is further subdivided into various codes particular to their own circumstances: some address hirelings, native as well as stranger (e.g. Deut. 24:14-15; Lev. 19:13; 25:39-40; Jer. 22:13), others, a seven-year limited term of servitude for men of one's own race (e.g. Ex. 21:2; Deut. 15:2-3), and others still grant the option of perpetually retaining slaves only in the case of foreign races (Lev. 25:44-46). Slaves and masters are elsewhere addressed generally (e.g. Ex. 21:20-21; Col. 4:1; Eph. 6:9).

---

[146] Tertullian, "The Chaplet, or De Corona," chapter 11
[147] Johann Albrecht Bengel, Gnomon of the New Testament, 1 Timothy 5

> ⁴⁴ Both thy bondmen, and thy bondmaids, which thou shalt have, shall be of the heathen that are round about you; of them shall ye buy bondmen and bondmaids.
> ⁴⁵ Moreover of the children of the strangers that do sojourn among you, of them shall ye buy, and of their families that are with you, which they begat in your land: and they shall be your possession.
> ⁴⁶ And ye shall take them as an inheritance for your children after you, to inherit them for a possession; they shall be your bondmen for ever: but over your brethren the children of Israel, ye shall not rule one over another with rigour.
>
> Leviticus 25:44-46

While modern churchmen are overjoyed to draw upon Leviticus 25 for reference to the fifty-year sabbath of Jubilee insofar as they can portray it as wealth redistribution and proto-socialism, few now countenance the weekly sabbath which undergirds it. Virtually none dare interact with the above section which sanctions (in at least some instances) the perpetual slavery of foreigners. Moreover, moderns are loath to admit that since the explication of the fifty-year sabbath has slave codes woven into it, it confirms that the fourth law's reference to manservants and maidservants in Exodus 20:8-11 truly does intend domestic servitude as normative to sabbath law. Treating the Jubilee as an aspect of the sabbath, Rushdoony tells us:

> *The essence of the sabbath is the work of restoration, God's new creation; the goal of the sabbath is the second creation rest of God. Man is required to rest and to allow earth and animals to rest, that God's restoration may work, and creation be revitalized. Every sabbath rest points to the new creation, the regeneration and restoration of all things.*[148]

If the sabbath as a day of recreation is literally 're-creation' exemplifying the redeemed social order, it is presented in the Fourth Word and Jubilee principle as an inherently stratified, hierarchical, familialist, nationalist, paternalist, and — in the language of cultural Marxism — 'racist' order.

The Jubilee return of all lands, leased or sublet, to the Israelite tribes and families to which they were originally apportioned exemplifies ethnic protectionism, ensuring that no Israelite line could be divested or uprooted either by kindred tribes or foreign nationals. Yes, the bloodlines of Israel were thus rooted to the land inalienably. Foreigners, though able to lease, had no right of allodial claim to the land. Sabbath law forthrightly mandates what are regarded as the most odious principles to post-WWII sensibilities — blood and soil.

As the winds of zeitgeist move through the Church, this unavoidable national-familial framework of ordered hierarchy in the covenant is not refuted, but

---

[148] Rushdoony, R.J. *The Institutes of Biblical Law*. 1973. p. 143

simply ignored or shunned. The only recourse left to our humanist-programmed brethren is some form of utopianism.

> *Man is reduced to economic man and viewed in terms of an externalism which destroys man. Utopianism not only presents an illusory or dangerous picture of the future, but it also distorts and destroys the present. Utopianism thus affords man no help as he works toward the future: it gives man illusions which beget only needless sacrifice and work and produce nothing but social chaos.*[149]

But the last category to be addressed in the fourth law under the authority of the householder is 'the stranger within thy gates.' We cannot miss that in the words of the catechism, strangers abided 'under the charge' of an Israelite house.[150] The law places the stranger and his labor directly under the paternal oversight of the domestic authority—in Hebrew, the bayith, the clan. Far from blurring the stranger's standing as a stranger, declaring him indistinguishable from an Israelite, or as an 'honorary' or 'naturalized' Israelite, the law insists upon his abiding distinction as a stranger. To eisegetically impose egalitarianism here, as if the stranger within one's gates was not to be regarded as that which the law calls him, is not only a hermeneutical error, and violence to the text, but nullification of the law. As obvious a fact as it is, we are compelled to underscore the point, that if the sabbath law speaks to the stranger as a category under authority to an Israelite family, then strangers exist. Even if bonded to a native's house, they abide as distinguished from said house. To claim belief in the sabbath, while denying that strangers differ at all from blood-natives, or while rejecting the ethnic paternalism presupposed in this law, is to argue that we should not allow the law to mean what it plainly says.

No, we see that the stranger sojourning under conditions of theonomy had legal standing only under the patronage of a native clan:

> [15] *So I took the chief of your tribes, wise men, and known, and made them heads over you, captains over thousands, and captains over hundreds, and captains over fifties, and captains over tens, and officers among your tribes.*
> [16] *And I charged your judges at that time, saying, Hear the causes between your brethren, and judge righteously between every man and his brother,* **and the stranger that is with him.**
>
> Deuteronomy 1:15-16

The stranger's standing, then, in matters juridical was, as with matters labor-oriented, contingent upon his being 'with' an Israelite. Whether a merchant, laborer,

---

[149] Ibid., p. 158
[150] Westminster Larger Catechism, question #118

or ambassador, the stranger's 'resident alien' status was held valid only under the bonded surety of an Israelite benefactor: this was indemnity to "'the stranger,' who according to the law could have a legal claim to no land in Israel,"[151] and would otherwise be left without the needful means of navigating what to him was a foreign polity and culture. This is what it means to 'love' the alien: to fulfill the law toward him. Aside from doing him no wrong, this is what it means to 'treat the alien as one born among you': legal representation by suretyship lending him the proxy of an Israelite's standing in court. Whatever legal entanglements come to the stranger, they did so only under the supervisory liability of his Israelite sponsor.

We now know by contemporary experience just how wise the law is in this respect, as the alternative — egalitarianism for the stranger in our lands — leaves the alien lost in an unfamiliar society, unaccountable in the land, and incentivized toward criminal predation upon the native populace. Absent the law's paternalism and protectionism, the stranger is a subversive element, hostile toward, rather than thankful for, the nation hosting him.

All of which Solomon took into the scope of his counsel, advising his son that the patron of a stranger, so contracted, must walk circumspectly and take precaution to well indemnify himself:

> 1 *My son, if thou be surety for thy friend, if thou hast stricken thy hand with a stranger,*
> 2 *Thou art snared with the words of thy mouth, thou art taken with the words of thy mouth.*
>
> Proverbs 6:1-2

Clark therefore summed up the stranger's status thus:

> *And in Mosaic law, it was not deemed improper to exclude strangers from participating in religious affairs, to exempt them from the benefits of the seven-year release, to give or sell them meat of animals dying of themselves, nor upon occasion to segregate and enumerate them. Thus "David commanded to gather together the strangers that were in the land of Israel" [1 Chron. 22:2], and Solomon "numbered" all the strangers that were in the land [2 Chron. 2:17].*
>
> *Though the law required that strangers be fairly treated, it was not intended that they should "devour" the land [Isa. 1:7] or the strength of the people [Hos. 7:9], nor that they should fill themselves with the wealth of the people through exploitation [Prov. 5:10]. On the contrary, it was evidently supposed that the strangers, with some exceptions, should constitute a subservient class, from whose ranks bondmen and hired servants might be obtained. . . . In Isaiah it is*

---

[151] Kellogg, S.H. *The Expositor's Bible: The Book of Leviticus.* Chapter XXI

said that "strangers shall stand and feed your flocks, . . . the sons of the alien shall be your plowmen and your vine-dressers" [Isa. 61:5], and "the sons of the strangers shall build up thy walls." Solomon, in building the "house of the Lord" and the "house for his kingdom," set the strangers apart, some to be bearers of burdens, others to be hewers in the mountain, and others to be overseers [2 Chron. 2:17, 18].[152]

As if to dispel any illusions that these strictures are in any way arbitrary, all matters social, labor-oriented, and litigious are in the sabbath law conceived as being anchored in the elements and divisions of creation itself. If 'thy stranger that is within thy gates' is constrained under the authority of an Israelite family to observe the sabbath on the grounds that 'in six days the Lord made heaven and earth, the sea, and all that in them is, and rested the seventh day: wherefore the Lord blessed the sabbath day, and hallowed it' (Ex. 20:11), then this enduring distinction between Israelite and stranger is, upon the Creator's authority, concession to and maintenance of complementarity in the created order. Nations violate it only at their own peril.

The Fifth Word
July 19, 2016

Honour thy father and thy mother: that thy days may be long upon the land which the Lord thy God giveth thee.

Exodus 20:12

The Catechism summarizes the scope of this law as enjoining "the performance of those duties which we mutually owe in our several relations, as inferiors, superiors, or equals."[153] Which is to say that this commandment exemplifies hierarchy, and cannot be understood apart therefrom. The included acknowledgment that the law here connotes varied duties 'to our several relations' patently condemns the New Age ethical abstraction of 'fairness' which touts 'treating everyone equally' as a sublime virtue. Social egalitarianism is denounced, then, by the fifth law as Gnostic myth.

Assuming the egalitarian presuppositions of the Neo-Theonomists, who have come to lobby for a nuclear family based not upon any physical relation, but upon

---
[152] Clark, H.B. *Biblical Law*, p. 219, §§ 329-330
[153] Westminster Larger Catechism, question #126

contract and cohabitation, the most that can be deduced from this annexation of promise to live 'long upon the land which the Lord thy God giveth thee' is a singular, personal length of days on one's parcel. But this interpretation, as we know, is at loggerheads with the express national context of the covenant, which is redundantly set before Israel, reminding them that the Covenant hallows not just their immediate domiciles and immediate family, but the span of their generations, preceding and proceeding: "Behold, I have set the land before you: go in and possess the land which the Lord sware unto your fathers, Abraham, Isaac, and Jacob, to give unto them and to their seed after them" (Deut. 1:8).

No, the inducement of the fifth word, delivered as it is in the context of the national Covenant upon promises made to remote ancestors, ensures the inheritance of the land (in conjunction with the promise of the second law) 'to a thousand generations' (Ex. 20:6): a promise of covenant legacy and national preservation. So did centenarian Faeroese patriarch, Graekaris Madsen, explain the fifth law:

> *My grandfather taught me to read and write and to obey the laws of God. He said,* 'Honor thy father and thy mother, *and all the ancestors from the very first to have settled here, and you will live long in the country.' That's what I've tried to do.*[154]

After all, if we are bound all our lives to honor father and mother, as they were likewise enjoined to honor their fathers and mothers, then we cannot avoid the implication of honoring those to whom our parents were likewise duty-bound to honor; in order to rightly esteem our father and mother, we are necessarily impelled to honor theirs, and those before them. And that with an eye toward the promise redounding to our own posterity in generations forthcoming.

Who could really imagine it otherwise? How could a child especially honor his father if he treated his father's father as a stranger? Clearly, the fifth law is a call to special love of one's ancestors for the sake of one's descendants as joint partakers, a lineage hallowed to God. Few relationships lay the reciprocity of the Golden Rule before our eyes in such stark relief as when we treat our sires as we wish to be treated by our sons.

Underlying this, however, we find that the codification of familialism-on-nationalism here is not the standalone objective, as St. Paul discloses the divine rationale behind the existence of the nations He "hath made of one blood all nations [ethne] of men for to dwell on all the face of the earth . . . That they should seek the Lord, if haply they might feel after Him, and find Him" (Acts 17:26-27). Which is to say that the normative life order for mankind, as decreed by God, is ethnonationalism; and that, for the purpose of fostering true religion. As Paul explains, the

---

[154] La Fay's 1972 interview with Graekaris Madsen, The Vikings, p. 119, emphasis added

relative social insularity of ethnic enclaves engenders a certain perspectivalism without which genuine religion does not flourish. The words of S.H. Kellogg are here illuminating:

> *If we are surprised, at first, to see this place of honour in the law of holiness given to the fifth commandment, our surprise will lessen when we remember how, taking the individual in the development of his personal life, he learns to fear God, first of all, through fearing and honouring his parents. In the earliest beginnings of life, the parent – to speak with reverence – stands to his child, in a very peculiar sense, for and in the place of God. We gain the conception of the Father in heaven first from our experience of fatherhood on earth; and so it may be said of this commandment, in a sense in which it cannot be said of any other, that it is the foundation of all religion. Alas for the child who contemns the instruction of his father and the command of his mother! for by so doing he puts himself out of the possibility of coming into the knowledge and experience of the Fatherhood of God.*[155]

The Fatherhood of God is made accessible to the minds of men by the analogy which precedes it in our natural experience—our apprehension of physical fatherhood. Likewise, then, with spiritual brotherhood: it is preceded and made comprehensible by physical brotherhood, and the motherhood of the Church by acquaintance with our own mothers. As is our sense of solidarity in the spiritual tribe and nation of our Christian creeds made significant through the covenantal apparatus of physical peoplehood. The abiding sanctity of kinship is the epistemological emissary of all spiritual relations in the Kingdom of God. We do not truly comprehend one without the other. We dare not dismiss the physicality of our being as invalid or immoral, for to dismiss either the physical or the spiritual is to lose the meaningfulness of both. This, therefore, is the reason why the Christian faith, historically, and in the fabric of biblical law, underscores the sanctity of kinship so—because these tropes are the chosen and necessary means of God to foster true morality and religion amongst the sons of men.

Our existence as 'sons of Abraham' in the 'spiritual nation of Israel' is an incomprehensible abstraction aside from the forerunning virtues of sonship under our own patriarchs in our physical nations. Regeneration relies upon natural generation for its basic context. And if the thing analogized be wholesome and true, that by which it is analogized cannot be otherwise: if the spiritual peoplehood of Christians is good, then so too must our foregoing physical peoplehood be good.

Aside from these realities, we cannot rightly understand the fifth law.

---

[155] Kellogg, S.H. *The Expositor's Bible: The Book of Leviticus.* Chapter XXI

The Sixth Word
July 20, 2016

Thou shalt not kill.
Exodus 20:13

Though it typically appears in our English translations as 'kill,' most exegetes note the Hebrew as being more approximate to murder, or 'the unwarranted taking of life.' But the uniform inexactitude of translation favoring 'kill' over 'murder,' while lending liberals a shallow excuse for anti-capital punishment rhetoric, does seem to aid in conveyance of other implied categories of negligent harm, such as manslaughter, mentioned elsewhere in biblical case law. Thus question 135 of the Westminster Larger Catechism states:

> *The duties required of in the sixth commandment are all careful studies, and lawful endeavors, to preserve the life of ourselves and others by resisting all thoughts and purposes, subduing all passions, and avoiding all occasions, temptations, and practices, which tend to the unjust taking away the life of any; by just defence thereof against violence, . . . comforting and succouring the distressed and protecting and defending the innocent.*

If the sixth law forbids all things which 'tend to the unjust taking away the life of any,' by the clear attestation of history, experience, and Scripture, no single thing endangers innocent life more than the twin forces of imperial government and racial integration. The two appear together so invariably that we may very well say that it is a distinction without a difference. If imperial statism, known in recent times as international socialism, internationalism, or the New World Order, aren't precisely the same thing as racial integration, they appear inseparable. Democide and genocide are Siamese twins.

But whatever else the UN may be and do, their 1946 resolution on genocide tenders a surprisingly sound definition from the Westminster perspective:

> *In the present Convention, genocide means any of the following acts committed with intent to destroy, in whole or in part, a national, ethnical, racial or religious group, as such:*
>
> a. *Killing members of the group;*
> b. *Causing serious bodily or mental harm to members of the group;*
> c. *Deliberately inflicting on the group conditions of life calculated to bring about its physical destruction in whole or in part;*
> d. *Imposing measures intended to prevent births within the group;*

e.   *Forcibly transferring children of the group to another group.*

Albeit, this resolution must have been ratified with tongues firmly planted in the collective cheek of the assembly, because the UN in its fundamental aims of international federalism (borderless planetary regime) under 'human rights156' marks them, (according to their own definition) among the chief culprits, especially with respect to acts C and D above. For they have certainly brought about these conditions in all European stock nations for the express purpose of 'diversifying,' i.e., diluting, overwhelming, supplanting, and/or expunging, the European-stock peoples.

   In all places where this agenda has been implemented, it has tendered the same result: establishment of C and D in policy invariably ushers in the overt violence defined in sections A and B: open borders to free-range non-white immigration, 'equal rights,' 'civil rights,' 'human rights,' disallowance of freedoms of association, property, and opinion, bombardment of the populace with anti-White egalitarian propaganda in schools, movies, television, and press, the massive expansion of government and government programs, devaluation of the currency (and savings), and affirmative action in all institutions for all but White males constitute socio-economic circumstances calculated to preclude child-rearing at replacement levels. These conditions invariably result in widespread and ever-escalating violence against our people at the hands of others. Wherever diversity is extolled and integration pursued, our people are being savaged day and night. The 'peace' brought to us by racial integration is plummeting standards of living, and levels of violence unknown to us historically outside theaters of war. All the necessary conditions for the perpetuation of our race have been systematically and methodically removed.

   Yet our neo-churchmen would have it no other way. In spite of all, they tell us the borders and segregation which so long preserved our Mayberry-esque innocence were by connotation of the great contrast with other races, infinitely greater violence than our present estimated 40,000 black-on-white rapes per annum, mass murder, and the roving bands of Diversity in every city hunting our women, children, and elders. All these present conditions set the trajectory which, if not arrested, spells the global extermination of the White race inside the next century. And as the Japhetic wing of the species is diminished, civilization recedes with us.

   In spite of the starkness of these realities, none of it seems to touch the conscience of Alienists. To hear them tell it, our mass-murder is the consummation of 'peace' long deferred. Our forced extinction is the Kingdom come.

---

[156] See also "The Inhumanity of Human Rights" on Faithandheritage.com.

Yet the catechism, question #136, reiterates forcefully that the sins forbidden in the sixth commandment include "provoking words, oppression, quarreling, striking, wounding, and whatsoever tends to the destruction of the life of any."

All posturing as Reformational thinkers notwithstanding, any assent to the sixth law amongst Alienists is now entirely divorced from the Westminster perspective, because they hold 'provoking words' against our people approximate to the Golden Rule. Our 'oppression,' worship. 'Quarreling' against our right to exist, the Dominion Mandate. Hordes of invading strangers 'striking [and] wounding' our people, the Great Commission. 'And whatsoever tends to the destruction of the life' of our children, the sublime good.

Conversely, they see any attempt, or even the slightest entertainment of 'just defense thereof against violence,' as the height of blasphemy, and our murderers as saints. And *any* defense on our part (including the bare acknowledgement of these realities), they have the temerity to call 'murder'! Worse, they tell us that our motive—the preservation of our people's lives—only enhances the charge by the magnified force of that most dubious Marxian penological concept—'racism.' Yes, in the eyes of the modern subverted churches of the West, simply noticing our genocide is actually worse than any one act of mass murder: in the minds of Alienists it is approximate only to the sum of murder attributed to man throughout history. For Whites to acknowledge the campaign of genocide against themselves somehow transfers the bloodguilt of that genocide onto the White dissenter himself.

Rushdoony pegged this 'party of love' aright:

> *Love, thus, as the great humanistic virtue, has become all-important. Those who belong to the party of love are the holy ones of the humanistic world even in the commission of crimes, whereas, the orthodox Christian, as a hate-monger by definition, is guilty even in the non-commission of a crime.*[157]

But beyond the subordinate legislation regarding manslaughter and indemnification against accidental injury, Rushdoony treated both the prohibitions on hybridization and all texts governing nature-conservancy as outworkings of the sixth word as well. For the hybridization of animals and crops generally allows the transmission of genetic disorders and blights which would not ordinarily adhere beyond the genetic strains in which they first arise.

Alienists argue that because men can procreate cross-racially[158], that then means all men are really of the same 'kind,' and the same race, and therefore, miscegenation does not qualify as hybridization. But the codes dealing with hybridization such as Leviticus 19:19 say just the opposite: that different 'kinds' are in

---

[157] Rushdoony, R.J. *Institutes of Biblical Law*, "The Sixth Commandment," p. 285
[158] Reynolds, Thorin."The Interfertility Argument" 10 Mar 2015. https://faithandheritage.com/2015/03/the-interfertility-argument/

many cases capable of reproduction resulting in chimeras. This is the whole point of hybrid laws—to prevent the conjugation of things which are just similar enough to commingle, but of clearly different breeds, nonetheless. To say otherwise is to reduce the hybrid laws to absurdity. So too would it fly in the face of the universal opinion of the historic exegetes who ever interpreted those codes as prohibitions on breeding hybrids.

This is why Rushdoony treated the subject of hybridization and eco-conservancy under the umbrella of the sixth law—because hybrids are usually of diminished qualities from their purebred parents, and tend to partial if not full sterility. In biology this concept is known as 'hybrid inviability,' which leads at length to the terminus of the mixed strains. Sometimes the sterility is immediate in the first generation of admixture; other times it becomes apparent in the second or third, or progressively as one examines the history of a mixed population. Positive fertility studies demonstrate conclusively that human pairings of homogeneous third and fourth cousins tend to be the most fertile.[159] The inverse corollary of which is that couplings further removed genetically prove less fertile. As it turns out, modern genetic studies affirm the biblical order: if seriously seeking to 'be fruitful and multiply,' one should wed homogeneously 'from one's close side' (the literal translation of Adam's rib). The dominion mandate works just as we would expect if it, the ethnic insularity codes, and our physiology were authored by the same Mind—synergistically and complementarily.

Concomitant with diminished fertility, when speaking of humans, this dynamic takes into its scope matters cultural and spiritual as well, because racially mixed populations never find social, ethical, or political equilibrium. As Yeats put it, "Things fall apart; the centre cannot hold."[160] Miscegenated societies grow sterile by the fact that they cannot reproduce and perpetuate the social virtues of their parent races. This results in either civil war, secession, and resegregation, or the low, protracted simmer which pits all the irreconcilable elements into heated violence; boiling off all virtues, it spoils the whole stew. Such as do not slowly die out of internal pressures are overcome by purer breeds whose corporate character remains unsullied, unalloyed, and unattenuated. The end of the mongrel society is, in any case, death.

Which is to say that I agree with Rushdoony's consideration of the topic relative to the sixth law. I very much commend the reader to the good reverend's writing on the topic, but I do not think the sixth word the only source, nor perhaps even the primary source, of the hybridization codes. As we shall see in the next segment, they also descend from the seventh law.

---

[159] deCODE Genetics."Third Cousins Have Greatest Number Of Offspring, Data From Iceland Shows." 8 Feb 2008. *ScienceDaily*.
[160] Yeats, W.B. "The Second Coming."

But to whatever extent our neo-churchmen veer from the Catechism's demand of indemnification and its express racial implications, they reveal themselves plainly hostile to the sixth word, evincing a radical mania in their minds seated in the place of God's law.

The Seventh Word
July 24, 2016

Thou shalt not commit adultery.
Exodus 20:14

However much liberal churchmen may wish to truncate the seventh word as pertaining only to intercourse in breach of a marriage vow, the Catechism stands as a constant rebuke of their designs, affirming that Christendom past understood this law to address much more. The Westminster divines agreed that the seventh commandment encapsulated within it prohibition of "fornication, rape, incest, sodomy, and all unnatural lusts; all unclean imaginations . . . unlawful marriages" (WLC, question #139). In essence, then, Westminster comprehended the seventh commandment as taking into its scope the whole realm of sexual infractions and deviancies. It encompasses not just breach of a marriage contract, but 'all unlawful marriages.' Which is to say there are some 'marriages' which are, in a manner, adulterous even when neither party 'cheats' on the other. The seventh law addresses all matters of promiscuity, marital, familial, social, political, national, racial, and even horticultural.

Why?

First, it is taken for granted that all case laws pertaining to joining one thing to another — especially sexually — throughout the books of Moses are but outworkings and applications of the seventh word to various circumstances. Or as Tertullian phrased it, "All acts of adultery, all cases of fornication, all the licentiousness of public brothels, whether committed at home or perpetrated out of doors, serve to produce confusions of blood and complications of natural relationship."[161]

Concomitant with the word *bastard*, the word *adultery* does not mean today exactly what it meant in times past. Others have well plumbed the lexicography of this subject, so I will only sketch the issue in loose strokes here: to begin with, the word *adultery* is derived of the Latin word *adulterare*, which, according to most

---

[161] Tertullian, *Ad Nationes*, Book I, Chapter 16

lexicons, means "to corrupt, or pollute, mix, commingle, or alloy, etc." In V.S. Herrell's words,

> *The most interesting thing that we learn [in the OE Dictionary], however, is from a note in the definition of the verb adulterate: 'repl[aced] by To commit adultery.' So, in fact, the verb adulterate and to commit adultery were at one point interchangeable.*[162]

The Oxford Etymological Dictionary does indeed corroborate this on the nounal form as well:

> *Adulteration (n) c. 1500, from the Latin, adulterationem (nominative adulteratio), noun of action from past participle stem of adulterare, 'corrupt, falsify, debauch,* commit adultery,*' from ad- 'to' (see ad-) + alterare 'to alter' (see alter).*

But the 1828 Webster's Dictionary tenders a redundant affirmation of the same with respect to all the adjectival and verbal forms of adulterate too:

> *ADUL'TERATE, verb transitive. [Latin adultero, from adulter,* mixed, *or an* adulterer*; ad and alter, other.] To corrupt, debase, or make impure by an admixture of baser materials; as, to adulterate liquors, or the coin of a country.*
> *ADUL'TERATE, verb intransitive.* To commit adultery. *obsolete*
> *ADUL'TERATE, adjective. Tainted with* adultery; debased by foreign mixture.

A survey of the whole family of words derived from the adulter root share in the essence of its basic definition:

- adulter: "to corrupt, debase, adulterate."
- adulterant: "that which adulterates, adulterating."
- adulterate: adj.: "spurious, counterfeit, of base origin, or corrupted by base mixture." verb: "to render spurious or counterfeit . . . by admixture of baser ingredients."
- adulterer: "one who adulterates, corrupts, or debases."
- adulterous: "pertaining to, or characterized by, adulteration; spurious, counterfeit, adulterate."

This is so because the root of adultery—*adulter*—is but a compound of *'ad'* and *'alter'*—literally, "by addition of something dissimilar, altering an original substance." This, by the most basic structure of the word, is its technical meaning. But

---

[162] Herrell, V.S. *The Sixth Law,* p. 42

according to its etymological history, the English terms *adulteration* and *adultery* arose contemporaneously in the 1500s, and though they were, according to the Oxford Dictionary, originally synonymous iterations of the same concept, adultery was the form which found its way into the Geneva Bible of 1599 and the King James Bible followed that pattern.

But we needn't beleaguer the point here by tracing the definitions of the Greek and Hebrew words that preceded adultery and adulteration; rather, I would recommend any interested in a detailed lexicography to look at Herrell's work in these matters. Suffice it to say that when large-scale translation into the English language came underway, adultery was merely an alternate iteration and synonym for adulteration, meaning, simply, 'mixing.' And this is how we arrive at our definition pertaining to extramarital sexuality: adultery, in the sense explicitly referenced by the seventh word, is a literal mixing of seed, namely the husband's and the adulterer's, within the adulteress. Even this most basic moral command, this fundamental, decalogical precept, is wrong principally because it is an unlawful mixing, as the term's etymology implies. The rest of the commandment's implications are derived from this core concept.

The Scripture confirms this etymological point in its frequent linking of sexual morality with the avoidance of undue mixture or confusion—adulteration. Take Leviticus 20:12, speaking of sub-categories of adultery (cf. v. 10), which the King James Bible describes as 'confusion,' and the Interlinear Hebrew Aramaic OT (by Hendrickson Publ.) translates as 'unnatural mixture.' John Gill frames it as "a shocking and shameful mixture . . . confound[ing] the degrees of relation and affinity."[163] Matthew Poole exposits this passage as an address of "perverting the order which God hath appointed, and mixing the blood which God would have separated."[164] Adultery here is associated with the overlap of disparate bloodlines. And in Ezekiel 16, where the the nation of Israel is upbraided for her harlotry with the Egyptians, Assyrians, and others, verse 32 describes Israel as "a wife that committeth adultery, which taketh strangers instead of her husband" (Ezek. 16:32).

Then there is the case of Solomon's renowned counsels against adultery, which is exactly what they are described as in all quarters of interpretation; no amount of prevarication can make these passages say other than what they insist on saying. Proverbs 6:26 certainly does describe the subject under consideration as adultery, telling us that "an adulteress hunteth for his life." As does 6:32: "Whoso committeth adultery with a woman lacketh understanding: he that doeth it destroyeth his own soul." Many other popular translations amongst Reformed readers, such as the ESV, manage to insert the words 'adultery' and 'adulteress' many more times in this area of Scripture. But the text warns clearly against "the lips of a strange woman" (5:3), "her ways . . . thou canst not know" (5:6), "lest thou give

---

[163] Gill, John. *Exposition On The Whole Bible*. 1763. Leviticus 20 Commentary.
[164] Poole, Matthew. *English Annotations on the Holy Bible*. 1685. Leviticus 20 Commentary.

thine honour unto others" (5:9), "lest strangers be filled with thy wealth; and thy labours be in the house of a stranger" (5:10). And the reader is advised to "drink waters out of thine own cistern . . . thine own well" (5:15), "let them be only thine own, and not strangers' with thee" (5:17), for "why wilt thou, my son, be ravished with a strange woman, and embrace the bosom of a stranger?" (5:20). Proverbs 6:23-24 go so far as to say: "For the commandment is a lamp; and the law is light; and reproofs of instruction are the way of life: To keep thee from the evil woman, from the flattery of the tongue of a strange woman." Many translations actually render the term 'strange woman' there as 'adulteress.' Which is to say that the association of 'adultery' with foreigners, of some distance or another, is popularly taken for granted by translators and signifies here more than just relations outside wedlock. While clearly encompassing marital infidelity, the adultery against which Solomon inveighs also incorporates the distinction between familiar and foreign, bringing miscegenation in view. Solomon even portrays kinship itself as the anthropomorphic manifestation of wisdom: "Say unto wisdom, Thou art my sister; and call understanding thy kinswoman: That they may keep thee from the strange woman, from the stranger which flattereth with her words" (Prov. 7:4-5). We cannot miss therein the study in contrasts: wisdom and understanding are posited as good kinswomen (a sister and a bride) to keep a young man from the embrace of stranger. He drives home the point ultimately by stating, "The mouth of a strange woman is a deep pit: he that is abhorred of the Lord shall fall therein" (Prov. 22:14). Yes, those whom God hates, he gives over to adulteration. Or, we might paraphrase Proverbs 22:14 as, 'He whom God hates, He also miscegenates.' But that is just a reiteration of the 'vengeance of the covenant' warned of in Deuteronomy 28 and Leviticus 26.

John Calvin argued against adultery in these same terms[165], speaking of "the adulterous woman" as engaged in "the clandestine admixture of seeds." Based upon this definition of adultery as 'admixture of seeds' he offers this apologetic:

For what else will remain safe in human society, if license be given to bring in by stealth the offspring of a stranger? To steal a name which may be given to spurious offspring? And to transfer to them property to be taken away from the lawful heirs?

Calvin explicitly ties marital infidelity to the mixing of seeds (and consequent risk of cuckoldry). His usage of this terminology was nothing if not consistent:

*Mules are the **adulterous** offspring of the horse and the ass. Moses says that Anah was the author of this connection. But I do not consider this as said in praise of his industry; for the Lord has not in vain distinguished the different*

---

[165] Calvin, John. *Commentary On Genesis*. Volume 2. Christian Classics Ethereal Library.

> *kinds of animals from the beginning. But since the vanity of the flesh often solicits the children of this world, so that they apply their minds to superfluous matters, Moses marks this unnatural pursuit in Anah, who did not think it sufficient to have a great number of animals; but he must add to them a degenerate race produced by unnatural intercourse. Moreover, we learn hence, that there is more moderation among brute animals in following the law of nature, than in men, who invent* vicious admixtures.

None of which are new observations with respect to Calvin's theology. In fact, mine would be regarded as a rather pedestrian reading of Calvin everywhere outside Reformed Alienist circles, as they have the unique and conflicted interests of venerating Calvin in the abstract, while simultaneously reviling the man's worldview in reality. At least when Alienist writers are consistent enough in their presuppositions to openly declare Calvin to be their vision of the devil, they can bring themselves to interact with the man's social theory as it really was. Meanwhile, Alienists who somehow imagine Calvin as teaching a unitarian theory of society abide as is oft the case of unnatural mixtures, deranged and sterile.

> *But the notion that what ails the world is confusion had much practical value for Calvin. . . . [W]hen Calvin associated disorder with obscurity, he could conceive of correcting it by sharpening the contours of the various entities composing the world; once one thing has been clearly distinguished, physically or conceptually, from others, it can be assigned its proper place in the order of things. . . .*
>
> *Thus he abominated 'mixture,' one of the most pejorative terms in his vocabulary; mixture in any area of experience suggested to him disorder and unintelligibility. He had absorbed deeply not only the traditional concern for cosmic purity of a culture that had restricted mixture to the sublunary realm but also various Old Testament prohibitions. Mixture, for Calvin, connoted "adulteration" or "promiscuity," but it also set off in him deep emotional and metaphysical reverberations. He repeatedly warned against "mixing together things totally different." . . .*
>
> *The positive corollary of Calvin's loathing of mixture was his approval of boundaries, which separate one thing from another. He attributed boundaries to God himself: God had established the boundaries between peoples, which should therefore remain within the space assigned to them. . . . "Just as there are in a military camp separate lines for each platoon and section," Calvin observed, "men are placed on the earth so that each nation may be content with its own boundaries."*[166]

---

[166] Bouwsma, William J. *John Calvin: A Sixteenth Century Portrait*, pp. 34-35. For the final quote Bouwsma cites Calvin's commentaries on Psalm 74:16 and Acts 17:26, and the wording matches the Fraser translation of his commentaries. The Beveridge translation of Calvin's Acts commentary reads as follows: "Now, we see, as in a camp, every troop and band hath his appointed place, so men are placed upon earth, that every people may be content with their bounds."

Rushdoony affirmed the same understanding of adultery as had Calvin—a 'mixing of seeds':

> *Clearly then, Biblical law is designed to create a familistic society, and the central social offense is to strike at the life of the family. Adultery is thus placed on the same level as murder, in that it is a murderous act against the central social institution of any healthy culture. Unpunished adultery is destructive of the life of the family and of social order. On the part of the wife, it is treason to the family and introduces an alien loyalty to the home, as well as an alien seed.*[167]

So adultery consists chiefly in mixing, not merely in violation of the sacred marriage vow, on which basis the Scripture and our fathers spoke in one voice against adultery as an introduction of foreign seed. All of which raises the question: what other admixtures, besides that of a familial outsider's seed with the husband's, does the Scripture consider adulterous? The Scripture of course mentions other seeds, but this perspective of the seventh word encompassing laws governing seeds, generally, isn't just a study in parallelism. By the authority of St. Paul, 1 Corinthians 9:8-10 confirms that the OT cattle laws have chiefly to deal not with cattle, but with human relations. Thus St. Augustine, writing on the subject of marriage, could describe "the sexual intercourse of man and woman, then, [as] . . . the *seed-bed*" of human society.[168]

In keeping with this understanding, S.H. Kellogg too exposited the seed and yoking laws of Leviticus 19 as extensions of the seventh commandment against adultery:

> *Most probable it appears that they were intended for an educational purpose, to cultivate in the mind of the people the sentiment of reverence for the order established in nature by God. For what the world calls the order of nature is really the order appointed by God, as the infinitely wise and perfect One; hence, as nature is thus a manifestation of God, the Hebrew was forbidden to seek to bring about that which is not according to nature, unnatural commixtures; and from this point of view, the last of the three precepts appears to be a symbolic reminder of the same duty, namely, reverence for the order of nature, as being an order determined by God.*[169]

Matthew Henry interpreted the seed and yoking laws in exactly the same way as well, describing Leviticus 19:19 as a generic 'law against mixtures,' entailing that:

---

[167] Rushdoony, R.J. *The Institutes of Biblical Law*, p. 395
[168] Augustine, *City of God*, Book XV, Chapter 16
[169] Kellogg, S.H. *The Expositor's Bible: The Book of Leviticus*, Chapter XXI

> We must acquiesce in the order of nature God hath established, believing that it is best and sufficient, and not covet monsters. Add thou not unto His works, lest He reprove thee; for it is the excellency of the work of God that nothing can, without making it worse, be either put to it or taken from it, Eccl. iii. 14. As what God has joined we must not separate, so what he has separated we must not join.[170]

If Henry cited Jesus therein on the subject of human marriage (Matt. 19:6; Mark 10:9) as a controlling clarification of this cattle law against 'the gendering of diverse kinds together,' he identified said cattle law as corresponding to human marriage, and therein, the seventh commandment against adultery. And naturally so since, out of the ten, the commandment contra adultery is the one which most directly addresses 'yoking.' (Albeit, the concept of 'seeds' corresponds to the fifth, sixth, and seventh commandments as well.) The same is affirmed by Paul in 2 Corinthians 6:14-18. And the case law in question (Lev. 19:19) is hemmed in on either side by codes commanding one to "bear no grudge against the children of thy folk [race]" (Lev. 19:18) and a ruling against marital infidelity with a bondwoman—i.e., one, who though domiciled on the demesne of a man's estate, and in bond to him, represents a line foreign to the covenant of his house (Lev. 19:20). All of which have typically been understood as a set in Calvinist thought, as all have in common a concern for purity of 'seeds' and 'yoking' in one respect or another.

But what did Henry mean by 'monsters'? The canonist of Christian common law, Sir William Blackstone, tenders the legal definition of the word as it had been comprehended in Henry's time:

> A monster . . . hath no inheritable blood, and cannot be heir to any land, albeit it be brought forth in marriage. . . . But our law will not admit a birth of this kind to be such an issue as shall entitle the husband to be tenant by the courtesy; because it is not capable of inheriting. And therefore, if there appears no other heir than such a prodigious birth, the land shall escheat to the lord.[171]

This is the sense in which Henry clearly intended the term: an illegitimate offspring without heritable blood, one born of bastardy, or by congenital defect rendered contrary to the nature of his parentage. A monster in Christian common law fell under the category of nullius filius—'kin to nobody.' While we yet retain the definition of 'monster' in the general sense of a creature unnatural, our fathers at the time understood it in a slightly less fantastical way than we: not as a matter of

---

[170] Henry, Matthew. *Commentary on the Whole Bible*. Leviticus 19 Commentary
[171] Blackstone, Sir William. *Commentaries on the Laws of England: In Four Books, Volume 1*. 1884. p. 246.

fiction, but a real category of people. Augustine even waxed long about the 'monstrous births,' 'monstrous races,' and 'monstrous peoples' among men.[172]

Aside from denoting those races which seem so unnatural, the term 'monster' was in Henry's day applied interchangeably with the terms 'bastard' or 'mongrel.' But the legal and linguistic force of all such terms were dampened in popular English vernacular with the popularization of more exacting categories, which H.L. Mencken documents in *The American Language: Supplement I*:

- *White father & Negro mother: mulatto*
- *White father & Indian mother: mestizo*
- *Indian father & Negro mother: chino*
- *White father & mulatta mother: quarteron or quadroon*
- *White father & mestiza mother: creole*
- *White father & Chinese mother: chino-blanco*
- *White father & cuarterona mother: quintero or octoroon*
- *Negro father & Indian mother: zambo or mustee*
- *Negro father & mulatta mother: zambo-negro*
- *Negro father & mestiza mother: mulatta-oscuro*
- *Negro father & Chinese mother: zambo-chino*
- *Negro father & zamba mother: zambo-negro*
- *Negro father & cuarterona or quintera mother: mulatto*
- *Indian father & mulatta mother: chino-oscuro*
- *Indian father & mestiza mother: mestizo-claro*
- *Indian father & Chinese mother: chino-cholo*
- *Indian father & zamba mother: zambo-claro*
- *Indian father & china-chola mother: Indian*[173]

But as Mencken explains, "It was upon the advice of [Black leader] Booker T. Washington that it [the Census Bureau] began calling all colored persons of African blood Negroes. *Mulatto, quadroon* and *octoroon* have now almost disappeared from American speech."[174] Mr. Mencken further explains that Booker T. Washington's advice of retiring said categories was not on account of any perceived offense in them, nor technical inaccuracy, but only due to the fact that "the divisions ran imperceptibly into one another." This is possibly because the quarters of society in which said mixtures occurred had a total disregard of genealogy, and were the least discriminate in their mating habits; thus under their own inclinations, they rapidly rendered the above categories useless by recombinant overlaps of hered-

---

[172] Augustine, *City of God*, Book XVI, Chapter 8
[173] Mencken, H.L. *The American Language: Supplement I*, p. 631
[174] Ibid., p. 631

ity, most undocumented. In this light, Washington's solution to declare the African-miscegenated (and inbred) non-White communities in America as included in the catch-all appellation 'Negro.' The positive consequent of which was the preservation of the White community against admixture, as all cross-breeds were allocated to the Black community; the negative consequent of which was the further adulteration of the Black community. But as noted, this policy of absorption of the mulatto into Black society was adopted at the advisement of Black leaders such as Booker T. Washington.

Antecedent of this development however, the mulatto—the crossbreed of White and Black races—acquired its nomenclature in Christendom directly from the mule, the hybrid of horse and donkey. It is this particular hybrid—the mule—which one finds universally referenced by Reformed exegetes such as Calvin, Gill, Henry, Poole, all our Bible dictionaries, the Church fathers, et al., as well as Josephus, and the rabbinic authorities, as the perspicuous object of the yoking and seed laws. As Smith's Bible Dictionary defines it, the mule is "a hybrid animal. . . . It was forbidden to the Israelites to breed mules." So does the ATS Bible Dictionary state, "A mixed animal. . . . There is no probability that the Jews bred mules, because it was forbidden to couple creatures of different species, Leviticus 19:19." And Easton's Bible Dictionary makes the identical statement:

> *It is not probable that the Hebrews bred mules, as this was strictly forbidden in the law (Leviticus 19:19). . . . They are not mentioned, however, till the time of David, for the word rendered 'mules' (R.V. correctly, 'hot springs') in Genesis 36:24 (yemim) probably denotes the warm springs of Callirhoe, on the eastern shore of the Dead Sea. . . . Mules are not mentioned in the New Testament. Perhaps they had by that time ceased to be used in Palestine.*

This term mulatto (mule), then, was applied to the Euro-Black hybrid specifically because the mule was the subject under which our historical exegetes had foremost applied the hybrid laws. Designating the crossbreed of White and Black races a mulatto was the application of God's law to the matter and the unmistakable announcement of his illicit status and disordered parentage. This terminology was the fruit of our Christian fathers having applied God's Law-Word to every area of life and defining the world in terms of it.

As such, commenting on Leviticus 19:19, Rushdoony lays before us the sweeping principle of these seed and yoking laws:

> *These laws forbid the blurring of God-ordained distinctions. The nature and direction of sin is to blur and finally erase all the God-ordained boundaries. . . .*

> God's laws are case laws. If vegetable seeds are not to be mingled, nor an ass and a horse crossbred, then in the human realm it follows that the confusion of God-ordained boundaries is even more serious.[175]

The matter at which Rushdoony's a fortiori argument is driving—miscegenation, the hybridization or adulteration of men—is directly proscribed in Deuteronomy 23:2, wherein we read, "No bastard shall enter into the assembly." Since many others have demonstrated the etymological force of the term bastard (one born of adulteration) and the corresponding Hebrew term—*mamzer*—underlying it,[176] I here will venture to say only that we know the word mamzer to connote one of mixed race. Without delving too deeply into the lexical quagmire, we know this to be the case by way of the fact that our foremost Bible translations render the same word in Zechariah 9:6 'a mixed race' or, as in the NASB, 'a mongrel race.' Eerdman's Bible Dictionary (1987 ed., p. 129) includes this note in its definition for mamzer: "At Zech 9:6 'a mongrel people' [KJV, JB "bastard"; NIV "foreigners"] refers to a nation of mixed population." Which, in turn, confirms Luther's translation of mamzer (in Deut. 23:2) as a 'mischling'[177]—literally, a "mixling."

As such, H.B. Clark, the father of the theonomic code book Biblical Law, could confidently assess biblical marriage policy:

> And under Mosaic law, the right to marry a woman was regarded as "appertaining" to one of her kindred. A woman who "possessed" an "inheritance" was entitled to marry whom she thought best, "only to the family of the tribe of her father."[178]

Which is reminiscent of Augustine's words:

> But the ancient fathers, fearing that near relationship might gradually in the course of generations diverge, and become distant relationship, or cease to be relationship at all, religiously endeavored to limit it by the bond of marriage before it became distant, and thus, as it were, to call it back when it was escaping them. And on this account, even when the world was full of people, though they did not choose wives from their sisters of half-sisters, yet they preferred them to be of the same stock as themselves.[179]

---

[175] Rushdoony, R.J. *Leviticus*, p. 230. Page 178 in the Scribd version.
[176] I also covered various exegetical and linguistic evidences for this definition in my article "Rahab the Hebrew: The Royal Genealogy Vindicated"
[177] The University of Michigan has a searchable version of Luther's German Bible, which shows Deut. 23:2 and Zech. 9:6 as the two instances of *mischling* for *mamzer*.
[178] Clark, H.B. *Biblical Law*, p. 127, §189
[179] Augustine, *City of God*, Book XV, Chapter 16

This, it must be noted, means that the conviction of the Patriarchs prior to Sinai, and in advance of the Mosaic law, was contra miscegeny. But there was on this matter no conflict between that patriarchal ethic and the deuteronomical codes which followed. As Clark says, "Mosaic law forbids the marriage of a man to a woman to whom he is closely related, or to a 'strange woman' — one of another race or nation."[180] Because the matrimonial ethics of Abraham and Moses were identical in this matter:

> A time-honored rule forbids marriages with persons of another nation, race or tribe. Abraham required his eldest servant to swear that he would "not take a wife unto my son of the daughters of the Canaanites, among whom I dwell," but would "go unto my country, and to my kindred, and take a wife unto my son Isaac." (Gen. 24:3, 4) And Mosaic law provides that "thou (shalt not) make marriages" with those of other nations, "thy daughter thou shalt not give unto his son; nor his daughter shalt thou take unto thy son." (Deut. 7:3; Ezra 9:12; Neh. 10:30). . . . [I]t was doubtless intended . . . to preserve the racial integrity of the Israelites."[181]

In Leviticus 21:14 we find a racial insularity code specifying whom Levites, as exemplars to their people, were allowed to wed: "A widow, or a divorced woman, or profane, or an harlot, these shall he not take: but he shall take a virgin of his own people to wife." Today, should one raise this verse for consideration, it is repudiated on the grounds that in its specification of the tribe of Levi, it must be speaking to a ceremonial aspect of the law only, not any abiding moral dimension. But the compilers of the Jamieson-Fausset-Brown Bible Commentary (Lev 21) say to the contrary, "The same rules are extended to the families of Christian ministers."

Henry applies it to the NT priesthood of all believers:

> As these priests were types of Christ, so all ministers must be followers of him, that their example may teach others to imitate the Saviour. Without blemish, and separate from sinners, He executed his priestly office on earth. What manner of persons then should his ministers be! But all are, if Christians, spiritual priests; the minister especially is called to set a good example, that the people may follow it.[182]

If the OT priests were a type of Christ and we, the 'priesthood of all believers' in the NT, are to emulate Christ, then we assume the same standard of holiness and

---

[180] Clark, H.B. *op. cit.*, p. 134, §199
[181] Ibid., p. 135, §201
[182] Henry, Matthew. *Commentary on the Whole Bible*. Leviticus 21 Commentary.

sanctification prescribed to the Levites. Which is to say that as marriage law, Leviticus 21:14 is patently normative, amongst both the Israelite tribes and contemporary Christians.

But if some expositors have cast these marital codes as specific to one tribe and priest-class only, many others, such as Henry, have concluded to the contrary that the definition of a lawful marriage does not change when we speak of priests. (This, we recall, was a major bone of contention between Rome and Geneva.) Rather, like requirements for elders in the NT (Titus 1:5-9; 1 Tim. 3:1-13), the marital code for priests emphasizes the minister's status as an exemplar to his brethren, which in itself is merely compliance with the law of kin-rule (Deut. 17:15). Also proving the normativity of this principle among the tribes, we see in the inducement proffered in verse 15 that the alternative to homogeneous marriage for priests was to 'profane his seed among the people.' Matthew Poole elaborates:

Neither shall he profane his seed *by mixing it with forbidden kinds, whereby the children would be disparaged, and rendered unfit for their priestly function.* Do sanctify him, *i.e. have separated him from all other sorts of men for my especial and immediate service, and therefore will not have that race corrupted.*[183]

This verse, then, redoubles the necessary conclusion that the moral standard for priests was the same standard to which all Israelites were to aspire. Because we are told that doing otherwise for a Levite would 'profane his seed (posterity)' amongst his fellow Israelites. For in the eyes of his kinsmen, a priest who did not wed a virgin of his own folk was not living out the example of a holy life. Because holiness—i.e., separateness, distinction, and sanctification to God—is exemplified by a holistic pursuit of purity, inward and outward.

This is precisely the way we find Leviticus 21:14, 15 to have been applied among Israelites in the eighth century B.C., as Tobit (of the tribe of Naphtali, not Levi), much like Solomon (of Judah) (Prov. 5:20), commanded his son Tobias to "take a wife of the seed of thy fathers, and take not a strange woman to wife, which is not of thy father's tribe" (Tobit 4:12).

When the prophet Ezra surveyed the apostasy of Israel (Ezra 9:1-2), he expressly mentions Levites and Israelites as culpable under the same marital codes— that "the people of Israel, and the priests, and the Levites, have not separated themselves from the people of the lands." He bewails the fact of Levites' mixture not with the other tribes of Israel, but only with non-Israelites: "For they have taken of their daughters for themselves, and for their sons: so that the holy seed have mingled themselves with the people of those lands." The holy (separated) seed is not regarded as specific to the Levites in this context, but described unitarily and nationally.

---

[183] Poole, Matthew. *English Annotations on the Holy Bible.* 1685. Leviticus 21 Commentary.

If some still object to the priest being a moral exemplar to the nation, none seem to object to the same mechanism at work in his NT equivalent, the elder. The requirements for elders and deacons (the priesthood of the NT) in Titus 1 or 1 Timothy 3 are accepted in virtual unanimity as being a standard of virtue to be aimed at by all Christians. For who will object that every Christian man ought to strive to be 'blameless' (1 Tim. 3:2) or that his wife ought to be 'faithful in all things' (1 Tim. 3:11)? No, ceremonial laws notwithstanding, if the codes governing the sanctification of elders (priests) in the NT are taken for granted as exemplars for Christians generally, there appear no grounds for assuming a unique marital-moral code on Levi in the OT. The insularity codes of Levi appear normative. Eusebius proves this point by cross-reference of the Levitical codes in question with the laws of inheritance and adoption in Numbers 27 and 36:

> *And the lineage of Joseph thus being traced, Mary, also, at the same time, as far as can be, is evinced to be of the same tribe, since, by the Mosaic law, intermarriages among different tribes were not permitted. For the injunction is, to marry one of the same kindred and the same family, so that the inheritance may not be transferred from tribe to tribe.*[184]

Reading the Levitical marriage codes with reference to the inheritance statutes applied in the case of the daughters of Zelophehad leaves no room for doubt that the law aims holistically to preserve the distinctions not only between Israelites and other nations but also between the tribes of Israel.

On a practical level, how could it really be otherwise? For if we granted the Alienist assertion that this mandate was given only to the Levite, not to the other tribes, it posits that the Levites were in themselves a strict ethno-nation living amongst, and yet segregated by law, from all the other tribes which were really multitribal, or multiracial. But not only would such an interpretation fail to prove Alienism, it would seem only to cause many more problems than it solves. Such an interpretation renders the law internally conflicted, both granting and denying ethnonationalism at once. Add to that the fact that it directly confounds that central Alienist assertion, that under God's law there are no tiered standards, but all laws apply equally to all. This, then, is the refutation of the Alienist cavils — that God's Word cannot contradict itself.

Plainly, in order for Levites to marry homogeneously from amongst Israelite stock, that stock must in fact exist. And to exist, it must abide as a limited and homogeneous entity, not admitting disparate races on the basis of statist abstractions. Any alternative renders the law incoherent. Inasmuch as the Levitical marital codes pertain to marriage, they are clearly expositions of the seventh word contra adultery and, therefore, moral in nature, not ceremonial.

---

[184] Eusebius Pamphilus, *Ecclesiastical History*, Chapter VII

Yes, as has been meticulously exposited by others, we know the prophets Ezra and Nehemiah held Israel as a whole to this same standard and separated those of Israelite lineage from their foreign wives and their adulterate children. According to Matthew Henry's commentary on Deuteronomy 23, this resolution of the prophets was carried out as the divine and authoritative interpretation of the law (see especially Neh. 13:1-3) to prevent "the separated seed of Israel mingling themselves" with strange peoples (Ezra 9:1, 2; 10:3). And because "they [had] dealt treacherously against the Lord: for they [had] begotten strange children" (Hos. 5:7). The word rendered 'strange' there in Hosea is *zuwr*, which means "foreign or alien," strongly related to *nokri*, which appears in Isaiah's admonishment against those who were "pleased with the children of foreigners" (Isa. 2:6). Where today are the ministers who yet will chastise those pleased with foreign children?

In the context of the national covenant of which the seventh law is part, the case is clear: heterogeneous unions do more than presage the national judgment (Deut. 28; Lev. 26): the two are coextensive. Infidelity is, in large part, its own judgment. No grimmer finality seems betokened in the ruling of any civil court than that issued of the court of heaven on this subject:

> *12Else if ye do in any wise go back, and cleave unto the remnant of these nations, even these that remain among you, and shall make marriages with them, and go in unto them, and they to you: 13know for a certainty that the Lord your God will no more drive out any of these nations from before you; but they shall be snares and traps unto you, and scourges in your sides, and thorns in your eyes, until ye perish from off this good land which the Lord your God hath given you.*
>
> Joshua 23:12-13

This is why, writing on the subject of unequal yoking in Deuteronomy 22:10 and 2 Corinthians 6:14, Rushdoony concluded holistically:

> *The burden of the law is thus against inter-religious, inter-racial, and inter-cultural marriages, in that they normally go against the very community which marriage is designed to establish. Unequal yoking means more than marriage. In society at large it means the enforced integration of various elements which are not congenial. Unequal yoking is in no realm productive of harmony; rather, it aggravates the differences and delays the growth of the different elements toward a Christian harmony and association.[185]*

The ad-alteration, 'unlawful marriages', or 'unequal yoking' of a seed — be it familial, societal, or racial — is a violation of the seventh law which results in the cuckoldry of hybridization and long-term sterility.

---

[185] Rushdoony, R.J. *The Institutes of Biblical Law*, p. 257

The Eighth Word
July 26, 2016

Thou shalt not steal.
Exodus 20:15

It isn't just about filching. Robbery comes in many forms.

Among the duties required in this law, Westminster Larger Catechism question #141 includes:

Faithfulness, and justice in contracts and commerce between man and man; rendering to everyone his due; . . . a provident care and study to get, keep, use, and dispose these things which are necessary and convenient for the sustentation of our nature, and suitable to our condition; . . . avoiding unnecessary . . . suretiship, or other like engagements.

As it pertains to property rights, the eighth commandment is intrinsically bound up with both the fifth and tenth commandments. For in the fifth we find that the inducement toward honoring our fathers and mothers is that we might thereby live long in 'the land which our God gives us.' The tenth, of course—a prohibition against coveting anything which is our neighbor's—forbids even the confusion of property in one's own heart, including all ideological views which might otherwise dilute ownership or undermine natural boundaries.

The term 'faithfulness' in catechism question #141 suggests much in itself, especially in terms of the present collision of Alienism with Kinism. And incredibly, 'rendering to everyone his due' strikes a chord, because Alienists insist that what is due from White Christians to non-Whites, Christian or otherwise, is our time, treasure, land, and children, and often our lives. Everything. Which is to say their standard goes far beyond God's law. However, the words 'a provident care and study to get, keep, use, and dispose these things which are necessary and convenient for the sustentation of our nature, and suitable to our condition' grants Christians individually, but also familially, tribally, nationally, and racially, the prerogative to secure their own existence with an eye toward the preservation of their respective natures. More than that, it actually *mandates* it.

Among other things, the Westminster position on the eighth word requires the self-defense of property, territory, and borders for the maintenance of our physical safety pursuant of our God-ordained peoplehood. This is so inasmuch as the case-law entailment of this commandment prohibits 'the moving of thy neighbor's landmark' (Deut. 19:14; 27:17), for which Hosea strongly indicted the princes of Judah, as they would not maintain the borders between the tribes or against foreign incursion (Hos. 5:10). Paul likewise drew upon this principle when he affirmed the continued demarcation of bounds between the nations (Acts 17:26). Even if this concept of property lines has its primary application to one's own estate, it is nonetheless treated in the text as extending unobstructedly to macro-territories of kinship groups as well. As the refrain goes, "races are but families writ large."

The 'sustentation of our nature, suitable to our condition' referenced in the catechism means self-preservation. This was the rationale behind Magna Carta, the Declaration of Arbroath, the Solemn League and Covenant, the Stamp Act, and the Declaration of Independence. This blood-and-soil principle is evident, too, in Cotton's Abstract of the Laws of New England, wherein we read that land grants were protected by allodial title "to such persons and to their heirs and assigns forever, as their property" (IV.1) and that "inheritances are to descend naturally to the next of kin, according to the law of nature, delivered by God" (IV.5), This aspect of Christian ethics is precisely the argument historically leveled in America for segregation and in South Africa for apartheid. As Griffin has summarized it:

> *Almost from their arrival in 1630, the Puritans instituted laws and practices designed to ensure that blacks would never be a part of their holy cities. . . . Their homes could not be next door to whites, but only in non-white residential areas. Blacks were excluded from the military, prohibited from serving on juries, and denied full citizenship, thus preventing them from voting.*[186]

For the alternative—neglect of 'the sustentation of our nature'—necessarily produces results '[un]suitable to our condition.' This is why even presently, White Alienists insist on raising their families in 'good neighborhoods' (read 'majority White'): because they know in their hearts that the alternative is to needlessly consign their children to social and physical conditions which White people find intolerable, and plainly unlivable. What seems to Black and Brown Christians normal life is to White Christians abject savagery, for Whites in proximity to large numbers of non-Whites experience a level of violence and rapine known to us nowhere but in historical theaters of open warfare.

Beyond the positive admonition to sustain our respective natures, question #142 lists among the sins forbidden in the eighth word, 'removing landmarks' (i.e., property lines and borders) and forbids 'depopulations' of peoples from their rightful territories. This explains Moses's having asked permission for the children of Israel to pass through the territory of their cousin-nation, Edom (Num. 20:16-21). He even offered to pay a toll for passage. This makes no sense at all unless Moses understood national borders as the legitimate property line of a people. Hoffmeier confirms just this:

---

[186] Griffin, Paul. *Seeds of Racism in the Soul of America*, p. 22f.

> The obvious question is, were ancient territorial borders taken seriously and was national sovereignty recognized? The answer is emphatically, yes. . . .
>
> It is worth noting that even a traveler, a foreigner, passing through the territory of another had to obtain permission to do so. . . .
>
> [N]ations could and did control their borders and determine who could pass through the land. On the individual, family, and clan level property was owned and boundaries established. . . . For this reason Mosaic law prohibited the removal of landmarks (Deut. 19:14).[187]

It is no coincidence, therefore, that wherever and to whatever degree Calvinism has held sway in any land, so too have ethno-nationalism, segregation, and paternalism. As Vos states it, in his commentary on Babel and the Table of Nations:

> Nationalism, within proper limits, has the divine sanction. . . .
>
> Now it is through maintaining the national diversities, as these express themselves in the difference of language, and are in turn upheld by this difference, that God prevents realization of the attempted scheme. . . . [T]here was [also] a positive intent that concerned the natural life of humanity. Under the providence of God each race or nation has a positive purpose to serve, fulfilment of which depends on relative seclusion from others.[188]

This is to say that apartheid, in some fashion, has ever been the purview of Reformed Christianity, because when our fathers defined the Scripture as 'the only rule for faith and practice,' they did not shrink from the prophet Nehemiah's rallying cry to his kinsmen as they rebuilt the walls (borders) of Jerusalem, one hand on their trowels, and one on their swords:

> And I looked, and rose up, and said to the nobles, and to the rulers, and to the rest of the people, Be not ye afraid of them: remember the Lord, which is great and terrible, and fight for your brethren, your sons, and your daughters, your wives, and your clans.
>
> Neh. 4:14

Irrespective of subscriptionist pretensions on the part of Alienists, Kinists are the sole remaining heirs and testators to the substance of the Westminster standard here and the doctrine of boundaries as it lies in Scripture.

This is certainly the case as Alienists in Reformed circles popularly argue, in the culture-of-critique fashion of the mid-twentieth century communists, that borders, like the nationalism which they presuppose, are but an artifice of eighteenth-century colonialism. (Never mind that the word 'bounds' appears eight times in

---

[187] Hoffmeier, James. *The Immigration Crisis*, pp.32, 33
[188] Vos, Geerhardus. *Biblical Theology*, p. 60

Scripture, or that the word 'borders' appears forty-two times, nor even that there are one hundred and fifty-six mentions of the singular term 'border' in Scripture: clearly, borders are no Enlightenment novelty.) Or, as I heard one OPC minister out of Long Beach, CA, absurdly argue from the pulpit back in the year 2001, "Israel's foremost sin, and the sin for which God judged them, was maintaining borders." Most Alienists flit back and forth between these two arguments like caged birds with only two perches from which to choose. Despite the precariousness of each, both of these excuses are subservient to the central liberal conviction that secure borders are exclusionary and prejudiced, and therefore, somehow contrary to Christian ethics. But Hoffmeier has rebuffed them:

> *Even in ancient times there were clearly delineated lands or countries, some large and others tiny. This is why the Old Testament speaks of the border of the land of Canaan (Ex. 16:35), Egypt (1 Kings 4:21; 2 Chron. 9:26; 26:8), and the borders of Israel (1 Sam. 27:1). . . .*
>
> *Israel's borders are given at different times and places in the Bible, sometimes in general terms, sometimes in great detail. For example, when the land is first promised to Abraham . . . 'from the river of Egypt unto the great river, the river Euphrates' (Gen. 15:18). In Joshua's day, however, when the twelve territories are divided up among the Israelite tribes, each territory within Israel is described in incredible detail, occupying seven chapters of the book of Joshua (13-19).*[189]

It wasn't just the borders of Israel which were considered sacrosanct under God's law. As Bahnsen argued so decisively:

> *Israel's obedience to God's law was intended to be an example to the nations. . . . The law morally binds the nations, and that means the magistrates of the world kingdoms are as much under ethical obligation as the fathers, craftsmen, or children of those nations.*[190]

Concluding this point Bahnsen says, "The moral obligation for rulers to guide and judge in terms of the holy law of God remains identical for both Israel and the world nations."[191]

If the applicability of Theonomy to contemporary nations outside Israel was Bahnsen's central thesis, he everywhere presupposed a legitimate plurality of nations preceding, persisting contemporaneously beside, and extending beyond the era of the Israelite Republic into the Christian age. Bahnsen's view of nations and borders then comports with Calvin's classic passage on the subject:

---

[189] Hoffmeier, James. *op cit.*, pp. 29-30
[190] Bahnsen, Greg. *Theonomy in Christian Ethics*, 3rd ed., pp. 346-347
[191] Ibid., p. 354

> *Now, we see, as in a camp, every troop and band hath his appointed place, so men are placed upon earth, that every people may be content with their bounds, and that among these people every particular person may have his mansion. But though ambition have, oftentimes raged, and many, being incensed with wicked lust, have past their bounds, yet the lust of men hath never brought to pass, but that God hath governed all events from out of his holy sanctuary. For though men, by raging upon earth, do seem to assault heaven, that they may overthrow God's providence, yet they are enforced, whether they will or no, rather to establish the same. Therefore, let us know that the world is so turned over through divers tumults, that God doth at length bring all things unto the end which he hath appointed.*[192]

Aside from Calvin's and Bahnsen's perspective here, Isaiah's descriptions of the Millennial age would be unintelligible: "Violence shall no more be heard in thy land, wasting nor destruction within thy *borders*" (Isa. 60:18). Such, too, is the case with the words of David: "My Son art Thou; today have I begotten Thee. Ask of Me, and I will give the nations as Thine heritage, and as Thy possession, the *bounds* of the earth" (Ps. 2:7-8). Christ is the Lord of all boundaries. His law institutes and maintains them. And as He swore to Israel (Deut. 28; Lev. 26), He has reserved the fall of their borders to aliens as the great curse to wipe unbent nations from the earth. Or as Isaiah says it, "Your land, strangers devour it in your presence, and it is desolate, as overthrown by strangers" (Isa. 1:7). "For the nation and kingdom that will not serve thee shall perish; yea, those nations shall be utterly wasted" (Isa. 60:12).

Of course, the inverse corollary of the prophet's words there is that the nation which serves God's Kingdom and keeps His law will live, and their land shall not be stolen by alien peoples. Which is to say that Theonomy intrinsically connotes nationalism.

Slightly oblique, however, to the matter of nationalism is monetary policy. Suffice it to say that the connection between them is still evident in everyday issues of *national* economy, *national* debt, GDP, exchange rates, interstate commerce, etc. Inasmuch as money matters are matters of property, they are a clear concern to the eighth word as well. If the catechism cites among things forbidden under the eighth word "fraudulent dealing, false weights and measures, . . . oppression, extortion, usury, bribery, vexatious lawsuits, . . . ingrossing commodities to enhance the price; unlawful callings, and all other unjust or sinful ways of taking or withholding from our neighbor what belongs to him," it would seem to indict the entire monetary apparatus of our day.

A seminal aspect of modern finance is fractional reserve banking. Much ink has been spilt and many tomes dedicated to this subject, so I will not elaborate

---

[192] Calvin, John. *Commentary on Acts*. Acts 17

overly much here. But I would offer a couple points for consideration: first, it is a sublimated species of usury—a matter worthy of discussion in itself.[193] Because inflation necessarily acts as a covert form of interest as well as a hidden tax. As the money supply is enlarged, wealth is quietly extracted from every man's savings. This is enslavement of the *Gemeinfrei*.

But the language historically applied to the subject of fractionalized currency is quite familiar to our broader discussion here; our fathers spoke of it as 'adulteration':

> *Nations have sometimes, for the same purpose, adulterated the standard of their coin; that is, have mixed a greater quantity of alloy in it. . . . The adulteration of the standard has exactly the same effect with what the French call an augmentation, or a direct raising of the denomination of the coin.*
>
> *An augmentation, or a direct raising of the denomination of the coin, always is, and from its nature must be, an open and avowed operation. By means of it pieces of a smaller weight and bulk are called by the same name which had before been given to pieces of a greater weight and bulk. The adulteration of the standard, on the contrary, has generally been a concealed operation. . . . When King John of France, in order to pay his debts, adulterated his coin, all the officers were sworn to secrecy. Both operations are unjust. But a simple augmentation is an injustice of open violence, whereas the adulteration is an injustice of treacherous fraud. This latter operation, therefore, as soon as it has been discovered, and it could never be concealed very long, has always excited much greater indignation than the former. The coin after any considerable augmentation has very seldom been brought back to its former weight; but after the greatest adulterations it has almost always been brought back to its former fineness. It has scarce happened that the fury and indignation of the people could otherwise be appeased.*[194]

This strikes at the substance of the biblical admonition to "just weights and measures" (e.g. Deut. 25:15; Lev. 19:36; Prov. 11:1) and raises the question of why Americans seem to have consented to the mass larceny and ostensible enslavement of our nation, especially since the Federal Reserve Act of 1913. But it also establishes the correspondence between the eighth word and the seed and yoking statutes which primary fall under the seventh word. The matter of adulteration transcends not only Rushdoony's emphasis on murder (the sixth word) and the question of illicit unions (the seventh word) itself, but by way of fraud and counterfeit, it is, as Smith testifies, an especially pernicious subset of theft also. Admittedly, this interpretation of inflation as a violation of multiple commandments is not a novel one. Among others, Franklin Sanders has made the same point:

---

[193] See S.C. Mooney's *Usury: Destroyer of Nations*, and Michael Hoffman's *Usury in Christendom*, and Calvin Elliott's *Usury: A Scriptural, Ethical, and Economic View*
[194] Smith, Adam. *Wealth of Nations*, p. 728

> Inflation is easy. That's just outright theft by fraud and adulteration, so start with the Eighth commandment, "Thou shalt not steal," and the Seventh Commandment, "Thou shalt not commit adultery." Then work your way through all the applications of those commandments to honest weights and measures.[195]

But Weaver has identified real property in land and borders as a seminal bulwark in society against the ethereal anti-national monetary schemes, saying:

> While we are looking at the moral influence of real property, let us observe, too, that it is the individual's surest protection against that dishonor called adulteration. If one surveys the economic history of the West for the past several centuries, he discovers not only a decline of craftsmanship but also, a related phenomenon, a steady shrinkage in the value of money. . . . A familiar term for this process is inflation, but, whatever it may be called, it represents the payment with depreciated media…[196]

> [P]roductive private property represents a kind of sanctuary against robbery through adulteration, for the individual getting his sustenance from property which bears his imprint and assimilation has a more real measure of value. . . . There is, moreover, a natural connection between the sense of honor and the personal relationship of property. As property becomes increasingly an abstraction and the sense of affinity fades, there sets in a strong temptation to adulterate behind a screen of anonymity.[197]

Albeit fiat currency and its consequent—inflation—are evident as unjust weights and measures, covert usury, and theft, we see that they have also generally been spoken of in the exact same terms as crossbreeding and adultery of seeds: adulteration. This intimates the near entwinement of the eighth word with the seventh; aside from theft, fractional reserve currency is an unequal yoking of media, an alloyed and fraudulent instrument, bastardized lucre, and in this oblique sense, adultery. Not only is adulterated media an enticement away from the land, but that initial turn toward fraud necessarily inaugurates a predatory economy resulting in the matricular cannibalization of all real property, and the dispossession of houses and nations. On the individual scale, this turn of heart to ascend, by hook or by crook, is an immediate renunciation of the life communal. This dynamic creates its own feedback loop, like a grassfire producing its own winds, which in turn whip their originating flames into a many-times-hotter conflagration. So laissez-faire capitalism, Marxism, and all intermediary subcategories of economism only

---

[195] Sanders, Franklin. "The Wages Of Sin (Are Paid In Fiat Money)." *The Money Changer*.
[196] Weaver, Richard. *Ideas Have Consequences*, p. 139
[197] Ibid., p. 141

compel neighbors and societies to the same predation with exponential effect toward total discorporation. Decoupled from the land, men feel the greater inducement to social anonymity and familial atomization, and nations trend toward further compromise and disintegration. When land or money recede from their true natures and functions—as Yeats poetizes—"Things fall apart; the centre cannot hold."

As Weaver notes, "Adulterated currency is a political weapon"[198] renowned in history as 'a destroyer of nations' as it thrives on perpetual war and the incremental estrangement of peoples from their ancestral lands. Its power as a political weapon has been the principal means of economic warfare at least since the 1630s; and it has since been used to divest, overthrow, enslave, and uproot whole peoples from their homelands—just the sort of depopulations warded against in the catechism. Herein we see the intimate overlap of adulteration of currency with the moving of thy neighbor's landmarks: these twin forces of theft act in a macabre synergy of macroeconomics to purge unworthy families, tribes, and nations from the land. Rushdoony's words on property and landmarks are poignant here, as he reconnects the eighth commandment contra theft to the sixth contra murder:

> *If it is a crime to alter property landmarks to defraud a neighbor of his land, how much greater a crime to alter social landmarks, the Biblical foundations of law and society, and thereby bring about the death of that social order? If it is a crime to rob banks, then surely it is a crime to rob and murder a social order.*[199]

Theft, no matter how petty, creates a cascading effect in the world which, if not redressed according to biblical law and penology, ultimately culminates in the overthrow of societies, and causes the land to vomit out whole lineages of men. As Rushdoony's a fortiori argument runs, the cumulative macro-effects of normalized petty theft are murderous unto genocide.

> *Because the Bible is a land-based book, and our faith tied to the earth as the Lord's (Ps. 24:1), the question is not an academic one. For modern man, land has become a commodity and an investment, not essentially a faith inheritance. Our modern outlook thus warps our perspective. For this reason, our federal government thinks nothing of allowing in as immigrants an increasing number of people who are religiously and racially hostile to us. They see no relationship between faith and land. As a result, the United States and the Western world have embarked on a suicidal course. They reject the concept of Christendom and embrace instead the humanistic "family of man," and thus immigration policies in the U.S. and Europe are based on myths and illusions of a destructive nature. Because neither*

---

[198] Ibid., p. 140
[199] Rushdoony, R.J. *The Institutes of Biblical Law*, p. 332

> land nor inheritance is now seen from the perspective of faith, we have problems in these spheres. The modern state sees itself as the primary owner, and hence eminent domain is basic to its life, and it therefore views itself as the primary heir with death taxes. Both a tax on the land and death taxes are anti-Biblical.
>
> A disregard for ties to the land has been one of the most destructive forces of the twentieth century. In Africa, artificial nations were created after World War II without regard for the fact that they encompassed rival warring tribes. Artificial unions such as Yugoslavia were created after World War I, bringing together differing peoples and religious groups. All such efforts have simply created chaos and conflict. The rationalistic planners of our time are Hegelians: for them, the rational is the real, and their rational ideas become a Procrustean bed on which humanity is tortured.[200]

As much as our identity in property and territory bespeaks our creaturely connection to the soil, it also reflects the *imago Dei* in man. For property and its governance are the recapitulation of God's sovereignty and providence. The Christian man must be provident over his own jurisdictions, which are, in keeping with his finite nature, limited. This, in conjunction with the reality that the *mishpachah* (clan-family) is presented to us as the central social unit in Scripture, depicts a dominion mandate of blood and soil. Again, this was well recognized by the Puritans, who stipulated, "Inheritances are to descend naturally to the next of kin, according to the law of nature, delivered by God."[201]

In principle, this was but a recapitulation of Levitical law, which specified that though aliens might lease a parcel of land from an Israelite clan, they could never own it; for at the year of Jubilee "each of you shall return to his possession, and each of you shall return to his family" (Lev. 25:10). All tracts of land sublet to strangers (and even to the neighboring tribes of Israel) were restored to the clans and tribes originally bestowed them by allotment. This protectionist measure secured all the Israelite lines against dispossession by strangers. As the Son of God is the Inheritor of all His Father's dominion, the same economy is reflected in the laws governing the sons of men: inheritance is defined by heritage and heirship. Even if some should be disinherited through unfaithfulness, the condition of inheritance through kinship was not fungible, and could not upon prescription to any creed be contracted to an outside party. In the common law of England this principle was understood as encompassing even the magistrate, as even kings were not allowed to trespass against the estate of any common man. This famed Anglo-Saxon concept of 'castle law' came about only by the undergirding principle in biblical law where the use and jurisdictions of property could no more be

---

[200] Rushdoony, R.J. *Numbers*, p. 290 in the Scribd version.
[201] Cotton, John. *An Abstract of the Laws of New England*, IV.5

adulterated or compromised than could their currency. The alternative in both cases was fraud and theft.

The concept of property—private, familial, communal, and national—removes objects and relations from all bids of contention. Property is then essential to the framework of genuine peace, laying to rest the anarchical contest which everywhere obtains in the absence of blood-and-soil dominion. The alternative to the Kinist view is what we have now—property tax, usurious mortgages, eminent domain, no-knock warrantless searches, usurpations by alien peoples, and depopulations of our folk, all facilitated by foreign banking clans who adulterate our money as a means to rob us of everything we have. The alternative to the Kinist view is that there are no areas or things over which one can truly claim dominion and moral custody under God. Aside from the Kinist understanding of these matters, there are only anarchistic or Marxian conceptions of property and value: barbarism.

The Ninth Word
July 27, 2016

Thou shalt not bear false witness against thy neighbour.
Exodus 20:16

Westminster Larger Catechism question 144 lists among the duties ascribed in the ninth word:

The preserving and promoting of truth between man and man, and the good name of our neighbour, as well as our own; appearing and standing for the truth; . . . fully, speaking the truth . . . in matters of judgment and justice, and in all other things whatsoever; . . . discouraging tale-bearers, flatterers, and slanderers; love and care of our own good name, and defending it when need requireth; . . . studying and practicing of whatsoever things are true, honest, lovely, and of good report.

Among the things conversely forbidden by the ninth word in question 145, we find:

All prejudicing the truth, and the good name of our neighbours, as well as our own, . . . suborning false witnesses, . . . pleading for an evil cause, . . . passing unjust sentence, calling evil good, and good evil; . . . concealing the truth, undue

> silence in a just cause, and holding our peace when iniquity calleth for either a reproof from ourselves, or complaint to others; . . . perverting [truth] to a wrong meaning, or in doubtful and equivocal expressions, to the prejudice of truth or justice; speaking untruth, lying, . . . stopping our ears against just defense.

Looking on American society in the throes of cultural revolution, and having narrowly survived the gulag erected under the same principles as those then sweeping America, Solzhenitsyn warned somberly: "Live not by lies." We did not heed him. So it is today that the entire Western world languishes under an all-pervasive web of lies which all men are demanded to tell in unison. If the above definition provided by the catechism doesn't set off fireballs in your mind around the unfolding secular orthodoxy of Political Correctness, which ostensibly mandates lying to some degree on almost every subject, odds are you are a cheerful collaborator in the lie. Or at the very least, benumbed to it.

What is political correctness? Merriam-Webster's dictionary defines the adjectival form as: "conforming to a belief that language and practices which could offend political sensibilities (as in matters of sex or race) should be eliminated." And the "simple definition" is "agreeing with the idea that people should be careful to not use language or behave in a way that could offend a particular group of people." Bill Lind elaborates:

> *If we look at it analytically, if we look at it historically, we quickly find out exactly what it is. Political Correctness is cultural Marxism. It is Marxism translated from economic into cultural terms. . . .*
>
> *Since reality contradicts [PC], reality must be forbidden. It must become forbidden to acknowledge the reality of our history. People must be forced to live a lie, and since people are naturally reluctant to live a lie, they naturally use their ears and eyes to look out and say, "Wait a minute. This isn't true. I can see it isn't true," the power of the state must be put behind the demand to live a lie. That is why ideology invariably creates a totalitarian state.*[202]

We are talking about a moral philosophy the core principles of which are to conceal, obfuscate, distort, and suppress the truth in any number of areas by the full spectrum of social, economic, and political force—legal or otherwise. To speak truth contrary to Marxian propaganda with respect to race, culture, gender, history, ecology, medicine, or any other topic is forbidden. Conversely, corporate assent to and programmed recitation of lies are declared mandatory. It is demanded of every man, woman, and child in every aspect of their lives to be an active participant in conspiracy against the truth.

---

[202] Lind, Bill. "The Origins Of Political Correctness." *Accuracy In Academia.* 5 Feb 2000.

From the perspective of the PC-initiate, no fate is too grim for him who dares tell the truth. If the legal consequences of such trespasses are severe and draconian, the social consequences are oft more so, and winked at by the legal system. Relegating truth-tellers to pariahhood is the goal. Or at least the goal short of a shallow grave.

As witnessed in recent events, when a Christian baker or wedding photographer dares not collude in the make-believe sham of 'gay marriage,' he is sued and harassed by mobs, myriad government agencies, and media: the official unofficial conclusion of the matter is banishment to the outskirts of society. Any with the temerity to reject what all know for a lie, whether in public or private, are subject to an avalanche of public scorn, including the ruination of career, calls for confiscation of the offender's children, imprisonment, and psychological reprogramming for all in his orbit of association. Total marginalization. And in the American prison system, confinement on any charge can be a death sentence—especially so for White Christians arraigned for trespass against the PC doctrines of race. When violence ensues on the politically incorrect, in or out of the judicial complex, and irrespective of all other facts, the hive-society—frothing zealots and demoralized reluctants alike—shrug their collective shoulders and mutter, "He had it coming." So as it pertains to violators of PC shibboleths, death threats are a matter of course, and people feel free to publicly wish for the children of such traditionalists to be molested by deviants so as to 'fix them.' Threats of rape and violence aimed even at the wives and children of those who speak truth on an array of subjects are now commonplace, and the system regards such horror aloofly, as a natural consequence and justified response from enlightened post-Christian society. All are expected to join in the collective hexing of the offender by voicing desires to see him killed, his wife violated, his children seized by the state and raised according to the sadistic whim of whatever privileged group his words or actions may have offended. Perhaps no harm was done another? No matter. Neither the substance of God's law nor any mitigating circumstances rise to consideration of the Alienist when one is perceived to run askance of cultural Marxism.

And that with an eye toward raising 'certain groups of people' above criticism, and demoting others—White Christian Males especially—below any level of respect. Inconceivably, Political Correctness contains within it the mutually exclusive concepts of egalitarianism, White guilt, equalitarianism, and deference to the Alien over the familiar. Whatever it does not level, it inverts. It is an ingrained visceral commitment to collective perjury. It taints and corrodes everything. This is, I regret to say, patently the social ethic now installed even in the churches. And as Otto Scott and Rushdoony noted, it leaves no Christian doctrine untouched:

> [Scott] I don't really know what the church today sermonizes against. Once we… when we really come to it, all sins seem to have shriveled down to racism.

[Rushdoony] Yes.
[Scott] Beyond that there is no sin.
[Rushdoony] Yes. That is very good. That is about the only sin that is left. And that is an odd thing to choose as a sin, because one of the characteristics of people all over the world has been a preference for their own. People prefer their own families. They prefer their own nationality or their own race, which is entirely legitimate as long as they don't abuse and mistreat others. I believe that the world has seen more racism in this century than ever before precisely because we are trying to equalize everything and we are trying to obscure the differences and say they don't exist. And when you do that, you are going to create a situation where there will be a bootlegged and resentful recognition of differences.
[Scott] Well, you drive underground what doesn't belong underground. The business of justice, the business of treating people fairly, the business of equality before law and meritocracy, so to speak, of making opportunities open to all, the whole idea of a civilized society is based on the idea of mutual respect. But respect is one thing. A denial of reality is something else. If in order to get along or to placate we have to pretend that everyone has the same intellect and intelligence, the same ability, then we have downgraded all intelligence and all ability.
[Rushdoony] Yes.
[Scott] It is usually a question of let's you and he be equal. Not you and I.
[Rushdoony] Yes. Well, by obscuring the fact of differences, what we have done is to create a climate in which any awareness of reality is gone.
[Scott] Well, it is dishonest.
[Rushdoony] Yes. You are not living in a real world if you don't recognize differences and say he is better than I am. He is of another color. And he or she is not as good as I am in this particular field where I am good.[203]

As Scott observed, this new ethical paradigm displacing Christian morality in the street and the pulpit is fundamentally dishonest. And about virtually everything. With lies thus institutionalized in all our institutional denominations, if one speaks of the distinctions between races in terms of color, crime, intelligence, athleticism, or even their mention in Scripture, he will be tried for heresy. If he speak of objective moral, aesthetic, or cultural standards, superiors and inferiors, the biblical definitions of nation and family, an honest approach to history, or even the objectivity and unity of truth, he will be slandered as 'worse than a pedophile' and driven from the communion table. The undergirding presuppositions of this ersatz orthodoxy are well-acknowledged for cultural Marxism. As Theodore Dalrymple commented on communist societies:

In my study of communist societies, I came to the conclusion that the purpose of communist propaganda was not to persuade or convince, nor to inform, but to

---

[203] Easy Chair episode "Envy," @ 24:42.

humiliate; and therefore, the less it corresponded to reality the better. When people are forced to remain silent when they are being told the most obvious lies, or even worse when they are forced to repeat the lies themselves, they lose once and for all their sense of probity. To assent to obvious lies is to co-operate with evil, and in some small way to become evil oneself. One's standing to resist anything is thus eroded, and even destroyed. A society of emasculated liars is easy to control. I think if you examine political correctness, it has the same effect and is intended to.[204]

To the extent that citing or even being suspected of favoring politically incorrect facts results in civil repercussions such as detainment, investigation, audit, arrest, all manner of litigious action, and even extradition, these thought-crimes are ever assumed to be actionable in the domain of the courts. Whereas, in Christian law, though lying is sin, petty lying incurs no civil penalty. However, another form of false witness—perjury—does. And since the the penology of perjury is being brought to bear in the case of 'hate crimes,' it is as if we are, each one of us, now ever on the witness stand. Except, in this inverted order, men suffer the recompense for perjury if they tell the truth, even in the most mundane matters, and for the most benevolent motives.

The legal artifice known as 'hate crime' is that wherein straight White Christian Men receive draconian punishment not for any injury wrongly done another, but for the mere suspicion of his thinking forbidden truths in proximity of minorities. And that, even when the minority be the majority.

The sacrosanct status ascribed to minorities upon which this legal artifice rests also drags the matter into the highest category of lying—blasphemy—speaking falsely or defamatorily about God. (Thus the matter touches also the third word.) For in the new orthodoxy minorities (or their archetypes) comprise a new pantheon of the gods. We know this because they are being venerated as gods, and to demure from recitation of the mandated lies exalting the new Baals, one is regarded as the worst sort of criminal—one depraved beyond comparison to any other category of criminal, reprobate beyond all remedy. Of course, to treat the matter so, they have to overtly declare good evil and evil good. So they have. The lie is total, pervading their deepest convictions, and the irrationality of that lie compels them to a ravening state, 'suppressing the truth in unrighteousness' (Rom. 1:18), and, therein, total reprobation.

In Christian and Anglo-Saxon law slander, lying about someone to his hurt, was always illegal. But in 1913, not coincidentally, just two months in advance of the Federal Reserve Act, the Anti-Defamation League of B'nai B'rith was born. Its charter states:

---

[204] Dalrymple, Theodore. *Frontpage Magazine* interview "Our Culture, What's Left of It," 31 Aug 2005.

> The immediate object of the League is to stop, by appeals to reason and conscience and, if necessary, by appeals to law, the defamation of the Jewish people. Its ultimate purpose is to secure justice and fair treatment to all citizens alike and to put an end forever to unjust and unfair discrimination against and ridicule of any sect or body of citizens.

Though defamation is taken in common speech as a synonym for slander or libel, which mean lying about someone, it is often prosecuted throughout the Western world as telling injurious truths—particularly when it regards 'minorities,' i.e., non-Whites and non-Christians. "The truth is no defense."[205] And the now-ubiquitous terminology of 'hate speech' is couched in this anti-defamation principle. These pseudo-Talmudic penological categories are entirely at odds with the traditional reckoning of the ninth word, which commands "speaking the truth . . . in matters of judgment and justice, and in all other things whatsoever." This means that Christians can in no way move nor act in harmony with the values of the Jewish ADL. They are at opposite poles of the ethical spectrum, as Judaism regards the whole of the New Testament to be the consummate defamation of the Jews. In fact, ADL chairman Abe Foxman describes the New Testament and Christian preaching as 'deicide libel.'[206] Under direction of the ADL, the federal government effectively treats those who believe "Jews are responsible for the death of Christ" as anti-Semites,[207] tacitly condemning all Bible-believing Christians—a resolution which portends much evil.

But Alienist churchmen—virtually the whole of the institutional church today—have taken to this anti-Christ bridle, affirming the ethics of the ADL as well as their sister organization, the Frankfurt School, to be the default Christian view. Even though granting such directly abrogates the Christian faith. It's incomprehensible.

The violence and madness endemic to these baptized lies led Rushdoony to affirm Henry Miller's terminology for our age—'the time of the assassins':

> [E]quality as a philosophical and religious faith is at work. All people are equals; woman is equal to man, and man is equal to God. As a result, there must be in principle a war against differences. Not only unisex but uniman is the goal, the bland, neutral person. Henry Miller sees the return to Paradise only through the destruction of history, meaning, law, and morality. There must be a time of total destruction, the "time of the assassins," and the new world can only come when the old world is forgotten. This means a period of anarchy, racial amalgamation,

---

[205] Weber, Mark. "The Importance of the Zündel Hearing in Toronto." *Institute for Historical Review.*
[206] Foxman, Abraham H. "Jews and Money: The Story of a Stereotype."
[207] See the polls provided in *Contemporary Global Anti-Semitism: A Report Provided to the United States Congress,* p. 31 (PDF p. 41), where Poles and Hungarians holding this belief are deemed antisemitic.

and universal human hermaphroditism ("the birth of male-and-female in every individual") and then the new world may appear.[208]

The 'new world' of Rushdoony's and Miller's appraisal was also predicted beforetime by Burke, Orwell, and others. It is the age of 'the Big Lie,' 'an age of consolidation,' a time for which Isaiah's words are well suited:

*And judgment is turned away backward,
And justice standeth afar off;
For truth is fallen in the street,
And equity cannot enter.*
(Isa. 59:14)

The Isaiahic imagery of Truth assaulted in the street, Equity restrained at the gate so as not to help her, Judgment turned away from the crime scene by compromised priests, and Justice standing aloof—it is a poignant anthropomorphic metaphor indeed; for in our day our daughters are raped and murdered in the streets by the little Baals of Political Correctness while we are restrained at the gate by blackguard magistrates and turned backward by subverted churchmen. They will not hear. They refuse to see. Though much acclaimed in the age of Alienism, truth, justice, judgment, and equity are only affirmed by a total inversion of content. And because genuine justice and equity have been outlawed, the revolutionaries can locate no point of objectivity to anchor them. Once Justice is defined as robbery, overthrow, dispossession, and genocide of White Christians, and equity as pretending that men and women are interchangeable, that gender is fluid, and that heathens and savage races are the cultural and spiritual equals or betters of White Christians, the revolutionaries themselves find their principles unlivable. Because all attempts at living that inverted ethic implodes civil society, even if attempted under the auspices of an egalitarian interpretation of Galatians 3:28. But the truth is worse in their eyes. They prefer the endless death which their views entail over truth. As it has been said, "those who hate Me love death" (Prov. 8:36).

But the Christian man is commanded to "give no heed to Jewish myths" (Titus 1:14)—think Frankfurt School Marxism and Boasian anthropology—but rather "cast down imaginations and every high thing which exalts itself contrary to the knowledge of God" (2 Cor. 10:5). As such, Alienism is inherently at odds with the ninth word, which is intelligible only under the assumptions of Kinism.

---

[208] Rushdoony, R.J. *The Institutes of Biblical Law*, p. 437

The Tenth Word
July 28, 2016

Thou shalt not covet thy neighbor's house, thou shalt not covet thy neighbor's wife, nor his manservant, nor his maidservant, nor his ox, nor his ass, nor any thing that is thy neighbor's.

Exodus 20:17

Though the tenth word is essentially a recapitulation of all the foregoing commands of the second table, among the aspects of this law which are overlooked or otherwise denounced in the liberalized churches is its foremost thrust: that which belongs to my neighbor does not belong to me and there is no justification to yearn for, devise, or otherwise justify means to make it otherwise. If it does not mean this, it means nothing.

> But it [the tenth word] describes not merely the emotion of coveting but also includes the attempt to attach something to oneself illegally. . . . The term "house" can in a narrow and special sense describe the dwelling-place, primarily the built house but also in every case the tent-"house" of the nomad; it can, however, also be used in a more or less wide or transferred sense to mean, for instance, the family.[209]

Yet, under the Alienist spirit which pervades at present—not by open contest or debate, but by subversion, arbitrary force, and psychological programming—the seminal and conspicuous meaning of this law is the very thing now roundly condemned for 'the heresy of racism'! Because the whole animating spirit of Alienism is a denial of limited jurisdictions, maintenance of boundaries, and distinctions between clans and the God-ordained unequal possessions of all kinship units, large and small.

The catechism is unequivocal here. The duties required in the tenth word include 'full contentment with our own condition,' (question #147), which is to say that my family's condition necessarily differs from those of other lines in manifold ways, and we should never begrudge another heritage their strengths, nor their rightful possessions, even when they differ from or exceed our own. But so-called "Civil Rights" (government-created minority privileges meant to trump the White Man's God-given rights) fly in the face of this law. As such, Affirmative Action quotas, social advancement, anti-discrimination policies in housing and business,

---

[209] Martin Noth, *Exodus*, p. 166

ongoing "reparations" via the hydra-like apparata of the welfare state (with manifold race-based benefits for minorities), and the illegal fourteenth amendment back of it all are aught but the diametric and institutional inversion of the tenth commandment; for all those revolutionary policies are established firmly upon the covetousness of non-Whites—Blacks and Jews, signally—toward their White neighbors. It is a policy of holistic civilizational larceny predicated on the institutionalization of what JFK called 'covert means.'[210]

Rather than upholding property rights and hallowing boundaries between peoples, and rebuking revolutionary ideologies as the catechism insists we ought, the leveling ethos (Marxian, Jacobin, and Gnostic) is now esteemed in the subverted churches as a law above the law. Alienism actually makes a sublime virtue of violating the tenth word. So much so that their usual refrains are things like "equality is the fruit of the gospel," "physical kinship is carnal and has been abolished in Christ," and even, "race-mixing is the gospel." They issue these blasphemous aphorisms with such hubris and contempt of all property, identity, and jurisdiction because their controlling hermeneutic—"the church is your TRUE family and physical relation is meaningless," predicated upon a misreading of Gal. 3:28—compels them to invert the law.

If things forbidden in the tenth word include "discontentment with our own estate; envying and grieving at the good of our neighbor, together with all inordinate motions and affections to anything that is his" (WLC #148), it means different clans have differing claims on property and different rights in regard to those jurisdictions, just as the tribes of Israel did, and so too with the Hebrew ethnicity altogether. So it was in the Christian era—especially after the fall of Rome—that the nations discipled to Christ observed the tenth word, as well as the eighth, as establishing the property rights both in principle and in fact. And thus feudalism under God's law came to reassert the nationalism previously infringed by the empire.

In terms of the American nation, the tenth word proscribed any and all ideological pretexts to confusion of what belongs to whom. This very much shaped our founding documents, which specify that ours was a republic founded for 'ourselves and our posterity' (U.S. Constitution Preamble), permitting only 'free white persons of good character' (Naturalization Act of 1790).

The Black's demand of citizenship and the Abolitionist's encouragement in the pursuit of that usurpation were covetousness of the greatest magnitude. The Jacobin imaginings of propositional nationhood codified in the 14th amendment were couched definitively in covetousness for our children's very birthright, and all the benefits thereof. Clearly, if we are commanded to 'covet nothing that is my neighbor's,' it includes all the desiderata being extorted from us on the part of alien

---

[210] President Kennedy, John F. "The President and the Press: Address Before the American Newspaper Publishers Association." 27 Apr 61.

peoples: argument for the full inclusion in our body politic of a strange people violates the law outright.

Yes, while Israel had one law for the native and the alien alike (Ex. 12:49), it clearly did not erase the legal distinction between the two categories because the law itself depends upon the legitimate existence of each in order for the law to be intelligible. Clearly, all such passages, then, are a notice of jurisdiction: the alien was bound to honor the law of Israel and had no claim to diplomatic immunity nor ignorance of the law. Countervailing this principle of one law for native and stranger, the Scripture nonetheless stipulates many inequalities in law between them, such as the fact that alien peoples sojourning in the borders of Israel could not own land (Lev. 25), could not ascend to leadership (Deut. 1:13; 17:15), could, per the words of Luther's translation, "not enter the body politic" (Deut. 23:2), and had no standing in court apart from paternalistic bondservice to an Israelite (Ex. 20:10; Deut. 1:16).

Meantime, the law also specified that while Israelites could not lend to kinsmen at interest, they could so lend to alien peoples in their midst (Deut. 23:20), and though Israelites could maintain a stable of slaves from their own race, the term of their slavery was seven years by law, while interminable chattel slavery was restricted to alien races bought with money (Lev. 25:44-46). However, the law stipulates that the alien in Israel had no reciprocal right to take Israelites for perpetual slaves; and even those Israelites who sold themselves to aliens under the seven-year term of bondservice had a special immunity mandating that they could be redeemed from their service by a kinsman at any time (Lev. 25:47-55). All of these overt inequalities between native and alien in law the Scripture regards as equity. In fact, this inequality the text calls "liberty to all the inhabitants of the land" (Lev. 25:10). It can do so because the modern Alienist notion of liberty is entirely false. Equality is not liberty. On the contrary, genuine liberty entirely requires inequality: privileges and immunities are implicit in the very institution of the family, and the family cannot be understood apart from them. So too with nation and race.

Inasmuch as we should countenance no ideologies which propose to legitimate covetousness in ourselves, neither shall we do so in others toward ourselves, nor even in others toward third parties apart from us. To do so is plainly antinomian.

The bane of communism, socialism, capitalism, propositionalism, civil rights, human rights, and all other leveling ideologies, the tenth word presupposes the legitimacy of privilege, hierarchy, aristocracy, segregation, private property, association, clan, and heredity. There is no escaping it. To love thy neighbor as thyself is to never begrudge him the privileges and immunities appropriate to him in his hereditary domain.

For all its sophistic mummery, Alienism is a repudiation of the tenth word in its every dimension. I mean, let's be realistic: the tenth law directly sanctions domestic slavery—a thing ubiquitously decried by Alienists as 'the greatest evil in American history'—a la reference to manservants and maidservants as things belonging to our neighbors. And yet, there it is, entwined inextricably in God's very law. The law's enumeration of slaves as domestic possessions simply crushes all pretensions of Abolitionism.

Since the commandment in question deals particularly with a state of mind (covetousness), it anathematizes all leveling ideologies directly. Yes, by prohibition of covetous thoughts, it outlaws all such philosophies as deny the legitimate boundaries, possessions, privileges and immunities of property vested in kinship groups such as the clan. Yes, popular as it may be in recent years, Alienism is directly anathematized by the tenth word.

As with all other points of the Decalogue, the tenth word can only be understood and reasonably accounted for in terms of traditional Calvinistic-Theonomic-Christian thought, which is to say, Kinism.

Closing Thoughts

My writing of this piece brings to mind the PCA's General Assembly of 2015, wherein the denomination founded in fundamental opposition to Marxism and racial integration sat in proverbial sackcloth and ashes denouncing the foundational principles of their own denomination as heretical, and by mute implication, their founders as heretics. This grand theological revolution comes exactly astride of the secular revolution which is presently purging all symbols of traditional Christian sentiment—especially things related to the Confederacy, the American founding, and European civilization—from both public and private acknowledgement. And for exactly the same reasons. Equal parts convenience and hypocrisy, but all sacrilege, this quorum announced the PCA's official adoption of a new religion to replace the old 'racist' faith of our fathers.

Remarkably, this explicit repudiation of their own heritage does not prevent these men from pretending to affirm a time-tested and ancient faith. Just as they rotely cite the Decalogue while deaf to its conspicuous meanings and implications, they drop citations from the venerable dead like unwanted pennies, but those references only rebuke them. They deny the existence of Kinism—which they insist is 'racism'—in the history of Christian thought as they simultaneously convene to denounce the founders of all our Reformed denominations for the high crime of 'racism'.

Yes, in the fourth century Augustine spoke not merely of all mankind but of "the Hebrew race," "the race of Israel," "the race called the Philistines," "monstrous races," "the race of David," "the race of the Roman people," "men of Greek race," "a foreign race," and "the people of God [as] composed of every race of men."[211] Far from Augustine was the babble of "only one race, the human race."

Fast-forward to 1993, when Carl F. Henry, among others, produced a joint resolution on Christian government containing these words:

> *God's Law and the Nations: We affirm . . . that God's moral law has applicability to all people and nations. . . .*
>
> *We deny that . . . diversity and tolerance should be imposed by laws or regulations enforcing political correctness or multiculturalism.*[212]

Ethnonationalism was, at that time, at least in conservative circles, still taken for granted as the Christian world order. The ersatz orthodoxy as it is held now — the idea that the gospel has abolished the nations and that the law prohibits limited filial associations and tribal jurisdictions — was apparently disregarded by Greg Bahnsen, too, when he penned what is arguably his magnum opus, *Theonomy in Christian Ethics*:

> *The law itself is blessed, and obedience to it brings great blessing for that people who honor God by heeding His commandments. When the law is ignored by a nation, then justice is perverted and wickedness abounds (Hab. 1:4). By contrast, an abundant, prosperous and holy people is the goal of a God-directed state (cf. Prov. 14:28-35). "Righteousness exalts a nation, but sin is a reproach to any people" (Prov. 14:34). . . . There are great national blessings for that society which follows the moral directives of God. . . . A nation will receive a blessing or curse from God's law based on their obedience or disobedience thereof (Deut. 11:26 ff.). The book of the law is emphatic that the Lord will greatly bless a nation for careful obedience to all His commandments (Deut. 15:4 f.). If a nation will respond properly to God's prescriptive will, then the law will not bring death, evil and a curse upon them, but rather it will promote their life, blessing and good (Deut. 30:15, 19). If a nation keeps the commandments and statutes of God, He will love them, bless them, and multiply their children, crops, and herds; furthermore there will be no barrenness or sickness among them (Deut. 7:12-15). The nation which hearkens to God's commands will be prospered . . . (Deut. 11:13-15). If the nation obeys all of God's law it will be exalted with blessed cities,*

---

[211] Augustine, *City of God*, Book XV, ch. 8; Book XVI, chs. 2, 3, 8; Book XVII, ch. 7; Book XVIII, chs. 13, 18, 45; Book XX, ch. 21

[212] Henry, Carl F.H. "A Summary Statement of the Consultation of Theology and Civil Law," qtd. in H. Wayne House, *The Christian and American Law*, pp. 289, 290

fields, children, crops, herds, rain, labor and economy (Deut. 28:1 ff.). If the nation hearkens to God's commandments and statutes in the book of the law with their whole heart God will bless their labor, procreation, crops, and herds (Deut. 30:6-10). If a nation will walk in God's law, then it will have . . . fruitful multiplication . . . (Lev. 26:3-13). . . .

God is faithful to His word and will abundantly bless that nation which honors Him and His law. To refuse to be blessed by God, saying, "No! there will be no such blessing before we reach heaven!' is manifestly absurd; it represents pessimistic recalcitrance. Why should a people refuse to be blessed? . . . To some degree the blessings which accrue to a nation which obeys God's law are a foretaste of the heavenly kingdom.[213]

Bahnsen took for granted the existence of a multiplicity of Christian nations, individually covenanted to God after the pattern of national Israel. And more recently still, Wyngaarden has affirmed the same:

More than a dozen excellent commentaries could be mentioned that all interpret Israel as thus inclusive of Jew and Gentile, in this verse, – the Gentile adherents thus being merged with the covenant people of Israel, though each nationality remains distinct.

This abiding distinction of the nationalities is also clearly implied by Isaiah. For, though Israel is frequently called Jehovah's People, the work of his hands, his inheritance, yet these three epithets severally are applied not only to Israel, but also to Assyria and to Egypt: "Blessed be Egypt, my people, and Assyria, the work of my hands, and Israel, mine inheritance." 19:25.

Thus the highest description of Jehovah's covenant people is applied to Egypt, – "my people," – showing that the Gentiles will share the covenant blessings, not less than Israel. Yet the several nationalities are here kept distinct, even when Gentiles share, in the covenant blessing, on a level of equality with Israel. Egypt, Assyria and Israel are not nationally merged. And the same principle, that nationalities are not obliterated, by membership in the covenant, applies, of course, also in the New Testament dispensation.[214]

Simply put, the scriptural witness is clear that "all peoples (races), nations (ethnicities), and languages should serve Him" (Dan. 7:14). Or as Strawbridge once adroitly argued:

The [Great] Commission to disciple and baptize nations, in the Biblical thematic development stands upon the very early division of the nations. In Biblical usage,

---

[213] Bahnsen, Greg. *Theonomy in Christian Ethics*, 3rd ed., pp. 468-470
[214] Wyngaarden, Martin J. *The Future of the Kingdom in Prophecy and Fulfillment: A Study of the Scope of "Spiritualization" in Scripture* (2008), p. 101f.

the term "nations" is equal to "all the families of the earth" (Gen. 12:3, 28:14, Acts 3:25; cf. Ps. 22:[27]). Moreover, in a Biblical survey of the term "nations," the terms "family" and "house" or "household" are explicitly and organically connected. For example, in the book that defines the beginning of family and nation, Genesis, "nations" is equal to "families."[215]

Rushdoony concurs:

> A man can never be considered in abstraction from what he is. To hold that we can discount a man's race, heritage, intelligence, religion, and moral character, and then somehow deal with the real man is a common liberal fallacy; the result is only an abstract idea of a man, not a living man.[216]

Far from a dispensable category or dismissible artifact, nationhood, contiguous as it is with the physical clan, is the relation ordained of God between man and man and between man and God. For the Scripture describes God's covenantal interaction with men in terms of their lineage, redemption, or reprobation house by house, nation by nation, and race by race. Apart from these realities, man is an anarchist without law.

The Ten Words, similarly consonant with the Scripture overall, cannot be made sense of inside an Alienist frame of reference. For Alienism denies the lawfulness and/or existence of all the essential categories and entities taken for granted therein as legitimate and real. This is why the Alienist vision of Christendom never obtained anywhere in Christendom past: if Alienism were the true Christian view, there would be some multicult imperial country on earth called Christiana where all the races were fused into a mocha blend from the beginning of the Christian era to present. But no such place exists. Nor did anything resembling it ever rise in covenanted lands until and where Jacobin-Marxism aggressively supplanted Christianity.

Before that, Christendom insisted upon and persisted as ethno-nations. Because we believed in God's law.

---

[215] Strawbridge, Gregg. "The Grandness of the Great Commission."
[216] Rushdoony, R.J. *The Institutes of Biblical Law*, p. 434

The Way We Were

August 18, 2016

Some time ago I happened across an article by Gary North wherein he did something uncharacteristic of a professor of that hybrid Libertarian-Postmillennial philosophy of the neo-Theonomists: he waxed nostalgic. More than nostalgic, he actually confessed things to have been objectively better in the past than the present. And it didn't even have anything to do with reflections on the freer market of yesteryear, the greater affordability of postage stamps, the superior quality of American steel, the production cost of rubber nipples, or the liquidity of the sundry widgets with which economists are generally absorbed. On the contrary, it ran a sentimental gamut from the innocence of golden-age cinema to the quaintness of small-town life in his childhood, to the patriotism of earlier generations, to Fourth of July orations, to public morality and a sense of shared culture lost. All very uncharacteristic of the sterile algorithms of better-living-through-chemistry, open-border, multicult economism for which his clique is otherwise known. One secondhand anecdote he mentions is poignant:

> *There is a scene in "It Happened One Night" (1934), where Clark Gable is riding in a bus. The bus is lighted inside, and everyone is singing. For years, I thought that scene was filler. My friend and master journalist Otto Scott, age 85, tells me that singing on Greyhound buses was common in those days, though with lights off. Strangers sang on buses.*[217]

Such a small and comforting grace, North laments the fact that by his time social cohesion had eroded to the point where this instinctual ritual was lost. Albeit a small segue, it strikes the deepest chord in the essay, bespeaking the underlying issue on which he otherwise will not directly look: it really couldn't happen today except in the most homogeneous enclaves. Beyond the fact that the multicult denizens of the land today share little in the way of folk expression and symbols, the songs of those disparate groups tend to be highly offensive to every group but their own. And none but such a homogeneous society with precisely the root depth which ours had could have produced the cultural architecture which he

---

[217] North, Gary. "What Ever Happened to July 4th Orations?" *LewRockwell*. 4 Jul 2003.

spied in impromptu choruses or the comparatively wholesome media milieu of his youth.

Here's an anecdote from my own life confirming North's observations of modern America's drift from innocence: a couple decades past when I attended a Fourth of July celebration at Knott's Berry Farm in Southern California, the event featured a line-up of very WASPy bands, some in colonial dress, others in mid-nineteenth century waistcoats and cumberbuns. They played everything from the National Anthem to the Ride of Paul Revere to Bunker Hill to Dixie. But all these Americana songs and motifs evoked not cheers, but boos, cursing, and mockery from the majority-Mestizo park-goers. Defiant, many screamed, "Viva la Raza!", "Viva la Mayheeco!" and many other things I'll not relay here. Alongside the Mestizos, the Blacks milling about beatboxed and rapped vulgarities interlaced with unintelligible gibbering in attempts to overshout what they derided as "racist Cracker music" and "goofy-ass Whiteboy music." Intent on intimidating and demoralizing the strawhatted and bowtied White musicians, they glowered and gyrated libidinously, waving middle fingers aloft, barking profanity at them. While they may all have appreciated the evening's fireworks, it was plain that none of these diverse "citizens" had come to celebrate the attainment of independence for the American colonies from Britain or our founding of a limited republic based upon Anglo-Saxon Christian Law. They had not the slightest inkling of such matters. Even if they had been propagandized K through 12 in the new mythos that they represent the true apotheosis of American identity, they could see naught in such traditional displays but triumphal White history and identity. They counted all the memes of Americana an affront to their new and true American identities. I feel slightly silly having to explain something so obvious, but such are our days: non-White people are generally quite offended by American history. The further back, the more so. Because it is European. Because America and the West are the legacy of the White Christian uniquely. What Whites—Gary North included—see as the 'good old days', non-whites tend to see as the absolute definition of evil.

Most remarkably, this heterogeneous view—that true Americanism is multiculturalism—is affirmed now as much by GOP laureate historian Harry Jaffa as by socialist historian Howard Zinn. Whatever their differences, each of these schools of thought retroactively imposes the same central assumptions upon our history—that multiculturalism, multiracialism, and religious pluralism are the lodestones of Americanism, supportive of "our highest ideal": equality. This grasping for equality is the native temptation of covetous and interloping aliens, but Americans once not long ago, and nigh to a man, repudiated such Jacobin notions. However, all the new state-sanctioned interpretations, different though they be in many ways, unanimously promulgate the vantage of the outgroup and subversive minorities intent on deposing and humbling "ourselves and our posterity" as the true American view.

But that is not to say that Leftist and Rightist egalitarianism do not differ. They do. Jewish Radicals such as Zinn, the SPLC, ADL, ACLU, and the myriad Afrocentrist groups markedly differ from Libertarians and NeoCons in that they openly revile all pre-Civil Rights history, including the triumph of our colonies, the taming of the wilderness, the winning of the West, the upholding of natural aristocracy, localism, the establishment of our republic, and all the graces of settled Christian society in the new world as the single darkest passage in human history. Meanwhile, the GOP/Libertarian axis (white as the driven snow, generally) such as North, have appropriated those same equality-mongering presuppositions and reconstrued them as somehow foundational and supportive of the America they knew prior to the Civil Rights revolution. Though they esteem the America of Laura Ingalls Wilder, Anne of Green Gables, Johnny Tremain, and the traditional outlook of historians like Israel Smith Clare, as well as Madison Grant, and favoring the historiography of the Dunning School, they yet profess the same central doctrine of nation and peoplehood in keeping with antichrist bloviator Michael Moore — the propositional nation over against Blood and Soil.

Even my own Mexican and Filipino friends who accompanied me that night, though multi-generational Christians all, and raised in America, reacted with glee at all the disgraceful hijinks of the other non-White ethnics present, while my White friends and I stood disgusted with the disrespect shown to the society under whose wing they sheltered. All else being equal, the only ones who identified with the symbols and tropes of the War of Independence and the symbols of our founding were my fellow Whites. Meanwhile, our non-White friends were only dismayed at our outrage. Things approaching the holy to us were at best trifling oddities to them, and at worst, great evils to be suppressed or abrogated. Yes, the only thing to prompt outrage from my non-White friends was the inexplicable reverence we Whites had for the colonial tableau and the great drama of our forefathers' battle against arbitrary government. They simply could not identify with our sires' fight for liberty under God, because our forefathers bore theirs no resemblance by creed nor breed.

Clearly, in order for strangers to sing impromptu songs of a folk-patriotic character together in the dark they must have a certain degree of shared experience preceding them for generations. They must have a similitude of values, identifying with the same heroes, tokens, symbols, and hereditary roots in the same civilization. They must trust one another instinctually. They must see themselves in their fellows. In short, they must be brethren rather than strangers.

The Stranger within my gate,
He may be true or kind,
But he does not talk my talk –
I cannot feel his mind.

I see the face and the eyes and the mouth,
But not the soul behind.

The men of my own stock,
They may do ill or well,
But they tell the lies I am wanted to,
They are used to the lies I tell;
And we do not need interpreters
When we go to buy or sell.

The Stranger within my gates,
He may be evil or good,
But I cannot tell what powers control –
What reasons sway his mood;
Nor when the Gods of his far-off land
Shall repossess his blood.

The men of my own stock,
Bitter bad they may be,
But, at least, they hear the things I hear,
And see the things I see;
And whatever I think of them and their likes
They think of the likes of me.

This was my father's belief
And this is also mine:
Let the corn be all one sheaf –
And the grapes be all one vine,
Ere our children's teeth are set on edge
By bitter bread and wine.[218]

Even those come of the same tribes may oft differ enough creedally that they cannot sing all the same songs. Such is the case amongst our churches, in that both psalter and hymnal Calvinists eschew all the repetitious "free-will" songs and often heretical ditties of Arminians and Charismatics. How much less, then, can they of foreign race, culture, language, and creed see the world through our eyes, speak the same sentiments, love the same heroes, and sing the same songs? Granting even that they learn our tongue, their own non-White identities import incongruous assumptions and irreconcilable perspectives to virtually every word uttered between us.

---

[218] Kipling, Rudyard. "The Stranger," 1908

It's obvious that this whole train of thought sits uneasy with North. Because in his worldview he really hasn't anyplace to put it, as Libertarianism itself is an apologetic for radical pluralism—the negation and repudiation of the very social solidarity for which we find him here pining. Under the rubric of his atomized theory of society he cannot locate the value of the commodities under consideration, because they do not appear on the NASDAQ. Even if that lost social capital compels him to acknowledge some great value in it, it cannot be appraised in pennypound. It has no trade value against sterling. And its loss cannot be construed as any net advancement of the millennium. His economic toolbox has no conceptual implements by which social capital and alienation can be weighed and measured. It is apparent that he has momentarily slipped the well-worn channels for which his barrow is fitted. We can see his wheels slipping the furrows. But falteringly, he seems to gain traction enough for an inkling of the fact that there are no palliative markets left to a dispossessed pariah people such as his have become.

But just as he would seem to begin writing in the voice of Robert Putnam of his *Heimat* and *Hiraeth*, it no doubt dawned on him that the tragedy of the revolution of sentiment under his inspection is diversity-driven and the necessary consequent of his own laissez-faire socio-economic theory no less than that of the statist central planners. At which point he leaves off this homesick scenic drive for the myopic monetary paths which he plods to this day, eyes firmly fixed on the consoling tracks laid by the money-changers who have auctioned the world he knew and the birthright of his children out from under them.

Back when this society was still largely ours, it was entirely expected to hear public expressions of the Christian faith—especially around the holidays. Like so many of us, North is haunted by the memory of White Protestant America as it was. Little things like Ernie Ford and Gordon MacRae singing "O Holy Night" on prime-time television. His was the first generation raised with television. Americans were tapping their feet to the Gilbert and Sullivan Minstrel Show. Agatha Christie's bestseller, *Ten Little Niggers*, was adapted to film under the title *And Then There Were None* in '45 and again under the original title in '49. Both the book and film adaptations were released with aplomb and met with praise in both America and England. Audiences saw no offense in Abbott and Costello's comedic adventure *Africa Screams*.

Though we still held a *de facto* cultural hegemony, North's young life was defined by the rise of the American suburb, a nationwide migration away from our cities which were otherwise being encroached upon by other races. Today it would be called 'White Flight,' but it was then taken for granted as nothing but good parenting to remove your children from the eminent danger which foreign races pose them. In the America North knew, playing Cowboys and Indians was taken for granted as the most wholesome thing imaginable for little boys. (It's considered a "hate crime" now.) The Ballad of Davy Crockett was beloved by all, unreservedly. Children were thrilled to hear the Daniel Boone theme song come over the airwaves every day. Prince Valiant was buttressed by Tarzan, Johnny Quest, Popeye, and Dick Tracey in the Sunday funny papers. Those characters unapologetically dispatched African and Indian Savages, Mohammedans, Oriental Huns, Japs, Goons from Goon Island, and all other existential threats to Western civilization. Even popular syndicated strips with titles like "White Boy," about a Christian child kidnapped by Sioux Indians, upheld the White race unflinchingly.

Though totally suppressed later, this was a time throughout which Walt Disney released scores of wonderfully traditional films celebrating the history and advance of European Christendom. But that was before Tom & Jerry episodes were prefaced with "trigger warnings." Before they began mass cartoon bans because they said words like "Mammy." It was also before they rewrote Mark Twain's books to purge them of a word which leftists deemed offensive well after the fact, discontinuing Nigger Jim. Prior, they banned *Gone With the Wind, Moby Dick, The Call of the Wild*, and—most ironically—*Fahrenheit 451*. The works of Rudyard Kipling—which bore swastikas on their covers, by the way—were cherished. Charles Lindbergh was still seen as one of the greatest heroes of the modern age; and that after his having published his famous article "Aviation, Geography, and Race" in *Reader's Digest*, calling for the natal solidarity of Europeans world.

In spite of the irrepressible division of the Brothers' War, *Dixie* was one of the most popular songs in America, both sides of the Mason-Dixon. And the Confederate war dead—defamed as "traitors" today—were reckoned heroes and patriots even by the descendants of those who fought for the Union. The Confederate Battle Flag was accepted universally as both a thoroughly Christian and sublimely American flag. Notwithstanding many contradictions by that day, Americans were yet unconsciously immersed in the tapestry of western, antebellum, colonial, medieval, and biblical narratives which comprise the legacy and milieu from which we proceed. It was our heritage, our identity. Our farmers were heroes to us alongside the knights, explorers, cavaliers, pilgrims, settlers, planters, minutemen, frontiersmen, and cowboys gone before. Norman Rockwell's iconic covers for the *Saturday Evening Post* glorified the normal as much as N.C. Wyeth's had in *Scribner's Magazine* before him. No one thought them scandalous at the time, but today all that bourgeois imagery is deemed infamous "White supremacy."

Even if many people had grown negligent of the Scripture personally, it yet permeated the culture to such a degree that if someone said, "Ho, what word, Uriah?", "Kane shall be razed!", or "the apple of his eye," everyone was through usage familiar with their meanings. Even the myriad para-biblical Aesopian folk sayings such as "a rolling stone gathers no moss" or references to "sour grapes" required no further explanation, as they do now. And even if the anticommunist movement of the 50s and 60s is retrospectively decried in Academia and the media as having been some fringe extremism outside *true* American sentiment, anticommunism was entirely mainstream then. The Dan Smoot Report newsletter boasted 33,000 paid subscribers, and his weekly show was broadcast prime-time on television and radio. It was back before Walmart and all the corporate chains ran all the mom-and-pop businesses into the ground, when bookstores and barbershops were still American institutions, and when the hardware store was locally owned. A great deal of Arminian and Charismatic error by that point notwithstanding, street preachers, public hymn sings (especially at Christmas), and Christian tracts were common idiosyncrasies of American culture. And our Anglo-Saxon language had not yet been redacted by the multicult to render so many mundane words contraband. North lived through the political formation of what came to be known as "The Religious Right." Well in advance of the Roe v. Wade issue, "The Moral Majority" roared to life in opposition to racial integration. That was before the bastards in D.C. actually used troops against American kids to force them to integrate with negroes. Literally at gunpoint. "This used to be America." Though American culture was, by North's time, already in precipitous decline, he had the tremendous benefit of civilizational furniture in the early 1940s which, in retrospect from the Obamanation of 2016, looks like "The Valley of Love and Delight."

As an aside, the question begs to be asked: why, throughout the course of all the responses to Black riots and murderous rampages, did the government insist on only non-lethal peacekeeping methods such as tear gas, batons, shields, rubber bullets, hoses, and so on, but opted to deploy 101st Airborne troops with loaded rifles and fixed bayonets against White children declining to attend school with negroes? This landmark violation of the Posse Comitatus Act against White children who wanted only to not be aggressed upon by Blacks bespeaks much in the way of the liberal view of race. And it continues today, as we see perennial Black riots met with non-lethal force as a rule, but woe betide the White ranching family that dares stand up for their God-given and constitutional rights, as the Bundies did recently. They are met with assault rifles, military snipers, and predator drones. But I digress.

As journalist-turned-satirist Lewis Grizzard put it:

> *I had a handle on things in 1962. It was the year I turned sixteen and got my driver's license... Whenever I wanted french fries in 1962, Mama would cut potatoes by hand and cook them for me. Movies hadn't become 'films,' most of them still made sense, and nobody in them — unless they were made in Sweden — got naked. I had a large collection of Elvis records in 1962 and hung out at my hometown truckstop that had an all-country jukebox featuring Hank Williams, Faron Young, Jim Reeves, Earnest Tubb, Kitty Wells, and Patsy Cline. I had a pretty blonde girlfriend. The best thing on television was Gunsmoke...*
> *I slept well in 1962.*

> But the very next year, somebody shot the president...
> Then the Beatles came.
> Then all hell broke loose.
> And changes began to unravel my simple, neat world. What once was good became bad. What once was unthinkable became acceptable...
> Girls wanted to be in the Boy Scouts. Later, homosexuals wanted to be in the Boy Scouts.
> The 'isms' came. Racism, sexism. The phobias came. Homophobia, xenophobia...
> Miami was lost to the Cubans. San Francisco was lost to the hippies, and then to the homosexuals...
> It's been thirty years since 1962... I still don't want to be around homosexuals, remain convinced Bernie Goetz did the right thing when he shot those punks on the New York subway...
> This book is dedicated to everyone just like me, the Lord have mercy upon us.[219]

The popular American memes and symbols of Mr. North's nativity are no longer admitted. They have been stricken from the books. All the little graces which defined America then are, in full Orwellian fashion, denounced as un-American today. For in multicult America, Columbus Day is an offense to Indians, Mexicans, Blacks, and Jews. Thanksgiving is repudiated by the same people for the same reasons. Christmas, as well, for that matter, as the whole liturgical calendar, is reviled by Jews and Muslims. Jews and Blacks have compelled an overwrite of the Christian observance of Lee-Jackson Day with the communist MLK Day. The Celtic Cross, the Crusaders' Cross, the St. Andrew's Cross, the Iron Cross, the Fiery Cross, and the Bent Cross are all now deemed 'hate symbols' and ostensibly outlawed on account of the various cultures flooding across our libertarian style borders. And all crosses are being purged from public view by courtcraft of the folks at the ACLU, SPLC, and ADL. Ten Commandments monuments, Confederate flags, and monuments to all our Confederate heroes, Founding Fathers, and colonial heroes are being removed, and their graves desecrated, in the name of this new Americanism*. Because crosses, Christian law, and American liberty are universally rebuked now as White supremacy.

The folk traditions and cultural characteristics which White Christians have taken for granted as judicious and universal goods, and the loss of which North himself laments, have proven in many respects affinities unique to us alone, naught but offensive presumption in the eyes of most other peoples. Certainly, those of other races who claim Christ will no doubt affirm the Golden Rule, and we have no reason to doubt their sincerity; however, the principle of doing unto others has been studiously applied amongst the Japhethite tribes so long that the gradual permutations and circumstantial implications of it have resulted in what

---

[219] Grizzard, Lewis. *I Haven't Understood Anything Since 1962*. Introduction.

we know as "manners," "etiquette," "propriety," "decorum," and social subtleties such as magnanimity and empathic altruism. Neither have many other races absorbed concepts such as "personal boundaries" for appropriate speaking distance, or the universal White assumption that you don't touch other people's things without permission, or that it's impolite to speak of personal matters in public, or to speak so loudly in public that others have no choice but to overhear one's personal discussions, or to play your music so loudly that your neighbors must partake in it too. While a little thing like Western table manners seems to the White mind like obvious implication of the Golden Rule, Christians of other races, in spite of their affirmation of the Apostles' Creed or even TULIP, have little conception of such civil graces as we know them. Because their peoples haven't spent millennia with the law etching into their habits and mannerisms as ours have. And it is part and parcel of the European's empathic altruism that we recognize the handicaps of other peoples and their histories in these respects. But even that forbearance on our part, when known to other races, is seen by them as a most patronizing condescension. On balance, the horns of that dilemma admit no out—if we hold Christianized and Americanized equatorial peoples amongst us to the same standards we expect of our own, we have laid a yoke on them which, while light as air to us, they can almost never bear. In which case they decry us for 'racists,' bigots, and White supremacists for expecting them to live by our millennia-calibrated cultural norms; and if we do the opposite, accepting their ethnic handicaps as the relative threshold of their capacities under God, or simply as different expressions of Christian folkways demonstrative of the pluriformity of Christian cultures, we are denounced for holding to a paternalist 'racism' of lowered expectations. All of which underscores the moral necessity of the separatism maintained up until about five decades ago. By house, community, state, region, and nation, segregation is obvious as the normative and only efficacious remedy.

Even if our turncoat pulpits are loath to admit it, the federal expungement of the color line, the orchestrated rise of miscegenation, and the planned proliferation of alien peoples amongst us has moved apace of the degeneration and apostasy of the White race in America as well. Everyone knows diversity and apostasy have blossomed synergistically in this country. Rather than making the stranger better, the strangers have only made us worse. Or as Matthew Henry phrased it:

They were sworn unto him [Tobiah], not as their prince, but as their friend and ally, because both he and his son had married daughters of Israel, v. 18. See the mischief of marrying with strangers; for one heathen that was converted by it ten Jews were perverted. When once they became akin to Tobiah they soon became sworn to him. A sinful love leads to a sinful league.[220]

---

[220] Henry, Matthew. *Commentary on Nehemiah 6.*

Albeit a hitpiece, Allan J. Lichtman's *White Protestant Nation* correctly identifies the impediment to shared experience and symbol introduced by ethnic diversity:

> *The conservative tradition is white and Protestant in part because black Protestant culture has followed its own path to cultural pluralism and liberal politics. Both religion and race have mattered for conservatives who view nationhood as anchored in white, native-stock peoples and their distinctive culture. . . . [C]onservatives have been cultural, religious, and at times racial nationalists, dedicated to protecting America's superior civilization from racially or culturally inferior peoples, foreign ideologies, sexual deviance, ecumenical religion, or the encroachment of a so-called one-world government.*[221]

Note his irrefutable point that all along Black Christianity in America has been monolithically liberal—even prior to the Civil Rights revolution and the invasion of other races, they were polarized against the traditional Protestant orthodoxy of the White majority. Even when race wasn't a factor, such as with respect to the Catholic Irish and Italians or the German 48ers, their variance from our Protestant faith was a profound impediment to their assimilation, but they at length did assimilate, many taking up our religion and ethics. But no racial outgroup has broken with their patterns of antagonism against our ancient liberties. Even when claiming the Christian faith for generations, non-Whites move in ethnic lockstep opposite not only Whites, but traditional Americanism and orthodox Christianity.

Or as Martin E. Marty has elucidated:

> *[E]thnicity is the skeleton key of religion in America because it provides 'the supporting framework,' 'the bare outlines or main features,' of American religion. . . .*
>
> *The black child in the ghetto or the Amerindian youngster may engage in ceremonies of civil religion. But they may think of something quite different from the world of the white child's pilgrims or founders when they sing of a 'land where my fathers died.' This is the land where their fathers were enslaved or killed. . . . The delineations of civil religion are never universal in origin, content, ethos, or scope; they are informed by the experience of the delineator's own ethnic subcommunities.*[222]

Marty's thesis is confirmed by that of another, one of the great historiographical works of recent times: *Albion's Seed* by D.H. Fischer, which posits that the conservative Christian character and founding institutions of America were due to the folkways of her homogeneous population of Teutonic-British origins. The thesis

---

[221] Lichtman, Allan J. *White Protestant Nation*, p. 4
[222] Marty, Martin E. "Ethnicity, The Skeleton of Religion in America"

of that work — this "Teutonic Germ theory" — which he recounts was the prevailing understanding of America's institutions and culture up until the mid-twentieth century, when abstract Boasian egalitarianism and statist social contract theories came to prominence in academia, as he testifies, at the insistence of Jewish professors. Yet none can gainsay him on the subject of the social attitudes of the American colonists. Fischer comments:

> [R]eform was regarded in Massachusetts as a process of recovery and preservation. Reformation meant going backward rather than forward, on the assumption that error was novel and truth was ancient in the world. The Protestant Reformation meant a reversion to primitive Christianity. In politics reform was a return to the ancient constitution. In society it meant a revival of ancestral ways.[223]

That is, Reformed theology compelled them to a deeply conservative attitude in terms of their ethnic lineage. The Puritans in New England and the Presbyterians of Virginia were equally protective of their ethnic genealogies, prizing of course equal yoking in race as indispensable to equal yoking in the spirit. All in accord with Scripture, of course.

Even Samuel Huntington has confessed as much:

> America is a founded society created by seventeenth- and eighteenth-century settlers, almost all of whom came from the British Isles. . . . They initially defined America in terms of race, ethnicity, culture, and most importantly religion.[224]

But John Jay affirmed the same long ago:

> With equal pleasure I have as often taken notice that Providence has been pleased to give this one connected country to one united people – a people descended from the same ancestors, speaking the same language, professing the same religion, attached to the same principles of government, very similar in their manners and customs, and who, by their joint counsels, arms, and efforts, fighting side by side throughout a long and bloody war, have nobly established general liberty and independence.[225]

Buchanan has tendered a concise explanation of this subject from biblical reference:

---

[223] Fischer, D.H. *Albion's Seed*, p. 56
[224] Qtd. in Buchanan, Pat. *State of Emergency*, p. 151
[225] Jay, John. *The Federalist No. 2*

> The 133rd Psalm speaks of an embryonic nation: "Behold how good and how pleasant it is for brethren to dwell together in unity!" The word occurs even earlier in the Old Testament. Genesis 10:32, after listing the descendants of Noah, relates: "these are the families of the sons of Noah, after their generations, in their nations; and by these were the nations divided in the earth after the flood."
>
> In Genesis 12, God makes His promise to Abram, "I will make of thee a great nation," and gives him a new name, Abraham, the "father of many nations." God promises to make a great nation of his son Ishmael. Arabs trace the origin of their peoples to Ishmael. God told Rebekah two nations were struggling in her womb: Esau and Jacob.
>
> "Nation – as suggested by its Latin root nascere, to be born – intrinsically implies a link of blood," wrote Peter Brimelow in the National Review in 1992. "A nation in a real sense is an extended family. The merging process through which all nations pass is not merely cultural, but to a considerable extent biological through intermarriage."
>
> Brimelow describes a nation as an 'ethno-cultural community – an interlacing of ethnicity and culture.[226]

The reason North is haunted by this *Hiraeth* and cannot reckon with the tragic erasure of his natal culture is because his abstract Austrian economic lens translates all the world into economic terms. Libertarianism casts nation as synonymous with economy. Yet the two are quite different things. As French historian Ernest Renan concluded, "A *Zollverein* is not a fatherland." An economic system is not a nation.

But plodding the same Libertarian-Millennial furrows as North, Doug Wilson opines, "Of course a healthy society has nothing to fear from immigrants. A free society is therefore one with open borders."[227] Absurdities such as this have become commonplace in neo-Reconstructionist circles of late, especially with the emergence of the apparatchik Bojidar Marinov, to whom our own Reverend McAtee has laid corrective hickory. Likewise has the good yeoman Dow thrashed SBC chairman Russell Moore on the matter. And even if the folks at Theonomy Resources are too dim to understand the material they are promoting, John Weaver has proven the righteous case for solvent borders for the maintenance of ethnic insularity beyond criticism.

But one cannot imagine a more foolish statement coming from a claimant of Christ—especially a supposed Theonomist such as Wilson—because it is 180 de-

---

[226] Buchanan, Pat. *State of Emergency*, pp. 141-142
[227] Wilson, Douglas. "The Camp of the Saints." *Blog & Mablog*. 30 Nov 2015.

grees from the position of R.J. Rushdoony, who not only held borders to be biblically mandated hedges between peoples, but emphasized that the preservation of those peoples themselves is the divinely-decreed object of borders.[228]

The Neo-Theos are walking in the steps not of Rushdoony, but of men like Milton Friedman. Friedman advanced the idea that open borders was the historic American position. But Friedman's theory of borders is no truer from the vantage of American history than from biblical prescription:

> *As you all know, until 1914 America had completely free immigration. Anyone could get on a boat and come to these shores; and if he landed on Ellis Island, he was an immigrant. Was that a good thing or a bad thing? You will find hardly a soul who will say it was a bad thing. Almost everyone will say it was a good thing.*[229]

Any standard American history will include something to this effect:

> *In the United States, opposition to immigration has a long history, starting in the late 1790s, in reaction to an influx of political refugees from France and Ireland. The Alien and Sedition Acts in 1798 restricted the rights of immigrants. Nativism first gained a name and affected politics in mid-19th century United States because of the large inflows of immigrants from cultures that were markedly different from the existing Protestant culture. Nativists objected primarily to Roman Catholics, especially Irish Americans. Nativist movements included the American Party of the mid-19th Century (formed by members of the Know-Nothing movement).*[230]

North, Wilson, Marinov, and Friedman are just plain wrong about the traditional American view of immigration. Both the Stamp Act and Declaration of Independence overtly mention the American Indians as outside our nation without qualification. The preamble to our Constitution specified that the republic was founded only for "ourselves and our posterity." And the founding congress's very first act expressly limited citizenship to White people, and suffrage was limited from colonial times to landed White males over the age of twenty-one. Thus, anyone of another race who came to our shores did so only under the terms of their never having the option of citizenship or suffrage. So it was that our founders arranged immigration policy with little incentive given to non-Europeans. They insisted ostensibly upon the old Israelite policy that no matter how long other races might

---

[228] Rushdoony, R.J. "Justice and World Law," 35:04.
[229] Friedman, Milton. Quote from *YouTube*. "Milton Friedman - Illegal Immigration only helps when its Illegal." TheAsianRepublican. 26 Sept 2012.
[230] *Wikipedia*. "Opposition to Immigration." United States.

tarry as denizens in the land, they were a "mixed multitude" forever camping apart and distinct from our nation.

Moreover, Dabney has left us a most detailed account of both Virgina's extensive colonial and post-independence measures against the importation of foreign races.[231] He concludes that account with a summary the founding sentiment held in common North and South:

> *And the reprobation of that national wrong [the slave trade forced upon us by the Crown], with regret for the presence of the African upon the soil, was the universal feeling of that generation which succeeded the Revolution. . . . They were sober, wise, and practical men, who felt that to protect the rights, purity, and prosperity of their own country and posterity, was more properly their task than to plead the wrongs of a distant and alien people. . . . They deprecated the slave trade, because it was peopling their soil so largely with an inferior and savage race, incapable of union, instead of with civilized Englishmen.*[232]

The moratorium on slave importation was predicated not upon the abuses of the trade itself—though that was certainly a concern—but upon the universal conviction that the proliferation of a foreign race on our soil presaged disaster for our people (the White race) on this continent. Which is to say that the slave trade was abolished foremost to prevent the influx of non-White races into our country. And though the state of Virginia was the first state in Christendom to outlaw their import/immigration, all the Christian nations quickly followed suit under the same rationale: separatism. Beyond the matter of their importation, whether we are speaking of Abraham Lincoln in America, or William Wilberforce in England, even the radical Abolitionists who came later generally argued their case not under the pro-miscegenationist doctrine of modern Alienists, but just the opposite, pursuant of a more rigid segregation—total deportation of the whole Black population. This had been the default position of Henry Clay's Whig party before it became a Republican one. In contrast to the later Republican plan of immediate forced expulsion of the whole African race stood the much more temperate position of the Confederates—that of generational manumission and gradual repatriation of the Africans to their ancestral homelands. But that is only to say that while North and South came to differ on the subject of how this slavery was to end, and how the Black man would be removed from our land, both hemispheres agreed on racial separatism. In fact, many Northern states outlawed even the temporary presence of Blacks in their borders at any time, for any reason.

Prior to the war a moderate and bipartisan attempt at African deportation was implemented under president Monroe. As the U.S. Department of State's Office of

---

[231] Dabney, R.L. *A Defense of Virginia*, pp. 44-54
[232] Ibid., pp. 53-54

the Historian explains that policy, "In 1816, a group of white Americans founded the American Colonization Society (ACS) to deal with the 'problem' of the growing number of free blacks in the United States by resettling them in Africa."[233] The roster of support for the ACS was a who's who of American Founders. Thomas Jefferson (the author of both the Virginia Constitution and the Declaration of Independence) and James Madison (the 'Father of the Constitution'), among others, were ardent supporters of this unabashed White Nationalist policy.

What's more, the Virginian House of Burgesses actually attempted banning all African immigration to the colonies many times prior to any such efforts by New England and prior to Independence, though all such motions were vetoed by the British Crown. But no sooner had Americans won our freedom than Virginia abolished the import of black slaves. They were the first state on earth to do so.

So then, from the colonial and founding eras, Americans had limited citizenship to Whites only and outlawed the import—the only means by which non-Whites could make these shores at the time—of Blacks. The authors of the Declaration of Independence and the Constitution organized deportations of said race explicitly for the sake of preserving our European stock here. And we went on to fight a grueling internecine war, brother against brother, in large part to determine how best to mitigate the damage of the non-White presence on this continent and under what policy they would best be removed from our shores.

Then came the saga of America's war with Mexico, including our men's sacrifice at the Alamo: Sam Houston's famous statement epitomized the American sentiment—"I didn't come to Texas to live under the Greaser's yoke." Make no mistake, Americans and Texans laid down their lives at the Alamo not for any Austrian economic model or anachronistic abstractions such as 'equality', but simply to keep the Mexicans out. The annexation of California was pursued on like grounds—to rescue the Spanish (White) Rancheros from Mestizo domination.

It wasn't until the late 1800s that the synergy of the industrial revolution and colonialism opened passage to America for sundry races, thereby making necessary overt codification of the principles always presupposed in our founding documents and religion. Americans' Christian, populist response was adamant nativism, which culminated in a slew of border-and-race-conservative legislation such as the U.S.-China Burlingame Treaty of 1868, the Angell Treaty of 1880, the Chinese Exclusion Act of 1882, the Gentlemen's Agreement of 1907, the Asiatic Barred Zone Act of 1917, the Immigration Restriction Act of 1921, and the Immigration Act of 1924 among others. None of which was throughout those years imagined for "un-American" in the least. On the contrary, everyone from the parson to the Supreme Court justice insisted that such measures were necessary applications of

---

[233] "Founding of Liberia, 1847." *Office of the Historian.* https://history.state.gov/milestones/1830-1860/liberia

Christian Common and Constitutional law applied to the circumstance of the increasing mobility of foreign races.

Though Lincoln's revolutionary, socialistic, and never-ratified 14th amendment inverted the purpose and meaning of the federal constitution by alchemically declaring the Africans in our midst 'Americans,' it was subsequently taken for granted by everyone from the Supreme Court Justice to the buggy whip maker that the African's new government-bestowed identity as an 'American' would forever retain an indelible asterisk, because even if they had been declared citizens by a contrivance of bureaucratic imagination, they simply weren't of the American genos as we knew God to have made us, nor as our founders had defined us. It wasn't until the mid-twentieth century when Arabs, Chinese, Mexicans, and others would have the same alchemy continually applied on their behalf through fiat courtcraft by Leftist-activist judges in denial of all foregoing Christian law. Because they were bent on deconstructing the American people as a means of deconstructing the world order of Christendom and, thereby, Christianity itself.

Yet prior to this, the case is conclusive that American policies on citizenship, the franchise, and border enforcement exemplified from the earliest times what may be called Theonomic White Nationalism and Racial Protectionism—concepts so taken for granted that they were known only as "patriotism." But today, we know them by the theological term Kinism.

So when Friedman postulated his open-borders libertarianism on the premise that America was 'always' an open-borders economic abstraction, he was lying through his teeth. And the new Alienist doctrine which men such as Marinov, McDurmon, Wilson, and North have built upon that lie is revealed for a most absurd mythology. Inasmuch as our fathers knew the ethnic protectionism of historic America only as patriotism, the alternative—racial egalitarianism, propositionalism, economism—posited equally by Austrian economists as much as Straussians, Fabians, and Marxists, would be understood by our Christian fathers as naught but Treason.

We were not advised about any of these changes. We were not consulted on the question of whether we wanted to overturn everything that made us who we were. It was done to us. They who have force-fed Americans this alien perspective via their academia-media monopolies—the likes of Emma Lazarus, *et al.*—have imposed this lie to the point that the alternative—patriotism—is nearly forgotten completely.

It is no mere coincidence that the loss of that halcyon social capital and all the little vestigial threads of common affection and symbol bequeathed to North's generation were perceptibly severed most harshly in the wake of the 1964 Civil Rights Act and the 1965 Immigration Act. These incantational hexes on Western civilization were twin forces of destruction, together elevating the alien over us and flinging wide the gates to their hordes. This, much more than any of the foregoing abolitionist and suffragette movements, marks what Grizzard coined "the coming of the 'isms'" — the mainstreaming of revolutionary and counterculture penological concepts like 'racism,' 'sexism,' 'xenophobia,' 'homophobia,' 'Islamophobia', etc. All of which were previously conceived as under the umbrella of Christian virtues of patriotism and patriarchy.

All of the things of which North bemoans our loss were secured in his youth only by an array of social supports which he himself decries. As Lichtman again explains through gnashing teeth:

Taken together, the prohibition of vice, anticommunism, conservative maternalism, evangelical Protestantism, business conservatism, racial science and containment, and the grassroots organizing of the Ku Klux Klan formed a stout defense of America's white Protestant, free enterprise civilization.[234]

North and all his ilk have planted their feet in the shifting sands opposite said position. The legal maxim, *Salus populi, suprema lex* — "The safety of the people is the highest law" — is but a synthesis of the second table of the Decalogue. But the neo-Theonomists spurn it. These gross inversions are not foremost the fault of non-Whites. Principally, the efficient cause is to be found inside the gates, in our own White churches. As an Austrian-Libertarian-Postmillennialist, the underlying assumption which North carries into consideration of American society is identical to that of the hardcore Atheists, Communists, Jews, Muslims, Wiccans, Mexican illegals, and Trotskyite NeoCons: the social contract theory. He accepts that American identity subsists by the alchemical stew of geographic proximity, civil creedalism, and the magisterial state.

Of signal import in John Jay's writing on America's "one connected people" of common ancestry, habit, tradition, and religion in Federalist No. 2 is that his words preceded our constitutional founding! That means Jay considered the American nation to have preexisted the American federal government. Such sentiments, if voiced today, are derided as 'racist' and outside the respectability of men like North and Trotsky.

Rounding into the year of our Lord 2016, we see now the forebodings of our forebears like de Tocqueville, R.L. Dabney, Madison Grant, *et al.*, met with all the confirmations of history. If their contemporaries affirmed their prescient perception of the natural consequences of race-egalitarianism, their posterity cannot but affirm them prophets, because we see now the fruit of the gnostic-abstractionist theories of nationhood in full bloom all about us. Though a keen critic of all the dysfunction of statism, North's gnostic view of nationhood guarantees the inexorable entrenchment of the very thing he reviles. His laissez-faire economism ensures to be overrun by aliens who not only vote for ever more government, but

---

[234] Lichtman, Allan J. *op. cit.*, p. 10

through the violence and general dysfunction endemic to their nationalities, actually *create a perceived need* for the very oppressive nanny-police state which the Libertarians otherwise abjure. Sheriff Taylor and Deputy Fife just don't stand a chance against all the equatorial warlords pouring into our borders. Which is why North's view aligns so seamlessly with the Straussians, the Fabians, and the Marxists who presently define the mainstream and presume to redefine *who we are*. The Misesian Theonomists have nonetheless thrown in with the core conviction of the Radical Left that American identity is conceptual rather than real: not national at all, but notional. If Mr. North may quibble over the centralization under Lincoln, and state compulsion in contracts, he nonetheless affirms the core convictions of all the cookie-cutter Leftists like James Forsyth:

> *Your family could have arrived on the Mayflower or in the back of a van, but if you believe in the values of this country as embodied by the Declaration of Independence, the Constitution, the Gettysburg Address, and the Civil Rights Act, then you are American.*

To which Daniel Larison has offered a poignant rejoinder:

> *There is nothing more artificial, more insubstantial and more dangerous than categorising a nation according to ideology—this is to make honest disagreement over political principles a betrayal of the nation itself. It is to make dissent into a kind of treason; it is to make fidelity to older traditions that contradict the reigning ideology a mark of disloyalty to the nation. Fundamentally it is also to confuse ideas for concrete realities and to give them the loyalty we owe to real things. It is to ignore the concrete realities of kin and place and our memory of our kin and place down through the centuries for the sake of abstractions. This sort of thinking may very well make it easier for people to enter the country, but it makes it impossible to say any longer what kind of country it is, where it came from or who we are as a people.*[235]

These men have disavowed nationalism for notionalism—a creedal nation, a nation without natality—which is no nation at all. Even those Christians who have bought into this concept have done so by reverse-engineering their lately appended political ideology (of only the last fifty years) into their theology; but rather than undergirding their abstractionist civics, their politics prove to entirely confound their religion. Citing biblical descriptions of a "spiritual nation" of Christians is all well and good. Creedalism is certainly indispensable to orthodoxy; however, our inclusion in the spiritual nation of believers is not even determined

---

[235] Larison, Daniel. "Who We Are." *The American Conservative*. 23 Aug 2006.

by *our* theology, but by the grace of God alone. For if our membership in the kingdom were predicated upon our present confession, we would be speaking of neither covenantalism nor monergism at all, but a works-righteousness and anthropocentric synergism. Regeneration precedes justification in the *ordo salutis*. God elects men apart from and prior to their actions—including our professions of faith.

Even on a practical level, if we adopted the idea that an ever-present confession was what sealed a person's place in the covenant, infants, the senile, and the mentally deficient would all face excommunication and, presumably, damnation. Even if these things have never been conceived in such a way (for not even Arminians treat their confessionally incapable children and elders in keeping with this anthropocentric view of membership), and even if they make nonsense of soteriology and communion, it grants them no real remedy in matters political, civic, or national. To bestow natality incantationally in this way not only stands all human history and biblical law on their heads, but openly defies all the biblical language of the table of nations (Gen. 10; 11), because none therein are so counted by their political subscriptionism, theology, or economic models, but are included exclusively on account of their lineage—and that secondarily reinforced by their respective linguistic-cultural expressions. Tirasians are counted as such not on account of their professing 'Tirasian values' or taking part in a 'free market,' but because they descended from Tiras and were born among their brethren. If the Tirasians adopted a theory of peoplehood such as the present egalitarianism, they would have quickly found themselves strangers in their own land, just as Mr. North bemoans now with respect to the American.

Yes, he may pine for a universal laissez-faire society under a minimal state, but in application, it fatally undercuts itself. Not only is Minarchy favored nigh exclusively by Whites, but the presence of violent minorities even dissuades most of us from such ideals. When Honduran headhunters are raping people to death in the streets, no-knock SWAT raids and mandatory curfews start sounding pretty good. While America was certainly founded on Christian principles of liberty, the later ingrafting of the anti-reality creed of racial equality necessarily abrogated that liberty. Our Christian fathers knew it long ago that the Jacobin virtues of *liberté, egalité, fraternité* were all mutually exclusive concepts: liberty cannot coexist with equality, and if universal equality is assumed, true fraternity is outlawed. The libertarian dream of maximal liberty and non-aggression comes closest to actualization only in the context of homogeneous societies. White ones, especially. Conversely, universal societies such as the fiduciary-multicult utopia dreamt by Libertarians only set an inexorable trajectory for iron-fisted centralization of power under the maximal state. This fact North can neither accept nor escape. In him stirs a faint voice of Christian conscience, but his ideology yet demands that he bless the curses, and pronounce them pure.

From the cloister of his temporarily safe White enclave he may yet console himself by putting his feet up on that antique American-made desk, and enjoy a cup of Earl Grey, while listening to his old Glenn Miller records once more, as the mocha-colored Americans* plot to burn everything he ever loved to the ground and strike it from all memory.

"Ecce Homo": Sheepdogs, Alpha Males, and the Man of God

October 4, 2016

Ecce Homo. "Behold the man." These were Pilate's words to the ravening throng screaming for Christ's blood. The Man, indeed. The exemplar of perfect manhood.

Endemic to Conservatives under Liberal occupation, we have played the part of Cassandra all along the way, warnings of the slippery slope ever on our lips and quills: racial integration would lead inexorably to sodomite marriage*, and to every other sundry permutation of sexual revolution which the devil can devise toward the total blurring and eventual abolition of gender differences and deconstruction of the family. Because nation and clan differ not so much in kind but in scale, as goes national (ethnic) identity so goes familial identity. And though Liberals scoffed at all our forebodings, assuring us that every fresh innovation of the moment was the sum of their goals, once attained they always pushed on to new depths of depravity only to turn around and assert again that their new landing was the ultimate goal with no agenda beyond. Even the inner wall of the court has collapsed under the crush of this process as the churches, too, at length yielded to sexual revolution, embracing gender equality nigh simultaneously with racial equality, and therefore, same-sex unions as readily as miscegenation.

Even purported Theonomist and author of several family-centric works, Doug Wilson, has come to accept married* sodomites as "the same as anyone else." Albeit excluding their wedding* day.

The gender-bending chemicals in the water must really be working because American Vision released an article arguing that associating physical strength with masculinity is paganism![236] Look, godliness is clearly not contingent on a man's relative health indicators such as physical strength, okay? Nobody ever argued otherwise. But you'd never know that from McDurmon's article; to hear him tell it, one of the great heresies besetting the church today is the doctrine which holds men enter the gates of heaven only by besting St. Peter in armwrestling. His may be the most straw-packed straw man argument against masculinity — and thereby patriarchy — I've encountered to date. And abjuring the cultiva-

---

[236] Since the time this article was written, the referenced article here has since been taken down and is no longer available

tion of physical strength is tantamount to pacifism, shirking one's God-given responsibility to defend life. After all, how ultimately differs McDurmon's position, that men should spurn physical strength, from John Piper's position that it is wrong to defend one's wife from a rapist by force? McDurmon's position is merely a resolve against effective defense of life, thus landing him in what amounts to the same stance as Piper—pacifism.[237]

Nonetheless, strength, not unlike the beard or a deep voice, is one of the God-ordained characteristics of the male gender set against the "weaker sex." It is symbolically denotative of the authority with which God has vested men in the family, church, and broader society. As such, David had no inkling of McDurmon's position when he sang, "He teacheth my hands to war, so that a bow of steel is broken by mine arms." (2 Sam.22:35; Psa. 18:34) Clearly, physical strength is an objective good and symbol of potency and dominion associated by God with the male gender. And since "man's chief end is to glorify God" (WSC Q.1) with all his strength (Deut. 6:5), strength is to be valued, even prized. It is a mighty gift emblematic of men's federal authority under God and to great effect in His service.

Need I even mention Samson, whose faithfulness was inextricably tied to his physical strength? And whose physical might was both derivative and symbolic of God's own dominion and power?

Meantime, as American Vision undermines Christian manhood, the same fellows turn around to "press the antithesis" in a startling direction—gynocracy! Yes, according to Bojidar Marinov, a wife is to be the manager of all her husband's property and of her own, in effect, leaving the man custodian of nothing. This is what Bojidar characterizes as "equality," and God's template for the Christian family. Yes, these putative leaders of the Theonomic movement have defaulted to the position of the lowest heathen societies.

Under these circumstances of such unmistakable subversion of covenant theology, it's no wonder at all that evangelicals and secular reactionaries are positing their own theories of manhood. Granted, because egalitarianism and feminism are polarizations away from Christian patriarchy and the manosphere is a reversed polarization away from the egalitarian/feminist paradigm, the Men's Rights Movement often finds its way back round to some traditional Christian positions. But not unaugmented.

Reaction isn't enough. For reaction is accounted for in advance by the culture destroyers and merely plays into their dialectic: thesis, antithesis, synthesis. Action, reaction, solution. And apart from God's Law-Word, all our cogitations against evil are infected with the same germ. For all the relative good that non-

---

[237] Desperandum, Nil. "John Piper on Guns: Suicidal, Arminian, Pacifist, and Statist." *Faith and Heritage*. 14 Feb 2013. https://faithandheritage.com/2013/02/john-piper-on-guns-suicidal-arminian-pacifist-and-statist/

Christian reactionary thought may stumble upon, we cannot embrace their categories without qualification and recontextualization under the Christian cosmos. In order to justify, anchor, and perfect it, we must predicate reactionary thinking upon, and calibrate it in terms of, divine revelation. There is no other objective starting point nor basis for the endeavor. Apart from God's Law-Word even the shrewdest minds are adrift and at the mercy of the dialectic.

But the two foremost reactionary paradigms today which purport to rescue manhood from the gynocracy are both ethological analogies based upon the social hierarchies of animals.

One is Killology. Though originally postulated as a system of military study and conditioning for battlefield psychology, it has since unfolded to encompass a more general theory of sociology which hopes to reprise manhood by casting society as divided between three types—sheep, wolves, and sheepdogs. Therein women, children, and weak men are sheep who need protection from wolves (sinister men), and the only ones to do this are the good (strong) men—sheepdogs. This perspective, which was articulated for public consumption first by Army War Psychologist Lt. Col. David Grossman, has since been adopted as the patent social theory in militia and patriot circles. Evangelical churches which especially prize veterans even host Killology courses at their churches. In fact, Grossman began the Sheepdog Seminars expressly for churches and he has succeeded in suffusing a right-wing evangelical culture with his Killology credo.

Lest anyone dismiss the seeming emphasis on killing in this new philosophy of rightish Evangelicals, proponents of said view cite the aphorism of Maj. Gen. James Mattis approvingly: "Be polite, be professional, but have a plan to kill everybody you meet." I ask you, reader, is this the disposition of the Christian man? Ever calculating against friend and foe alike? I submit to you that such a man has no actual friends, only prospective enemies and collateral damage.

The other paradigm purporting to redeem manhood is a subset of what is called Game theory, Alpha Game, or simply, Game—a set of algorithms loosely patterned after the pack hierarchies of social animals like wolves and apes. So advocates of this view delineate the pecking order of human society. And as you might imagine, as a study in algorithms, the notoriety of Game theory has largely been advanced by awkward Gamers and Strategists intent on memorizing the "cheat codes" to social interaction for their personal service. This perspective is interwoven with economic, psychological, sexological, and even marketing strategies. Call it counting cards with people, hotwiring your friends, or just plain old manipulation, in an age so leveraged against White men and a Church demuring from biblical identities, Game has filled the void and defined masculinity for many Gen Xers and Millennials, and may be said to comprise its own wing of the Alt Right, if not permeating the whole. Besides this, because of their intersection and overlap in Alt Right circles it has gained ground in some contrarian Christian circles as well—Trad Cats, Orthodox, and the like, mostly.

Within this system the gold standard of manhood and ostensible enlightenment is the class known as the "alpha male." Even if the application of Game hasn't gone entirely mainstream in the public consciousness, this denotation of masculinity certainly has. As has the related "beta male" concept. Though some proponents of this perspective insist that the social stations of men are predetermined and unalterable, life coaches and ascendant masters abound eager to disciple lower-ranking males in the ways of alphahood—true manliness.

Although these concepts are widely used to facilitate womanizing, some, embracing an "omega male" status and confronted with the caustic nature of modern feminism, have resorted to the antithesis, asexuality.

Foremost though, devotees of this paradigm are chasing the status they call alpha. Though technical definitions of that status differ depending on who is describing it, the tally is likely to include traits like *loud* alongside *confident* and *arrogant* next to *fearless*. I've even seen descriptions which include *overbearing*. The alpha persona seems to encompass both charisma and general belligerence. If the alpha character is intimidated by neither adverse social settings nor rabid enemies, he is also described as so cocksure as to tolerate no peers nor superiors. Because the alpha has to be the boss in every circumstance. All of which should sound familiar as the concept of Nietzschean man asserting his 'will to power,' in concert with which Nietzsche also posited his 'God is dead' doctrine.

While I certainly do not intend to dissuade our men from recapturing their boldness and courage, or the willingness to struggle for our Folk, that struggle is rightly defined only in terms of the Christian faith. I certainly appreciate the social rejection of feminism, but the alternative offered in the alpha ideal is equivalent to Austrian economics' value in critiquing statism: both demonstrate facility in deconstructing their perceived antitheses—but that's as far as it goes. Neither have viable worldviews of their own. In as much as a libertarian-built world inexorably lays the groundwork for the very centralization which it decries, alpha Game actually feeds into the feminist paradigm that men are all self-serving manipulators, fakes, sexual predators, and con-men. Even if the Game paradigm successfully deconstructs feminist social grids, at length, because it does not posit any restoration of the clan-centric society under the objective values of God's Law, it sets the stage for only a deeper jading of our women against our men. If the Hippies couldn't "live on love," how much less can our people live on posturing, manipulation, and self-aggrandizement?

Granted, the technicians of this system draw some shrewd observations about behavioral patterns, but treating human interaction as merely a means to obtain sex, treasure, and praise, they also smuggle in a hedonistic philosophy which runs the gamut from self-help for the socially inept to building a better sociopath. This is why so many who subscribe to Game theory count themselves "black-pilled," embracing egoism and nihilism. It is the perspective one would script for some extraterrestrial mandroid hoping to infiltrate and subdue the human species.

Borrowing as they do from ethology, both these theories of masculinity — Killology and Game — are based upon the assumption that men are naught but complex animals. Allowing such to define the desired traits and virtues of manhood is to consent to the evolutionary presuppositions which underlie those systems — or, speaking to its more candidly theological character, animism. And the old fundamentalist saw against evolution, "teaching kids they are animals will only produce animals," is then applicable in regard to these perspectives. Even if they are taught in church seminars.

Of my personal friends and acquaintances who are committed evangelicals and acolytes of Killology, all dismiss Just War Theory with open contempt. If an enemy (a term they have no small difficulty defining) pitches a rock and misses, the sheepdogs advocate total war against not just his family, but typically too, his neighbors and associates, if not his nation. Typically speaking, men of this mindset are also big believers in preemptive action based upon suspicion. Yes, they reckon distrust is ample reason to start war after war. Thus they endorse Israeli policy with respect to Palestinians and neocon foreign policy for the greater Mideast. They recognize no principle of proportionality or moderation in the *lex talionis*, only ruthlessness. They look on chivalry in disdain. Winning is all that matters, no matter the cost in innocent life. If confronted with the collateral damage of massacred non-combatant children, they respond, "So? It isn't my fault their fathers aren't better at protecting them. They should have trained harder if they wanted to win. And they shouldn't have tugged on Superman's cape." I have been told something very close to this very thing face-to-face by more than one such sheepdog.

For all its parabolic presentation and in spite of pretense of approximating Christian resistance theory, Killology is really naught but an apologetic for the militaristic barbarism native to and serving the interests of Zionism — psyche conditioning for *shabbos goy*.

Keeping, then, in mind the aggressive militaristic externality of Killology, and the aggressive social internality of Game, the two accord with the dichotomy of externally-focused Zionist foreign policy and the internally-focused hedonism pedaled to undermine American domestic life. And appraising the politics of each lens, there is correspondence in fact; Killologists tend to be right-wing neocon types and Game devotees identify with the Alt Right which Richard Spencer (who coined the term) defines as "the New Left" — a big tent of total-state NS types, Euro Imperium folks, atheists, perennialists, nihilists, satanists, eco-nuts, anarcho-futurists, and a handful of "Dark Enlightenment" Trad Cats and Orthodox. The Protestants involved are so only out of what they perceive as a total dearth of positive movement in their own circles and a lack of alternatives. It is in times such as these that the line between principle and pragmatism tends to blur. And in essence, the Christians pursuing the alpha motif do so for the same reasons they identify with the Alt Right—because flawed as the rightist heathens' positions may be, their rejection of cultural Marxism is superior to Christians' embrace of cultural Marxism.

But these twin Manosphere analogies—society as a wolfpack vs. society as wolves, sheep, and sheepdogs—miss the mark because neither are predicated on biblical grounds. Although the Bible does tender a social analogy which sounds similar: society as divided primarily among sheep, goats, wolves, and the Shepherd. But the similarity is superficial at best because the biblical paradigm is truly an analogy, not an ontological description of man undergirt by evolutionary or animist presuppositions. That is, the Scripture speaks of Christians as 'sheep' in much the same way that it speaks of the Church as the bride of Christ. The designation of sheep in that analogy is meant only to communicate our reliance on and protection by our Good Shepherd (Christ), not to suggest men to be mere animals, nor to admonish us to emulate any animal behavior. Even if it often proves to be the behavior of many Christians, nowhere do we gather the impression from the text that because we are called sheep we have a mandate to wander about oblivious, grazing and bleating dumbly. No more so than its calling us a bride effects a sex change upon the elders.

Both Killology and Game implicitly condemn the identity of the sheep in the biblical analogy. In Killology 'sheep' are the weak and foolish, and in Game they correspond to Betas and Deltas, again, the weak and the foolish.

The sheepdog and the alpha male are one and the same in that they seek their own status and bow the knee to none but their own egos. But striving toward humility, the Christian gentleman mortifies the self, serves God, and fears no man (Lk. 14:7-11). Where the sheepdog/alpha fights in and for his own pride, Christ's man fights for the glory of the Lord of Hosts at the hearthside no less than the battlements; he lays down his life upon the hearthstone and is therefore at home on the rampart.

Chesterton has counterpoised the contest between alpha heathen and selfless Christian man in the words of Alfred the Great to the Viking lord Guthrum:

> *That on you is fallen the shadow,*
> *And not upon the Name;*
> *That though we scatter and though we fly,*
> *And you hang over us like the sky,*
> *You are more tired of victory,*
> *Than we are tired of shame.*
>
> *That though you hunt the Christian man*
> *Like a hare on the hill-side,*

The hare has still more heart to run
Than you have heart to ride.

That though all lances split on you,
All swords be heaved in vain,
We have more lust again to lose
Than you to win again.

Your lord sits high in the saddle,
A broken-hearted king,
But our king Alfred, lost from fame,
Fallen among foes or bonds of shame,
In I know not what mean trade or name,
Has still some song to sing;

Our monks go robed in rain and snow,
But the heart of flame therein,
But you go clothed in feasts and flames,
When all is ice within;

[…]
Pride juggles with her toppling towers,
They strike the sun and cease,
But the firm feet of humility
They grip the ground like trees.[238]

It is a paradox to the heathen mind which conquers by the superstitions of pride, that it is in love and humility that the Christian man becomes indomitable. This is the testimony of all the martyrs. The passion and power of the heathen gods of ego begins and ends in the shallow faculties of man, a being embrittled and fractured by sin, but the perseverance of the saints begins and ends with God whose faculties are infinite and whose being defines all Good. The weakness of God is stronger than the might of men. At the Lord's birth He was deemed such a threat to the state that the governor of Judea dispatched armies against an infant, and in spite of their organized resources, the Babe eluded them. As a Youth He engaged the theologians, lawyers, and scholars and through the Scriptures prevailed against the greatest minds again and again. Apprenticed in construction by his adoptive father Joseph, He grew into great physical strength and like unto Samson, He entered the temple which had become equivalent to the Wall Street Stock Exchange, bludgeoned and scourged the usurious moneychangers, bankers, merchants, and

---

[238] Chesterton, G.K. "Ballad of the White Horse."

all their armed guards, driving them from the temple; one Man driving a thousand, He proved the consummate Warrior. Unflinching, He faced down demoniac ghouls, cast out demons, and after extreme fasting, sought out the devil himself for battle in the wilderness, and prevailed. He calmed the storm with a word. And threw a phalanx of soldiers to the ground, again, with but a word. But He also healed the sick, lame, and blind, and even rose men from the dead. Christ, the zenith and source of all power and authority, and the perfect expression of Manhood, walked this earth not with vain bravado or posturing, but gently in total power under total control, in the mastery over the flesh and the allure of social elevation. Though unyielding with His enemies and speaking truth with all power, He walked in meekness and was a servant to His friends and His Father. He loved His mother and other women besides, but unlike Adam fell thrall to no womanly anxieties. Far from living to climb the social ladder and the gratification of appetite therein, in obedience to the Father and for love of His people He subjected Himself to utter shame and ignominious death. He counted righteousness and the glory of God of more worth than His appearance. No torture could rend confession, apology, or pleas for mercy from His lips; no power in creation could compel Him to concede the authority of Roman interrogation. Even as He hung upon the cursed tree He was possessed of more raw power than all the armies in heaven and earth, but He indulged no temptation to use it in His defense, preferring our defense and God's glory therein. He died unbent and unbroken. And arose in glory.

He is greater than any sheepdog. He is the Shepherd. He is far more than any alpha. He is Alpha and Omega. In the humility and peace of His service is man's greatest strength, and apart from His service, all is vanity. All other examples of masculinity, no matter how august or how commanding, are but His shadow falling across the earth. Whether we speak of those neo-theonomists who eschew the emblems and duties of manhood through pacifism, or those neocon evangelicals and Alt Righters who posture at manhood through emulation of animals pursuant of the praise of men, all make themselves less than men. The precondition and taproot of the Patriarchy of old for which all these are blindly groping is found in the very thing from which they aver at all cost—relinquishment of pride. To be a real man one must fear and obey God, thinking His thoughts after Him. To be a man in full, take up your cross and follow Him. *Ecce Homo*.

The Golden Rule: The Equity of Ethnonationalism

October 20, 2016

Therefore all things whatsoever ye would that men should do to you, do ye even so to them: for this is the law and the prophets.

Matthew 7:12

This most simple summary of the Law, while perhaps being the best known biblical aphorism lingering in the collective mind, is all but entirely misunderstood today. Though misconception of spiritual things is to be expected of unbelievers, as they are intent on suppressing the truth, it is exceeding strange to see claimants of Christ adopting the unbeliever's interpretation of Christ's words here. But this is precisely what has happened.

Everyone from the Hindu to the atheist affirms the Golden Rule. I won't bore the reader with the quotes proving that point, but there are ample citations available demonstrating a similar-sounding principle in all the major world religions; suffice it to say it is confirmed by virtually every source touching the subject—the Golden Rule is a universal value posited by Confucius, Buddha, Rabbi Hillel, et al., independent of Christ and the Christian tradition.

But this is so only if we interpret the Golden Rule in the same way that the modern Alienist church does. This fact alone—that the modern churches find themselves arguing that 'the sum of the law and prophets' (Matt. 7:12) is a universal ethic embraced by all religions—should itself refute them. For Paul solemnly admonished the Colossians in 2:8 that the Christian man must be on guard against "the traditions of men and the rudiments of the world," i.e., the assumptions held in common by the heathen. If concord with all the cults is a boon in their eyes, they prove themselves doubly blind.

Albeit this ethical-theological stigmatism is not entirely new. In his Defense of Virginia, Dabney addressed the same spirit invading under the banner of abolitionism in his day (also accessible via the Dabney Archive):

But a more special word should be devoted to the argument from the Golden Rule.... [A]s leading Abolitionists continue to advance the oft-torn and tattered folly, the friends of truth must continue to tear it to shreds. The whole reasoning of the Abolitionists proceeds on the absurd idea, that any caprice or vain desire we might entertain towards our fellowman, if we were in his place, and he in ours, must be the rule of our conduct towards him, whether the desire would be in itself right or not. This absurdity has been illustrated by a thousand instances. On this rule, a parent who, were he a child again, would be wayward and self-indulgent, commits a clear sin in restraining or punishing the waywardness of his child, for this is doing the opposite of what he would wish were he again the child. Judge and sheriff commit a criminal murder in condemning and executing the most atrocious felon; for were they on the gallows themselves, the overmastering love of life would very surely prompt them to desire release. In a word, whatever ill-regulated desire we are conscious of having, or of being likely to have, in reversed circumstances, that desire we are bound to make the rule of our action in granting the parallel caprice of any other man, be he bore, beggar, highwayman, or what not. On this understanding, the Golden Rule would become any thing but golden; it would be a rule of iniquity; for instead of making impartial equity our regulating principle, it would make the accidents of man's criminal caprice the law of his acts. It would become every man's duty to enable all other men to do whatever his own sinful heart, mutatis mutandis, might prompt…

It is clear, then, that our Saviour, by His Golden Rule, never intended to establish so absurd a law. The rule of our conduct to our neighbour is not any desire which we might have, were we to change places; but it is that desire which we should, in that case, be morally entitled to have. . . . The Apostle Paul gives precisely the true application of this rule when he says: "Masters, give unto your servants that which is just and equal." And this means, not emancipation from servitude, but good treatment as servants; which is proven by the fact that the precept contemplates the relation of masters and servants as still subsisting.

Dabney's essay is a sledgehammer, as is David Carlton's expansion thereon.[239] Both reprise the unpopular truth that antebellum slavery was indeed consistent with the Golden Rule and loving thy neighbor. I do not presume to improve on the case they've made. I'm content to focus more minutely on the matter of the modern church—even the supposed conservative denominations such as PCA and OPC—having come to interpret the Golden Rule in conformity with the counterfeit humanist ideal found in every sect of heathendom.

As is plain, Alienists are overjoyed at the application of the humanist lens to Christ's words with respects to racial integration and interracial marriage. Their moral outrage at those who question the humanist ethos is visceral. They can conceive nothing in the conservative's objection to miscegeny but violation of the Golden Rule and, by implication, apostasy. With a degree of sanctimony which they seem to muster for no other cause or argument, they thunder, "How would

---

[239] Carlton, Davis. "Slavery: Its Morality, History, and Implications for Race Relations in America, Part 2." *Faith and Heritage*. 18 May 2012. https://faithandheritage.com/2012/05/slavery-its-morality-history-and-implications-for-race-relations-in-america-part-2/

you like someone to declare *your* marriage a sin?! Do unto others as you would have them do unto you!" Any traditionalist who does not wilt before the Alienist's thoughtless zeal is damned for a heretic. Which, of course, would be of little concern if it weren't for the fact that they have infiltrated all the positions of influence in the institutional churches now. Nonetheless, on the merits of their argument an honest man can hardly stifle his laughter. But it does not rise to genuine mirth, only sardonic exasperation.

For not only did our sires uniformly denounce miscegenation and from the largest platforms, but the meager 4% margin who actually approved of miscegenation in 1958 were not Christians at all. That number was comprised of the hardest of the hard Left: Jews, atheists, communists, and Jewish atheist communists. Meantime, our fathers pronounced only the most solemn omens concerning the logical entailments thereof. Indeed, our segregationist fathers forecast that the egalitarian interpretation of the Golden Rule sanctioning interracial unions necessarily implied the sanction of everything from sodomite unions to human sacrifice and cannibalism. As Richard Weaver famously warned, ideas have consequences.

But the anti-Christ Left mocked our fathers' logical forecasts as "ignorant paranoia" and "Chicken Little slippery-slope hysteria."

However, not only did our fathers' arguments accord with Scripture and logic, but all their prognostications therefrom were likewise borne out in time. The same rationale—'Do unto others' seen through the humanist lens—went on to necessarily condone first "same-sex unions" and then "gay marriage." If no one should be suffered to interfere with love* between two consenting parties, then acceptance of miscegenation on those grounds validated sodomite marriage* intrinsically. It also gave us contraceptive-based family planning, as well as abortion. No-fault divorce, too. And the Warren Court went on to apply the principle over the breadth of many more such subjects, just as our fathers' forebodings warned. So much so that his biography by Newton would be titled *Justice for All: Earl Warren and the Nation He Made*. Describing modern America as 'made' by Earl Warren is fairly apt even if he was only following the ideological course set by the likes of Justice Brandeis.

But in his wake, the engines of the court are still stoked hot as the furnaces of hell, forging from that first ore one new abominable permutation after another. All under the auspices of 'doing unto others' with respect to the institutions of family and nation—all under euphemisms like 'reproductive rights,' 'civil rights,' and 'human rights.'

Truth be told, the entirety of the Sexual Revolution hinged upon that first matter of race. This, of course, is not at all a controversial statement except amongst those Christians who, having lately been coached into the Alienist view of race, do not yet apply the principle consistently. But if a margin of them retain yet some reservations against post-genderism, they are capitulating rapidly.[240]

In practice the humanist view assumes egalitarianism, but is ironically undergirded by moral relativism and self-deification. The Devil, as from the beginning, calls for equality between man, woman, God, and the other—the Devil being the 'other' in the story, of course.

Even the Church of Satan subscribes to a form of the Golden Rule. Anton LaVey taught: "Do unto others as they do unto you." While this is really a repudiation of the Golden Rule, in practice it winds up the same as the ethic taught by the Alienists under the auspices of the Golden Rule. First, it starts with an assumption of equality on the part of its adherents—that all equally deserve what they expect of others, and that all have the equal right to judge their fellows by their high estimation of their own deserts. The assumption of reciprocity therein introduces a corollary: if everyone treats everyone else as he is treated, the necessary implication is that one must treat others as one wishes to be treated, else one could never be treated as one wishes. So by way of self-interest, it winds up back at the more common expression of the Golden Rule anyway. But secondly, it assumes the previous and primary rule of satanism posited by Aleister Crowley: "Do as thou wilt." And it is clear from Dabney's argument above that because the liberal's own preferences are cast as every man's duty, Crowley's law is actually the cornerstone assumption of the liberal Christian. The Alienist position differs from the satanist's on this point only with respect to their relative directness and candor. But their underlying assumptions are the same. As Rushdoony observed:

> *The demand of humanism (and of its child, socialism) is for a universal ethics. In universal ethics we are told that, even as the family gave way to the tribe, and the tribe to the nation, so the nation must give way to a one-world order. All men must treat all other men equally. Partiality to our family, nation, or race, represents a lower morality, we are told, and must be replaced by a 'higher' morality of a universal ethics.*[241]

If granted, the Alienist view of a 'universal morality' nullifies the tenth commandment. For the call to level all expectations of treatment, entitling every slave to the estate of every master, is itself to declare all covetousness holy, which precipitates a like nullification of the eighth commandment, blessing every larceny. In fact, citing Christ's summary of the Law—which is what Jesus expressly describes the Golden Rule to be—the Alienist ultimately interprets that summary as a neutralization of all that it summarizes.

---

[240] Murphy, Caryle. "Most U.S. Christian groups grow more accepting of homosexuality." *Pew Research Center*. 18 Dec 2015. https://www.pewresearch.org/fact-tank/2015/12/18/most-u-s-christian-groups-grow-more-accepting-of-homosexuality/
[241] Rushdoony, R.J. *Roots of Reconstruction*, p. 574

But despite its ubiquity amongst the humanist sects, even that leveling—due to assumptions held by Whites in particular, and consonant with the notion of "colorblindness"—is itself deemed a deep offense to non-Whites. When Whites treat everyone as *we* wish to be treated, it is described by other races as consonant with "White supremacy." But that's just to say that the humanist conception of the Golden Rule does not pay the universalized dividends which its proponents imagine. Insofar as we are speaking of White Alienists, presumption of equality is still subject to the personal preferences and social norms of White people, the inescapability of which is willfully ignored by said liberal Whites, but appears to all other peoples as nothing but an ethno-ethical imperialism, and an especially obtuse form of hypocrisy. Thus proving the internal contradiction thereof, as well as its unlivability.

What, then, does the Golden Rule actually teach?

Though a summation of the Law in itself, the Golden Rule proclaimed by Christ is also a restatement of Moses's foregoing summary of the law—"love thy neighbor as thyself" (Lev. 19:18)—which Jesus also identified as the second greatest commandment (Matt. 22:36-40), subordinate to the commandment to "love the Lord thy God with all thine heart, and with all thy soul, and with all thy might" (Deut. 6:5). As the first pertains to man's duties to God, and the second, his duties toward other men, it is apparent that the first and second greatest commandments are coordinate with the two tables of the Decalogue. So, be it the second greatest commandment or the Golden Rule, it is apparent that our interpretation of either such summary must accord with the law each abbreviates; else it is no summary at all. To suggest otherwise is only to propose a foreign law system at odds with and overlaying God's Law, thus implying some essential incoherence not only in Christian ethics, but in the divine Word itself, and, ultimately, in God back of it—a perspective approaching the old heresy of Marcionism. That is to say that the popular conception of the Golden Rule, in and out of the churches, amounts to blasphemy and nascent heathenism.

As religion always impacts language, this confusion has come synchronistically with a confounding of basic terms: in this case the difference between egalitarianism and equity. Where the modern churchmen have colored the Golden Rule as a pledge of equality, certain words had to be redefined to strip us of terminology by which we might reprise the biblical view. Granted, the standard dictionaries today tell you that these words—equity and egalitarianism—are synonyms, but as this is an age of such unified deceit, we turn to the elder dictionaries, from a time when the West was still monolithically Christian, for a true definition. This is the first entry in Webster's 1828 on the word *equity*: "1. Justice; right. In practice, *equity* is the impartial distribution of justice, or the doing that to another which the laws of God and man, and of reason, give him a right to claim. It is the treating of a person according to justice and reason."

Quite different from egalitarianism, treating all men according to the justice of God's law means categorical and bounded proportionality relative to one's identity, without which there is no actual relation to other men and things. Even the alternate usage of equity, pertaining to real estate, communicates the idea that right is tied up with one's relative station and identity. The homesteader or householder is both literally and figuratively "entitled." It is not equality, but equity, at which the Golden Rule aims.

In order to comprehend the Golden Rule as consistent with God's Law and Scripture in general, it must presuppose all the ordered inequalities hallowed in the scope thereof: the special rights of a man to his own property encompass not only the plot and structure of his house but the lineal blood conception of his house also. This is how the fourth commandment conceives wife and children among our "possessions" and how the tenth likewise conceives our neighbor's wife and children as his possessions separate from ours. Thus does the law demand a reciprocity of respect, each man for the unequal estate of his neighbor. Suffice it to say that if the law forbids coveting and all confusion of ownership with respect to one's neighbor's wife, children, slaves, livestock, and estate, then men have lawful claims of exclusive rights over many things. In this same way, though Israel was admonished to treat the alien "as one born among you," the alien was nonetheless precluded by law from titles of land, political office, and intermarriage with Israelites. Meaning that the alien never ceased being acknowledged for what he was — an alien. Not only do I have no equal rights to my neighbor's estate, nor to equal standing in house, nor to citizenship amongst nations of other races, but the mere fancy that I could is itself a plain violation of the law per the tenth commandment — and because it is a summary of the law, a violation of the Golden Rule itself.

So when the liberal, under the auspices of the Golden Rule, imputes to heathen foreigners the birthright of our children without distinction, he undercuts the very principle he imagines to vindicate himself. To honor the Golden Rule, we must do unto every man as we would *rightly* have done to us were we in his circumstance. And each man's rights differ according to circumstance. 'Doing unto others' means my neighbor has equal right not to my wife and children, but to his own; by the same principle, a man of another people is entitled to citizenship not in my nation, but in his own. The Golden Rule in no way mandates that blacks are entitled access to my sisters and daughters, only to their own. The children of the world are not entitled to my love and care in anything like an equal proportion to my own children. In fact, the Scripture overtly condemns those "pleased with the children of foreigners" (Isa. 2:6; cf. Hos. 5:7) in place of their own children. The hour demands emphasis of these basic truths, because the churches have suddenly spurned God's design for the family in favor of the delusions pursued by Angelina Jolie.

If "My house shall be called a house of prayer for all nations" (Isa. 56:7), those nations (*ethne*) must exist, and to perpetuate themselves as limited entities as the

Scripture presupposes, they can only abide in some form of segregation. All of which is to say that the Golden Rule is consonant not only with familism, but also with nationalism. Sanctioning unequal privileges of lineage, inheritance, and class, with respect to historic Christendom, entails that dread bane of Alienism — White privilege. But so too for Black privilege, and Yellow, and Brown, and Red: all have privilege and supremacy relative to their own domains. The only equality in it is that every man and nation is equally entitled to their unequal rights under God.

Charlottesville and the Kalergi Clergy

August 25, 2017

"It is usually considered good practice to examine a thing for oneself before echoing the vulgar ridicule of it."

J. Gresham Machen, *Christianity and Liberalism*

We all know what happened at Charlottesville. And as expected, the MSM spun a narrative inverse of reality. Establishment GOP mouthpieces quickly joined the Marxist chorus denouncing 'White Supremacy' and depicting Antifa as the wholesome mainstream repelling Nazi stormtroopers marching in to lynch all the Blacks, effeminates, dyslexics, and left-handed Indigo children who make up the utopia of modern Charlottesville.

But Christians can all surely see through this cartoonish narrative. Can't they?

Odd as it is, and their theological peccadillos notwithstanding, the ministerial corps of America took to their podcast posts, manned the Twitter turrets, and it was blog-bombs away in unprecedented unanimity denouncing one side in particular. Was it the aggressor side? Was it the side who brought offensive weapons like bats, knives, rocks, bleach, acid, and flamethrowers? Was it the side that demands unlimited abortion? Was it the side with topless lesbians screaming about their menstruation? Was it the side calling for the overthrow of history? Was it the side threatening the mass rape of the others' women and children? Was it the side demanding and promising genocide? Was it the side which monolithically demands the outlawing of various aspects of Christianity, or the Christian Faith *in toto*?

The answer to all of these is *no*.

Jack Graham led his lily White church in a benedictory oath saying, "We stand together as a church . . . to say in the strongest terms that we condemn any sort of racial bigotry, white supremacy, prejudice, and intolerance."

Hordes of rampaging black-hood Communists, Black thugs, blue-haired lesbians, sodomites, pedophiles, catamites, Talmudists, witches, and Satanists attacked lawfully assembled demonstrators gathered *to speak* against the Marxist erasure of Christian history and Western Man, and pastor Jack identifies the latter group as the singular enemy of the church? White people who believe in history are the problem?

Just what in the literal hell is going on here?

Tim Keller chimed in denouncing any desire for preservation of our monuments and symbols, or any favorable view of our heritage, as categorical *Nazism!* Which only confirms either that he has no idea what Nazism is, or that he is intent on purposeful distortion. He even singles out "particularly Anglos" as having a moral imperative to disavow any and all positive association with our own history and people! Which is to say, according to Keller, *if you are White, your salvation depends upon repudiation of your Christian heritage!*

Rod Dreher, who wrote an entire book on the R2K premise that Christians should abandon the public sphere, broke his ostensible vow of silence to condemn the rally and self-defense of the Rightists as "White racial terrorism."

Russ Moore, president of the Southern Baptists' ERLC, writing for the Washington Post and NY Times (the fact that he gets a stage in such anti-Christian publications is telling, isn't it?), declared any White retaining affection for his people or their history "satanic to the core" and the literal manifestation of the Beast of Revelation.[242] *Yeah, he really went there.*

Pensacola *Christian* College actually expelled Allen Armentrout *for the sin of saluting the Lee Memorial with the cross of St. Andrew in hand.* And because he stood taciturn in the face of venomous anti-Christs and post-gender bipeds of the African persuasion threatening violence on him. So acknowledgment of the venerable dead is now an excommunicable offense. So much for *Foxe's Book of Martyrs*, then.

Professor Mark Eckels said via Facebook, "I stand with my Black brothers and sisters against racial hatred #Charlottesville."

Um, your 'Black brothers and sisters' were the ones flagrant in their 'racial hatred.' And not just at Charlottesville, but everywhere, all the time. Realize, the genocide of the White race is not conspiracy theory in their eyes, but a proposition openly embraced and celebrated! As they tell it, the end of the White man is mandatory and anyone who is insufficiently enthusiastic about it deserves to be executed with welding torches and have their families *raped to death by Blacks*. This is absolutely mainstream thought amongst them. It's the argument they defer to in every other exchange.

Meantime, the White Right you've singled out as the villains are merely attempting to gain a platform to object to that genocide, and be White in public, for goodness' sake!

Jemar Tisby, president of RAAN, said in a Washington Post article (again, ask yourself why *he* gets a pass to write in such an anti-Christian venue), "The church remains instrumental in dismantling the racial caste system in America."

---

[242] Moore, Russell. "Russell Moore: White supremacy angers Jesus, but does it anger his church?" *The Washington Post*. 14 Aug 2017. https://www.washingtonpost.com/news/acts-of-faith/wp/2017/08/14/russell-moore-white-supremacy-angers-jesus-but-does-it-anger-his-church/

Let me remind you, RAAN stands for *Reformed African-American Network*. Which operates in the open as a racial advocacy group within the Church! And not only with the forbearance of White people, but the jubilant acclaim of the same. If Mr. Tisby wants to discuss the 'racial caste system', let's start with why he enjoys an unquestioned latitude to seek the good of his race, and speak to Christian issues from a racial vantage, when White Christians are denied the basic right to exist; and the subsequent question of why his race is presumed to have moral authority to lecture mine on the consummate evil of Whiteness, but no reciprocity is allowed to Whites to criticize Blacks in any capacity, nor even to disagree with their appraisal of Whites. The plain fact is, this entire society is presently set up in deference to non-Whites and demands the erasure of Whites from the very civilization we built.

Joel McDurmon tweets, "Still think I'm crazy on racism? Think there's no anti-black hate anymore? Grieve for #charlottesville and repent; do something."

Yes, Joel, you're certifiable. The term 'racism' is nothing less than the indictment of the theonomic social order of love for one's family, folk, and fatherland. Y'know, the theonomic movement you're presently turning on its head?

And there was nothing about the UTR rally demonstrative of special hatred of Blacks. If anything, it was hatred of our ongoing genocide and the satanic zeitgeist driving it. 'Anti-black hate' is the SPLC's cartoon narrative, and you know it. No one was chanting, "We hate niggers!" They were chanting, "You will not replace us!" I mean, even if both sides were advocating the genocide of the other, rebuking only one party would reveal your partisanship; but it's worse than that, because the two aren't saying the same thing. And you are attacking the party making the benign statements, in deference to the party making the most malevolent statements. More than statements, in fact, the party you identify with is everywhere *acting on* their genocidal ideation, murdering White men merely for being White.

Hey, Joel, enjoy those thirty shekels of shame, or however much Soros is paying you, because it's the only reward you have coming.

Jeff Durbin opens his *comedy* show by saying, "As Christians, we condemn, completely, racism. Racism is essentially hatred. It's hatred for another person, another image-bearer of God, because of the color of their skin."

I have never met *any White* who fits that criteria. I mean, as someone who has been called racist a lot, I can tell you, I have no hatred for any particular color. But I do hate evil, and the large majority of Blacks are monstrously evil. Not least of which for their insistence that my people have no right to live—a position nigh universal to them. No, to the extent that Blacks are hated, it is in MLK's historic words, "not on account of their color, but the content of their character."

And though motives vary, the Right are not motivated by hatred of anyone so much as a sense of priority for their own children and culture, and a sense of responsibility to ancestors, posterity, and God.

Most funny, though, is that Durbin's definition of 'racism' is all but unanimously condemned by Blacks as 'blatant White Supremacy.' So, yeah, he only provokes the very people he means to appease. For all his virtue signalling, the Antifa folk to whom he's catering regard Durbin indistinguishable from the 'Nazis.' He may deceive himself into believing he is on the side of the downtrodden minorities, but as an anti-abortion cis White Christian, Durbin is to them only a target, and the only people who might defend him are the mean ol' 'racists' he condemns.

Durbin also resorts to that old bumpersticker slogan—"No race but the human race"—as if it were some foundational Christian doctrine. Truth is, it's hardly older than corduroy bell bottoms, and was entirely unknown to us prior. In the New Testament alone the terms *ethnos, genos, genea,* and so forth are applied to many limited racial groups. Or as Schaff famously spoke to the Christian doctrine of slavery:

> *Wherever the governmental idea holds the mercenary so completely in check and yields to the influence of Christian morality, it may be a wholesome training school for inferior races, as it is in fact with the African negroes, until they are capable to govern themselves.*[243]

See, Jeff, prior to the sexual revolution and the artifice of 'civil rights,' Christians—especially our Reformed luminaries—did not entertain this 'one race, the human race' concept. To them, all such talk was decried for *New Ageism, Liberalism, Communism, Unitarianism, Jacobinism, Monism, Docetism, Gnosticism,* or *Humanism.*

And really, Jeff? A red Karl Marx t-shirt? I'm sure you meant it in that ironic hipster way, but it's not ironic. It's entirely *apropos* to your message.

But Durbin's interview of Doug Wilson is most interesting. They address the collapse of American culture as the result of our nation having slid into liberal apostasy. Which is spot on. But when he asks Wilson about the racism of the Charlottesville rally, he throws him a curve ball by bringing up the ubiquitous accusations of 'racism' hurled at Wilson himself. In the latter context he answers, "Racism is anybody who is winning an argument with a Liberal." Bravo, Doug.

But no longer addressing the charge leveled at himself, he turns on a dime to condemn the Charlottesville rally-goers under the same presuppositions as the secular Liberals condemning him:

> *The Church of Jesus Christ is cosmopolitan. And I want to argue that is the only way you can overcome ethnic divisions and hostilities, racial animosity. If you*

---

[243] Schaff. *Slavery and the Bible.* p. 24

> *dispense with Christ, people are always going to default to their own tribe. . . . If you look at the Charlottesville white supremacists, white nationalists, white separatists . . . that group was almost certainly not educated in white supremacist academies. They were educated in the government schools. And they were taught identity politics, and then they went and looked in the mirror to see what group they belonged to. And if you don't have a transcendent reality overarching the whole thing, like the Lord Jesus Christ . . . you're going to give way to this sort of identity politics.*

I'm sorry, this is utter hogwash. His very first premise is false. And so too, then, all that follows therefrom. No matter where we look in Scripture, the Church is not a mocha polyglot, but rather, "a Kingdom of races, nations, and tongues" (Dan. 7:14; Rev. 7:9; *etc.*) discipled *as nations* (Matt. 28:19-20).

And the notion that White heritage has been coached by the secular school system is a plain inversion of reality. The entirety of state education is organized to suppress two things—White identity and the Lordship of Christ. That's no coincidence. They were wed for two millennia. And remember, the monument around which this scandal orbits is tribute to an age of greater pro-White tribalism before the entrenchment of the common schools, when Christianity was ascendant and 'anti-racism' was a thing yet undreamt.

Regardless, the tribalism to which secular liberalism defaults is Intertribalism: *the very cosmopolitanism that Durbin and Wilson claim to be the Christian position!*

But you won't believe what happens next. Durbin asks, "Why does socialism suck?" To which Wilson retorts:

> *Socialism is driven by envy and malice and the whole egalitarian impulse to level everything. It's an impulse that's scratching at difference, and wants to eradicate every difference; and if they can't elevate themselves, they want to tear down the other. . . . Egalitarianism is the central rot. And what you're doing is you want to rebel against the station which God assigned to you. God gave me certain limitations; I'm in the box that is my personal identity. I am me. . . . I can't be somebody else. I need to just receive what God has given me with gratitude and not try to level everything.*

Thus refuting everything he said prior. You just can't make this stuff up. They simply cannot keep the story straight. Sorry, fellers, you can't sell both propositions at once: either Christianity abolishes all difference, or anti-Christianity (Socialism) does, but both can't be true at the same time.

Granted, we Kinists have our own reservations concerning the UTR action, as the unity called for affected an unequal yoke between believers and the eclectic confederation of Libertarians, anarchocapitalists, anarchofuturists, some genuine National Socialists, Strasserites, and the like. Which unfortunately muted the

Christian message and sets the stage for more secular drift toward heathen Imperium.

But to quote a Kinist friend, "The Alt Right is leading because Christians consider Nigel Lee and Geerhardus Vos to be racists." So either way, in order for Christians to take the lead against the Marxists, the issue must be put to bed amongst our churchmen—there is no moral equivalence between Nationalism and the Multicult Comintern.

Just as occurred in the French Revolution, under Spanish Republicans, and during the Bolshevik Revolution, so long as the ministerial corps default to Antifa's social theory, Christendom shall only fall further into eclipse. And the *Kalergi Clergy* abetting them will, like all the useful idiots, find themselves strangled with their own guts.

On that last day, Wurmbrand, Solzhenitsyn, and a great cloud of martyrs shall testify against our contemporary Balaams who succor the enemy for worldly approval, for mammon, and for fear of the Jews. So much so that they even fear those biblical words 'for fear of the Jews.'

Nationalism as Christian Apologetics

September 4, 2017

I met a fellow a couple years ago whose testimony, according to the prevailing wisdom, cannot exist: you see, as he told it, he came to Reformed Christian faith through White Nationalism. Not out of, but *through*.

Now, this is interesting because we have since seen more of this very thing among others. It is not a fluke, but a quantifiable dynamic. And it works like this:

To merely perceive the PC anti-White mania and genocide underway as evil is induction into the Right by default. And so convicted, this apprehension of evil impels a man down an epistemological path groping for the moral framework that provides for the existence of true good and evil, especially with regard to the subject which set him searching in the first place. And as we will show, the initial apprehension of that evil itself confirms the Christian metaphysic uniquely, both as regards epistemology and ethics.

Though he may wander in jungles of egoism, through Youngian forest mist, and across the hardclay wastes of materialism, he keeps coming back round to the border of the great primordial garden of delight where evil was first distinguished, and that dread mountain shaped like a skull—the only place of evil's authoritative definition and judgment. He finds predication for objective morality and the distinction between good and evil ultimately where our fathers found it—*in Christ alone*.

Most recently, we saw this very dynamic writ large in Bill Nye and Rachel Bloom's children's song "My Sex Junk," which proved so abhorrent in its denial of distinction that even atheists came out of the woodwork confessing that if such debauchery is the ultimate destination of secularism (and everyone knows it is), man has no choice but to turn to Christ.

So too in regard to the nightmarish Pizzagate scandal. Stefan Molyneux for one has conceded the case many times now—something to the effect that:

> *If it all comes down to this ultimate choice between rule by an international cabal of literal devil-worshiping, baby-eating pedophiles and their pet acid-attacking, mass-raping Jihadis on one hand, or that old-time Christianity on the other, sign me up with the Big Guy!*

Even arch-atheist Richard Dawkins grants that Christianity is humanity's only weapon against Islam, and that his own faith—Humanism—has no ethical power against it. He, like many others of his ilk, are coming to speak of Christianity as a 'survival strategy' apart from which humans aren't likely to long survive as a species. Which is but a sterilized way of admitting that Christianity is *necessary*.

But this is not a matter of anecdote alone. Augustine famously identified in evil itself a hostile witness to the absolute standard of the Christian God. Be it wicked men or angels, or the horrors of the modern dystopia, the very apparent impropriety of a thing breaking with its design testifies by inverse corollary to the objective Good from which it deviates.

The evils besetting our people are in Bahnsen's terminology, God Himself 'pushing the antithesis', demonstrating the indispensability of God's order for society through 'the impossibility of the contrary.' And as Humanism has eclipsed Christianity at present, some are awakening to the fact that apart from the old world order of Christendom, there is no measure by which to condemn the Nyes, Blooms, Podestas and Abramoviks of the world, nor allow for all the norms of behavior and bonds of fidelity and meaning that make life livable. Men simply cannot live that way. That way lies death on all sides and leaves man without a standard to even appraise life over death.

Beyond anecdote and arguments *via negativa* is the plain disclosure of Scripture that God segregated the peoples *"that they might grope for Him, seek Him, and find Him."* (Acts 17:27)

So inasmuch as a man is given to see the cosmopolitan multicult as nullifying all constraints on evil, the alternative of wholesome identitarian social order finds its own ultimate predication in the Christian worldview alone.

And, if you'll notice, this pedagogical chain that anchors man's identity essentially to God's own identity mirrors the same process toward conversion in the soteriological realm. In both corporate and personal conversion the order of operation is the same:

1) Apprehension and conviction of evil (sin)
2) by reference to the alternative in Nationalism (God's Law),
3) which, being predicated on the Lordship of Christ alone,
4) forms the ordained means toward conversion of nations no less than men.

This, then, is why Calvin in his *Institutes of the Christian Religion* identifies *national* election as the *primary* means of election for men. Because the Law, having been given as a national covenant, is tied up metaphysically with the life of nations. And thereby the man who is convicted of the error of internationalism is, whether he knows it or not, leaning on the law of God as tutor, and being driven by it, in search of salvation, back to its Author—the Author of our being who engineered man's social needs and the life communal in accord with the Law that He would issue for the governance thereof. When we witness to a man we speak to his sin and the ways in which he has fallen short of God's standard to convict him of his need of the Savior; so too with the nation. So the salvation of men and nations occurs by the same mechanisms, as they are magnitudes of the same thing.

Now, I don't know if Molyneux or Dawkins will ultimately convert, but the fact that so many like them are coming around to confess that the Christian worldview is the only haven they know against social chaos and the death of meaning, is certainly the sort of precursor we expect to see in the process of conversion.

I'm not saying that those making such concessions, or even those calling for a civilizational reprisal of Christendom, are all subscribing immediately to the *Heidelberg Confession* or reciting the *Shorter Catechism*; but Nationalists are the only sociopolitical wing wherein affirmative talk of traditional family life, the indispensability of masculinity, femininity, and traditional gender roles, the necessity of Christian hegemony, and even traditional liturgy are normative phenomena. Most within the churches actually demure from confessing historic Christian culture superior to other cultures. Worse, many insist the culture of Christendom was actually inferior to just about all others! And while the majority of churches today encourage careerism for women, facilitate no-fault divorce, support government schools without qualification, promote women to leadership roles, encourage unequal yoking of all sorts, embrace degenerate anti-Christian arts and music, discourage patriotism to family, country, and folk, and even abet the proliferation of other gods over Christ, the Nationalists tend to go the opposite direction on all these things. Which actually identifies them, like the pre-conversion Bereans, as being "more noble-minded" than the post-conversion Cretans who were all "evil beasts"; because the Nationalists have greater commonality ethics-wise with the historic church than do our contemporary pulpits.

Of course, many Nationalists will content themselves with the *outward* forms of Christian culture, and never attain to the inward substance, but are all the irreverends preaching anarcho-tyranny and the multicult comintern as the gospel or its consequent in any better position? Worse by far, I'd say.

Fact is, Nationalism does not impede the gospel in the least, but rather nurtures it. According to Matthew 28 and Acts 17:27, Nationalism is the fertile soil in which the gospel is meant to flourish. Meantime, the Babelism taken for granted presently in the subverted churches is, by contrast, a "rocky soil" which, allowing for no roots, ultimately chokes out tender shoots. (Matt. 13:1-8)

And there really is no such thing as Covenant Theology apart from the matrix of Patriarchy, Familism, and Nationalism. Because Covenantalism is intrinsically wrapped up with lineage and peoplehood. Which is presupposed even in that essential covenant practice of paedobaptism, for heaven's sake.

So if the churches are presently averse to Nationalism, we realize that to be a very recent phenomenon at odds with not just Christian history, but the most basic preconditions to Christian order.

Thus the rising trend of Nationalists groping Christward, to the source of all preexisting order and the ultimate predication for it, is to be expected. Because the Covenant is the ultimate precondition to that ordered freedom and identity to which the theodicy of the multicult drives them by default. So of all missionary fields, this is the one most ripe for harvest. And the one entirely ignored by the churches in favor of every other group on earth, no matter how resistant to Christian doctrine and ethics. So much so that the impastors now cast Christian social theory as consonant with that of Antifa! Insane as that is.

I foresee, however, that on account of my acknowledgment of *means* in God's election, someone will accuse me of mingling Calvinism with Arminianism or Rationalism. Should this objection be raised, I preemptively refer any such detractors to the Confession:

> *As God hath appointed the elect unto glory, so hath He, by the eternal and most free purpose of His will,* foreordained all the means thereunto.
>
> WCF 3:6

And as noted, Calvin identified the *primary* means of election to be national. (Calvin's Institutes, chapter 21) Moreover, Solomon argues simply, *"Righteousness exalteth a nation; but sin is a reproach to any folk."* (Prov. 14:34) Or, as rendered so concisely in the Septuagint, *"sins diminish tribes."*

If Solomon says Nationalism is associated with righteousness and the the reproach and diminution of a race connotes sin, Nationalism is not only consistent with righteousness, but essential. For to have a *godly* nation, *you must have a nation*. In spite of the gnostic delusions of our churchmen, this unmovable truth, "the expectation of the nations," is revealed from heaven to shepherds keeping watch by night, and increasingly, to a generation dispossessed watching the heavens from the heath. And glory to God, as much as Christ came to earth in terms of Nationalism, Nationalism finds its justification in Christ alone.

An Open Letter to the American Church: A Response to RAAN's Charlottesville Declaration

October 23, 2017

Immediately following the Charlottesville incident the Reformed African American Network (RAAN) issued "The Charlottesville Declaration: An Appeal to the Church in America," which has since been endorsed by an expanding roster of clergy and clerisy eager to virtue signal in accord with rappers, hip-hop personae, and the secular mainstream. It begins with these words:

> *In Charlottesville, VA, the violence of white supremacy visited our nation once again; its demonic presence has not been exorcised from us. From the founding of this nation until the present hour, the idolatry of whiteness has been a prodeath spirit within our republic.*

Drafted by putative Christians Rhodes and Tisby, this encyclical posits that America's natal spirit is 'demonic' because it was founded, as all other nations are, on an ethno-religious basis.

But the ethnic character of other nations earns them no such condemnation. After all, RAAN objects neither to the adamant Black Supremacy taken for granted in African nations. And they remain conspicuously silent on the matter of the many African nations that have not only oppressed, but even genocided their White minority populations! RAAN doesn't even object to those states that at present maintain anti-White exterminationist policies (e.g. Zimbabwe and South Africa). They warrant no criticism whatever in their estimation. Far from 'demonic' in fact, RAAN regards the unapologetic Black Supremacy of those nations a positive good in the world.

Though they focus their animus foremost at America for affirming the life and legacy of our own folk, just as every nation in history has, RAAN's singular contempt for Whiteness makes plain that their objection is against all Eurostock nations, irrespective of territory.

> *It is easy for us to scapegoat the domestic terrorists who incited violence that ended in the deaths of three Americans. We can call them extremists who do not represent American values, but upon closer examination, the ideology deployed*

as a weapon in Charlottesville haunts every institution of the country, including the Church.

Wait. The White people who turned out in Charlottesville to protest the removal of our historic Christian monuments are 'domestic terrorists'? Because they protested the secular crusade against our heritage? Because they defended themselves against attackers who outnumbered them five to one? Or simply because they dared to be White?

Do they really not comprehend that if you deem objection to the Bolshevik-style erasure of our history and culture 'terrorism' you have conceded the secular case against all Christian history? To take such a stance you have actually sanctioned the outlawing of the Bible itself! How do they not see this?

Even their supportive argument for the thesis that 'incitation of violence' defined the Charlottesville protestors as 'terrorists' is a direct blow against the Christian faith. If taking a stance hated by the secular world is 'incitation to violence', and thereby 'terrorism', you have conceded completely to the abolishment of the Christian faith!

Never mind that the term 'terrorism' was coined during the Jacobin revolution to describe liberal government suppression of Christian heritage by intimidation—the very thing that RAAN here endorses.

And declaring American history and culture contrary to 'American values' is a self-contradictory statement. RAAN's conception of American values abolishes all traditional American values in favor of arbitrary government and the anti-American heathen hordes.

Moreover, if you reject the values that you admit from the nation's founding permeated 'every institution of the country, including the Church,' as inconsistent with 'American values,' you once again negate yourself. Because you use the term 'American values' to signify all things contrary to American ideals and identity.

Thus, it is with great concern for the soul of this nation that we, the undersigned, covenant to "cry loud and spare not" (Isaiah 58:1) against America's national sin, beginning within the body of Christ. White supremacy—often called by many names including racism, white privilege, "alt-right" and the KKK—is an insidious doctrine that in manifold ways steals, kills, and destroys the inviolable dignity of all God's children (Genesis 1:26-28).

If 'racism' is America's national sin, and you define racism according to Critical Race Theory as "the inborn prejudice and power of all White people" (as RAAN does), all you are condemning is the existence of White people. Keeping with the leftist zeitgeist, RAAN holds that the existence of White history, culture, and people 'steals, kills, and destroys the inviolable dignity of all God's children'. Do I need to point out that this position takes for granted that White people aren't ultimately human? Or that in this ideology, Whiteness is cast as the proximate definition of evil?

Irony most acute: no Ku Kluxer ever promulgated a theory of race more hostile toward Blacks than is RAAN's doctrine against Whites.

> *It suppresses the truth of God (Romans 1:18), and walks out of step with the true Gospel (Galatians 2:14). All that is left for an unrepentant stance toward sin is God's justice and judgement. Alas, many of the Lord's followers remain hard of heart and hearing, making God's judgement upon this nation seemingly inevitable.*

Galatians 2:14 is an especially odd prooftext for RAAN's case. It reads: "But when I saw that they walked not uprightly according to the truth of the gospel, I said unto Peter before them all, If thou, being a Judaean, livest after the manner of Gentiles, and not as do the Judaeans, why compellest thou the Gentiles to live as do the Judaeans?"

Ruminate on this a moment. RAAN and the secular horde are compelling White people to forswear and abrogate our identity. Black identity certainly is not on the chopping block, nor any other but the identity of White Christians. So inasmuch as Paul rebukes the Judaizer impulse in the early church to suppress the identities of the Gentiles (the predominantly European nations, incidentally), he therein also rebukes RAAN.

But their citation of Romans 1:18 is even more self-indicting: "For the wrath of God is revealed from heaven against all ungodliness and unrighteousness of men who suppress the truth in unrighteousness."

Realize, the White folks who protested in Charlottesville did so in objection to the memory-holing of our history and the leftist rewriting of American identity. Which is to say, they were the vocal opposition to those 'suppressing the truth in unrighteousness.'

This brings to mind the gauntlet thrown down by Obama and Holder, who repetitiously called White America "a nation of cowards" because we have supposedly avoided "an honest conversation about race." RAAN representatives have echoed these same sentiments. But the fact is, whenever White people have attempted to have 'an honest conversation about race,' the immediate response from the Black community is not only disagreement, but hysteria, assault, riots, doxing, demands that the state strip Whites of whatever vestigial rights remain to us, pronouncements of damnation, threats against our wives and children, calls for our necessary extermination, and gloating over our diminishment and looming extinction.

The castigation and intimidation heaped on any White who dares speak the truth in regard to history, culture, and race is the most elaborate and obvious suppression of truth today. It is also the unapologetic agenda of RAAN.

With James Cone they have concluded, "If God is not for us [non-Whites] and against White people, then he is a murderer, and we had better kill him."[244]

In RAAN's lexicon 'truth' is whatever excuses their behavior and hurts White people. And just like Eric Holder, they aren't interested in any conversation about race that doesn't further their empowerment over Whites. That's the truth.

Judgment begins with the household of God, which has been particularly instrumental in the creation and maintenance of racial inequity.

The trouble here is twofold.

On the one hand, the Bible knows nothing of any equality between men, save perhaps that they are all equally men, all sinners, and all liable to die. But even if all are equally men, no two are equal men. And as respects the idea of *racial* equality, Scripture rather takes for granted everywhere that there are some ethnicities especially "fierce," some "mild," some "mighty," some "terrible from their beginning onward," some "more noble-minded," some "wicked beasts," some holy, and some wholly reprobate. Noah prophesied entirely unequal destinies over his sons and the races whom they were to sire (Gen. 9); the peoples who sprang of Jacob and Esau were unequal. The Bible spares not even the subject of inequalities of appearance between the races as it praises David's and Solomon's "fair and ruddy countenance" and Israelite bodies being "whiter milk" and "brighter than ivory"; and this over against references to the Ethiopian's dark skin in the context of "soiled garments," the "leopard's spots" (a predator), and, in the same passage, even sin itself. God's law-order is not equalitarian in the least, but fundamentally pluriform and hierarchical.

On the other hand, RAAN's entire worldview is itself fundamentally opposed to equality among the races anyway. Because they hold White people to be uniquely evil, and regard Blacks and Browns more naturally sanctified. More extreme than the Bible's treatment of the Ethiopian's dark hide as a metaphor for sin, RAAN holds Whiteness to be an actual sin. And the most grievous sin, at that.

Even while holding all legal, institutional, and social supremacy over Whites, they plead for equality as if they were the party systematically marginalized and handicapped by the state. And their descriptions of the 'equality' they seek is nothing but Black Supremacy top to bottom.

Because, as Rushdoony said, "The goal of the equalitarians has always been power, and equality has been an argument to tickle the sick conscience of a faithless and shaky ruling element."

---

[244] Cone, James. *A Black Theology of Liberation.* 1969

Or in a better known reference, as Orwell said, "All animals are equal, but some are more equal than others."

From the French Revolution to the Bolshevik Revolution to the Cultural Revolution, this has not changed. That revolutionary spirit, after all, was introduced when Satan preached equality to our first parents. All the rabble since are only aping that first community organizer.

> *From Puritan pilgrims to Evangelical revivalists, churchmen have been seduced by the spirit of the age, calling evil good and good evil. The blood of indigenous peoples, Africans, and other people of color cries out from American soil to God our Maker. As premature calls for peace seek to silence the pregnant rage of this generation, the words of Scripture come freshly to mind: "Do you think I came to bring peace on earth? No, I tell you, but division" (Luke 12:51-53).*

Just pause and marvel at the absurdity of this narrative: because they defended their families from bloodthirsty savages and enforced God's law, our martyr-fathers are accused of falling thrall to evil zeitgeist, while RAAN obversely presupposes the 'pregnant rage of this generation' to be wholesome somehow. As if our Reformation-era fathers who organized their whole lives on Scripture were morally inferior to modern communists, atheists, witches, Buddhists, Muslims, Jews, Satanists and gender-fluid dragonkin who share RAAN's 'pregnant rage' against historic Christendom.

Really.

You cannot hold to the same *avant garde* view as contemporary heathendom and claim the moral high ground over the heroes of Christian history whose entire social ethic was consciously gleaned from Scripture. RAAN is doing nothing less than pronouncing their excommunication on the historic Church for not being politically correct. They declare thereby the gates of hell the new gates of heaven.

But they transcend even this hypocrisy with one yet greater: having denounced 'division' practiced by the Puritans and Presbyterian divines who settled this New Canaan for our covenant nation, RAAN invokes the words of Christ that sanction division (Lk. 12:51-53). And no less so than had the White Reformers, it is indeed an *ethnic* division which they see their new Christianity as mandating. Pay attention here:

> *Because of this, we do not need cheap grace, cheap peace, cheap reconciliation. We need a revival of spirit, a revolution of values, and the abundance of righteous justice in this land.*

A repudiation of 'cheap' grace, peace, and reconciliation in favor of 'revolution' and 'justice' against White Christians, all following a prooftext about Christ bringing division (lit. a sword)? This is consonant with the 'by any means necessary' talk of the Black Panthers, Nation of Islam, BLM, and Antifa. I daresay, any signatories to this encyclical who understand that it calls for more aggressive race war against White people is no member of Christ. And those who do not see the genocidal objective in it are, quite frankly, fools.

> *Now is the time for the Church to again be the moral compass for this nation. Now is the time for a prophetic, Spirit-led remnant to bear credible "word and deed" witness to the glorious Gospel of Jesus Christ. As in the generation that preceded us, we especially call upon those born-again disciples who still cherish the authority of Scripture and the enablement of the Spirit.*

Heretofore they had only denounced the historic Church, and with special emphasis against our Reformation-era fathers. But with an about-face, they now affirm the church as a moral light. Their equivocation on the word 'church' is understandable only by reference to all they denounced prior. Clearly, the only church they deem valid is the African community, the occasional unitarian abolitionist, and some miscegenated anti-White satellites born out of the cultural revolution of the 60s.

> *We declare that old time religion is still good enough for us in this new era, religion that provides us a full-orbed Gospel of evangelism and activism. May we be salt and light witnesses against the kingdom of darkness, knowing that we war not against flesh and blood, but against principalities, against powers, against the rulers of the darkness of this world, against spiritual wickedness in high places (Ephesians 6:12).*
>
> *To this end, we call upon white leaders and members of the Evangelical church to condemn in the strongest terms the white supremacist ideology that has long existed in the church and our society. Nothing less than a full-throated condemnation can lead to true reconciliation in the Lord's body.*

In context, the forces of darkness to which they here allude are White people generally, and White Christians, especially. Remember, this statement by RAAN is in response to White people objecting to the erasure of our history, and the suppression of our Protestant faith, as well as our cultural and physical genocide.

The enemy which their 'old time gospel' of the 60s is to overthrow is White America, Christendom, and the orthodox Christian faith that underpins them.

> *Additionally, this condemnation must not be in word only, but also in deeds that "bring forth fruits worthy of repentance" (Luke 3:8). As Dr. King notes in Letter from Birmingham Jail, white apathy is worse than white supremacy.*

'Deeds' which *compel* repentance in others against their will. At minimum, this means acts of intimidation and coercion. To confirm this, just ask yourself how everyone would read the same words published by a "White American Network" calling on people to engage in deeds of condemnation against Blacks to compel changes in their theology and politics.

Right, everyone would insist it was a terror pledge. Those who penned it would be excommunicated from church and society. The FBI might even descend on its authors in full force.

As an aside, RAAN's citation of MLK Jr.—a habitual adulterer, whoremonger, blasphemer, paid communist provocateur, and denier of the Trinity, the virgin birth, original sin, and the divinity of Christ and His resurrection—conveys all we need to know about their definition of Christianity: while professing orthodox White Christians their enemies, they profess spiritual kinship with King, who was nothing but reprobate scum.

Moreover, the apathetic White liberals whom MLK and RAAN identify as their enemies alongside 'White Supremacists' like the Pilgrims are liberals like James White! Because he professes to be a 'colorblind' racial egalitarian! RAAN themselves have harried Dr. White hither and yon with accusations of 'racism' and 'White Supremacy'. Because, just like BLM, RAAN concludes that Liberalism is White Supremacy too![245] Which only proves RAAN's claimed longing for equality is a farce. What they demand is Black Supremacy over Whites.

> *We also appeal to the black church to urgently remember its historic role of living within the pastoral-prophetic tension in U.S. Christianity. We call black Christians and others back to a prophetic vocation embodied in the ministries of Lemuel Haynes, Frederick Douglass, Sojourner Truth, Maria W. Stewart, Richard Allen, Charles Price Jones, Charles Harrison Mason, Nannie Helen Burroughs, Ida B. Wells-Barnett, Mary Mcleod Bethune, Fannie Lou Hamer, Gardner C. Taylor, J. Deotis Roberts, and John Perkins. Now is the time to remind the nation and ourselves of the personal and social power of the Gospel.*

I'm sorry, but the Black church's historic role in Christianity has been the embodiment of the outer extremities of heresy, generally passing off in the place of Christianity what can only be called voodoo. Or as that august doctor of Roman-occupied North Africa stated it:

> *Ham . . . can only stand for the hot breed of heretics. They are hot, because they are on fire not with the spirit of wisdom, but the spirit of impatience; for that is*

---

[245] Mikelionis, Lukas. "Black Lives Matter shouts down ACLU: 'You protect Hitler, too!'." *Fox News*. 5 Oct 2017. https://www.foxnews.com/us/black-lives-matter-shouts-down-aclu-you-protect-hitler-too

> the characteristic fervour in the hearts of heretics; that is what makes them disturb the peace of the saints.[246]

And RAAN's inclusion of a roll call of heretics to bolster their argument only further confirms that Augustine's commentary on Hamites applies still.

> Lastly, we invite Christians of good will to join in reading, learning, and acting on insights found in the ways in which the Church both legitimated and resisted white supremacy throughout the last several centuries. Armed with saving knowledge and theological and historical truth, we can persuasively call for repentance and be repairers of the breach. White supremacy will be cast out and dismantled, God willing, by prayer and fasting. We fight for victory in the name of Jesus our Lord! Amen.

By this point, it should be apparent what RAAN means by 'Christians of good will'. It includes Black, Brown, Red, and Yellow folk irrespective of creed, and excludes all traditional and orthodox White Christians.

When they speak of being armed with 'knowledge' and 'truth' by which they can 'persuasively call for repentance,' they mean that as adepts of Cultural Marxism and Critical Race Theory, they are prepared to intimidate and compel White Christians to renounce everything we have ever known to be true in regard to history, civics, ethics, and back of all that, theology.

When they prophesy thereby that 'White Supremacy will be cast out and dismantled,' we can only take them to mean the same White supremacy they identified in the Charlottesville protest—the history and heroes of Christendom, and all objectors to our organized genocide.

This then is RAAN's mission: the suppression of White people's speech and rights of association and assembly; the subordination of Whites in church, state, and general society; the secular state abolishment of White history (which is an approximate overlay of Christian history); and its replacement with a Cultural Marxist narrative revolving around other peoples (especially Blacks) that lays blame for all non-White dysfunction to the account of Whites; the abolishment of the American nation of "free White persons of good character" (Act of 1790) and ultimately all Eurostock nations; and the intimidation of Whites into affirming and abetting all of the above.

But these revolutionary objectives are by no means unique to the prelates at RAAN; if not the totality of their religion, these things are the clear preoccupation in virtually all Black churches. To them, the 'gospel' is synonymous with the destruction of White America.

---

[246] Augustine. *City of God*.

Listen, I'm not saying all the Charlottesville demonstrators were Christians. Even if the majority professed Christian faith, a fair number no doubt claimed no allegiance to Christ. And there were no doubt agent provocateurs aplenty in their ranks bent on making them appear, if at all possible, the aggressors. And for what it's worth, this writer doesn't see much to be gained by 'uniting the Right,' because to whatever degree we concede to an ecumenical sentiment, we only grant the very liberalism we should be standing against. But the general concern and objective of the demonstration was nonetheless theologically sound and entirely defensive in orientation.

RAAN's declaration, on the other hand, was pure maniacal heresy.

Ehud Cross-Examined:
A Reader Asks Some Pointed Questions

April 13, 2018

Someone recently forwarded this salvo of questions to me. They originate with a young man close to our circles with skin in the game, so to speak. He asks:

How could Joseph's marriage to an Egyptian and Jacob's recognition of Ephraim and Manasseh as legitimate heirs — despite their dilution of Israelite blood through their Egyptian mother — be legal?

This is a most understandable question. Because Egyptians as we know them today are of multiple castes and had different racial identities at different times prior. But herein too lies the answer. A careful reading of Genesis 42 confirms that at their reunion Joseph's brothers took him to be an Egyptian. They could not even distinguish him — their own brother — from the majority population of Egypt at the time. This is because Egypt was at the time likely ruled by the Hyksos — Semitic shepherds who had taken the reins from the founding dynasties whom we now know to have been a Japhethic people. Either way, the admission of Joseph's wife and children as legitimate was in terms of their Semitic heritage, which was on sight more or less indistinguishable from the Israelite ethnicity.

The same thing would apply to Moses's marriage to an Ethiopian woman (I understand she was white or at least not black), but even if similar in genetic background, [Ehud] sets forth that the ban extends even to a brother nation like Edom in order to maintain racial purity. If this was the case, how was it possible for such a marriage to be legitimated?

Calvin and Henry, among others, are deliberate in clearing Moses of the charge of marrying an *ethnic* Ethiop. As we've discussed before,[247] there is only one wife of Moses named in text: Zipporah. And Zipporah was the daughter of Jethro, the high priest of Midian. The Midianites were descended from Midian, the son of Abraham by way of his second wife, Keturah. So Zipporah would have been a Semite of close relation to Israel. The reason for her being called an 'Ethiop' by

---

[247] Carlton, Davis. "Kinist Orthodoxy: A Response to Brian Schwertley, Part 5." *Faith and Heritage.* 28 Jan 2015. https://faithandheritage.com/2015/01/kinist-orthodoxy-a-response-to-brian-schwertley-part-5/

Moses's relatives is on account not of race, but of geography, because Midian's territory bordered on (and sometimes within) the land of Ethiopia/Cush. If this sounds strange, realize we have the same exact dynamic today as the Dutch tend to look down on their Boer cousins who settled South Africa. They disdain their "Afrikaner" kinsmen on account of certain social and political divergences. The Dutch, being now an especially liberal element, resent the Boer history of having clung to Calvinist orthodoxy as well as the resultant policy of apartheid.

Similarly, fresh from Egyptian slavery, many Israelites likely resented the Midianites' practice of slave-driving. After all, it was Midianites who first sold Joseph to Potiphar (Gen. 37:36). And as slavers dwelling between Egypt and Cush, the Midianites would have been a central cog in the sale of Africans into Egyptian slavery.

And the idea of Moses having married someone of another *racial* type is a novelty entertained only as of the past few years under the circumstance of a liberal eclipse which throws all biblical doctrines into question and disrepute. Prior to which, the normative perspective was that Moses's wife was of the same Semitic race as Moses and Israel, but resented on political and historical grounds; and those social grievances were what prompted Miriam's slur against Zipporah.

Deuteronomy 23:7-8 says that both Edomites and Egyptians were to be allowed into the congregation after the third generation. As far as I have understood the meaning of congregational admittance, this would mean full rights as a citizen, including land ownership, public office and marriage among the rest of the nation?

Yes, there were restrictions—'to the third generation'—against Edomite and Egyptians. Even if they are treated on an ethnic basis, the distinction between them and Israel was not racial because the Edomites were a Semitic people whom the law in question stipulates to have access to Israelite citizenship explicitly on the grounds that (irrespective of conversion status) the Edomite "is thy brother." And as we've said, the Egyptians whom Israel knew in the time of their sojourn there were Hyksos-Semites, so we do not take the provision allowing for their assimilation to pertain to the Japhethic dynasties of Egypt which preceded them, nor the Nubian dynasty which followed after them, only to the Semitic Egyptians amongst whom Israel had residence.

And think of it—without overt caveat, anytime someone references Germans, Swedes, Englishmen, or Europeans in general, no one assumes them to mean the Arabs, Africans, and Orientals rapidly flooding into Europe today. Because we still think of Europeans in the ethnic sense that we've always known and it would be artificial in the extreme to count a community suddenly relocated from Somalia to England as "Englishmen." Because they simply aren't Anglo-Saxons. But given enough time, men will be habituated to the new drifts of peoples in those lands to the extent that they may begin to speak occasionally of Germans in the geographic rather than ethnic sense, inclusive of the profuse admixtures. This is the sense to which the law regarding the assimilability of Egyptians compels us—the grant of their integration with Israel pertained only to the *sort* of Egyptians known to Israel during their sojourn there. And this is especially clear when we see later in Israel's history that the prophets Ezra and Nehemiah came to regard Egyptians as no longer assimilable under the law (Ezra 9:1, etc.). The law had not changed. But we know from the prophets' authoritative administration of the law, not to mention classical history, that the definition of "Egyptian" had.

Deuteronomy 21:10-14 deals with the matter of female captives taken in war. I cannot imagine this law as a forecast of the eventual infighting between the Hebrews. Why was the offspring of such ethnic mixing still considered legitimate as indicated by the complete lack of sanctions or legal disadvantages mentioned in connection with such unions?

A survey of the commentaries on this subject is fruitful. I shall quote Ellicott, not because he says anything so different than the others, but merely for his succinctness here:

> When thou . . . seest among the captives a beautiful woman.—*This could not be among the seven nations, of whom it is said (Deuteronomy 20:1-6), "thou shalt save alive nothing that breatheth." But it may well apply to the recent case of the Midianitish maidens (Numbers 31:15-18), who had been taken captive in great numbers, and would naturally be reduced to slavery.*[248]

So, yes, in fact, it seems this law accords precisely to the circumstance of Israelites having taken Midianite warbrides in Numbers 31. As it turns out, it is the only such instance mentioned in Scripture. And as Ellicott notes, because the law elsewhere emphatically forbids certain mixed marriages, this particular allowance cannot be viewed as a contravention or nullification of those codes, but rather, must be understood as somehow congruent with them. And again, Ezra's and Nehemiah's prophetic interpretation of the law accepted no loophole for bridegrooming among foreign peoples: *"Now it came to pass, when they had heard the law, that they separated from Israel all the mixed multitude."* (Neh. 13:3) The word translated as 'mixed multitude' there is *ereb*, which Strong's Exhaustive Concordance defines as *"a mixture, (or mongrel race) – Arabia, mingled people, mixed (multitude)."*

There is a conspicuous inconsistency in arguing that the grant of warbrides in Deuteronomy 21 allows for miscegenation in all circumstances except the one outlined in the text. That is, none who've made this case endorse the practice of going to war against another people, exterminating a woman's whole family, abducting her, and then forcing her to marry her family's slayer. They instead cite this *ad*

---

[248] Ellicott, Charles. *Bible Commentary*. Deuteronomy 21.

hoc provision (which they don't even truly endorse) granted to Israel as remedy to the Midianite issue as justification for doing something quite different: "Because God granted Israel to do (X) in a certain circumstance, we may therefore do (Y) in a very different circumstance." It is simply an incoherent line of argument.

Furthermore, there is the lawful provision discussing a priest's daughter who marries a foreigner (Leviticus 22:12-13). The law states that the outsider husband of a priest's daughter may not eat of the holy things, but the Lord still recognizes the marriage and no shame is ascribed to the family of the priest. Does not the very existence of such a by-law, as well as the law in Deut. 21:10-14, indicate that the Lord both anticipated and regarded as legitimate inter-ethnic unions under certain circumstances and with the fulfillment of particular covenant requirements?

This word 'stranger' which occurs in Leviticus 22:12 is *zuwr*. Depending on context, it can mean an alien by race, by nation, by tribe, by community, by clan, by house, or by covenant. This passage in particular is singled out by the Brown-Driver-Briggs Lexicon as an instance pertaining *"to the family of another household, children of another household than God's, especially of another family than priests, not belonging to the tribe of Levi."*

Which explains why more than half of our English translations make some attempt to clarify the matter by translating that passage as denoting family or tribe, rather than race. To wit, both the ESV and NASB render *zuwr* there as "a layman," the CSB and HCSB both use "a man outside a priest's family," the CEV and GNT opt for "someone who isn't a priest," the JPS Tanakh 1917 says "a common man" (i.e., not a Levite), the DRB uses "any of the people" (i.e., of the other tribes of Israel), and other sundry permutations of the same.

Relative to which, too, is that we always adjudicate the less clear by the more clear. In this case, the more clear is nearby in the same book: "*A widow, or a divorced woman, or profane, or an harlot, these shall he not take: but he shall take a virgin of his own people to wife. So that he shall not profane his seed among his people: for I the LORD do sanctify him.*" (Lev. 21: 14-15)

This use of the word 'people' is significant. The Hebrew term is *am*, which Strong's defines as *"folk, men, nation, people. From **amam**; a people (as a congregated unit); specifically, a tribe (as those of Israel); … folk, men, nation, people."*

Whereas the LXX uses the word *genos*, which Strong's Lexicon renders *"kindred, offspring, stock, tribe, nation, nationality descended from a particular people."* And which Thayer's Lexicon defines preeminently as "race".

But it isn't an etymological matter only, as Ezekiel elaborates on the ethnic holiness of the Levites thus: *"Neither shall they take for their wives a widow, nor her that is put away: but they shall take maidens of the seed of the house of Israel, or a widow that had a priest before."* (Ezek. 44:22)

Now, if we seek coherence from the interplay of these passages as we are obliged to do, a definitive doctrine takes shape: that Levites could only bridegroom from amongst the tribes of Israel, but if the daughters of Levites married men from amongst the other tribes of Israel, their husbands were not granted the priestly benefits by that union. To squeeze more than that out of it so as to admit miscegenation puts the principle of Levitical holiness, and even the concept of tribal and national distinction emphasized here, at odds with themselves. Which is the same thing as pitting the Scripture against itself. And that is something the Christian cannot abide.

However, God very clearly recognized both the fallen nature of people and the difficult circumstances that are beyond their control in providing the legitimate alternatives of remarriage for both widows and divorced women both in the Old and New Testaments.

This point is well taken. We agree. While circumstance of illegitimate birth (and many other circumstances, besides) does impact perspective, and therefore, spirit as well, it is not wholly determinative. The disposition of a man's soul toward God and His Word is more important than belonging to any particular race, nation, tribe, or house. Because membership in the household of faith sustains such a one.

But the fact remains that a saving faith does not alchemically transform a Chinaman into a Swede simply because he earnestly desires it. Part of the Christian faith is having the humility to accept our own designs and domains under God.

Mercifully, for the borderman—one born neither one thing nor the other—the mandate of equal yoking applies to him as much as anyone else. We all have a mandate from God to seek our like in bridegrooming. Obviously, this is subject to opportunity, but the positive injunction remains—"be ye not unequally yoked," "gender not diverse kinds," "be ye holy." The Samaritans, being a mixed people after all, came about in just this way too—through a grouping of illegitimate offspring. In time, they became a people of their own and due their relation to Israel, they were the next nation after the Israelites to hear the gospel preached in their streets.

With regard to Ezra and Nehemiah's reforms, with the above considerations in mind, I don't see how the inclusion of Egyptians and/or other Hebrew-related people groups in the inter-marriage indictment can be held to have the same meaning as the listed Canaanite nations wholly banned and segregated from the Israelite communities.

Well, they weren't held to exactly the same standard. As I'm sure you know, segregation was not the extent of 'the ban' on Canaanites. God had commanded Israel to make total war on them forever. They were to be exterminated, men, women, and children. Yes, under the administration of Ezra and Nehemiah, Israel only segregated from them, but considering the fact of the mingled presence of so many other nations with them, and the delicate circumstance of their recent wide-scale admixture with Israel, it seems a special mercy that separation was the only thing mandated there.

Israel did, however, at the insistence of the Prophets, segregate from the other nations (such as Egyptians) there too, even from their mixed offspring born thereby. It was perhaps the most heartbreaking episode in Israel's history, but, most bittersweet, it was also their time of their national restoration and renewal.

They were flagrantly violating the covenant at numerous points and their unions with other peoples could just as easily have been violations based on different issues rather than on the single prohibition of avoiding mamzer *offspring.*

There were no doubt many matters at issue, but the law which the Prophets emphasized were those contra miscegenation specifically (Ezra 9:2) and when they heard the law they did not separate from idolaters, but from all the *ereb* (Neh. 13:3), which, as covered,[249] has reference to foreign peoples and mixed offspring. Circumstantially, nothing proves this more than their putting away the mixed children whom they had themselves raised. As we read in 1 Corinthians 7:14, "For the unbelieving husband is sanctified by the wife, and the unbelieving wife is sanctified by the husband; else, your children would be unclean, but they are holy." Covenantally speaking, the faith of one believer (his identity in Christ) overflows the other members of their house with grace—especially if it is the head of household who believes. This is foundational federal theology, and indispensable to covenantal thinking in Old and New Testaments. Which in turn means the issue for which the foreign wives and children were put away in Ezra and Nehemiah had to be something other than their errant faith. This, again, confirms the face value of the ethnic terminology used there such as *ereb*.

Since Israel had not been back in their homeland for three generations at this point, the Egyptians and Edomites had not yet reached the required religious and cultural saturation to be considered eligible for marriage.

That's not quite accurate. Cyrus settled the first Israelite envoys back in Israel around 536 BC. Ezra would not arrive on the scene until the late 450s BC, and Nehemiah later still about 445. Their concerted restoration effort occurred then roughly a century after the first waves of refugees returned. That is plenty of time for many of their admixtures to have satisfied the third-generation stipulation. We see further confirmation of this in that both Ezra and Nehemiah make

---

[249] Desperandum, Nil. "Further Commentary on the Mamzer of Deuteronomy 23." *Faith and Heritage.* 1 Sept 2014. https://faithandheritage.com/2014/09/further-commentary-on-the-mamzer-of-deuteronomy-23/

recourse to the genealogies all the way back to the first settlers from the previous century to confirm everyone's lineage—a needless action if they were facing a single generation of mixing. But many—adults included—could not validate lawful descent genealogically and were consequently among those sent away. Even the fact that the mixed children were speaking foreign languages and could not speak Hebrew at all testifies to a large-scale and generationally ingrained process of degeneration.

Edomites aren't mentioned among the offending groups in the book, but Egyptians are. But as of the 25th dynasty, Egypt was under the dominion of an entirely different people; Semites no longer, the Egyptians were, by that time, primarily Nubians or a heavy mixed offshoot thereof. So there is little reason to believe the 'third generation' provision would have applied to them at that point.

How would the mamzer *prohibition have been applied to the hosts of Gentiles, who considering their ignorance of the laws of Israel and the record of Biblical history itself, seemed to have no problem with ethnic inter-marriage and the results of producing mixed offspring?*

Nations have always had some special affinity for their own. The outstanding exceptions to which have generally occurred only by imposition of empires. Whether by top-down diktat, or by bottom-up agitation of one tribe or another, all are artificial as they defy God's ordained social order, which is nationalism.

In the classical world both nationalism and racial categorization were well observed by the Greeks as well as Romans to a degree that Paul's discursive on illegitimacy in Hebrews 12 echos Greek law contra miscegenation:

> *A classical parallel to 'then are ye bastards, and not sons' is supplied by Aristophanes, Birds 1650-2, 'for you are illegitimate and no trueborn son, since your mother is a foreign woman,' where, however, the nothos [bastard] is the child of mixed marriage which was not recognized as legal in Athens of the fifth century B.C.[1. F.F. Bruce, The New International Commentary on the New Testament, Hebrews 12, p. 358]*

Even if imperfectly conceived under the various schools of paganism, race consciousness, nationalism, segregation, and anti-miscegenation laws were normative to the ancient world. And the exceptions wherein integration was promoted were invariably in terms of the most aggressive anti-Christ imperial orders such as Babylon, Assyria, Babel, the Soviet Union, and the UN.

You've also asked some specific questions about Ruth, Timothy, and others which have been addressed by others before me on this site and elsewhere. Regrettably, for the sake of time (this is already a lengthy reply) I must leave those points to be made by others.

As an aside, how would this apply to the tens of millions of mixed race individuals and families today?

This question is posed parenthetically, but it is really a seminal question for us. How we can most equitably apply these principles to our contemporary world and personal lives is so counter-cultural at this moment, and yet so essential that we dare not lay the matter down. For to do so is to relinquish society and the earth to Lucifer, "the weakener of the nations" (Isa. 14:12). But prior to answering, I will first incorporate your final question.

A final question ending on a personal note...

If it can be proven from Scripture the above questions/propositions-to-the-contrary are simply misunderstandings on my behalf and the mamzer ban applies to anyone of mixed race (regardless of the extent or type of miscegenation), how would I conduct myself as a believer of mixed blood?

With my ancestry approximately 70% European (Dutch, German and English) and the rest being a mixture of African and Asian influence, I have been raised solely in White culture and society. My entire identity is that of a White Christian (my somewhat mixed ancestry notwithstanding). What rules and guidelines should I follow for my illegitimate status? And are there any legal consequences from a Biblical perspective for my biological parents in terms of remarriage and their lives going forward?

I know a fair number of Christians in this approximate scenario—some related to me by blood, in fact. And if you took a survey of professing Kinists today, you'd find a significant margin to have similar situations among their relatives as well. So we are not insensate to the difficulties attending this issue. But as Christians we should be working at all levels to restore and reassert God's order for society. In the macro, this means cultural revival and civil policy that affirms and sustains our respective nations under Christ; in the micro—especially for already mixed broods—it means doing all that we can to ameliorate the situation by guiding our mixed multitude not to compound the blurring of boundaries, but to seek their like for the purposes of marriage. This may be the greatest affront to the modern egalitarian mind, but it conforms both to the biblical image mandate of equal-yoking and to practicality, because we all know those unions built on greater similarity are necessarily more coherent and durable. Your case—a mulatto raised immersed in Euro-stock culture—is actually a prevalent scenario today. Far more so than the reverse. And no one of only European, African, or Oriental stock would be able to fully identify with your experience. To have a wife who truly sees the world from the perspective of your identity, she needs be as much like you as possible in all things. So the Kinist answer is no occasion to despair. Far from it. It actually affords you the greatest likelihood of personal fulfillment and a secure marriage. Because the *telos* of God's design and law work in confluence with our practical needs.

The temptation before you, however, which must be resisted at all costs, is that caustic revolutionary spirit against the peoples from whom you are set apart, which is tantamount to revolution against the God who ordered the world into these identities. And it would be the easiest thing in the world for you to embrace a combative stance, or even visceral hatred, of White people because the humanist zeitgeist encourages it so ubiquitously today. But if you are numbered among the elect, I pray and trust that He will keep you walking *contra mundum.*

According to His law, by His grace,
Ehud

The Blackwashing of Christian History and Beyond

Part 1

July 15, 2018

And when the Philistine looked about, and saw David, he disdained him: for he was but a youth, and ruddy, and of a fair countenance.

1 Sam. 17:42

An emerging facet of the Alienist heresy yet unaddressed is the blackwashing of Church history. Within the Reformed fold specifically, it is Peter Leithart who sometime around 2010 began peddling the notion that the Church fathers such as Origen, Cyril, Lactantius, Cyprian, Tertullian, Athanasius, Augustine, et al. were Black Africans. And per this revolutionary hagiography, he insists Christianity is to be understood as originating in and built natively upon African spirituality: "Western theology is, in fact, an African export, as is much of Eastern Christianity."[250]

But Leithart seems to have picked this thesis up contemporaneous with the release of Thomas Oden's 2010 book How Africa Shaped the Christian Mind.

Read that title again. Understand what is in the offing here: the Christian Church is being demanded to confess Afrocentrism, a thing heretofore undreamt in the Reformed, Evangelical, Roman, and Eastern churches alike.

Adopted seemingly overnight without a scintilla of circumspection, we witness now its implications and their implementation. This inversion of historical narrative necessarily portends revision of all areas of theology. For instance, corollary to this new Afrocentric ecclesiology, Ken Ham has introduced the theory that Adam and Eve were dark Brown to Black in color. Yes, he describes it as "middle-brown," but looking at the pictures he uses to denote it on page 99 of his book One Race, One Blood—they aren't Italians, Greeks, or Iranians. They are clearly Africans. And looking at this graphic published by Ham's AIG, his outfit (the preeminent creationist ministry today) is promulgating the notion not only that the African type is prototypical Man, but also that Whiteness is presumed to denote the mark of Cain! So the fair European phenotype is cast as the symbol of

---

[250] Leithart, Peter. "What Africa Can Teach the North."

murder. This in spite of the fact that the scriptural language suggests precisely the opposite by the first man's name—Adam, and the family of words of which it is part (adom, edom, etc.), is alternately translated as 'clay', 'ruddy', 'rosey', 'red', 'blushing', 'fair', 'white'.

Accordingly, we see this paradigm shift is even now beginning to work its way into Bible translations; specifically, the passage quoted at the top of this piece—1 Samuel 17:42 is, as of the 2011 publication of the International Standard Version, suddenly being rendered, "When the Philistine looked and saw David, he had contempt for him, because he was only a young man. David had a dark, healthy complexion and was handsome." This isn't just a slight divergence. It posits a diametrically opposite vision of David from the one known heretofore.

Back of Leithart, Oden, Ham, and the translators of the ISV bible, this Afrocentric view of salvation history ultimately stems from the work of Black Liberation theologian James Cone. In his 1969 book *Black Theology & Black Power* we read:

> *For white people, God's reconciliation in Jesus Christ means that God has made black people a beautiful people; and if they are going to be in relationship with God, they must enter by means of their black brothers, who are a manifestation of God's presence on earth. The assumption that one can know God without knowing blackness is the basic heresy of the white churches. They want God without blackness, Christ without obedience, love without death. What they fail to realize is that in America, God's revelation on earth has always been black, red, or some other shocking shade, but never white. Whiteness, as revealed in the history of America, is the expression of what is wrong with man. It is a symbol of man's depravity. God cannot be white even though white churches have portrayed him as white. When we look at what whiteness has done to the minds of men in this country, we can see clearly what the New Testament meant when it spoke of the principalities and powers. To speak of Satan and his powers becomes not just a way of speaking but a fact of reality. When we can see a people who are controlled by an ideology of whiteness, then we know what reconciliation must mean. The coming of Christ means a denial of what we thought we were. It means destroying the white devil in us. Reconciliation to God means that white people are prepared to deny themselves (whiteness), take up the cross (blackness) and follow Christ (black ghetto).*

When first published, Cone's view was laughed to scorn by all mainstream communions. But no longer. Though entirely foreign to historic Christianity, this Afrocentric paradigm is being adopted now by the same denominations absent cursory examination or circumspection. While contrary in every detail to orthodoxy, it fulfills the confirmation bias impressed upon them by the modern neurolinguistic programming of Christ's enemies. Which is really the only explanation for their collective amnesia: their very memories (of Christianity prior to Cultural Marxism) have been retroactively overwritten by the warlocks of propaganda to the extent that they can no longer even conceive of the faith known to our fathers; or even of the faith they themselves knew in their youth. (Which I shall prove in the case of John Piper in an upcoming article.)

But behold now the unfolding implications of this new Afrocentric Christianity:

> *African biblicism has arisen because of the revolutionary impact of vernacular Bible translations. Mbiti says: "When the translation is first published, especially that of the New Testament and more so of the whole Bible, the church in that particular language area experiences its own Pentecost. The church is born afresh, it receives the Pentecostal tongues of fire. As in Acts 2, the local Christians now for the first time "hear each of us in his own language."*[251]

So because Africans prove innate charismatics, the definition of authentic Christianity and 'biblicism' becomes charismata, which means continued word gifts, which, for all intents and purposes, means an open canon, and in practice, no quantifiable standard, person to person — which is all thoroughly heretical. Some 'biblicism', there, Pete.

> *Africans have no use for the pansy Jesus of modern liberalism. They want a savior with the testosterone to fight for them. No pale Galileans need apply.*[252]

My jaw drops every time I read that portion. Leithart is clearly channeling James Cone who ignominiously wrote, "If God is not for black people and against white people, then God is a murderer and we'd better kill him." (Cone, Black Theology & Black Power) But I'm still taken aback at Leithart's blithe baptism of obvious racial animus toward 'pale' (i.e., White) people. Even more so for his surreal description of the alternative to this anti-White sentiment as 'liberalism' and a 'pansy Jesus'. So the African Christianity he holds forth here is one which sees itself as having a racial and religious mandate against White Christians and orthodox Christendom, generally. And this anti-White sentiment, he assures us, is the real Christianity — the empowerment of Africans to overcome White Christians! Which is all a little too coincidentally confluent with the ethos and eschatology of our zeitgeist. Sheer coincidence, I'm sure.

And if any White Christian said something equivalent — that 'they would only bow to a savior with the testosterone to fight for them against the dark-skinned peoples' — they would rightly be accused of forging a god in their own revanchist image. In fact, this is the very thing of which Kinists stand so wrongly accused

---

[251] Ibid.
[252] Ibid.

(and by the very same Alienists preaching race war on Whites!). Kinists make no such claim of any onus on God's part to favor Whites, nor any mandate to war on other races. Just the opposite, Kinists hold that God demands as a matter of Christian love, that we are to honor the bounds and belongings of other peoples. Meantime, Leithart, the African religion which he lauds, and the Alienist convivium are preaching just such a tribal deity.

Reminiscent of Xerxes's emissary at the Hellespont, in his essay "Evolving Toward Africa" Leithart calls for traditional Christians to lay down all defense of the faith against this takeover. As he explains it, the duty his god demands of Whites is to "assume a posture of reception" with respect to this new African theology, ethics, and cultural dominance.

Whence comes such an onus? Aside from the bald assertion that unless we acquiesce to Afrocentric charismata with its overtly anti-White ethos, yield the rewrite of the Christian history and faith, the dispossession of our children, and genocide, we are damned.

We could laugh to tears at all of this nonsense if not for the fact that it is actually being taken seriously within the majority of the churches at present. Which of course raises the question of whether or not these people can be considered Christian in any sense of the word.

In part 2 we shall quench this strange fire.

Part 2
July 17, 2018

As established in part 1, this large and rapidly expanding "Woke Church" (Afrocentric/Anti-White) ideology spilling over one doctrinal bulkhead after another is predicated on what we may call the Leithart/Oden thesis that Christianity is an essentially Hamitic faith. But back of which, ultimately, is James Cone's satanic assertion that *"God is Black and salvation comes only by embrace and worship of Blackness."*

If you think connecting Leithart's and Oden's ideas to Cone's is a stretch, realize that the churches whom they've influenced have already come to presuppose Cone's doctrine. Think of it—the whole 'woke church' narrative is punctuated by reference to the *imago Dei* in non-Whites. The implied accusation this tactic always carries is that to see no mandate for our doctrinal, national, cultural, and familial suicide, or any lack of obedience to minority demands, is somehow a denial of Blacks being human. And the only way not to be accused of denying the *imago*

Dei in Blacks or POCs is to obey them without question. Which is to say, *worship them*.

As much as we'd rather dismiss the whole 'woke' bailiwick as inconsequential jailhouse Black Power nonsense, the governments of our denominations have been intimidated into confessing it wholesale. In fact, between the writing of parts 1 and 2, such proved the undertow at both the 150th SBC Conference and PCA 46th General Assembly. Both these supposed mossback battalions have officially announced their conversion to the new Nimrodianism in place of Christianity.

All curiously apace with the blackwashing of history underway outside the Church.

Even if the push to Afrocentize Christianity begs address on a widening front, we can start by looking at the initial foothold taken in Reformed and evangelical circles by the Oden/Leithart thesis. In condescending scolds they remind us that Tertullian, "The Father of Western Theology," was Black. But was he?

All the standard sources on the man relay his having lived in Roman-occupied North Africa circa 155-240 AD, and come of Berber blood.

Who are the Berbers? Today we may find examples of Arabic-Negro groups claiming Berber heritage alongside Italic and blonde Celtic-looking tribes. And as respects language, the Berber tongue is not confined to any one race. But that is emphatically *not* the case being made in the Oden/Leithart thesis. The argument they are making is more strictly racial—that the Berbers, as natives of the African continent, must be accounted Blacks, categorically.

Never mind too that it is at loggerheads with the standard ethnic description the Berbers make of themselves:

> *The Berbers or Amazighs are an ethnic group indigenous to North Africa. They are distributed in an area stretching from the Atlantic Ocean to the Siwa Oasis in Egypt, and from the Mediterranean Sea to the Niger River. They Belong to the Caucasian–Mediterranean Race.*[253]

The 'Caucasian-Mediterranean Race' also overlaps large swaths of Syrians and Iranians who on sight could pass for Romanians or even Germans. Old Carthage was visibly of the same stock as Greece and Italy. Which, by appearance and civilizational bent, was of close blood to Alexandrian Egypt and Macedon (Acts 16:9). Ranging from a middle-olive cast to the hue of freckled Celts, the Mediterranean breed is, by sight as well as all classical and biblical history, Japhetic. And it isn't just me saying that:

---

[253] "Who Are the Berbers (Amazigh)." *The Berber.* https://theberber.wordpress.com/who-are-the-berbers-amazigh/

The first reference to the Ancient Berbers goes back to a very ancient Egyptian period. They were mentioned in the pre-dynastic period, on the so-called "Stele of Tehenou" which is still preserved in the Cairo museum in Egypt. That tablet is considered to be the oldest source wherein the Berbers have been mentioned.

The second source is known as **The Stele of King Narmer.** *This tablet is newer than the first source, and it depicted the Tehenou as captives.*

The second oldest name is **Tamahou.** *This name was mentioned for the first time in the period of the first king of the "Sixth Dynasty" and was referred to in other sources after that period. According to* **Oric Bates**, *those people were white-skinned, with blond hair and blue eyes.*[254]

An easy way to vet this fact is simply to look at the busts of the Berber kings stretching back to well before the Christian era. Not one shows hint of any Hamitic strain. Or compare the busts of Carthaginian general Hannibal Barca with that of Julius Caesar. Though born to opposite sides of the Mediterranean, they could be brothers. And either could today be realistically portrayed in film by the likes of Norwegian/German actor Lance Henriksen.

It is to these Caucasic tribes of North Africa and the Near East that so many Church fathers belonged.

But the one singled out as proving beyond all shadow of doubt the thesis of a Black foundation is St. Athanasius, the so-called 'Black dwarf'. This moniker cited ubiquitously at present, the Afrocentrists assure us, is proof positive that Athanasius was Black.

As it turns out though, if you follow the rabbit trail of what is now a lengthy run of citations, they lead back to a solitary source:

Among those who were present at the Council of Nicea there was a young man, so dark and short that his enemies would later call him 'the black dwarf.' This was Athanasius, Alexander's secretary...[255]

Yes, it was Puerto Rican liberationist professor Justo González who first introduced this description of Athanasius. The year was 1984.

That's it. Nothing precedes it. Leithart's *big gun* in this fight turns out to be nothing but the active imagination of an infamous late-twentieth-century liberation theologian—i.e., *an overt Communist heretic* who was himself forced to recant the theory nearly a decade ago. Quietly, of course, his 2010 edition of the work in question has been redacted to omit any mention of the 'Black dwarf.'

---

[254] "Berber." *New World Encyclopedia.* https://www.newworldencyclopedia.org/entry/Berber
[255] González, Justo. *The Story of Christianity:* Vol. 1, Ch. 19, p. 199

So as the churches are presently hammering out the implications of this new 'Woke Theology', the Communist canard on which it is all based is long since debunked. *Absurd* doesn't begin to describe it.

Especially since the traditional description of Athanasius as having *"a slight stoop, a hooked nose and small mouth, a short beard spreading into large whiskers, and light auburn hair"*[256] clearly precludes Black features. And it was this traditional description that informed all portraiture of him from the earliest times.

And since from these two—Tertullian and Athanasius—was Hamitic identity imputed to the other fathers, we needn't address them all. Because all the lesser cases are predicated on false assumptions drawn from the stronger ones (e.g., "Athanasius was from North Africa and he was called 'Black dwarf,' so all the North African fathers were Black"), they fall as a set.

Led away after these maleficent cognitive biases, the Alienists continue grasping at the most dubious straws to exalt all emblems of darkness over light. But it is precisely here that we have a great solace: the fact that these 'Woke' innovations are so transparently false, and their consequences so catastrophic, means theirs is a fuel which burns hot and fast, and shall quickly be snuffed out. As they reimagine the Church as a Hamitic spirit, the shades they invoke will, by their identification therewith, necessarily possess them. As another renowned North African father, Augustine, has said in *The City of God*:

> *Again, the name Ham means 'hot'; and Noah's middle son, separating himself, as it were, from the other two, and remaining between them, is included neither in the first fruits of Israel nor in the fullness of the Gentiles; for what does he signify if not the 'hot' race of the heretics, who burn not with the spirit of wisdom, but with impatience? For it is with impatience that the breasts of the heretics are wont to glow; and it is for this reason that they disturb the peace of the saints.*

---

[256] Schaff, Phillip. *A Select Library of Nicene and Post-Nicene Fathers of the Christian Church*

Covenant vs. Coven: Liberalism as Witchcraft

October 22, 2018

In a gripping exchange between the Prophet Samuel and King Saul over the state's obligation to obey God's Law, Samuel levels this remarkable simile: *"Rebellion is as the sin of witchcraft."* (1 Sam.15:23)

In context, because the term 'rebellion' is aimed at the king and his failure to obey God's command, it condemns outright the so-called divine right of kings, statism, and political pragmatism. Kings are not at liberty to rule by caprice or utility. The word of the king does not equate to the Word of God. Or as Henry summarizes it, *"Those are unfit and unworthy to rule over men who are not willing that God should rule over them."*[257]

Of course, that Samuel's use of simile does not draw *complete* equivalence between rebellion and witchcraft in a penological sense is proven by the fact that rebellions in general are not prosecuted as witchcraft in Scripture. But the prophet's resort to said simile nonetheless confirms a certain commonality between witchcraft and more mundane forms of rebellion.

In its essential sense, then, it means *legal positivism* — the notion that men have nomological autonomy and can create law themselves — is a subdued form of divination. For all pretext of men actually *making* law is to usurp the throne of Lawgiver and conjure a counterfeit reality.

Where our Christian fathers maintained that *"Law cannot be created, merely discovered"* (Blackstone) and *"No law can be suffered to contradict the law of God"* (Ibid.), they demarcated the political antithesis of Enlightenment *ideology* and *liberalism* as fundamentally antinomian.

For this reason it has long been noted that the work of John Locke (the putative "father of liberalism") was an application of *Lex, Rex*, but purged of the theonomy of Rutherford's sovereign God. Endeavoring to ameliorate the appearance of his rebellion before the eyes of Christendom, Locke appropriated some of the outward form while discarding the inward substance. But even his dissimulation could not abide without immediately lobbying for the decoupling of law from God's plenary revelation in deference to man's imagination.

Even if Lockean liberalism counted itself an enemy of divine right royalism, they shared in the presupposition of legal positivism — that man, either individual

---

[257] Henry, Matthew. *Commentary on the Whole Bible*. 1 Samuel 15.

or in state aggregate, has leave to legislate an alternate reality. Which, as established, is the core of witchcraft.

The correspondence of liberalism to witchcraft is comically apparent in the contemporary phenomenon of the tattooed trollops, lesbians, spinsters, and all the cat ladies who comprise the ranks of feminism today: angry, licentious, painted women living outside male headship in the company of their "fur babies" (literal *familiars*) who call their god by feminine pronouns, make regular use of horoscopes and yogic meditations, and prize abortion as a sacrament. The average feminist is an uncanny facsimile of the archetypical hedgewitch burned into the collective memory of European fairy and folktales.

Beyond a question of similitude, even if all feminists do not self-identify as witches, all self-declared witches do identify as feminists and liberals. So these vectors overlap to a degree beyond mere coincidence.

As noted elsewhere,[258] Rachel Held Evans's interpretation of the Proverbs 31 woman as a blanket affirmation of womanhood whatever form or path it takes is but a repackaged law of Thelema granting women the latitude to 'do as thou wilt'. So while claiming Christianity, the women under her tutelage are found to be functional Thelemites.

Though distinct from Wicca, the technical definition of Thelema, *"the Science and Art of causing Change to occur in conformity with Will,"* makes it of precisely the same essence—witchcraft. More's the pity, Lori Alexander has shone a bright light on the fact that the faith taken for granted amongst women (and facilitated by certain cunning men) in the churches today is of this same rebellious spirit.[259]

But by this point, the institutional church has adopted the catechism of the Frankfurt School, trading in the seven deadly sins for penological hexes such as sexism, ageism", anti-Semitism, homophobia, xenophobia, and racism. So the church visible is presently in the place of the old Galatian church when Paul asked incredulously, *"Who hath bewitched you?!"* (Gal. 3:1) These neologisms, and the alien nomology they presuppose (not to mention the scientific propaganda by which they have been promulgated), are literal spells cast over our people. The whole bailiwick of "human rights" is nothing less than occult incantation. "Intersectionality," deference to alien "narratives" and their psychobabble shibboleths are fundamentally incantational and sorcerous. All of these presume to speak into being a world which neither is nor can be.

Albeit their powers of illusion over those they have ensorcelled prove quite potent.

---

[258] Would, Ehud. "Season of the Witch, Part 1: The Feminist War Against the Family." *Faith and Heritage*. 22 Nov 2017. https://faithandheritage.com/2017/11/season-of-the-witch-part-1-the-feminist-war-against-the-family/
[259] Malsbury, Colby. "When Shrews Attack: The Pathetic Saga of the 'Debt-Free Virgins Without Tattoos' Fracas." *Faith and Heritage*. 6 Aug 2018. https://faithandheritage.com/2018/08/when-shrews-attack-the-pathetic-saga-of-the-debt-free-virgins-without-tattoos-fracas/

Even the etymology winks at this fact as *liberalism*, like its preceding iteration, *libertinism*, is namesake of the Roman god Liber whose rites St. Augustine described as the most vile "mixture of seeds" (plant, human, and animal). So Liber's foundational meaning was always rebellion against the Christian cosmos.

So we see the matter at issue—*fiat nomology as witchcraft*—applies to more than kings and avowed witches. It pertains to all ideologies, libertarianism as much as communism, and to ecclesiocracy as much as name-it-and-claim-it charismata.

All the multicult narratives imposed on us today are incantations meant to conjure a different cosmic order over against the Christian cosmos. The pluralist-isms which have subdued our institutions are literal spells against Christ's Lordship and the peoples thereof. The liberaldom which presently occupies the West is, by denial of theonomy in favor of autonomy and heteronomy, an empire of ostensible witchcraft.

As modern Christendom gives place to so many forms of autonomy, is it any wonder that blatant witchcraft is on the rise? As in the case of Saul who would not learn from Samuel's rebuke of his similitude to witchcraft (1 Sam.15:23), the church has, by sundry paths, made her way to Endor (1 Sam. 28) and the embrace of overt witchcraft.

But it is not the latter consequences which we should fear most, for they have inherent in them a rod of chastisement by which God may effect repentance in us. It is the more innocuous seeming strains of the same which have taken us there. They are, in fact, more dangerous for their subtleties.